First World War
and Army of Occupation
War Diary
France, Belgium and Germany

14 DIVISION
Headquarters, Branches and Services
Adjutant and Quarter-Master General
1 January 1916 - 31 December 1916

WO95/1879/2

The Naval & Military Press Ltd
www.nmarchive.com
Published in association with The National Archives

Published by

The Naval & Military Press Ltd

Unit 10 Ridgewood Industrial Park,

Uckfield, East Sussex,

TN22 5QE England

Tel: +44 (0) 1825 749494

www.naval-military-press.com

www.nmarchive.com

This diary has been reprinted in facsimile from the original. Any imperfections are inevitably reproduced and the quality may fall short of modern type and cartographic standards.

© **Crown Copyright**
Images reproduced by permission of The National Archives, London, England, 2015.

Contents

Document type	Place/Title	Date From	Date To
Heading	WO95/1879/2 14 Div General Orders Jan-Dec 1916		
Miscellaneous	14th Division Routine Orders 1916		
Miscellaneous	Sketch Maps, Chapter 2 5.		
Miscellaneous	Crowford		
Miscellaneous	14th (Light) Division. Routine Orders.	01/01/1916	01/01/1916
Miscellaneous	14th (Light) Division. Routine Orders.	02/01/1916	02/01/1916
Miscellaneous	14th (Light) Division. Routine Orders.	03/01/1916	03/01/1916
Miscellaneous	14th (Light) Division. Routine Orders.	05/01/1916	05/01/1916
Miscellaneous	14th (Light) Division. Routine Orders.	06/01/1916	06/01/1916
Miscellaneous	14th (Light) Division. Routine Orders.	08/01/1916	08/01/1916
Miscellaneous	14th (Light) Division. Routine Orders.	09/01/1916	09/01/1916
Miscellaneous	14th (Light) Division. Routine Orders.	10/01/1916	10/01/1916
Miscellaneous	14th (Light) Division. Routine Orders.	11/01/1916	11/01/1916
Miscellaneous	14th (Light) Division. Routine Orders.	12/01/1916	12/01/1916
Miscellaneous	14th (Light) Division. Routine Orders.	13/01/1916	13/01/1916
Miscellaneous	14th (Light) Division. Routine Orders.	14/01/1916	14/01/1916
Miscellaneous	14th (Light) Division. Routine Orders.	15/01/1916	15/01/1916
Miscellaneous	14th (Light) Division. Routine Orders.	16/01/1916	16/01/1916
Miscellaneous	14th (Light) Division. Routine Orders.	17/01/1916	17/01/1916
Miscellaneous	Notice.		
Miscellaneous	14th (Light) Division. Routine Orders.	18/01/1916	18/01/1916
Miscellaneous	14th (Light) Division. Routine Orders.	19/01/1916	19/01/1916
Miscellaneous	14th (Light) Division. Routine Orders.	20/01/1916	20/01/1916
Miscellaneous	14th (Light) Division. Routine Orders.	21/01/1916	21/01/1916
Miscellaneous	14th (Light) Division. Routine Orders.	22/01/1916	22/01/1916
Miscellaneous	14th (Light) Division. Routine Orders.	23/01/1916	23/01/1916
Miscellaneous	14th (Light) Division. Routine Orders.	24/01/1916	24/01/1916
Miscellaneous	14th (Light) Division. Routine Orders.	26/01/1916	26/01/1916
Miscellaneous	14th (Light) Division. Routine Orders.	27/01/1916	27/01/1916
Miscellaneous	14th (Light) Division. Routine Orders.	28/01/1916	28/01/1916
Miscellaneous	14th (Light) Division. Routine Orders.	29/01/1916	29/01/1916
Miscellaneous	14th (Light) Division. Routine Orders.	30/01/1916	30/01/1916
Miscellaneous	14th (Light) Division. Routine Orders.	31/01/1916	31/01/1916
Miscellaneous	14th (Light) Division. Routine Orders.	02/02/1916	02/02/1916
Miscellaneous	14th (Light) Division. Routine Orders.	03/02/1916	03/02/1916
Miscellaneous	14th (Light) Division. Routine Orders.	04/02/1916	04/02/1916
Miscellaneous	Notices.		
Miscellaneous	14th (Light) Division. Routine Orders.	05/02/1916	05/02/1916
Miscellaneous	14th (Light) Division. Routine Orders.	07/02/1916	07/02/1916
Miscellaneous	14th (Light) Division. Routine Orders.	08/02/1916	08/02/1916
Miscellaneous	14th (Light) Division. Routine Orders.	09/02/1916	09/02/1916
Miscellaneous	14th (Light) Division. Routine Orders.	10/02/1916	10/02/1916
Miscellaneous	14th (Light) Division. Routine Orders.	11/02/1916	11/02/1916
Miscellaneous	14th (Light) Division. Routine Orders.	14/02/1916	14/02/1916
Miscellaneous	14th (Light) Division. Routine Orders.	15/02/1916	15/02/1916
Miscellaneous	14th (Light) Division. Routine Orders.	16/02/1916	16/02/1916
Miscellaneous	14th (Light) Division. Routine Orders.	18/02/1916	18/02/1916
Miscellaneous	14th (Light) Division. Routine Orders.	21/02/1916	21/02/1916
Miscellaneous	14th (Light) Division. Routine Orders.	22/02/1916	22/02/1916
Miscellaneous	14th (Light) Division. Routine Orders.	23/02/1916	23/02/1916

Miscellaneous	14th (Light) Division. Routine Orders.	28/02/1916	28/02/1916
Miscellaneous	14th (Light) Division. Routine Orders.	01/03/1916	01/03/1916
Miscellaneous	14th (Light) Division. Routine Orders.	03/03/1916	03/03/1916
Miscellaneous	14th (Light) Division. Routine Orders.	04/03/1916	04/03/1916
Miscellaneous	14th (Light) Division. Routine Orders.	05/03/1916	05/03/1916
Miscellaneous	14th (Light) Division. Routine Orders.	06/03/1916	06/03/1916
Miscellaneous	14th (Light) Division. Routine Orders.	07/03/1916	07/03/1916
Miscellaneous	14th (Light) Division. Routine Orders.	08/03/1916	08/03/1916
Miscellaneous	14th (Light) Division. Routine Orders.	09/03/1916	09/03/1916
Miscellaneous	14th (Light) Division. Routine Orders.	10/03/1916	10/03/1916
Miscellaneous	14th (Light) Division. Routine Orders.	11/03/1916	11/03/1916
Miscellaneous	14th (Light) Division. Routine Orders.	12/03/1916	12/03/1916
Miscellaneous	14th (Light) Division. Routine Orders.	13/03/1916	13/03/1916
Miscellaneous	14th (Light) Division. Routine Orders.	14/03/1916	14/03/1916
Miscellaneous	14th (Light) Division. Routine Orders.	16/03/1916	16/03/1916
Miscellaneous	14th (Light) Division. Routine Orders.	18/03/1916	18/03/1916
Miscellaneous	14th (Light) Division. Routine Orders.	20/03/1916	20/03/1916
Miscellaneous	14th (Light) Division. Routine Orders.	21/03/1916	21/03/1916
Miscellaneous	14th (Light) Division. Routine Orders.	22/03/1916	22/03/1916
Miscellaneous	14th (Light) Division. Routine Orders.	23/03/1916	23/03/1916
Miscellaneous	14th (Light) Division. Routine Orders.	24/03/1916	24/03/1916
Miscellaneous	14th (Light) Division. Routinc Ordcrs.	25/03/1916	25/03/1916
Miscellaneous	14th (Light) Division. Routine Orders.	26/03/1916	26/03/1916
Miscellaneous	14th (Light) Division. Routine Orders.	27/03/1916	27/03/1916
Miscellaneous	14th (Light) Division. Routine Orders.	28/03/1916	28/03/1916
Miscellaneous	14th (Light) Division. Routine Orders.	29/03/1916	29/03/1916
Miscellaneous	14th (Light) Division. Routine Orders.	31/03/1916	31/03/1916
Miscellaneous	Notices.		
Miscellaneous	14th (Light) Division. Routine Orders.	01/04/1916	01/04/1916
Miscellaneous	14th (Light) Division. Routine Orders.	02/04/1916	02/04/1916
Miscellaneous	14th (Light) Division. Routine Orders.	03/04/1916	03/04/1916
Miscellaneous	14th (Light) Division. Routine Orders.	04/04/1916	04/04/1916
Miscellaneous	14th (Light) Division. Routine Orders.	05/04/1916	05/04/1916
Miscellaneous	14th (Light) Division. Routine Orders.	06/04/1916	06/04/1916
Miscellaneous	14th (Light) Division. Routine Orders.	07/04/1916	07/04/1916
Miscellaneous	14th (Light) Division. Routine Orders.	08/04/1916	08/04/1916
Miscellaneous	14th (Light) Division. Routine Orders.	10/04/1916	10/04/1916
Miscellaneous	14th (Light) Division. Routine Orders.	12/04/1916	12/04/1916
Miscellaneous	14th (Light) Division. Routine Orders.	13/04/1916	13/04/1916
Miscellaneous	14th (Light) Division. Routine Orders.	15/04/1916	15/04/1916
Miscellaneous	Notices.		
Miscellaneous	14th (Light) Division. Routine Orders.	16/04/1916	16/04/1916
Miscellaneous	Divine Services For Easter.		
Miscellaneous	14th (Light) Division. Routine Orders.	17/04/1916	17/04/1916
Miscellaneous	14th (Light) Division. Routine Orders.	19/04/1916	19/04/1916
Miscellaneous	14th (Light) Division. Routine Orders.	20/04/1916	20/04/1916
Miscellaneous	14th (Light) Division. Routine Orders.	21/04/1916	21/04/1916
Miscellaneous	14th (Light) Division. Routine Orders.	24/04/1916	24/04/1916
Miscellaneous	14th (Light) Division. Routine Orders.	25/04/1916	25/04/1916
Miscellaneous	14th (Light) Division. Routine Orders.	26/04/1916	26/04/1916
Miscellaneous	14th (Light) Division. Routine Orders.	27/04/1916	27/04/1916
Miscellaneous	Notices.		
Miscellaneous	14th (Light) Division. Routine Orders.	29/04/1916	29/04/1916
Miscellaneous	14th (Light) Division. Routine Orders.	30/04/1916	30/04/1916
Miscellaneous	14th (Light) Division. Routine Orders.	01/05/1916	01/05/1916
Miscellaneous	14th (Light) Division. Routine Orders.	03/05/1916	03/05/1916

Miscellaneous	14th (Light) Division. Routine Orders.	05/05/1916	05/05/1916
Miscellaneous	14th (Light) Division. Routine Orders.	06/05/1916	06/05/1916
Miscellaneous	14th (Light) Division. Routine Orders.	07/05/1916	07/05/1916
Miscellaneous	14th (Light) Division. Routine Orders.	09/05/1916	09/05/1916
Miscellaneous	14th (Light) Division. Routine Orders.	11/05/1916	11/05/1916
Miscellaneous	14th (Light) Division. Routine Orders.	12/05/1916	12/05/1916
Miscellaneous	Divine Services For Sunday-14th May, 1916		
Miscellaneous	14th (Light) Division. Routine Orders.	15/05/1916	15/05/1916
Miscellaneous	Notices.		
Miscellaneous	14th (Light) Division. Routine Orders.	16/05/1916	16/05/1916
Miscellaneous	14th (Light) Division. Routine Orders.	17/05/1916	17/05/1916
Miscellaneous	14th (Light) Division.	18/05/1916	18/05/1916
Miscellaneous	14th (Light) Division. Routine Orders.	19/05/1916	19/05/1916
Miscellaneous	14th (Light) Division. Routine Orders.	21/05/1916	21/05/1916
Miscellaneous	14th (Light) Division. Routine Orders.	22/05/1916	22/05/1916
Miscellaneous	14th (Light) Division. Routine Orders.	23/05/1916	23/05/1916
Miscellaneous	14th (Light) Division. Routine Orders.	24/05/1916	24/05/1916
Miscellaneous	14th (Light) Division. Routine Orders.	26/05/1916	26/05/1916
Miscellaneous	14th (Light) Division. Routine Orders.	27/05/1916	27/05/1916
Miscellaneous	14th (Light) Division. Routine Orders.	28/05/1916	28/05/1916
Miscellaneous	14th (Light) Division. Routine Orders.	29/05/1916	29/05/1916
Miscellaneous	14th (Light) Division. Routine Orders.	30/05/1916	30/05/1916
Miscellaneous	14th (Light) Division. Routine Orders.	31/05/1916	31/05/1916
Miscellaneous	14th (Light) Division. Routine Orders.	01/06/1916	01/06/1916
Miscellaneous	14th (Light) Division. Routine Orders.	02/06/1916	02/06/1916
Miscellaneous	Divine Services. Sunday-June 4th, 1916		
Miscellaneous	14th (Light) Division. Routine Orders.	04/06/1916	04/06/1916
Miscellaneous	14th (Light) Division. Routine Orders.	05/06/1916	05/06/1916
Miscellaneous	14th (Light) Division. Routine Orders.	06/06/1916	06/06/1916
Miscellaneous	14th (Light) Division. Routine Orders.	08/06/1916	08/06/1916
Miscellaneous	14th (Light) Division. Routine Orders.	10/06/1916	10/06/1916
Miscellaneous	Notices.		
Miscellaneous	14th (Light) Division. Routine Orders.	11/06/1916	11/06/1916
Miscellaneous	14th (Light) Division. Routine Orders.	12/06/1916	12/06/1916
Miscellaneous	14th (Light) Division. Routine Orders.	13/06/1916	13/06/1916
Miscellaneous	14th (Light) Division. Routine Orders.	14/06/1916	14/06/1916
Miscellaneous	14th (Light) Division. Routine Orders.	15/06/1916	15/06/1916
Miscellaneous	14th (Light) Division. Routine Orders.	16/06/1916	16/06/1916
Miscellaneous	14th (Light) Division. Routine Orders.	17/06/1916	17/06/1916
Miscellaneous	14th (Light) Division. Routine Orders.		
Miscellaneous	14th (Light) Division. Routine Orders.	20/06/1916	20/06/1916
Miscellaneous	14th (Light) Division. Routine Orders.	22/06/1916	22/06/1916
Miscellaneous	14th (Light) Division. Routine Orders.	24/06/1916	24/06/1916
Miscellaneous	14th (Light) Division. Routine Orders.	25/06/1916	25/06/1916
Miscellaneous	14th (Light) Division. Routine Orders.	27/06/1916	27/06/1916
Miscellaneous	14th (Light) Division. Routine Orders.	28/06/1916	28/06/1916
Miscellaneous	14th (Light) Division. Routine Orders.	30/06/1916	30/06/1916
Miscellaneous	14th (Light) Division. Routine Orders.	01/07/1916	01/07/1916
Miscellaneous	14th (Light) Division. Routine Orders.	02/07/1916	02/07/1916
Miscellaneous	14th (Light) Division. Routine Orders.	04/07/1916	04/07/1916
Miscellaneous	14th (Light) Division. Routine Orders.	05/07/1916	05/07/1916
Miscellaneous	14th (Light) Division. Routine Orders.	06/07/1916	06/07/1916
Miscellaneous	14th (Light) Division. Routine Orders.	07/07/1916	07/07/1916
Miscellaneous	Church Services For Sunday 9th July, 1916		
Miscellaneous	14th (Light) Division. Routine Orders.	08/07/1916	08/07/1916
Miscellaneous	14th (Light) Division. Routine Orders.	09/07/1916	09/07/1916

Miscellaneous	14th (Light) Division. Routine Orders.	11/06/1916	11/06/1916
Miscellaneous	14th (Light) Division. Routine Orders.	12/07/1916	12/07/1916
Miscellaneous	14th (Light) Division. Routine Orders.	13/07/1916	13/07/1916
Miscellaneous	14th (Light) Division. Routine Orders.	14/07/1916	14/07/1916
Miscellaneous	14th (Light) Division. Routine Orders.	15/07/1916	15/07/1916
Miscellaneous	14th (Light) Division. Routine Orders.	16/06/1916	16/06/1916
Miscellaneous	14th (Light) Division. Routine Orders.	17/07/1916	17/07/1916
Miscellaneous	14th (Light) Division. Routine Orders.	19/07/1916	19/07/1916
Miscellaneous	14th (Light) Division. Routine Orders.	20/07/1916	20/07/1916
Miscellaneous	14th (Light) Division. Routine Orders.	21/07/1916	21/07/1916
Miscellaneous	14th (Light) Division. Routine Orders.	22/07/1916	22/07/1916
Miscellaneous	14th (Light) Division. Routine Orders.	23/07/1916	23/07/1916
Miscellaneous	14th (Light) Division. Routine Orders.	24/07/1916	24/07/1916
Miscellaneous	14th (Light) Division. Routine Orders.	25/07/1916	25/07/1916
Miscellaneous	14th (Light) Division. Routine Orders.	27/07/1916	27/07/1916
Miscellaneous	14th (Light) Division. Routine Orders.	02/08/1916	02/08/1916
Miscellaneous	14th (Light) Division. Routine Orders.	07/08/1916	07/08/1916
Miscellaneous	14th (Light) Division. Routine Orders.	08/08/1916	08/08/1916
Miscellaneous	14th (Light) Division. Routine Orders.	09/08/1916	09/08/1916
Miscellaneous	14th (Light) Division. Routine Orders.	10/08/1916	10/08/1916
Miscellaneous	14th (Light) Division. Routine Orders.	12/08/1916	12/08/1916
Miscellaneous	14th (Light) Division. Routine Orders.	14/08/1916	14/08/1916
Miscellaneous	14th (Light) Division. Routine Orders.	16/08/1916	16/08/1916
Miscellaneous	14th (Light) Division. Routine Orders.	18/08/1916	18/08/1916
Miscellaneous	14th (Light) Division. Routine Orders.	20/08/1916	20/08/1916
Miscellaneous	14th (Light) Division. Routine Orders.	22/08/1916	22/08/1916
Miscellaneous	14th (Light) Division. Routine Orders.	23/08/1916	23/08/1916
Miscellaneous	14th (Light) Division. Routine Orders.	01/09/1916	01/09/1916
Miscellaneous	14th (Light) Division. Routine Orders.	02/09/1916	02/09/1916
Miscellaneous	14th (Light) Division. Routine Orders.	03/09/1916	03/09/1916
Miscellaneous	14th (Light) Division. Routine Orders.	05/09/1916	05/09/1916
Miscellaneous	14th (Light) Division. Routine Orders.	07/09/1916	07/09/1916
Diagram etc			
Miscellaneous	14th (Light) Division. Routine Orders.	09/09/1916	09/09/1916
Miscellaneous	14th (Light) Division. Routine Orders.	12/09/1916	12/09/1916
Miscellaneous	14th (Light) Division. Routine Orders.	14/09/1916	14/09/1916
Miscellaneous	14th (Light) Division. Routine Orders.	15/09/1916	15/09/1916
Miscellaneous	14th (Light) Division. Routine Orders.	16/09/1916	16/09/1916
Miscellaneous	14th (Light) Division. Routine Orders.	18/09/1916	18/09/1916
Miscellaneous	14th (Light) Division. Routine Orders.	20/09/1916	20/09/1916
Miscellaneous	14th (Light) Division. Routine Orders.	24/09/1916	24/09/1916
Miscellaneous	14th (Light) Division. Routine Orders.	25/09/1916	25/09/1916
Miscellaneous	14th (Light) Division.	27/09/1916	27/09/1916
Miscellaneous	Traffic Orders, 14th Division.		
Miscellaneous	14th (Light) Division. Routine Orders.	29/09/1916	29/09/1916
Miscellaneous	14th (Light) Division. Routine Orders.	30/09/1916	30/09/1916
Miscellaneous	14th (Light) Division. Routine Orders.	01/10/1916	01/10/1916
Miscellaneous	14th (Light) Division. Routine Orders.	02/10/1916	02/10/1916
Miscellaneous	14th (Light) Division. Routine Orders.		
Miscellaneous	14th (Light) Division. Routine Orders.	05/10/1916	05/10/1916
Miscellaneous	14th (Light) Division. Routine Orders.	06/10/1916	06/10/1916
Miscellaneous	Routine Orders.	07/10/1916	07/10/1916
Miscellaneous	14th (Light) Division. Routine Orders.	08/10/1916	08/10/1916
Miscellaneous	14th (Light) Division. Routine Orders.	09/10/1916	09/10/1916
Miscellaneous	14th (Light) Division Routine Orders.	10/10/1916	10/10/1916
Miscellaneous	14th (Light) Division. Routine Orders.	12/10/1916	12/10/1916

Miscellaneous	14th (Light) Division. Routine Orders.	14/10/1916	14/10/1916
Miscellaneous	14th (Light) Division. Routine Orders.	15/10/1916	15/10/1916
Miscellaneous	14th (Light) Division. Routine Orders.	16/10/1916	16/10/1916
Miscellaneous	14th (Light) Division. Routine Orders.	17/10/1916	17/10/1916
Miscellaneous	14th (Light) Division. Routine Orders.	18/10/1916	18/10/1916
Miscellaneous	14th (Light) Division. Routine Orders.		
Miscellaneous	14th (Light) Division. Routine Orders.	20/10/1916	20/10/1916
Miscellaneous	14th (Light) Division. Routine Orders.	21/10/1916	21/10/1916
Miscellaneous	14th (Light) Division. Routine Orders.	22/10/1916	22/10/1916
Miscellaneous	14th (Light) Division. Routine Orders.	23/10/1916	23/10/1916
Miscellaneous	14th (Light) Division. Routine Orders.	24/10/1916	24/10/1916
Miscellaneous	14th (Light) Division. Routine Orders.	25/10/1916	25/10/1916
Miscellaneous	14th (Light) Division. Routine Orders.	26/10/1916	26/10/1916
Miscellaneous	14th (Light) Division. Routine Orders.	28/10/1916	28/10/1916
Miscellaneous	14th (Light) Division. Routine Orders.	29/10/1916	29/10/1916
Miscellaneous	14th (Light) Division. Routine Orders.	30/10/1916	30/10/1916
Miscellaneous	14th (Light) Division. Routine Orders.	31/10/1916	31/10/1916
Miscellaneous	14th (Light) Division. Routine Orders.	03/11/1916	03/11/1916
Miscellaneous	14th (Light) Division. Routine Orders.	04/11/1916	04/11/1916
Miscellaneous	14th (Light) Division. Routine Orders.	05/11/1916	05/11/1916
Miscellaneous	14th (Light) Division. Routine Orders.	06/11/1916	06/11/1916
Miscellaneous	14th (Light) Division. Routine Orders.	07/11/1916	07/11/1916
Miscellaneous	14th (Light) Division. Routine Orders.	08/11/1916	08/11/1916
Miscellaneous	14th (Light) Division. Routine Orders.	10/11/1916	10/11/1916
Miscellaneous	14th (Light) Division. Routine Orders.	11/11/1916	11/11/1916
Miscellaneous	14th (Light) Division. Routine Orders.	12/11/1916	12/11/1916
Miscellaneous	14th (Light) Division. Routine Orders.	13/11/1916	13/11/1916
Miscellaneous	14th (Light) Division. Routine Orders.	14/11/1916	14/11/1916
Miscellaneous	14th (Light) Division. Routine Orders.	15/11/1916	15/11/1916
Miscellaneous	14th (Light) Division. Routine Orders.	16/11/1916	16/11/1916
Miscellaneous	14th (Light) Division. Routine Orders.	17/11/1916	17/11/1916
Miscellaneous	14th (Light) Division. Routine Orders.	18/11/1916	18/11/1916
Miscellaneous	14th (Light) Division. Routine Orders.	19/11/1916	19/11/1916
Miscellaneous	14th (Light) Division. Routine Orders.	20/11/1916	20/11/1916
Miscellaneous	14th (Light) Division. Routine Orders.	21/11/1916	21/11/1916
Miscellaneous	14th (Light) Division. Routine Orders.	22/11/1916	22/11/1916
Miscellaneous	14th (Light) Division. Routine Orders.	23/11/1916	23/11/1916
Miscellaneous	14th (Light) Division. Routine Orders.	24/11/1916	24/11/1916
Miscellaneous	14th (Light) Division. Routine Orders.	25/11/1916	25/11/1916
Miscellaneous	14th (Light) Division. Routine Orders.	27/11/1916	27/11/1916
Miscellaneous	14th (Light) Division. Routine Orders.	30/11/1916	30/11/1916
Miscellaneous	14th (Light) Division. Routine Orders.	01/12/1916	01/12/1916
Miscellaneous	14th (Light) Division. Routine Orders.	02/12/1916	02/12/1916
Miscellaneous	14th (Light) Division. Routine Orders.	03/12/1916	03/12/1916
Miscellaneous	14th (Light) Division. Routine Orders.	04/12/1916	04/12/1916
Miscellaneous	14th (Light) Division. Routine Orders.	05/12/1916	05/12/1916
Miscellaneous	14th (Light) Division. Routine Orders.	06/12/1916	06/12/1916
Miscellaneous	14th (Light) Division Routine Orders	09/12/1916	09/12/1916
Miscellaneous	14th (Light) Division Routine Orders	10/12/1916	10/12/1916
Miscellaneous	14th (Light) Division Routine Orders	11/12/1916	11/12/1916
Miscellaneous	Return Shewing Amount of Fuel Drawn For Week Ended		
Miscellaneous	14th (Light) Division Routine Orders.	12/12/1916	12/12/1916
Miscellaneous	14th (Light) Division Routine Orders	13/12/1916	13/12/1916
Miscellaneous	14th (Light) Division. Routine Orders.	15/12/1916	15/12/1916
Miscellaneous	14th (Light) Division. Routine Orders.	16/12/1916	16/12/1916

Miscellaneous	14th (Light) Division. Routine Orders.	18/12/1916	18/12/1916
Miscellaneous	14th (Light) Division. Routine Orders.	20/12/1916	20/12/1916
Miscellaneous	14th (Light) Division. Routine Orders.	21/12/1916	21/12/1916
Miscellaneous	14th (Light) Division. Routine Orders.	22/12/1916	22/12/1916
Miscellaneous	14th (Light) Division. Routine Orders.	23/12/1916	23/12/1916
Miscellaneous	Christmas Services		
Miscellaneous	14th (Light) Division Routine Orders.	24/12/1916	24/12/1916
Miscellaneous	14th (Light) Division Routine Orders.	25/12/1916	25/12/1916
Miscellaneous	14th (Light) Division. Routine Orders.	27/12/1916	27/12/1916
Miscellaneous	14th (Light) Division. Routine Orders.	29/12/1916	29/12/1916
Miscellaneous	14th (Light) Division. Routine Orders.	30/12/1916	30/12/1916
Miscellaneous	14th (Light) Division. Routine Orders.	31/12/1916	31/12/1916

WO95/1879 - 2

14 Div General Orders

Jan - Dec 1916

14th Division.

Routine Orders,
1916.

S. S. Wilson

O.C Southern Brigade,
K.A.R.
Dar-es-Salaam.

SKETCH MAPS,

C H A P T E R 2 5.

Affair of Kasanga

1). The Southern Area of Operations.

2). ~~Spinx~~ Sphinxhaven -- 30th May 1915.

3). The Defence of Saisi, June - August 1915.

4). The Caprivi Zipfel.

Crawford

14TH (LIGHT) DIVISION.

ROUTINE ORDERS.

1st January, 1916.

1070. TRAFFIC CONTROL.

Orders re Traffic Control in 14th Divisional Area are issued herewith to all concerned.

1071. LEAVE.

To enable the Major-General to make a fresh allotment of Leave on a fair basis with the number of vacancies allowed to the Division, Officers Commanding all units are requested to render through usual channels to this office not later than 9 a.m. on Wednesday January 5th, a return made up to January 1st inclusive, showing as accurately as possible, the number of "All ranks" who have not had leave to England of any kind, Sick or otherwise, and also have been in this country :-
(a) 4 months and over.
(b) 3 but not exceeding 4 months,
(c) Under 3 months.
This return will include all ranks whom Commanding Officers now include in their Leave Rolls under existing Leave Rules which have been circulated.
It may be necessary to call for a somewhat similar return monthly, in order to maintain a fair apportionment.

1072. CASUALTIES.

All Units in the Division will render through usual channels a Return (numbers only) of all Casualties to 12 noon December 31st 1915 since arrival in this country under the following headings :-
Officers   (a) Killed. (b) Wounded, (c) Missing,
Other Ranks (a) Killed. (b) Wounded. (c) Missing.
Casualties originally reported under one of these headings but since definitely known to come under another should be correctly shown in the Return now called for. e.g. "Wounded" known to have died of wounds or "Missing" Known to have been killed to be shown under (a)
Returns to reach this office as soon as convenient, but not later than Monday January 10th 1916.

1073. SANITATION.

As much rubbish as possible from the trenches is to be sent back with returning transport each night in sacks and sandbags. None is to be sent loose.
Rubbish in excess of what can be dealt with in transport camps is to be sent to the Divisional incinerator at A.18.c. Some of the rubbish of the 49th Division is now lying dumped in sacks ready for removal in this way. This is to be sent back at once.
The Divisional incinerator at A.18.c is available for destruction of rubbish from all Units.
The incinerator at A.16.c is not to be used.

(over)

1074. OAT SACKS.

Units are again reminded of the necessity of returning the empty oat-sacks to the Supply Officers. As these sacks are used for packing vegetables for issue, neglect on this point may cause a shortage in the issue.

1075. POSTAL REFILLING.

Tomorrow and following days Postal Refilling will take place at F.27.b.10.3. Sheet 28 at 10.30 a.m.

[signature]

LIEUT-COLONEL,
A.A.&.Q.M.G.
14TH (LIGHT) DIVISION.

NOTICE.

DIVINE SERVICE 2-1-16.

WESLEYANS PRESBYTERIANS ETC.

9 a.m. At ELVERDINGHE, for troops in the vicinity, at Church Army Hut.

11 a.m. At 44th Field Ambulance, Rue Boeschepe, POPERINGHE, for 44th Field Ambulance, 8th R.B. and 8th K.R.R.C. This service will be followed by Communion Service,

14TH (LIGHT) DIVISION.

ROUTINE ORDERS.

2nd January, 1916.

1076. SANITATION.

As this is the season at which Enteric Fever and allied diseases become prevalent, the attention of all ranks is directed to the necessity of boiling all Milk, and chlorinating all water supplies.

The following extract from D.R.O. No. 568 is published for information and compliance :-

"In future water carts will be cleaned out twice a week with Permanganate of Potash, under the personal supervision of the regimental Medical Officer.

1077. MATERIAL (Collection of).

Brick rubble is available in ELVERDINGHE under the following arrangements :-

Units requiring rubble will obtain passes from the C.R.E., 14th Division for the number of loads they need.

On production of pass to Military Police at D.14.b.3.6., N.C.Os in charge of wagons will be allowed to collect bricks.

The Police will check the number of loads taken by each unit and report, through A.P.M. to C.R.E. daily.

Bricks may only be carted away by night but parties may be sent to prepare wagon loads of bricks in the day time.

The C.R.E. will give the necessary requisition for bricks removed, monthly, to the Bourgmaster of ELVERDINGHE according to the number of loads reported by the Military Police as having been taken.

1078. WIRELESS TELEGRAPHISTS.

The names of any N.C.Os and men, other than those now serving with the 14th Divisional Signal Company, who have had experience in wireless telegraphy, are to be forwarded by all units, through the usual channels, to this office by noon 5th instant. Particulars to be stated.

1079. GOGGLES.

Any anti-gas goggles made of rubber with film eye-piece and rubber band, in possession of Units are to be replaced.

Indents for replacement to be forwarded to D.A.D.O.S. without delay.

LIEUT-COLONEL,
A.A. & Q.M.G.
14TH (LIGHT) DIVISION.

14TH (LIGHT) DIVISION.

ROUTINE ORDERS.

3rd January, 1916.

1080. DISCIPLINE.

It has been observed that N.C.Os and men continue to ride on transport wagons going to the forward dumps.
Wagons of all kinds going to these forward dumps are to carry economical loads, that is to say, they must be loaded with stores to the full weight or bulk which they can carry over the route to be traversed.
No men are to be allowed on any wagon.

1081. SICK WASTAGE.

The following is the Sick Wastage Return for week ended noon 1st instant :-

	O.	D.R.		O.	O.R.
14th Div.H.Q.,A.S.C.Att.		1	5th K.S.L.I.		5
14th Div. Cavalry,		1	9th K.R.R.C.		10
14th Div. Cyclists,		1	9th R.B.		3
46th Bde R.F.A.		Nil	6th Somerset L.I.	1	1
47th Bde R.F.A.		Nil	6th D.C.L.I.	1	5
48th Bde R.F.A.		2	6th K.O.Y.L.I.		5
49th Bde R.F.A.	1	6	10th Durham L.I.		6
14th D.A.C.		4	11th L'pool R		1
61st Field Co. R.E.		Nil	8th M.M.G.Bty		Nil
62nd Field Co. R.E.		1	14th Div.Train,		7
89th Field Co. R.E.		Nil	14th Supply Column,		4
14th Signal Co.		Nil	42nd Fd.Amblce A.S.C.		
7th K.R.R.C.		6	attached,		1
8th K.R.R.C.	1	4	43rd Field Amblce.		Nil
7th R.B.		6	44th Field Amblce.		1
8th R.B.		8	16th Mob.Vet.Section.		Nil
5th Ox & Bucks,		5	25th Sanitary Sec.		Nil

Totals Officers 4, Other Ranks 94.

LIEUT-COLONEL,
A.A.&.Q.M.G.
14TH (LIGHT) DIVISION.

N O T I C E.

LOST: On 2nd inst on the POPERINGHE-PROVEN road near Chateau de Couthove, a dark brown Gelding Mule, with head collar and chain attached. No.10 off fore, 799 near fore, very wild and difficult to handle.
Information to O.C., 14th Div. Cavalry.

14TH (LIGHT) DIVISION.

ROUTINE ORDERS.

5th January, 1916.

1082. CARPENTERS.

Infantry Units will forward, through the usual channels, the names of all men on their strength who are Carpenters by profession.

Names to reach this office by 12 noon 8th inst.

1083. GRENADES - DEFECTS IN.

Corps Routine Order No.336 dated 3rd inst is re-published:-
"It has been reported that there has been isolated cases where perforations have been found in the wall between the Striker and Detonator Wells of the MILLS Grenade.

It is doubtful whether the perforations would cause an accident, but to be on the safe side, if when Grenades are being assembled, any are found so perforated, they should be returned to an Ammunition Railhead with a note saying why they are returned.

(Authority: D.D.O.S.,2nd Army 81/8, d/1/1/16.)
6th Corps No.Q.636/24."

1084. MISCELLANEOUS.

Arrangements have been made for washing and drying socks at the Divisional Baths, but it should be understood that this is supplementary to regimental arrangements, and is intended solely for the benefit of troops in the trenches.

The following number of pairs can be dealt with daily from the Infantry Brigades stated :-

41st Infantry Brigade	...	400 pairs
42nd " "	...	200 "
43rd " "	...	400 "

for LIEUT-COLONEL,
A.A.&.Q.M.G.
14TH (LIGHT) DIVISION.

NOTICE.

LOST on 1st January at Div.H.Q. a Light Draught HORSE - Black, Height 15.3, Age 6 or 7 years, white star on forehead, cross clipped on near side of neck, R.F.A. on hoofs.

Information to Camp Commandant, 14th Division.

14TH (LIGHT) DIVISION.

ROUTINE ORDERS.

6th January, 1916.

1085. DIVISIONAL BATHS.

Commencing on January 8th, Units attending the Baths should arrive in parties of 50 every 20 minutes. The Baths will be allotted on this basis in future, thus permitting a greater number to be dealt with than hitherto.

1086. APPOINTMENT.

2nd Lieut. F. Berisford, 10th Durham Light Infantry is granted the local rank of Captain while in Command of 14th Divisional Mining Company, with permission to wear the badges of that rank.

L Worthington Wilmer Maj
for.
LIEUT-COLONEL,
A.A.&.Q.M.G.
14TH (LIGHT) DIVISION.

N O T I C E.

FOUND: Brown GELDING, 166 on near fore, 14 on off fore.

Black MARE, 216 on near fore, A O C on near fore.

Apply, D/48th Brigade R.F.A.

14th (LIGHT) DIVISION.

ROUTINE ORDERS.

8th JANUARY 1916.

1087. CARDS FOR GALLANT & MERITORIOUS SERVICE.

Cards for Gallant and Meritorious Service have been awarded the following.
The Major General Commanding heartily congratulates the recipients.

7th K.R.R.C.

  No. 2851, A/C.S.M. J.Jones.
  "   6364, Sergt   S.Wilson.
  "   R8004, Rfn   Milward.
  "   A3079, "   Ledbrooke.
  "   R6454, "   W.Nixon.

8th K.R.R.C.

  No. 157, Corpl   W.E.Crewe.
  "   8353, Rfn   G.F.Snow.
  "   8354, "   L.N.Hutton.
  "   429, "   W.Lewington.

7th Rifle Brigade.

  No. 2502, A/Cpl H.Watts.
  "   2685, "   R.Parry.

8th Rifle Brigade.

  No. B3199, Sergt A.W.Kimberley.

5th Oxford & Bucks L.I.

  No. 10694, Corpl F.Hancock.

9th K.R.R.C.

  No. 10350, Rfn   Underwood.

6th Somerset L.I.

  No. 15264, C.S.M. T.Peppin.

6th D.C.L.I.

  No. 10821, Pte Brackenbury.
  "   11015, L.Cpl C.D.Smith.
  "   15066, "   G.Schofield.
  "   14933, "   E.Muldary.

11th King's Liverpool Regt.

  No. 12343, Corpl W.Smith.

'A' Batty. 47th F.A.Bde.

  89303, Sergt F.G.Sawyer.

'B' Batty. 47th F.A.Bde.

  84022, Gr G.Griffiths.

14th Divn Ammunition Column.

  45538, Bdr A.Copsey.

61st Field Coy R.E.

  42059, Sappr A.Hill.
  4044, "   A.Thompson.

44th Field Ambulance.

  31667, Sergt R.Eastham.

1088. HONOURS & REWARDS.

Recommendations for Honours and Rewards for the fighting at HOOGE in July last, continue to be received.
For the future no recommendations for reward for services rendered prior to December 1st 1915 are to be submitted to this Office.

1089. TRANSPORT.

Orders as regards transport for the Trenches and Canal Bank are circulated herewith.

1090. CLOTHING.

Owing to the very heavy issues of shirts to the troops, no shirts will be issued in lieu of vests. The supply of vests is now sufficient to meet demands.

1091. GUM-BOOTS.

All Units in possession of gum-boots thigh, will render a weekly certificate to reach this Office by 6 pm on Thursdays, showing number of boots destroyed by enemy fire, number sent back with sick and wounded to Field Ambulances, number lost through exigencies of the Service and numbers lost by neglect. The period covered by the Certificate will be from 12 noon on Wednesdays to 12 noon following Wednesday.

The number of boots still on hand should be stated at the foot of the Certificate.

The Certificate will be rendered by each Infantry Brigade as regards the whole Brigade.

1092. ELVERDINGHE - ADMINISTRATIVE COMMANDANT.

O.C., 11th King's Liverpool Regt is appointed Administrative Commandant, ELVERDINGHE.

The ELVERDINGHE area will include as much of Squares B 13 b, B 14, B 15 a and B 15 c as lies within the zone of the British Army.

Infantry Brigades and R.A. will notify the Administrative Commandant of all reliefs affecting this Area and of any troops withdrawn or added to those in the Area.

The Administrative Commandant will allot all accomodation within the Area and will be responsible for sanitation and camp stores.

He will be responsible for policing the grounds of the CHATEAU, but outside the grounds the A.P.M., 14th Division will make all police arrangements.

Troops allotted to the ELVERDINGHE Area will invariably send an advance party on the day previous to the arrival of the main body, to report to the Administrative Commandant and to be shown the exact allotment of the Area.

Officers Commanding are responsible that these advance parties acquaint themselves with all local orders and that these are communicated to the troops as soon as possible, and that every man in the Area is made acquainted with the local orders.

The Administrative Commandant will report all damages caused by the Troops, to Division Headquarters.

1093. RUBBISH - DISPOSAL OF.

The method of disposing of rubbish by conveying it to Divisional Incinerators is to be discontinued from this date, and the following adopted -

(a) Units in the Trenches and at ELVERDINGHE and Artillery in action will bury it.
(b) Other Units will construct camp incinerators, where such do not already exist, and will burn all rubbish on the spot.

1094. TRAFFIC CONTROL.

The Road G 26 Central (Sheet 28) to L 17 d 7.3 (Sheet 27) is closed to all traffic bound S.E. between the hours 8 am and 9 am, and will be available for light traffic in a N.W. direction between the hours of 2 pm and 5 pm.

1095. FORAGE.

From the 11th instant inclusive, the hay ration per horse will be reduced to 6 lbs until further orders. Owing to a shortage, as much hay and straw as possible should be saved.

1096. **FIRE EXTINGUISHERS.**

Units and Administrative Commandant will render a Return through the usual channels, by 13th instant, showing:-

    (a) Number of fire extinguishers on charge, if any

    (b) Where situated.

L Worthington Wilmer Major
for Lieut Colonel.
A.A. & Q.M.G., 14th (Light) Divn.

NOTICES.

LOST. On January 3rd from Wagon Lines of B/47th F.A.Bde, just East of POPERINGHE on main YPRES road, a Bay Gelding about 15.2, white star and stripe also fetlock, Marked near hind quarter 83 B.47 also on off hind hoof B 47, last seen going towards VLAMERTINGHE carrying complete set of draught harness.
Information to Wagon Lines B/47 Bde R.F.A.

DIVINE SERVICES, Sunday 9th January.

Church of England.

    9.30 am in Barn occupied by 25th Sanitary Section for Division Headquarters.

Roman Catholic.

    Mass at 10 am also Service at 3 pm at B Huts, Brandhook Road for all R.C.Troops in vicinity. Guide will be posted at Cross Roads.

    9 am - Mass at No, 1 Camp, A 16 Central.
    11 am - Mass at ELVERDINGHE.
    11 am - Mass at POPERINGHE.

Wesleyans, Presbyterians, &c.

    9 am - Service at Church Army Hut, B Huts for Troops in vicinity.

    11.30 am - Service at ELVERDINGHE CHATEAU for 5th Oxford & Bucks L.I. and 11th Liverpool Regt.

    4 pm - Service at A 16 c. for t 5th K.S.L.I.

14TH (LIGHT) DIVISION.

ROUTINE ORDERS.

9th January, 1916.

1097. LAMPS.

A report of the number of lamps in possession of Units and of caretakers of camps is to be rendered to this office by 13th instant.
The following lamps will be separately shown :-

      Hurricane Lamps,
      Hanging Lamps,
      Table Lamps,
      Lanterns, tent, folding.

The report will show which of these lamps, if any, form part of the authorised equipment of the Unit concerned according to A.F. G.1098.
Each Camp is to be shown separately in this report.

1098. SICK WASTAGE.

The following is the Sick Wastage Return for week ended noon 8th instant :-

Unit	O.	O.R.	Unit	O.	O.R.
14th Div.Cavalry,		3	5th K.S.K.L.		5.
14th Div.Cyclists,		Nil.	9th K.R.R.C.	2	8
46th Bde R.F.A.		2	9th R.B.		8
47th Bde R.F.A.		6.	5th Somerset L.I.		6
48th Bde R.F.A.		2.	6th D.C.L.I.		8
49th Bde R.F.A.		3.	6th K.O.Y.L.I.		6
14th D.A.C.		2.	10th Durham L.I.		4.
61st Field Co. R.E.		1.	11 L'pool R(RAMC attd)		1
62nd Field Co. R.E.		1.	11 L'pool R		3
89th Field Co. R.E.		Nil.	8th M.M.G.Bty.		Nil.
14th Signal Co.		Nil.	14th Div.Train.		4.
7th K.R.R.C.	1	8	14th Supply Column,		Nil.
8th K.R.R.C.	1	7	42nd F.A. ASC attd.		1.
7th R.B.		17	43rd F.A.		Nil
8th R.B.	1	8	43rd F.A. ASC attd.		1
5th Ox & Bucks,		14	44th F.A.	1	
			26th Mob.Vet.Sec.		Nil.
			25th Sanitary Sec.		Nil.

Totals Officers 7 O.Rs 128.

[signature]

LIEUT-COLONEL,
A.A.& Q.M.G.
14TH (LIGHT) DIVISION.

14TH (LIGHT) DIVISION.

ROUTINE ORDERS.

10th January, 1916.

1099. WAGONS, G.S.

Units other than Artillery, will report through the usual channels to reach this office by 12 noon 13th instant, the number of Wagons G.S. in possession outside those authorised by A.F. G.1098, stating from what source they were obtained.

1100. INDENTS.

Brigades will indent on C.R.E. for such Sniperscopes, periscopes, and rifle batteries as they require, and will distribute them as may be necessary.

1101. BILLETING.

Attention is called to G.R.O.684 of 28th February, 1915, and the instructions issued therewith, and republished in Extracts from G.R.Os.

Units taking up new billets will invariably acquaint the local authority of their requirements before taking up the billets, except in the area nearest to the enemy, in which the troops are close-billeted. In this area it is sufficient if troops notify the local authority of the numbers in occupation of each billet at the time when they enter the billet. In other areas the local authority allots the troops to different billets on different occasions so as to equalise the incidence of billeting over the whole commune.

1102. FUEL.

Infantry Battalions will fetch their own coal from the coal store according to the existing time tables until January 15 inclusive. After that date it will be delivered by the Divisional Train.

(over).

1103. **COMMISSIONS.**

Names are required of any young engineers serving in the ranks who are recommended and desirous of being granted <u>temporary</u> commissions in the rank of Second Lieutenant in the Royal Engineers, for appointment to Labour Battalions.

<u>Only those N.C.Os and men who have enlisted for the period of the war are eligible for these commissions.</u>

Candidates should be Civil engineers possessing at least one of the following qualifications :-
- (a) Associate members of the Institute of Civil Engineers.
- (b) Have passed the examination of the Institute and worked as engineers for 3 years.
- (c) Have served an apprenticeship in the United Kingdom, Canada or Australia with a recognised firm.
- (d) Possessors of a civil engineering degree of a University and have worked as Engineers for 3 years.
- (e) Have worked and received pay as engineers abroad for 3 years.

Applications will be forwarded on Form M.T.393, accompanied by all particulars as to technical qualifications.

All intending candidates should be interviewed by the C.R.E. or Senior R.E. Officer available in the Division or other formation to which they belong, and reported on as to their general fitness for commissions.

LIEUT COLONEL
A.A.&.Q.M.G
14TH (LIGHT) DIVISION.

14TH (LIGHT) DIVISION.

ROUTINE ORDERS.

11th January, 1916.

1104. LIGHTS ON MOTOR VEHICLES.

Attention is called to C.R.O. 328 of 1st January.
Complaints have been received that Motor Vehicles with strong head lights go East of STEENJE windmill and nearly to ELVERDINGHE. This practice is to cease.
A.P.M. will report any breach of this order to Divisional Headquarters.

1105. ADMINISTRATIVE.

Battalions and other units in the ELVERDINGHE area will be responsible for the Policing of the whole of the area assigned to them by the Administrative Commandant, ELVERDINGHE, and for the care of all Government Stores in the area assigned to them, notwithstanding that the general Police arrangements of the whole area will be supervised by the Administrative Commandant.
The accommodation of the men will be told off under directions of the O.C.Battalion or other Unit and the men are to occupy the Tents, or huts, or dug-outs to which they are told off. They must not be allowed to make use of unoccupied tents, huts or dug-outs on their own initiative. These unoccupied places must at all times be kept clean and clear of rubbish.

1106. PREVENTION OF LICE.

A supply of Oxford Grease and Powder is now available and Units should indent for the same as soon as possible. The Ointment should be rubbed well into the seams of the Coat and trousers while <u>at the same time</u> the underclothing is thoroughly dusted with the powder.

1107. PASSES.

The attention of all ranks is directed to G.R.O.589, which is re-published for information :-
"No officers or men will, except on duty, visit the area occupied by the French or Belgian Armies without authority from General Headquarters.
In the case of officers permitted to visit the Belgian area of operations they will report themselves on arrival to the Headquarters of the British Mission".

1108. DEFENSIVE CHEMICAL CORPS.

Commanding Officers will forward through the usual channels the name of 1 N.C.O. per battery R.A., and 1 N.C.O. per Company R.E. and Infantry, who can be recommended for a course of instruction with the 2nd Army Defensive Chemical Corps.
N.C.Os recommended should be intelligent and have some previous chemical training.
Names to reach this office by January 15th.

(over)

1109. RECOMMENDATIONS FOR PERMANENT COMMISSIONS.

    Reference D.R.O. 557 dated September 16th 1915, it is noted that the applications of candidates which have been returned from time to time are often re-submitted and no further remarks or recommendations are made.

    If an officer has improved since his application was first submitted it is all to his advantage if this is stated when his application is again sent in - the stronger the recommendations made, the more chance the candidate has of being recommended for a permanent commission.

LIEUT-COLONEL,
A.A.&.Q.M.G.
14TH (LIGHT) DIVISION.

14TH (LIGHT) DIVISION.

ROUTINE ORDERS.

12th January, 1916.

1110. OFFICERS - TRANSFERS TO R.F.C.

Applications from Volunteers for duty with the Royal Flying Corps are to be submitted through the usual channels whether the candidate is recommended or not. In no case is a Commanding Officer to decline to forward an application. The suitability of a candidate and the advisability of withdrawing him from his Unit will be reserved for decision at G.H.Q.

Commanding Officers will invariably state their reasons for recommending or declining to recommend an application.

1111. TUBE HELMETS.

The return called for in D.R.O.1056, dated 26th December, 1915, will, in future, be rendered by all Units.

1112. MATERIAL - Collection of.

In all cases where requisitions are given for material such as bricks, timber etc., the purpose for which the materials are taken must be indicated on the duplicate sent to the Branch Requisition Office and whether the materials have been taken from houses ruined by enemy shell fire.

LIEUT-COLONEL,
A.A.&.Q.M.G.
14TH (LIGHT) DIVISION.

NOTICE.

LOST: On 7th inst: from wagon travelling in direction of POPERINGHE, BAG containing Acquittance roll, A.B. 152, and Coy Roll Book.
Information to O.C., 10th Durham L.I.

14TH (LIGHT) DIVISION.

ROUTINE ORDERS.

13th January, 1916.

1113. PHOTOGRAPHY.

Attention is directed to G.R.Os 1137 and 1348. No Officer or soldier, or other person subject to Military law is permitted to be in possession of a Camera.

Commanding Officers will take steps to see that any camera which may now be in the possession of any officer or soldier, is returned immediately to England. Films or plates will be destroyed. Any Officer or soldier, or other person subject to Military Law, found in possession of a camera will be placed in arrest and the case reported to General Headquarters for instructions as to disposal.

This order will be repeated in order issued by all units and will be promulgated to all troops serving with the 14th Division and to all drafts or new units which join the 14th Division.

1114. DRINKING WATER.

Units in the new area will fill their water carts from sources as follows :-

Area.	Source of Supply.	Scoops of Chloride of lime required per Cart-load.
Elverdinghe.	Pumps in Elverdinghe Village	1
	Pump in Elverdinghe Chateau,	1
	Steentje Mill,	1.
Other Units East of Poperinghe Canal	Steentje Mill.	1.
Camps Nos.1 & 2.	Laiterie (Poperinghe)	Nil.
Camps " 3 & 4.	Pumps & Well at St.Sixte,	1.
Poperinghe.	Laiterie,	Nil.

1115. TUBE HELMETS.

It is notified for information that wet does not effect the chemical solution in which Tube helmets are saturated to any extent, so long as the Tube helmet is kept in its container. If a helmet becomes so sodden that it is impossible to breathe through it, it must be replaced.

1116. ENTRIES IN FIELD CONDUCT SHEET.

G.R.O. 1349 dated 9th inst., is re-published :-
"Cases continue to come to light where vague entries in the Field Conduct Sheet (Army Form B.122) such as "Conduct to the prejudice of good order and military discipline" or "Improper Conduct" are made. The nature of the offence must invariably be stated, e.g., Conduct to the prejudice of good order and military discipline— "Alcoholism".

- 2 -

117. **UNCENSORED LETTERS.**

G.R.O. 1353 dated 9th inst., is re-published :-
"As cases still occur in which men proceeding on leave take with them uncensored letters in order that they may be posted in England, General Routine Order No.612 is re-published for information :-
612 - Uncensored letters.
With reference to Routine Order No.195, dated 12th October, 1914, many cases have recently come to notice in which men proceeding on leave have taken with them uncensored letters in order that they may be posted in England. In future men about to proceed on leave will be informed that if at any time during their journey they are found in possession of uncensored letters, they will be placed in arrest and sent back to their units".

LIEUT-COLONEL,
A.A.&Q.M.G.
14TH (LIGHT) DIVISION

NOTICE.

FOUND: On the night of 12/13th Jan. between Bridge 4 and BRIELEN,
(1) BLACK MARE, clipped ◇ on neck, Officer's colonial saddle and Bridle.
(2) Chestnut GELDING, white star on forehead, clipped ◇ on neck, universal saddle and bridle.
Apply to Transport Officer, 6th D.C.L.I.

The following extracts from a letter to the General Officer-Commanding in Chief from Admiral of the Fleet Sir John Jellicoe, G.C.B., K.C.V.O., are published for information :-
" I must write these few lines to endeavour to express my thanks and, indeed, the thanks of all of us in the Grand Fleet, for the splendid treatment which the first batch of officers and men received on the occasion of their visit to the trenches. From one and all comes the same story.
First, of gratitude for their reception.
Second, of the loudest praise and enthusiasm for the extraordinary cheerfulness and wonderful spirit imbuing all ranks of the Army under the worst possible conditions.
I made a stipulation that each officer and man going to France should recount his experiences to his shipmates in a lecture, on return. They are all doing it with great zest and their one story is of the spirit of your officers and men.
I feel that you should know the impression created on Officers and men who themselves are accustomed to pretty rough conditions.
It must give a great feeling of confidence to command such men.
May I take this opportunity of asking if you will let officers and men know how great is our admiration for them, how closely we watch their gallant fight, and how we long to help them.
The day when we can do so may yet come"

14TH (LIGHT) DIVISION.

ROUTINE ORDERS.

14th January, 1916.

1118. GUM BOOTS THIGH.

Men are still observed walking about near their billets and in places like POPERINGHE wearing gum boots thigh. This is contrary to C.R.O. 339 dated 7th inst and must at once cease.

The excuse usually given is that the man's ankle boots have been lost or destroyed in the trenches. In future any man not in possession of ankle boots for any reason will remain in his billet until they have been replaced.

Any man found walking about in Gum Boots thigh under the circumstances not covered by C.R.O. 339 will be placed in close arrest.

If several cases are reported in the same unit, it will be for consideration whether gum boots thigh shall not be withdrawn from the unit.

This order is to be repeated in the orders of all units of the Division and read on three successive parades.

1119. RATIONS.

The practice of overdrawing rations in order to provide for unforeseen emergencies is not permitted.

Drafts have recently arrived at such short notice that units have been unable to obtain rations for them between receiving notification of the draft and the time of arrival. To meet the case of drafts arriving without sufficient notice, O.C., Divl Train will arrange for 500 rations to be always available for issue on the day of receipt of special supplementary indents.

O.C. Divl Train will be informed by Divl Headquarters as soon as notification of the arrival of reinforcements is received and he will then comply with such supplementary indents for rations as may be made necessary by the arrival of drafts.

Units are not to keep a stock of rations.

1120. HONOURS AND REWARDS.

When leave is granted to N.C.Os and men to whom the Victoria Cross has been awarded but who have not received the decoration, the following information is to be furnished before the leave begins, by the O.C. Unit direct to the Director of Personal Services, a copy of the letter being sent through the usual channels to Divisional Headquarters:-
Regimental Number,
Rank and Name,
Corps,
Period of Leave.
Full address while on leave.

If this information is available at the War Office it will be possible for arrangements to be made for the attendance, if required, of these N.C.Os and men at Buckingham Palace.

(over)

1121. KNOBKERRIES.

Units requiring Knobkerries or Knobkerry collars should indent on the C.R.E.

Laytham ?

LIEUT-COLONEL,
A.A.&.Q.M.G.
14TH (LIGHT) DIVISION.

NOTICES.

LOST. MARE, Chestnut, white blaze full length of face, a few dry scabs on both hind legs. Long undocked tail.
GELDING, Black, ∧ on near hind.
Both animals lost about 3 a.m. this morning.
Information to Transport Officer, 11th L'pool R (Pioneers).

LOST. L.D.HORSE, Black Gelding, white star. Strayed from lines of rear Section, D.A.C. at L.1.a. Sheet 27, on night of 7th inst.
Information to O.C., 14th Divisional Ammunition Column.

DIVINE SERVICES.

C. of E.
9.30 a.m. At Divl Headquarters.

R.C.
Mass at 10 a.m., also service at 3 p.m. at "B" Huts, Brandhoek Road for all R.C. troops in vicinity. Guide will be posted at Cross-roads.
9 a.m. Mass at No. 1 Camp, WOESTEN.
11 a.m.   "   " ELVERDINGHE Chateau.
11 a.m.   "   " POPERINGHE, (Notre Dame).

WESLEYANS & NONCONFORMISTS etc.

9.a.m. At Cyclists H.Qrs for Cyclists and Cavalry.
11 a.m. At "B" Huts for 5th Ox & Bucks L.I.
11 a.m. At The College, POPERINGHE, for 44th Fd.Amblce.
3.p.m. At "A" Huts for 10th Bn. Durham L.I.
3.p.m. At "B" Co. 8th K.R.R.C.
5.30 p.m. At H.Q.7th K.R.R.C. for 7th K.R.R.C. or troops Billeted at A.16.Central.

=========

14TH (LIGHT) DIVISION.

ROUTINE ORDERS.

15th January, 1916.

1122. SICK.

Commencing on the afternoon of the 15th inst., a ward for "Detained" men will be opened at the Section 42nd Field Ambulance at A.28.a. This is for the accommodation of such slight "sick" as do not require admission to a Field Ambulance, but who, at the time, are not quite fit for duty in the trenches.

These men will be sent to the "Detained Ward" on the afternoon that their battalion proceeds to the trenches, and will be returned to it on the day following the night of its relief.

They must take with them their rations for the following day, or else a message must be despatched, as early as possible, to the O.C. Section, 42nd Field Ambulance, stating the probable number that will be sent.

C. Parsons Bapt
LIEUT-COLONEL,
A.A.&.Q.M.G.
14TH (LIGHT) DIVISION.

NOTICE.

DIVINE SERVICE.
C of E. There will be a celebration of the Holy Communion on Sunday January 16th, at the Church Army Hut, Brandhoek, at 11-30 a.m.

The R.A. Band, which has been brought over from England, will play in the 6th Corps area from 15th to 19th inclusive.

On 16th, 17th, 18th, and 19th the R.A. Band will play at the 6th Division Fancies Theatre at 6 p.m.

On 17th it will play at the Church Army Hut, BRANDHOEK, at 2 p.m.

Other fixtures will be notified when arranged.

14TH (LIGHT) DIVISION.

ROUTINE ORDERS.

16th January, 1916.

1123. LOADING WAGONS: 6TH CORPS PARK.

From 17th instant inclusive, the loading of wagons at 6th Corps R.E. Park will be arranged by Chief Engineer 6th Corps.
Loading parties from 14th Division will not be required.

1124. PAYMENTS FOR BILLETING.

Attention is directed to 2nd Army Routine Order No. 280 of 7th instant.
Army Forms W.3401 should be indented for from Base Stationery Office, and taken into use forthwith.

[signature]

LIEUT-COLONEL.
A.A.&.Q.M.G.
14TH (LIGHT) DIVISION.

NOTICE.

The R.A. Band, which has been brought over from England, will play in the 6th Corps area from 15th to 19th inclusive.
On 16th, 17th, 18th and 19th, the R.A. Band will play at the 6th Division Fancies Theatre at 6 p.m.
On 17th it will play at the Church Army Hut, BRANDHOEK at 2 p.m.
Other fixtures will be notified when arranged.

14TH (LIGHT) DIVISION.

ROUTINE ORDERS.

17th January, 1916.

1125. DISCIPLINE - USE OF DRUGS.

General Routine Order No. 1360 dated 15-1-16, is re-published :-

"In consequence of certain acquittals in recent cases of alleged drunkenness, it is pointed out for information that if a person subject to Military Law takes a drug, and the effect of that drug, either by itself, or in conjunction with alcohol, is to render him unfit for duty, that person may be lawfully convicted of the offence of drunkenness, from whatever motive he may have taken the drug, unless he takes it, having previously reported sick in the proper manner, upon the order of the medical officer.

In the case of a medical officer, the opinion of another medical officer will be necessary before taking a drug that may render him unfit for duty."

1126. CENSORSHIP - GREEN ENVELOPES.

G.R.O. No. 1361 dated 15-1-16 is re-published :-

"1. The use of the green envelope for multiple letters is intended to enable men to send more than one letter a week of a private nature, which they may not wish to submit for censorship to their immediate commander. They are only to contain letters from the person who signs the certificate on the cover: the practice of enclosing letters from more than one writer is forbidden.

2. The existence of these envelopes is not to be used as a means to absolve officers from the duty of regimental censorship, or to induce or compel men to send all their letters in these envelopes.

3. Letters sent to the Base Censors for forwarding are not to be enclosed in any outer covers other than the officially issued green envelope.

1127. SICK WASTAGE.

The following is the Sick Wastage Return for week-ending noon 15th instant :-

Unit	B.D.R.	Unit	O.O.R.
14th Div.Cavalry,	1	9th K.R.R.C.	14
14th Div.Cyclists,	Nil.	9th R.B.	14
46th Bde R.F.A.	1 5	6th Somersets,	1 9
47th Bde R.F.A.	3	6th D.C.L.I.	9
48th Bde R.F.A.	5	6th K.O.Y.L.I.	5
49th Bde R.F.A.	1	10th Durhams,	7
14th D.A.C.	4	11th L'pool R(Pioneers)	11
61st Field Co. R.E.	Nil.	8th M.G.Btty,	1
62nd Field Co. R.E.	Nil.	14th Divl Train,	2
89th Field Co. R.E.	1.	14th Supply Column,	Nil.
14th Signal Co.	Nil.	42nd Field Amblce.	1
7th K.R.R.C.	5.	42nd Field Amblce,ASC attd	1
8th K.R.R.C.	5.	43rd Field Amblce,	Nil.
7th R.B.	11.	44th Field Amblce.	Nil.
8th R.B.	8.	26th Mob.Vet.Section,	Nil.
5th Ox & Bucks,	14.	25th Sanitary Section,	1.
5th K.S.L.I.	6.		

Total Officers 2 O.Rs 146.

N O T I C E.

R.A. BAND will perform at HOSPITAL FARM on 19th inst.,
at 2 p.m.

14TH (LIGHT) DIVISION.

ROUTINE ORDERS.

18th January, 1916.

1128. **GUM BOOTS - THIGH.**

Gum Boots thigh certified on weekly Certificate as "Destroyed by shell fire" and "Lost through the exigences of the service" will be replaced each week under orders from Divisional Headquarters.

Gum Boots thigh returned to D.A.D.O.S. and evacuated to Field Ambulances on wounded will be replaced on submission of receipts to Divisional Headquarters.

These replacements are subject to there being sufficient numbers of boots in stock at the time.

Steps must be taken to prevent the evacuation of gum Boots thigh with sick to Field Ambulances.

1129. **CLIPPING OF HORSES.**

The conditions subject to which horses are clipped are re-published for information :-
1. At least a saddle patch is to be left on Riding horses.
2. At least a blanket patch is to be left on draught horses.
3. The hair is not to be removed from the legs below the forearm and stifle..

Subject to these conditions the question of clipping will, in future, be left to the Unit commanders.

[signed] C.E. Hamilton

LIEUT-COLONEL,
A.A.&.Q.M.G.
14TH (LIGHT) DIVISION.

NOTICE.

R.A.BAND will perform at HOSPITAL FARM on 19th instant at 2 p.m.

STOLEN. Four BICYCLES, from PUSH BYKE FARM, on or about the 4th instant. Each cycle had a distinguishing mark on rear mud-guard, of a white disc, and a white number on the cross bar, Nos 33, 35,167 and 197.
Information to O.C., 14th Divisional Cyclist Co.

STOLEN. On morning of 17th instant, from 42nd Infantry Bde Transport Lines (G.12.c.4.8) BICYCLE, marked 9th R.B.
Information to B.T.O., 42nd Infantry Brigade.

14TH (LIGHT) DIVISION.

ROUTINE ORDERS.

19th January, 1916.

1130. ADMINISTRATIVE.

O.C., "B" Battery, 47th Bde R.F.A. is appointed Administrative Commandant of BRIELEN village. He will allot the accommodation there in accordance with instructions from Divisional Headquarters.

All buildings etc. in BRIELEN other than the billets allotted to their own unit, are out of bounds to the troops.

Changes of Units occupying BRIELEN are to be notified in advance to the O.C.,"B" Battery, 47th Bde, R.F.A.

1131. SICK.

Reference D.R.O. No.1122 dated 15th instant, for "42nd Field Ambulance" read "43rd Field Ambulance".

C.C.Hamilton

LIEUT COLONEL,
A.A.&.Q.M.G.,
14TH (LIGHT) DIVISION.

NOTICE.

LOST: On the 17th instant from H.Qrs 49th Bde R.F.A. Dark Chestnut HORSE, Height 15.1, age 10 years, Marks:-
Face - Star, Blaze, Snip into both nostrils underlip
Body - Complete with set of appointments, /⋀ mark on near hind quarters, Four white stockings, No.94 on near fore and B/49 on off fore.
Information to O.C."B"/49th Brigade R.F.A.

14th (LIGHT) DIVISION.

ROUTINE ORDERS.

20th JANUARY 1916.

1132. TRENCH COOKERS.

Any Trench Cookers which are not required should be returned to R.E. at once for return to 2nd Army Workshops.

1133. FIRES.

With reference to G.R.O.1575.
Courts of Enquiry will be assembled by Brigadier Generals Commanding Infantry Brigades, or G.O.C.,R.A., in the case of fires occurring in localities occupied by troops under their command alone.

When a fire occurs in a locality by other Divisional Troops or by Units of more than one Infantry Brigade or of Artillery and other Troops, a report will be sent to Divisional Headqrs by wire immediately after the occurrence, with a view to the assembly of a Court of Enquiry under Divisional arrangements.

1134. HONOURS & REWARDS.

A List of Special Promotions and Military Decorations awarded to Officers, Warrant Officers, Non-commissioned Officers and men 14th (Light) Division and notified in the London Gazette of January 14th is published herewith.

1135. HONOURS & REWARDS.

Clasp to Distinguished Conduct Medal.

Reference D.R.O. No.1033 dated 18th December 1915
No. B/1652, Corporal W.HOBDAY, 8th Bn The Rifle Brigade having been awarded a Distinguished Conduct Medal in the London Gazette dated 14th January 1916 a clasp to that Medal has now been awarded him in recognition of his bravery on the 23rd November 1915.
(Authority M.S./H/1425 dated 16th January 1916)

1136. DISCIPLINE ON LEAVE.

G.R.O. No.1338 dated 19th January is republished.
"All N.C.O's and men will be warned before proceeding on Leave that they are forbidden to bring bottles of liquor with them to the train or boat when returning from leave."

1137. BOUNDS.

C.R.O.362 dated 19th January 1916 is republished.
"The estaminet BLANKE LINDE (Sheet 27, F.17.c.2,5) is put out of bounds for troops until further orders from the 19th instant inclusive."

1138. **RUM JARS.**

C.R.O. number 368 dated 19th January is republished.
Owing to the difficulty of obtaining jars in England, rum is now being shipped to this country in casks. Endeavours will be made to decant as much of this as possible at Base, in order that the difficulty and inconvenience of handling casks in the Field may be thereby minimised. To effect this, it is imperative that all available jars in sound condition should be returned to Base. Steps will be taken to ensure that this is done.
(Authority: D.D.S & T., 2nd Army, S/191/15, dated 17/1/16).   6th Corps, Q/1456.

1139. **IDENTIFICATION OF VEHICLES.**

C.R.O. number 369 dated 19th January 1916 is republished.
All Units will forward through the usual channels to this office by noon, 22nd instant, a report, stating whether the H.T. and M.T. vehicles (excluding cars and motor cycles) on their charge, have had the recently approved signs for identification purposes painted on them. If not, this should be done at once, and the cause of delay stated on the report.   (6th Corps, Q85/1.)

LIEUT-COLONEL,
A.A.&.Q.M.G.
14TH (LIGHT) DIVISION.

14TH (LIGHT) DIVISION.

ROUTINE ORDERS.

21st January, 1916.

1140. COMMISSIONS.

It is notified for information that Candidates who are granted Regular Commissions under Army Order 333 and who remain with their former Unit, should retain the Temporary Rank they held in that Unit prior to being gazetted into the Regular Army.
(Authority M.S. T/934 dated 17th January, 1916).

1141. ADMINISTRATIVE.

Reference D.R.O. 1130 dated 19-1-16:
O.C., 47th Brigade R.F.A. is appointed Administrative Commandant of BRIELEN village from this date.
Captain C.H. Harbinson, R.A.M.C. is appointed Sanitary officer for BRIELEN village.

LIEUT-COLONEL,
A.A.&.Q.M.G.
14TH (LIGHT) DIVISION.

NOTICES.

DIVINE SERVICES,
C OF E. Holy Communion 11 a.m. at 62nd Field Co.R.E. Recreation Room.
Divine Service 9 a.m. Divisional Headquarters.

WESLEYANS, PRESBYTERIANS ETC.
9-30 a.m. Cyclists and Div. Cavalry at Convent, STE SIXTE.
11.0 a.m. 8th K.R.R.C. or troops stationed at A.16.Central.
2-30 p.m. 44th Field Ambulance, at College, POPERINGHE.
3-30 p.m. 7th K.R.R.C. at "B" Coys H.Qrs, POPERINGHE.
6-0 p.m. Divisional Train at H.Qr. Coy.

LOST. Between Divisional Rest Station and Divisional Headquarters, TOOL BAG, containing 1 Inner Tube, 2 Sparkling Plugs, 1 Set Belt fasteners and 1 New Driving Belt.
Information to 46th Field Ambulance.

14TH (LIGHT) DIVISION.

ROUTINE ORDERS.

22nd January, 1916.

1142. MUNITION WORKERS.

Reference this office circular No. 1448/33/A relating to Munition Workers, a Return showing No., Rank., Name, Unit., and Trade of all N.C.Os and men skilled in any of the Trades mentioned in above Circular, and who have not already been interviewed by Munition Investigators, will be forwarded by Officers Commanding all Infantry Units direct and by other Units through the usual channels so as to reach this office not later than 6 p.m. 24th instant. Orders will then be issued for the assembly of these men at convenient points on the morning of the 26th instant for interview by Munition Experts.
Nil Returns to be rendered.

Rendered nil

1143. COMMISSIONS IN REGULAR ARMY.

It has been ruled that Candidates who are granted Commissions in the Regular Army under Army Order No.333 will take their date in the Regular Army from the date of the C in Cs recommendation.
Applications for Ante-dating will not be entertained.

1144. ROAD MAKING.

A limited number of fascines for road-making are now available at F.19.c.5.9. (Sheet 27) Indents to C.R.E.

for LIEUT-COLONEL,
A.A.&.Q.M.G.
14TH (LIGHT) DIVISION.

NOTICE.

FOUND: On the VLAMERTINGHE - ELVERDINGHE road on 18th instant, Chestnut GELDING, blood, Blaze fore, White fetlock, about 14 hands. Harness with universal saddle.
For information, apply O.C., 13th Brigade R.G.A.

Ref. 1142 above - Please render return direct to A.A.&Q.M.G. 14th Div.

14TH (LIGHT) DIVISION.

ROUTINE ORDERS.

23rd January, 1916.

1145. LIMBER HOOKS FOR G.S. WAGONS.

1. It has been brought to notice that Limber Hooks for G.S. Limbered wagons are demanded from time to time by Units.
2. The fitting of these entails the removal and renewal of 6 or 12 rivets as the case may be, depending on the pattern of Hook supplied.
3. As many units must necessarily lack facilities for carrying out this service, it is doubtful whether all the hooks supplied have been utilised.
4. No applications are received for a supply of rivets with these hooks, although it is evident that the old rivets cannot be used again.
5. Units will report to this office, by noon, 26th instant, through the proper channels, whether they have any Limber Hooks on charge which cannot be used owing to their not being able to fit them. All such hooks are to be returned to Ordnance Workshops forthwith.

1146. SANITATION.

In order to ensure complete supervision of sanitation in the Division, the areas occupied by troops will be supervised by Field Ambulance Commanders as follows :-

O.C., 42nd Field Ambulance.
Area bounded on the North by the International boundary, on the East by POPERINGHE CANAL, on the West by the POPERINGHE - CROMBEKE road (passing through F.10.d. Sheet 27) and on the South by the interdivisional boundary.

Also camps in occupation by 14th Division in the area between the POPERINGHE - PROVEN and POPERINGHE - ABEELE roads.

O.C., 43rd Field Ambulance.
Area bounded as follows :-
North - International boundary.
East - KEMMELBECK Stream.
South - Interdivisional boundary (14th & 6th Divisions)
West - POPERINGHE CANAL.

O.C., 44th Field Ambulance.
Area in occupation by 14th Division with the following boundaries :-
North - Interdivisional boundary (14th & 6th Divns)
West - POPERINGHE CANAL and road POPERINGHE - ABEELE.
South - Intercorps boundary (VI & V Corps).
East - KEMMELBECK Stream.

(over).

1147. COURTS-MARTIAL.

From the number of cases recently brought to notice of officers detailed for Courts-Martial being ineligible to sit thereon from lack of the necessary qualifications, it appears that the number of young officers detailed to attend the various Field General Courts-Martial, is insufficient to ensure the requisite number of officers fit and qualified to sit on such Courts-Martial being forthcoming when required.

Brigade Commanders will arrange, in future, for at least two, and if possible more, young officers to attend for instruction, each Field General Court-Martial which assembles under their orders.

1148. SICK WASTAGE.

The following is the Sick Wastage Return for week-ended noon 22nd instant :-

Unit	O.	O.R.	Unit	O.	O.R.
14th Div. Cavalry,		1	9th K.R.R.C.	1	15
14th Div. Cyclists,		1	9th R.B.		6
46th F.A. Bde,		3	6th Somersets,	1	8
47th F.A. Bde,		1.	6th D.C.L.I.		6
48th F.A. Bde,		7.	6th K.O.Y.L.I.		6.
49th F.A. Bde,		2.	10th Durhams,		4.
14th D.A.C.		6.	11th L'pool R,		5.
61st Field Co. R.E.	1	-	8th M.M.G. Battery,		Nil.
62nd Field Co. R.E.	1	2	14th Div. Train,		1.
89th Field Co. R.E.		Nil.	14th Supply Column,		Nil.
14th Signal Co. R.E.		Nil.	42nd Field Amblce.		Nil.
7th K.R.R.C.		5.	43rd Field Amblce.		Nil.
8th K.R.R.C.		9.	44th Field Amblce,		2
7th R.B.		12.	26th Mob.Vet.Section,		Nil.
8th R.B.		6.	25th Sanitary Sec.		1.
5th Ox & Bucks,		8.	M.M.P.		2,
5th K.S.L.I.		4.			

Totals Officers 4. Other Ranks, 123.

for LIEUT-COLONEL,
A.A.& Q.M.G.
14TH (LIGHT) DIVISION.

14TH (LIGHT) DIVISION.

ROUTINE ORDERS.

24th January, 1916.

1149. FUEL.

Reference D.R.O.1102 dated 10th instant, the cartage of fuel other than coal is not undertaken by the Divisional Train. Units will send their own wagons for wood and coke.

1150. ACCIDENTS – Grenades.

Corps Routine Order No. 384 dated 23-1-16 is re-published :–
"In the event of any accidents with grenades occurring in future, wires will at once be sent to Corps and Divisional Headquarters, giving full details regarding the nature of the particular grenade which caused the accident, stating whether the same was of British or local manufacture. The remainder of the grenades in the same lot as the faulty one will be put on one side for examination later by an expert.

The above action will in no way interfere with the necessity of holding a Court of Inquiry, which should invariably be done if the accident involves death or injury to any of the personnel."

The wire referred to above will be addressed to Divisional Headquarters and repeated to Brigade H.Q.

1151. SALVAGE.

Salvage parties will be careful not to overlook any ironwork parts of vehicles which may be derelict in their areas, but will collect them and send them to A.O.D.

O.C. Units will also be careful to send to A.O.D. for transmission to the Base any ironwork of unserviceable or replaced components of vehicles in their possession.

Particular attention is to be given to the following articles :–
Turnbuckles and hinges,
Rave stays,
Bugles and plates, tugs and nuts of draught poles.
Fittings of tailboards.

1152. CLIPPING HORSES.

D.R.O. No. 1129 dated 18-1-16, is cancelled.
No horses are to be clipped without reference to Divisional Headquarters.

1153. MACHINE GUN MOUNTINGS.

On the formation of Brigade Machine Gun Companies, Battalions in possession of Disappearing Mountings will transfer them with the Vickers guns to the Brigade Machine Gun Companies.

Brigade Machine Gun Companies will indent on A.O.D. to complete the scale of one Disappearing Mounting per 4 guns authorised.

LIEUT-COLONEL,
A.A.&.Q.M.G.
14TH (LIGHT) DIVISION.

14TH (LIGHT) DIVISION.

ROUTINE ORDERS.

26th January, 1916.

1154. HONOURS AND REWARDS.

VICTORIA CROSS.

Extract from "London Gazette":-

HIS MAJESTY THE KING has been graciously pleased to award the VICTORIA CROSS to the undermentioned Non-Commissioned Officer:-

No. S/107, Corporal ALFRED DRAKE, 8th Bn. The Rifle Brigade (Prince Consort's Own)

For most conspicuous bravery on the night of November 23rd, 1915, near La Brique, France. He was one of a patrol of four which was reconnoitring towards the German lines. The patrol was discovered when close to the enemy, who opened heavy fire with rifles and machine gun, wounding the officer and one man. The latter was carried back by the last remaining man. Corporal Drake remained with his officer, and was last seen kneeling beside him and bandaging his wounds regardless of the enemy's fire. Later, a rescue party crawling near the German lines found the officer and corporal, the former unconscious but alive and bandaged, Corporal Drake beside him dead and riddled with bullets. He had given his own life and saved his officer.

1155. GAS HELMETS.

Indents are to be submitted at once to D.A.D.O.S. for P.H. pattern helmets, at rate of one per officer and man, to replace one of the P tube helmets now in use.

The former are now available and should be drawn without delay.

The wooden packing cases containing the P.H. pattern should be utilised for packing the P tube helmets when returning the latter to Ordnance Stores.

LIEUT-COLONEL,
A.A.&.Q.M.G.
14TH (LIGHT) DIVISION.

NOTICE.

LOST. Black KIT BAG, marked GATES, W.G. No.032590, M.T. A.
Believed to have fallen off lorry whilst travelling between GODEWAERSVELDT and POPERINGHE on 17-1-16, between 10 and 11 a.m.
Kindly return to O.C., 14th Divl Supply Column.

14TH (LIGHT) DIVISION.

ROUTINE ORDERS.

27th January, 1916.

1156. **BILLETING DISTRIBUTION LISTS.**

Reference D.R.O.1124 dated 16-1-16, there is no objection to an informal copy of the official Distribution List being left with the Mayor for his information at the time when the Billeting Certificates are put before him for his signature.

It is important that nothing should interfere with the due receipt by the Branch Requisition Office of the original., i.e., official Distribution List.

(Authority 2nd Army Q/1515/17 dated 24-1-16).

1157. **PROMOTION.**

No. 32067, Private W.H. Colbran, R.A.M.C., attached 14th Divisional Headquarters is promoted to the rank of Corporal, with effect from 15th January, 1916.
(Authority R.A.M.C.Orders, New Army, No.2., dated Record Office, 15th January, 1916).

1158. **COLLECTION OF MATERIAL.**

The system by which units requiring material from ELVERDINGHE obtain passes for the number of loads required is not affected by Corps Routine Order No.393. The passes are still required and will be checked by the Military Police.

Units requiring bricks etc., from BRIELEN will obtain passes from C.R.E. 14th Division in the same way as passes are obtained for bricks etc., from ELVERDINGHE.

Military Police will check passes as at ELVERDINGHE.

No bricks or material will be taken without passes.

LIEUT-COLONEL,
A.A.&.Q.M.G.
14TH (LIGHT) DIVISION.

N O T I C E.

LOST. A BICYCLE, No.114, from HOSPITAL FARM, on 11th inst.
Information to O.C., 14th Divisional Signal Co.R.E.

14TH (LIGHT) DIVISION.

ROUTINE ORDERS.

28th January, 1916.

1159. **DAMAGE TO CROPS.**

General Routine Order No. 1377 dated 26-1-16, is re-published :-
"The attention of all ranks is again directed to the need for care in avoiding damage to newly sown fields and young crops.
Officers and men off duty, whether on foot or on horseback, are forbidden to leave recognised roads and paths to take short cuts across tilled fields.
Games are not to be played in grass fields unless permission has been received from, or some arrangement has been made with the farmer to whom the field belongs.
Troops on duty and undergoing training must take the greatest care to avoid crossing newly sown land and young crops. If for the success of the manoeuvres or training it is essential to do so, arrangements must be made by the officer in command of the troops who do the damage, to report his action to the G.O.C. formation, who will at once take steps to recompense the farmer whose property has been damaged.
This order does not in any way affect the movement of troops in the face of the enemy.
See also General Routine Order No.613, d/8th February, 1915."

1160. **ABSENTEES.**

General Routine Order No.1379 dated 26-1-16 is republished :-
"General Routine Orders Nos.679 and 1071 are cancelled. Commanding Officers will in future transmit Absentee Reports concerning men absent in the United Kingdom, direct to the Officer i/c Records of the unit at home, who will also be informed direct of the return of any soldiers who have previously been reported as absent.
Reports of Absentees in this Country will, as heretofore, be sent to the A.P.M. of the formation concerned".

[signature]

LIEUT-COLONEL,
A.A.&.Q.M.G.
14TH (LIGHT) DIVISION.

NOTICES.
DIVINE SERVICES.

WESLEYANS, PRESBYTERIANS, NONCONFORMISTS ETC.
- 9.30 a.m. 5th Ox & Bucks, Div.H.Qrs, 42nd Bde Transport at Church Army Hut, "B" Huts.
- 9.30 a.m. 14th Cyclists & D.L.O.Y. at St.Sixte Convent.
- 11. a.m. 5th K.S.L.I. & Liverpools at ELVERDINGHE Chateau.
- 11. a.m. 8th R.B. at A.16.Central.
- 2.30 p.m. 44th Field Ambulance, at College, POPERINGHE.
- 3. p.m. 42nd Field Ambulance at Rest Station.
- 3.30.p.m. 7th R.B. at "B" Coy. Quarters.
- 6. p.m. Div. Train at No. 4 Coy. Camp.
- 6.30 p.m. 5th Ox & Bucks etc., at Church Army Hut, "B" Huts.

R. C.
- 9 a.m. Holy Mass at Woesten Rd, No. 1 Camp.
- 11 a.m. " " " ELVERDINGHE Chateau.
- 11 a.m. " " " Notre Dame, POPERINGHE.

14TH (LIGHT) DIVISION.

ROUTINE ORDERS.

29th January, 1916.

1161. LEAVE.

On 1st and 2nd February leave train departs VICTORIA 12.55 p.m. and from 3rd to 7th inclusive at 9.15 a.m.
Further times will be published as received.

1162. SANITATION OF CAMPS.

Instructions regarding the Sanitary measures to be adopted in all Standing Camps of the Division are issued herewith to all concerned.

[signature]

LIEUT-COLONEL,
A.A.&.Q.M.G.
14th (Light) Division.

NOTICES.

DIVINE SERVICES.

CHURCH OF ENGLAND.

9-30 a.m. Divine Service at Divl Headquarters.
11. a.m.   "   "   " 61st Field Co. Recreation Room
12. noon. Holy Communion, Church Army Hut, "B" Huts.
6.30 p.m. Divine Service 89th Field Co. Recreation Room.

14TH (LIGHT) DIVISION.

ROUTINE ORDERS.

30th January, 1916

1163. HONOURS AND REWARDS.

Under authority granted by HIS MAJESTY THE KING, the following decoration has been awarded for Gallant Conduct in the Field :-

DISTINGUISHED CONDUCT MEDAL.

No.A.15. Sergeant J. Presslee, 7th Bn. K.R.R.C.

The Major General Commanding heartily congratulates Sergeant Presslee. The Army Commander and Corps Commander have also requested that their congratulations may be conveyed to him.

1164. CAPES.

Units will report through the usual channels, by noon 1st February, whether the "Capes, Mackintosh," and "Capes W.P., Cyclists" issued to units, have proved satisfactory as regards their water resisting qualities.

1165. SICK WASTAGE.

The following is the Sick Wastage Return for week-ended noon 29th instant :-

Unit	O.	O.R.	Unit	O.	O.R.
14th Div. Cavalry,		Nil.	9th K.R.R.C.		21
14th Div. Cyclists,		Nil.	9th R.B.		5
46th F.A. Bde,		2.	6th Somersets,		10
47th F.A. Bde,		3.	6th D.C.L.I.		10
48th F.A. Bde,		3.	6th K.O.Y.L.I.	1	10
49th F.A. Bde,		1.	10th Durhams,		11
14th D.A.C.		3.	11th L'pool R		14
61st Field Co. R.E.		Nil.	8th M.M.G. Battery,		Nil.
62nd Field Co. R.E.		1.	14th Div. Train,		5.
89th Field Co. R.E.		1.	14th Supply Column,		Nil.
14th Signal Co.R.E.		Nil.	42nd Field Amblce.		Nil.
7th K.R.R.C.		10.	43rd Field Amblce.		Nil.
8th K.R.R.C.		13.	44th Field Amblce.		Nil.
7th R.B.		4.	26th Mob.Vet.Section,		Nil.
8th R.B.	1	10.	25th Sanitary Section,		Nil.
5th Ox & Bucks,		14.	M. M. P.		Nil.
5th K.S.L.I.	1	13.			

Totals Officers 3, Other Ranks 164.

LIEUT-COLONEL,
A.A.&.Q.M.G.
14TH (LIGHT) DIVISION.

14TH (LIGHT) DIVISION.

ROUTINE ORDERS.

31st January, 1918.

1166. **HONOURS AND REWARDS.**

Under authority granted by HIS MAJESTY THE KING, the following decoration has been awarded for Gallant Conduct in the Field :-

DISTINGUISHED CONDUCT MEDAL.

No.97515, Sapper B. Prior, 89th Field Coy. R.E.

The Major General Commanding heartily congratulates Sapper Prior. The Army Commander and Corps Commander have also requested that their congratulations may be conveyed to him.

1167. **STRENGTH - OFFICERS.**

Officers will not be struck off the strength of their Unit until notification of the result of Medical Boards is received from G.H.Q. or 2nd Army.

1168. **SIGNAL SERVICE.**

The Signal Office at ST JAN TER BIEZEN will be closed at 9 a.m. on February 3rd.
Orderlies from units at present served by that office should be attached daily to Corps H.Q. where all messages will be sent.

1169. **ROADS.**

The POPERINGHE - ELVERDINGHE Road is in a very bad state. Until repairs are carried out, Lorries and Buses will, when proceeding Eastwards, use the main ELVERDINGHE Road up to A.18.d, thence to Hospital Farm and ELVERDINGHE; returning by the main ELVERDINGHE - POPERINGHE Road direct.

LIEUT-COLONEL,
A.A.&.Q.M.G.
14TH (LIGHT) DIVISION.

NOTICE.

LOST. From Wagon Lines of A/48th Brigade R.F.A. on the night of 28/29th inst: BLUE ROAN MARE, No. 94 on near side, Saddle patch, A/48 on near hind quarters.
Also DARK BROWN GELDING, No.2 on near side, saddle patch, A/48 near hind quarters, also scar stifle off side.
Information to O.C., 48th Brigade R.F.A.

14TH (LIGHT) DIVISION.

ROUTINE ORDERS.

2nd February, 1916.

1170. HONOURS AND REWARDS.

(i) Under authority granted by HIS MAJESTY THE KING, the following decorations have been awarded for Gallant Conduct in the Field :-

DISTINGUISHED CONDUCT MEDAL.

22456. Corpl A.W.Booth,   6th Bn. K.O.Y.L.I.
18181. Pte E. Sutton,   6th Bn. K.O.Y.L.I.

The Major General Commanding heartily congratulates Corporal Booth and Pte Sutton. The Army Commander and Corps Commander have also requested that their congratulations may be conveyed to them.

(ii) The undermentioned names should be added to the List of Promotions and Honours issued with D.R.O. 1134 of 20th January, 1916:

Awarded the DISTINGUISHED CONDUCT MEDAL.

No. 40031, Pionr.C.F.Halden, 14th Div.Signal Co.R.E.
" 11650. Pte. A.G.Gittins, 6th Bn. D.C.L.I.

1171. DEMOLITION OF UNINHABITED HOUSES.

G.R.O.1385, d/30.1.16 is republished for information :-
" It has been brought to the notice of the Commander-in-Chief that cases have occurred where a British Officer has authorised the demolition of an uninhabited house, which was in good condition, for the purpose of obtaining materials for repair of roads, construction of stables, horse standings, etc.
Such action is unjustifiable unless necessitated by the urgency of the military situation, and Army Commanders will issue strict orders to prevent any recurrence of acts of this nature by the troops under their command. They will take severe disciplinary action in case of any infraction of the orders issued by them on the subject".
The only officer who will authorise demolition of houses in 14th Div. Area is the C.R.E., 14th Division and no houses in that area are to be demolished without his authority.

1172. REMOUNTS.

D.R.O. No. 1063 dated 28.12.15 is cancelled.
In future animals sent to the Mobile Veterinary Section should be struck off strength at once.

1173. MOTOR VEHICLES.

Officers Commanding Units in possession of Motor Vehicles will take immediate steps to ensure that all Officers, N.C.Os and men of their units are acquainted with the restrictions imposed by A.R.O. 245 dated 31st January, 1916, and will report by February 7th whether all officers, N.C.Os and men are acquainted with this order or not and the reason for any exception.

LIEUT COLONEL,
A. & Q.M.G.
14TH (LIGHT) DIVISION.

14TH (LIGHT) DIVISION.

ROUTINE ORDERS.

3rd February, 1916.

1174. HONOURS AND REWARDS.

The undermentioned have been awarded cards "For Gallant and Meritorious Service" by the Major-General Commanding :-

62nd Field Coy. R.E.

    No. 25251. Sapper Morris,   F.

6th Bn. Somerset Light Infantry.

    No. 10205. Corporal Bees,   R.

6th Bn. Duke of Cornwall's Light Infantry.

    No. 10904. Sergeant Pullen-Burry, O.A.

6th Bn. King's Own Yorkshire Light Infantry.

    No. 18751. Pte England, T.   (Killed in action)
         1951.   "   Stooper, C.   (Killed in action)

1175. TRANSPORT.

Baggage wagon horses in possession of Infantry Battalions will be sent back to the companies of the Divisional Train to which they belong on February 7th by 12 noon.

One G.S. Wagon per Infantry Battalion of those loaned to them by Divisional Artillery will be handed back to the Divisional Artillery in Infantry Transport Lines at 11 a.m. on February 7th. Divisional Artillery will arrange to take them over at that hour and remove them to artillery camps.

1176. COMMISSIONS.

When applications are submitted on A.F. M.T.393 recommending N.C.Os and men for Commissions, and the applicant expresses a desire to be posted to a particular Infantry Battalion, a certificate should be forwarded with the application stating that the Officer Commanding that particular unit is willing to accept the applicant as an officer in his Battalion.

1177. MAIL & LEAVE BOATS.

Communications are not to be sent to the Base Commandant, BOULOGNE, asking for information as to the sailing of Mail and Leave Boats. Information on this subject, when received in sufficient time at those Headquarters, will be communicated to all concerned.

                          LIEUT-COLONEL,
                          A.A.&.Q.M.G.
                          14TH (LIGHT) DIVISION.

NOTICE.

LOST, from Huts G.6.d.0.2. Sheet 28, BICYCLE, marked 196 R.E.
    Also S.M. scratched on tool-bag.
    Information to C.R.E., 14th Division.

14TH (LIGHT) DIVISION.

ROUTINE ORDERS.

4th February, 1916.

1178. DRINKING WATER.

Reference D.R.O.1114, dated January 13th:
The following additional sources of drinking water are available.
Where water is not chlorinated it must be boiled.

Area.	Source of Supply.	Location. (Sheet 28)	Scoops of Chloride of lime required per Water-cart.
Area West of POPERINGHE Canal.	Pump Estaminet "Do Rust Plaats"	A. 9.a.0.2.	1.
	Well at Drooguentak Farm,	A.21.b.1.3.	1.
Area between POPERINGHE CANAL and KEMELBECK Stream.	Alexandra Farm,	B.19.a.3.8.	1.
	Hospital Farm,	B.19.d.1.1.	1.
	Pump, (2 watercarts)	B.25.d.9.4.	1.
Area East of KEMELBECK Stream.	Pump, Isly Farm (1 Watercart per diem)	B.29.d.9.7.	2.
	" Brabant Farm (2 do)	B.29.d.8.2.	1.
	" Malakoff Farm	B.22.d.1.1.	½
	" Polissier Farm,	B.21.c.9.9.	2.
	" in Farmhouse,	B.28.b.7.9.	1.
	" in Rodan Farm,	B.22.d.1.8.	1.
	Underground tank "Chateau de Trois Tours" BRIELEN,	B.28.a.5.0.	1.
	Houses in BRIELEN labelled "Drinking water"		

1179. LEWIS GUN CARTRIDGES, S.A.A.

Units will report to this office, through the usual channels, by noon 6th instant, if any difficulties have been experienced in the extraction of S.A.A.Cartridges of K and G Manufacture when used with the Lewis Gun.

for LIEUT-COLONEL,
A.A.&.Q.M.G.
14TH (LIGHT) DIVISION.

NOTICES.

LOST: on night of 26th January, BAY GELDING, Light Draught, Markings, 405 on near fore, 14 D.A.C. on off fore, 405 cut on hair near side of neck.
Information to O.C., 14th Div. Ammunition Column.

DIVINE SERVICES.
for Sunday next, 6th February, 1915.

C. of E.
- 9.30 a.m. Divine Service, Divisional Headquarters,
- 12 noon. Holy Communion at Church Army Hut.
- 6.30 p.m. Divine Service, 89th Field Co. R.E.

R. C.
- 9 a.m. Mass at Woosten Road.
- 11 a.m. " " Elverdinghe Chateau,
- 11 a.m. " " Notre Dame, POPERINGHE.

WESLEYANS, PRESBYTERIANS, NONCONFORMISTS ETC.

- 9.15 a.m. for 14th Div.Cyclists & D.L.O.Y. at Ste.Sixte Convent.
- 10. a.m. " 5th K.S.L.I., 42nd I.B.Transport, 61st Co.R.E. at Church Army Hut, B Huts.
- 10.45 a.m. " 7th K.R.R.C. at A.16.Central in Recreation Barn.
- 11.30 a.m. " 9th K.R.R.C., 11th L'pool R at Elverdinghe Chateau.
- 2. p.m. " 45th Field Ambulance at The College, POPERINGHE.
- 3.30 p.m. " 8th K.R.R.C. at B Coys Quarters.
- 3.30 p.m. " Headquarters, & Signal Co. at Signals Marquee.
- 6.30 p.m. " Troops in vicinity at Church Army Hut, B Huts.

=========

14TH (LIGHT) DIVISION.

ROUTINE ORDERS.

5th February, 1916.

1180. INDENT FOR RATIONS.

The revised form of A.F. B.55 will be taken into use forthwith.

A certificate will be rendered through the usual channels, to reach this office by 12 noon, 9th inst., that this has been done.

1181. WATER CARTS.

Reference D.R.Os 533 of 10th September, 1915, and 568 of 19th September, 1915:

Permanganate of Potash is no longer obtainable. Chloride of Lime must be used instead.

1182. POSTAL REFILLING.

On and after tomorrow the 6th instant, Postal refilling will take place at the Advanced Railhead, where supplies are dealt with, at 11 a.m.

LIEUT-COLONEL.
A.A.&.Q.M.G.
2 14TH (LIGHT) DIVISION.

T.O. 9th K.R.Rif.C.
Passed for yr. information & necessary action, please.
Please return to O.R. Sgt.
Cuthbery
2/Lt. D.A./Adjt
8/2/16

14TH (LIGHT) DIVISION.
ROUTINE ORDERS.

7th February, 1916.

1183. WINTER FOOTGEAR.

All boots, gum, short, and boots, Lumbermens, and Stockings will be handed in to D.A.D.O.S. forthwith.
A report that this has been done will be rendered to this office by 12 noon 10th inst., through the usual channels, stating number handed in of each type.

1184. METHOD OF COMPLAINTS.

G.R.O. No. 1390 dated 4-2-16 is republished:
"The system under which complaints of officers and soldiers should be preferred (as laid down in para. 439, King's Regulations, and Sections 42 and 43 Army Act) should be brought prominently to the notice of all ranks, as cases have occurred wherein irregular methods have been employed, thus giving rise to much unnecessary enquiry and correspondence. All ranks should be warned that any departure from the authorised procedure will be severely dealt with."

1185. SICK WASTAGE.

The following is the Sick Wastage Return for week-ended noon 5th instant :-

Unit	O.	O.R.	Unit	O.	O.R.
14th Div. Cavalry		Nil.	9th K.R.R.C.		11.
14th Div. Cyclists,		1.	9th R.B.		8.
46th Bde R.F.A.		8.	6th Somerset L.I.		5.
47th Bde R.F.A.		4.	6th D.C.L.I.		11.
48th Bde R.F.A.		2.	6th K.O.Y.L.I.		6.
49th Bde R.F.A.		3.	10th Durham L.I.		7.
14th D.A.C.		5.	11th L'pool R,		8.
61st Field Co. R.E.		Nil.	8th M.M.G. Battery,		Nil.
62nd Field Co. R.E.		1.	14th Div. Train,		2.
89th Field Co. R.E.		1.	14th Div. Supply Column,		Nil.
14th Signal Sn. R.E.		1.	42nd Field Amblce,		1.
196th L.D. Co. R.E.		1.	A.S.C.Attd.42nd Fd.Amb.		1.
7th K.R.R.C.		8.	43rd Field Amblce,		Nil.
8th K.R.R.C.		5.	44th Field Amblce,		2.
7th R.B.		4.	26th Mob.Vet.Section,		Nil.
8th R.B.		14.	25th Sanitary Section,		Nil.
5th Ox & Bucks L.I.		10.	M. M. P.		1.
5th K.S.L.I.	1	9.			

Totals Officers: 1, Other Ranks: 156.

C. Ransom Taylor
for LIEUT-COLONEL,
A.A.&Q.M.G.
14TH (LIGHT) DIVISION.

P.S. Gumboots knee in possession of Corps are being collected today & sent down with transport. Please send in those & those in poss. of Transp. & send in return to order repeat here.
Cutt. 8/2/16.

14TH (LIGHT) DIVISION.

ROUTINE ORDERS.

8th February, 1916.

1186. MOTOR CARS & MOTOR CYCLES.

All units other than the Supply Column which are in possession of Motor Cars or Motor Cycles will report weekly by 12 noon Sunday, the number of Motor Cars and Motor Cycles which are not in running order, showing the cause and the date when they became non-effective.

1187. TRANSPORT.

D.A.C. Wagons in possession of Infantry battalions will be handed back to D.A.C. in Infantry transport camps as follows :-

41st Infantry Bde,	10th February,	11 a.m.
42nd Infantry Bde) 43rd Infantry Bde)	11th February,	11 a.m.

1188. WINTER CLOTHING.

Fur coats and winter clothing not required, or in excess, should be returned at once to D.A.D.O.S.

for LIEUT-COLONEL,
A.A.&.Q.M.G.
14TH (LIGHT) DIVISION.

14TH (LIGHT) DIVISION.

ROUTINE ORDERS.

9th February, 1916.

1189. REFILLING POINT.

Refilling point will be the road A.20.b.4.0. to A.8.b.9.4. for all units East of the Line PROVEN - ST JAN TER BIEZEN from the 11th instant.

O.C., 14th Divl Train will arrange refilling points for other units and will communicate them to the units concerned.

1190. LEAVE.

Arrangements have been made to give printed slips, or to stamp the leave papers, of Officers and men who may be detained at FOLKESTONE.

1191. PERMANENT COMMISSIONS.

It has been decided that officers of the Territorial Force and temporarily commissioned officers who have been granted permanent commissions in the Regular Army under Army Order 333 of 1915, and are temporarily retained in their original Territorial or Service Unit, may retain their Territorial or Temporary rank up to the time that it is found possible to release them from these units.

The date of relinquishment of such rank should be notified to this office as early as possible.

(14th Corps No.M.S./50/51).

1192. CHAFFCUTTERS.

A report will be rendered by 12 noon the 11th inst, stating the number of chaff-cutters in possession. The report should not include those belonging to inhabitants and used by agreement or hire.

C.L.L. Hamilton

LIEUT-COLONEL,
A.A.&.Q.M.G.
14TH (LIGHT) DIVISION.

NOTICE.

FOUND. MULE, strayed into the lines of 46th B.A.C., on 7th instant. Marks:- 209 on off fore, 70/407 on near fore, clipped tail.

Apply O.C., 46th Brigade Ammunition Column.

14TH (LIGHT) DIVISION.

ROUTINE ORDERS.

10th February, 1916.

1193. IRON RATIONS.

All units will report through the usual channels to Divisional Headquarters, by 16th instant, that every Officer and man is in possession of a serviceable iron ration.

1194. LEAVE.

Officers on leave in England who, from sickness or other causes, are compelled to apply to War Office for an extension of their original leave, should state the unit with which they were serving when they proceeded on leave.

1195. COLLECTION OF MATERIAL.

The collection of bricks and material from YPRES will cease from Sunday the 13th inst., inclusive.

1196. ORDNANCE STORE.

The D.A.D.O.S. Store in POPERINGHE will be closed for issues and receipts from 5 p.m. the 12th instant.

1197. FORAGE RATION.

On and after the 13th instant, the full 10 lbs of hay per horse will be sent up to railhead.

LIEUT-COLONEL,
A.A.&.Q.M.G.
14TH (LIGHT) DIVISION.

14TH (LIGHT) DIVISION.

ROUTINE ORDERS.

11th February, 1916.

1198. HONOURS AND REWARDS.

The undermentioned have been awarded cards "For Gallant and Meritorious Service" by the Major-General Commanding :-

10th Bn. Durham Light Infantry.

No. 20060. Cpl. W. Blenkinsopp,
    17883. " R.W. Chamley,
    25917. L/Cpl A.L.Course,
    26035. Pte F. Livermore,

6th Bn. (P.A) Somerset Light Infantry.

No. 9652. Pte J. Miller.

1199. TRAVELLING WARRANTS.

G.R.O. No.1397 d/9-2-16 is republished :-
"From this date no claims for refunds on tickets lost by soldiers when on leave, or requests for the cancellation of repayment warrants will be entertained.
In the event of a lost ticket being recovered, it should be forwarded by the officer commanding, through the usual channel, to the War Office, together with particulars of the warrant issued on repayment, when steps will be taken to effect a refund."

1200. DISTRIBUTION OF GIFTS AND COMFORTS FOR THE TROOPS, SENT THROUGH THE DIRECTOR-GENERAL OF VOLUNTARY ORGANIZATIONS.

G.R.O.No.1398 d/9-2-16 is republished :-
"1. A Department has been formed to organize, and as far as possible centralize, the despatch of gifts and comforts to the men of the various Expeditionary Forces. This Department is designated the "Department of the Director-General of Voluntary Organizations".
2. The goods provided for the benefit of the troops by this department will be distributed through the Military Forwarding Establishment, and commanding officers should inform the Assistant Military Forwarding Officer, Havre, of the particular articles needed by their units, in order that distribution may be made with the least possible delay.
3. On and after February 13th, the distribution of mufflers and mittens will also be made by the Assistant Military Forwarding Officer, Havre, and the portion of General Routine Order No. 1204, dated 13th October,1915, referring to these comforts, is hereby cancelled."

1201. LEAVE.

Jewish soldiers, who, in the ordinary course, would be granted leave of absence during the months of March and April, should as far as possible, be permitted to take their leave, the period of which would include 17th and 18th April, (The Jewish Feast of Passover).

1202. FORAGE.

G.R.O. 1399 d/9-2-16 is republished :-
"The following will be substituted for para 3 of General Routine Order No. 1235 dated 29th October, 1915, as amended by General Routine Order No. 1250 dated 6th November, 1915 :-

Para 3 - Forage.

	Oats, lbs	Hay, lbs
*Shires or Clydesdales,	19	15
*Horses, draught, of Heavy Brigades R.G.A. and other Horses, draught, heavy, of the Army,	15	15
All officers' chargers, and other horses over 15 hands, ½ inch,	12	12
Cobs, other than officers' chargers,	10	12
Mules of 15 hands and upwards employed on heavy draught work,	12	12
Small Mules,	6	12

Equivalents.
    1 lb crushed maize = 1 lb oats.
    1 1/8 lbs bran = 1 lb oats.

General Routine Orders Nos. 113, 158, 225, 238, 276, 298, 299, 323, 410, 412, 440, 481, 570, 819, 903, 1007, 1013, 1020, 1052, 1089 and 1182 are hereby cancelled.

* Issues are made on a flat rate of 17 lbs oats per heavy draught horse. It is left to Officers Commanding units to distribute this ration as they think fit."

1203. COMPENSATION CLAIMS - COLLECTION OF.

G.R.O. No. 1146 dated 11-9-15 is republished :-
"In conformity with French practice in the case of troops quitting cantonnements, arrangements will, whenever possible, be made for an officer to remain behind for at least three hours in each commune to receive and deal with claims for damage, which it was not possible for the inhabitants concerned to submit to the Commanding Officer prior to the departure of the troops."

1204. HORSES LEFT ON THE MARCH.

In the event of sick animals being left behind in billets, notice must be sent in writing to the local Maire, and to the A.D.V.S. of the Division, giving a description of the animal and the address at which left.

LIEUT-COLONEL,
A.A.&Q.M.G.
14TH (LIGHT) DIVISION.

14TH (LIGHT) DIVISION.

ROUTINE ORDERS.

14th February, 1916

1205. PRECEDENCE OF OFFICERS HOLDING TEMPORARY RANK.

2nd Army Routine Order No. 300 d/11-2-16 is republished:
" An officer granted higher temporary rank for the period during which he is holding an appointment will continue to take precedence in that rank from the date on which it was granted until he vacates the appointment, irrespective of whether he is granted substantive or brevet promotion to that rank during the period in question.
(Authority M.S.,G.H.Q., No.9670 dated 2-2-16)."

1206. LEAVE.

Officers, N.C.Os and men proceeding on Leave from ARNEKE Station should report to R.T.O. ARNEKE at 7 p.m. Train leaves 7.40 p.m. for HAZEBROUCK, where the night will be spent.
Train leaves HAZEBROUCK 6.13 a.m. for BOULOGNE.
The Leave Train from POPERINGHE runs as usual and can be used by Units situated nearer that Station than to ARNEKE.

1207. VETERINARY SERVICE.

The Mobile Veterinary Section is situated at C.27.a.6.4. Sheet 27 on the WORMHOUDT - LEDRINGHEM road.

1208. SICK WASTAGE.

The following is the Sick Wastage Return for week-ended noon 12th instant :-

	O.	O.R.		O.	O.R.
14th Div. Cavalry,			9th K.R.R.C.	2	15
14th Div. Cyclists,			9th R.B.	Nil.	10
46th Bde R.F.A.			6th Somerset L.I.	3.	7
47th Bde R.F.A.			6th D.C.L.I.	5.	10
48th Bde R.F.A.			6th K.O.Y.L.I.	2.	14.
49th Bde R.F.A.		1	10th Durham L.I.	3	10
14th D.A.C.			11th L'pool Regt,	5.	12
39th T.M.Battery,			8th M.M.G.Battery,	1.	Nil.
61st Field Co. R.E.			14th Div. Train,	Nil.	1.
62nd Field Co. R.E.			14th Div.Supply Col.	2.	Nil.
89th Field Co. R.E			42nd Field Amb.	Nil.	1.
14th Signal Co.R.E.			43rd Fd.Amb.ASC Attd.	Nil.	1.
7th K.R.R.C.		1	44th Field Amb.	11.	2.
8th K.R.R.C.			28th Mob.Vet.Sec.ASC Attd	12.	1.
7th R.B.		1	25th Sanitary Section,	9	Nil.
8th R.B.			M.M.P.	11.	Nil.
5th Ox & Bucks L.I.			A.O.C.att.47th F.A.Bde,	10.	1.
5th K.S.L.I.				8.	

Totals Officers 3, Other Ranks 169.

1209. RETURNS.

Commencing Saturday next, Officers Commanding Brigade Machine Gun Companies will render A.F. B.213 through the usual channels, by 6 p.m. each Saturday.

LIEUT-COLONEL,
A.A.&Q.M.G.
14TH (LIGHT) DIVISION.

14TH (LIGHT) DIVISION.

ROUTINE ORDERS.

15th February, 1916.

1210. LAND - OCCUPATION OF.

O.C. Units will render, through the usual channels, to Divisional Headquarters, returns as per attached pro-forma, for all land used by them.

The purpose for which the land was used must be shown in the column of remarks, e.g., "used for drill only" "used for bombing" "used for horse lines" etc.

Pasture land will not be used for bombing and as far as possible arable land not yet ploughed, or if ploughed at all events unsown will be used for this purpose.

Attention is called to G.R.O.1377 as to damage to crops by troops. Unnecessary damage will be charged to the troops.

D.R.O. 1219

1211. LEAVE.

From the 18th instant inclusive, the present allotment of leave is cancelled. Further instructions will be issued later.

1212. RETURNS.

All units will render through the usual channels, by midday 17th, a return showing all Officers and men absent from their units on extra regimental employment.

1213. BOUNDS.

The Estaminet "AU PONT" (C.21.a.0.10) is closed to troops for 10 days from the 14th instant inclusive.

LIEUT-COLONEL,
A.A.&.Q.M.G.
14TH (LIGHT) DIVISION.

14TH (LIGHT) DIVISION.

ROUTINE ORDERS.

16th February, 1916.

1214. HONOURS AND REWARDS.

Under authority granted by HIS MAJESTY THE KING, the following decorations have been awarded for Gallant Conduct in the Field :-

MILITARY CROSS.

Lieutenant G.L. Wood,   10th Bn. Durham L.I.

DISTINGUISHED CONDUCT MEDAL.

17883, Corporal R.W. Chamley, 10th Bn. Durham L.I.
20060. Corporal W. Blenkinsopp, 10th Bn. Durham L.I.

9652. Private J. Miller,   6th Bn. Somerset L.I.

The Major-General Commanding heartily congratulates the recipients. The Army Commander and Corps Commander have also requested that their congratulations may be conveyed to them.

1215. "W" Ammunition.

Instructions regarding the return of "W" S.A.A. to railheads for transmission to the Base are cancelled.
This ammunition has been found satisfactory for use in Rifles and all patterns of machine guns.

1216. TRAFFIC INSTRUCTIONS & CONVEYANCE OF STORES BY RAIL.

3rd Army Routine Orders Nos 78 and 210, dated 2nd October, 1915, and 15th December, 1915 respectively are circulated herewith.

1217. RETURNS.

Units will render a return direct to the A.D.V.S. by 12 noon 19th instant showing by classes, any animals surplus to establishments and those required to complete.

LIEUT-COLONEL,
A.A.& .Q.M.G.
14TH (LIGHT) DIVISION.

NOTICE.

FOUND. Bay HORSE, about 16 hands: found on WATOU road about 3 miles from POPERINGHE.   No distinctive marks.
Apply Town Major, POPERINGHE.

The Field Cashier will attend at The Chateau, WORMHOUDT (C.11.d.5.9. Sh.27) at 2 p.m. and at ROUTRECUE (E.20.d.8.9 Sh.27) at 3.30 p.m., to-morrow 17th instant.

14TH (LIGHT) DIVISION.

ROUTINE ORDERS.

18th February, 1916.

1218. HONOURS AND REWARDS.

The undermentioned have been awarded Cards "For Gallant and Meritorious Service" by the Major-General Commanding :-

<u>62nd Field Co. R.E.</u>

    No.40889, Sergt A. Reeves, R.E.
        40030. Corpl D. Brever, R.E.
        46815, Corpl T. Dunsire, R.E.

<u>5th Ox & Bucks L.I.</u>

    No.16685. L/Cpl F.H. Timms,

<u>6th Bn. K.O.Y.L.I.</u>

    No.18175. Pte. P. Richardson,

1219. LAND - OCCUPATION OF.

Returns, in accordance with D.R.O.1210 dated 15th inst., of land occupied in this area, will be forwarded to Div'l Headquarters by 8 p.m. tomorrow, 19th instant.

Date of vacating will be the date on which the unit is ordered to leave.

LIEUT-COLONEL,
A.A.&.Q.M.G.
14TH (LIGHT) DIVISION.

14TH (LIGHT) DIVISION.

ROUTINE ORDERS.

21st February, 1916.

1220. RETURNS.

A return will be sent through the usual channels to this office, by noon 23rd instant, giving the names of any experienced well-sinkers serving with their units.

J. E. Brundy, Major
for. LIEUT-COLONEL,
A.A.&Q.M.G.
14TH (LIGHT) DIVISION.

NOTICE.

FOUND: at FLESSELLES, on morning of 21st February, Dark Brown MARE, 14 to 15 hands, B.18 on near hind, White star of forehead, White spots on back, Cross on neck.
Apply A.P.M., 14th (Light) Division.

14TH (LIGHT) DIVISION.

ROUTINE ORDERS.

22nd February, 1916.

1221. HONOURS AND REWARDS.

Under authority granted by HIS MAJESTY THE KING, the following decoration has been awarded for Gallant Conduct in the Field :-

DISTINGUISHED CONDUCT MEDAL.

10803, Pte R. Baker,   6th Bn. Somerset L.I.

The Major-General Commanding heartily congratulates Pte Baker. The Army Commander and Corps Commander have also requested that their congratulations may be conveyed to him.

1222. TELESCOPIC SIGHTS FOR RIFLES.

Reference C.R.O.500 dated 21st February, 1915:
Report will be rendered so as to reach this office by noon 25th instant.

1223. REPORTS.

Reports will be rendered by Infantry Brigades and R.A. by noon 25th inst., whether it is considered desirable to increase the ration of milk, making a corresponding decrease in the Jam Ration, so that no extra expense to the public may be incurred. An increase of 20% in the Milk Ration is suggested.

LIEUT-COLONEL,
A.A.&.Q.M.G.
14TH (LIGHT) DIVISION.

NOTICE.

LOST: On the morning of the 21st, MARE, 14½ hands, white Star on forehead, white stocking near hind leg. Information to Transport Officer, 11th L'pool Regt (Pioneers).

14TH (LIGHT) DIVISION.

ROUTINE ORDERS.

23rd February, 1916.

1224. CHAPLAINS.

The following are the postings of the Church of England Chaplains of this Division :-

Rev. T.W.A. Jones,	41st Inf. Bde.
Rev. A.F. Marsham,	41st Inf. Bde.
Rev. C.H. Bailey,	42nd Inf. Bde.
Rev. G.R.C. Cooke,	42nd Inf. Bde.
Rev. W. Telfer,	43rd Inf. Bde.
Rev. G. Wreford-Browne,	43rd Inf. Bde.
Rev. W.P. Jones,	Divisional Troops.
Rev. C.H. Meyrick,	Divisional Troops.

1225. RETURN.

Units will forward by noon 25th instant, through the usual channels, nominal rolls of all Officers, N.C.Os and men who are detached from their units for duty, showing how they are employed.

1226. ANTI-GAS HELMETS.

Attention is directed to General Routine Order 1405 regarding the removal of tape slings from the Anti-Gas waterproof helmet cases.

1227. DISCIPLINE.

3rd Army Routine Order No. 311 d/21-2-16 is republished :-

"1. PURCHASE AND SALE OF SPIRITS OR ALCOHOLIC DRINKS. Beer, cider and the ordinary light wines are the only form of alcoholic drinks which may be bought or accepted by the troops at any kind of hotel, estaminet, shop or private house.

The sale, purchase or acceptance of spirits or liqueurs of any kind is forbidden.

2. TAKING OF ALCOHOLIC DRINK TO BILLETS.- N.C.Os and men are forbidden to take beer or any form of alcoholic drink to their billet.

3. REGIMENTAL CANTEENS.- Beer may be bought for supplying Regimental Canteens, but the hours for the sale of beer or other form of alcoholic drink in these canteens must not be different from those laid down for estaminets in G.R.O.1107, viz :- 11 a.m. to 1 p.m. and 6 p.m. to 8 p.m. At other times the canteen may be used as a recreation room."

1228. EXERCISING.

3rd Army Routine Order No. 313 d/21-2-16 is republished :-

"Horses and Mules are not to be exercised on any roads shown as lorry routes on the 3rd Army Traffic Map.

(over)

1229. ANTI-GAS GOGGLES.

Reference G.R.O. 488 dated 19-2-16:
Return will be rendered so as to reach Div'l Headquarters by 6 p.m. 24th instant.

1230. AREAS - ADMINISTRATION OF.

The Divisional area has been divided into Administrative Areas under the B.G.C.,R.A., B.Gs.C.,Infantry Brigades, O.C., 11th L'pool Regt, and O.C., 14th Amm.Sub-Park. The extent of these areas has been communicated to all concerned.

General and other Officers in charge of areas will be responsible for allotting accommodation, for the policing of the area, and for the sanitation, water supply and precautions against fire.

They will be in charge of all camp equipment allotted to units of the Division in their area, and they will attach to their Staffs an Officer to assist them in looking after it. Camp equipment will be issued by D.A.D.O.S. to units, notification of the quantities issued being sent to the Officer in charge of the Area through Div'l Headquarters.

1231. INDENTS.

Latrine Buckets at the rate of 4% are to be demanded by all units from D.A.D.O.S., Latrine Screens and Hurricane Lamps are to be demanded as may be necessary.

1232. RETURN.

A return will be rendered by all units, through area Commanders, so as to reach this office by noon on the 11th March, showing the number of the following stores in their possession, distinguishing between those actually in use and those not in use :-

Trench Shelters,
Paulins,
Marquees,
Tents, C.S.L.
Tent Bottoms, sets.

LIEUT-COLONEL,
A.A.&.Q.M.G.
14TH (LIGHT) DIVISION.

NOTICE.

FIELD CASHIER will attend at Divisional Headquarters MONDAYS AND THURSDAYS 2.30 to 4 p.m. beginning 24th February, 1916.

14TH (LIGHT) DIVISION.

ROUTINE ORDERS.

28th February, 1916.

1233. CLAIMS.

Officers Commanding Units, when leaving Billets must obtain a signed claim from any householder who has a claim to make.

The C.O. will enquire into the Claim and report upon it when forwarding it to Div. Claims Officer.

1234. CARD PASSES.

Officers and others holding Card Passes are requested to forward them to the A.P.M., in exchange for new Passes, on the 29th inst.

1235. HAIRCUTTING.

The Issue of Scissors, haircutting, and Clippers, hair, to all units, in the proportion of one pair of each per Company, is authorised by 3rd Army Routine Order No. 200. Commanding Officers will therefore make regimental arrangements for haircutting. No charge to be made against the men, nor will any payment to barbers be allowed.

1236. VERMOREL SPRAYERS, MARK II.

Demands for printed illustrated lists of the parts of Mark II Vermorel Sprayers should be forwarded through Ordnance Officers of formations, and not direct by units.
(Authority D.D.O.S., 3rd Army No.O/29/2 dated 5/2/16)
6th Corps Q/8.

1237. GLYCERINE.

It is notified for information that the issue of glycerine will be a Supply Service in future.
(Authority D.O.S., No.O.S.B/333 dated 31/1/16)

1238. PERMANENT COMMISSIONS IN THE REGULAR ARMY.

Recommendations for permanent commissions in the Regular Army, under Army Order No. XV, of the 27th August, 1915, should reach this office not later than the 10th of each month.

1239. BANDS.

It has been decided that the authorised establishment of drums, fifes, and pipes (or bugles in the case of Rifles or Light Infantry) may be maintained in any infantry Battalion which desires to have them. No addition to existing transport will be allowed.
(Authority Q.M.G., Q/2387, dated 15/6/15).
6th Corps Q/32.

(over)

1240. M.T. VEHICLES, - Damage to.

When cars and lorries become damaged, and it is likely that, on further enquiry, the driver may be proved to be responsible, he should not be sent to the Base M.T. Repair Shops with the vehicle until enquiry is complete, and a decision regarding responsibility is given.
(Authority D.D.S.&.T.,3rd Army No.S.T./1023,d/12/12/15)
6th Corps Q.34.

1241. MOTOR ACCESSORIES - DEMANDS FOR.

With reference to the Director of Transport's Circular No. 122, of the 13th December, 1915, demands for spare parts will, in future, be made weekly (on Fridays) unless of special urgency, to warrant an intermediate demand.
Indents on Army Form W.3338 will be rendered to the Advanced M.T. Depot in duplicate.

1242. DISCIPLINE.

1. All men leaving the village in which they are billeted, must be in possession of a regimental pass, signed by an officer, and be properly dressed in walking out order.
2. All Warrant Officers, N.C.Os and orderlies, either mounted, on cycles, or on foot, when proceeding out of the villages in which they are billeted, must be properly dressed, wearing belts or bandoliers.
3. An Officer should invariably accompany horses while at exercise, or, when going or returning from watering.
4. All horses and mules in the 6th Corps area, hooked into vehicles, will proceed at a walk, except by order of an officer, which should always be obtained in urgent cases. Draught horses are not to be trotted when at exercise, or, when going or returning from watering.

1243. POSTINGS TO INFANTRY BATTALIONS.

Several instances have recently occurred of officers being reported as killed or wounded, while serving with Trench Mortar Batteries and other formations, without any authority having been issued for their attachment to such formations.
It is notified for information, that postings to Infantry Battalions are carried out in the office of the A.G., G.H.Q., and it is in the interests of units that approval for these detachments should be obtained from that office, as, in the absence of such approval, the officer is still borne on the strength of his unit, and no action is taken to fill a vacancy that in reality exists, but of which, other than locally, there is no knowledge.

C. Parson Capt
for LIEUT-COLONEL,
A.A.&.Q.M.G.
14TH (LIGHT) DIVISION.

NOTICE.

LOST. BICYCLE, No. 21523, marked 49th Brigade R.F.A. in white letters on rear mud-guard. Missed whilst detraining on the morning of the 20th instant at LONGUEAU Station. Information to O.C., 49th Brigade R.F.A.

14TH (LIGHT) DIVISION.

ROUTINE ORDERS.

1st March, 1916.

1244. HONOURS AND REWARDS.

Under authority granted by HIS MAJESTY THE KING, the following decoration has been awarded for Gallant Conduct in the Field :-

DISTINGUISHED CONDUCT MEDAL.

No. 2651,	Corporal J. Edwardes,	10th Durham L.I.
14003,	Private W. Lolly,	-ditto-
1905.	Corporal J. Self,	9th Bn. Rifle Bde.
10863.	Private A. Prentice,	5th Ox & Bucks L.I.
16685.	L/Corporal F.H. Timms,	-ditto-

The Major-General Commanding heartily congratulates the recipients. The Army Commander and Corps Commander have also requested that their congratulations may be conveyed to them.

1245. SICK WASTAGE.

The following is the Sick Wastage Return for week ended noon 27th February, 1916 :-

	O.	O.R.		O.	O.R.
14th Div. Cavalry		1	9th K.R.R.C.		42.
14th Div. Cyclists,	1	1	9th R.B.		39.
46th Bde R.F.A.		1.	6th Somerset L.I.	1	39.
47th Bde R.F.A.		2.	6th D.C.L.I.	1	22.
48th Bde R.F.A.		5.	6th K.O.Y.L.I.		13.
49th Bde R.F.A.		Nil.	10th Durham L.I.		15.
14th D.A.C.		8.	11th L'pool R,		5.
39th H.M. Battery,		Nil.	8th M.M.G. Battery,		Nil.
61st Field Co. R.E.		Nil.	14th Div. Train,	1	-
62nd Field Coy.R.E.		1.	14th Div. Supply Col.		Nil.
89th Field Coy.R.E.	1	1.	42nd Field Amb.		4.
14th Signal Co.R.E.			43rd Field Amb.		Nil.
A.S.C.Attd.		1.	44th Field Amb.	1	-
7th K.R.R.C.		1.	26th Mob. Vet Sec.		Nil.
8th K.R.R.C.		7.	25th Sanitary Sec.		Nil.
7th R.B.		6.	M.M.P.		1.
8th R.B.	1	25.	Army Chaplains Dept.	1	-
5th Ox & Bucks L.I.		5.			
5th K.S.L.I.		15.			

Totals Officers 8, Other Ranks 260.

1246. LORRY TRAFFIC.

It has been observed that lorries do not go as slowly as orders prescribe, and, that damage to roads results. The rear lorries of convoys are the chief offenders, as they go too fast in trying to recover ground lost. Periodical short halts for convoys should be arranged, to enable lorries to catch up without increasing speed.

Lorries will reduce their speed to 4 miles per hour when passing, or being passed by, faster moving vehicles.

1247. **RIDING HORSES – Replacement of.**

Units will take the necessary steps to ensure that all saddlery which becomes surplus, owing to the substitution of bicycles for riding horses, is returned to the Base.
(Authority: D.D.O.S., 3rd Army No.0/117/2, dated 14/2/16)
6th Corps Q/62.

1248. **SPECIAL ANTI-GAS HELMETS FOR ARTILLERY.**

The scale of issue of special anti-gas helmets with rubber sponge rims goggles for Artillery, is altered to 6 helmets per gun, in place of 24 per battery.
Indents for any additional helmets should be forwarded through the usual channels.
(Authority D.G.280/2/38 dated 3/2/16 – 0/18/12)
6th Corps Q/8/3.

1248. **TRAFFIC CONTROL.**

The DOULLENS-ARRAS Road is closed to all traffic by day East of LE BAC DU SUD.
By night this road may be used by all traffic East of a line running North and South through BERNEVILLE.
The following roads are temporarily closed to all traffic :-

   LARBRET – BAVINCOURT
   GOUY – MONCHIET
   SAULTY – BAVINCOURT
   BAVINCOURT – GOUY
   GOUY, (V.6.b –(2000 yards S.W. of BAC DU SUD)

Not more than 2 vehicles at a time and not more than 30 men at a time will pass under the railway at the Western entrance to DAINVILLE in daylight. At least 200 yards will be left between parties.

LIEUT-COLONEL,
A.A. & Q.M.G.
14th (Light) DIVISION.

NOTICES.

LOST: On 15th February, 1916, between BRANDHOEK and ZEGGERS CAPPEL, a SACK, containing Boots, Clothing, 2 French Dictionaries, etc.
Information to H.Qrs, 14th Div'l Artillery.

LOST: At WARLUZEL, on or about the 26th February, a Civilian SADDLE. Maker's Name Avery or Murphy, Fermoy.
Finder please return to O.C., 11th King's L'pool Regt.

14TH (LIGHT) DIVISION.

ROUTINE ORDERS.

3rd March, 1916.

1249. MOTOR CAR LIGHTS.

Motor cars standing in villages East of the Line HABARCQ - GOUY at night will have their lights either extinguished or covered up.

No lights will be used by motor vehicles on the ARRAS - DOULLENS road or any road East of the Line WARLUS - BERNEVILLE.

1250. DISCIPLINE.

(a) Offences which should be reserved for superior authority are still being dealt with by Commanding Officers. Attention is directed to para.487, King's Regulations, which must be strictly complied with.

(b) The Commander-in-Chief notes with displeasure the slackness displayed by the troops in the matter of saluting. This is especially noticeable among men apparently off duty walking about in towns and villages. Officers will take steps to check this lack of discipline, and report to the unit concerned the names of men who fail to salute them.

Officers Commanding Units will deal severely with men whose names may be brought to their notice in this respect.

1251. ADDRESS.

It is notified for information that the 26th Mobile Veterinary Section is at BARLY.

1252. VENTILATION OF BILLETS.

Officers Commanding Units will ensure that there is at least one door or window to every room in which men are billeted, and that either the door or window always remains open at night.

This is especially necessary in the case of rooms which have no chimney.

Capt.
for
LIEUT-COLONEL,
A.A.&.Q.M.G.
14TH (LIGHT) DIVISION.

14TH (LIGHT) DIVISION.

ROUTINE ORDERS.

4TH MARCH, 1916.

1253. CLAIMS - PAYMENT OF.

The Command Paymaster, Base, having raised the question of the validity of receipts given my Maires on behalf of their interessés, the French Mission has been consulted on the subject.

Maires of Communes cannot sign for the inhabitants. Payments, should therefore, be made, not to Maires, but direct to the claimants concerned.
(Claims Commission G/469.)

1254. TOWN ORDERS - ARRAS.

Reference Town Orders, ARRAS, Orders Nos. 2, 4, 6, 14, and 16, will be read to all units on 3 successive parades, and a report rendered to Divisional Headquarters by March 7th that this has been done.

These orders will also be read over to all troops each time they enter ARRAS to be quartered there, and a complete copy of the orders will be posted in every billet.

1255. ADMINISTRATIVE.

A Garrison Sergeant Major will be detailed by Div'l Headquarters to keep the billeting lists and to take charge of all Garrison Stores in each of the undermentioned villages:
- DAINVILLE,
- BERNEVILLE,
- SIMENCOURT,
- FOSSEUX and
- BARLY.

Major Rundle, K.S.L.I., will be attached to Divisional Headquarters and will supervise the work of the Garrison Sergeant Majors.

Application for billets will ordinarily be made to Garrison Sergeant Majors. When units are moved into any of the villages, notification will be sent beforehand to Major Rundle at Divisional Headquarters.

1256. TRAFFIC CONTROL.

No lorries will proceed East of BERNEVILLE without special authority from Div. H.Qrs. This authority only holds good for one journey on the date of issue.

LIEUT-COLONEL,
A.A.&.Q.M.G.
14TH (LIGHT) DIVISION.

NOTICE.
DIVINE SERVICE.

C. of E. Church parade at Eastern end of BERNEVILLE village, near Battn. Headquarters, 5th K.S.L.I. on Sunday March 5th, Band of 6th Somerset L.I. will attend.

O.C. Coys
Please initial

A. Ed.
B. RSI
C. Whn.
D. ISR

14TH (LIGHT) DIVISION.

ROUTINE ORDERS.

5th March, 1916.

1257. SPIES.

Persons in French, Belgian or British Uniform have recently been seen in the British area, behaving in a suspicious manner, and in each case have escaped examination owing to prompt action not being taken.

In future, the papers of any person of whatever apparent rank, whose words or actions are suspicious, should be at once examined by any officer, N.C.O. or man on the spot. If this leaves any doubt whatever, the suspect should be immediately arrested and taken to the nearest British Officer, who will be responsible that he does not escape.

If the Officer is not satisfied, he should send the suspect to the nearest A.P.M., or direct to the Headquarters of the nearest Brigade, Division or Corps, who will have enquiries made by a Liaison or Intelligence Officer.

Every French or Belgian Officer or man attached to a British formation should produce an identification card issued and stamped by the French or Belgian Mission, and signed and stamped by a Liaison Officer and by a British Staff Officer or Officer Commanding a unit.

French and Belgians not attached to British formations should, when they enter our area, produce papers clearly establishing their right to do so.

It should be remembered that it is better to cause inconvenience to a number of innocent persons than to let one spy escape.

1258. LOOTING.

Any person found :-
    (1) In the act of looting,
    (2) In the possession of loot,
    (3) In a furnished house in which he is not billeted, and which is unoccupied,

will immediately be placed under arrest, and subsequently tried by Field General Court Martial.

In each case the offender is liable to suffer death by being shot.

1259. TRAFFIC.

(1) No traffic other than single Motor Cars or Ambulances may proceed East of the MAROEUIL-DAINVILLE Railway during the hours of daylight.

(2) a. No lorry transport is to be used when it is possible to use horse transport, except when distances are too great.

    b. Horse transport only will be used for Supply work from WANQUETIN Eastwards.

(3) During the hours of darkness, and while Divisions are occupying their present areas, the Northern Division will have sole use of the WARLUS-DAINVILLE Road, Reference Map Sheet 51c, from L.31 - L.29, and the Southern Division R.1 - R.8 - L.30 or R.1 - L.34.

(4) The following road is closed for the time being to lorry traffic:- Ref. Map, Sheet 51c.
From J.32.central to K.31.c.

- 2 -

1260. AEROPLANE PRECAUTIONS.

Every unit will mount an aeroplane guard on its billets daily and provide the sentry with a whistle.

Administrative Commandants of Villages will see that there is a sentry with a whistle at intervals of not less than 100 yards along each street.

Any sentry who sees or hears an aeroplane will at once blow 3 BLASTS on his whistle. This signal is to be repeated by all other aeroplane sentries.

Every officer, N.C.O. and man will immediately get into a building or if there is no building available will stand still close to a wall. Horses and vehicles will pull to the side of the road and halt.

The N.C.O. of the main Guard will come out into the street and look at the aeroplane. When satisfied that the aeroplane has gone or that it is British or French, he will cause TWO BLASTS to be blown on the whistle of the sentry of the main Guard. Traffic will then be resumed.

No one but the N.C.O. of the village Main Guard is authorised to give the signal for the resumption of traffic.

Troops and vehicles on roads or in fields in the open country will halt and remain perfectly still when an aeroplane is in view, but vehicles on the crest of hills will move down below the crest before halting. The Police will take the name of any officer and will arrest any N.C.O. or man infringing this order.

Troops billeted in villages are on no account to stand or loiter in the streets when off duty.

They must remain in their billets or in the courtyards at the back of the houses out of view from aircraft.

Transport must not remain halted in the streets of villages these must be kept absolutely clear. When the transport of a unit is about to leave a village, the vehicles must be kept in the yards until ready to march. On no account must it be formed up and kept waiting in the streets.

Empty vehicles are not to be left standing at the sides of the streets.

Watering parties must not halt in the streets.

Football is prohibited.

1261. EXERCISING HORSES.

Horses will be exercised between the hours of 4 a.m. and 6 a.m. only.

1262. WATERING HORSES.

Administrative Commandants of villages will detail hours of watering horses for each unit in such a way that no great quantity of horses is moving at the same time.

Units will adhere strictly to the hours laid down.

No man is to be allowed to take more than 2 horses to water at a time.

(Over).

1263. ADMINISTRATIVE.

With reference to D.R.O.1255:
The senior Officer in each village is O.C. Troops there
The following Officers are appointed Administrative Commandants :-

DAINVILLE.	=	2/Lieut.H.Brereton,	11th L'pool R.
BERNEVILLE,	=	Major T.C.Rundle,	5th K.S.L.I.
SIMENCOURT,	=	Major C.G.Mansfield-Clarke,	B.T.O.42nd.
FOSSEUX,	=	Major F.C.A.Hurt,	D.L.O.Y.
BARLY,	=	Capt.M.A. Towler,	14th Div.Cyclists.

These officers will be responsible for local discipline and sanitation and for the distribution of billets in consultation with the Maires of villages. The Garrison Sergeant Major, when appointed, will work under them.

M.M.P. will be allotted to them by the A.P.M. They are authorised to demand such local Police from units as may be necessary, reporting their action to Div'l Headquarters.

A Sanitary party will be detailed by the O.C. Sanitary Section to each village. Administrative Commandants are authorised to demand any fatigue parties necessary for sanitary duties, from the troops in their village.

Administrative Commandants will demand from the troops in their village any fatigue parties necessary for clearing the drains of the roads and when necessary for scraping the roads and clearing snow.

Administrative Commandants are responsible that aeroplane Guards are posted and that M.M.P. and local police enforce the orders as to action while aeroplanes are about. O.C.Troops in each village is responsible that every assistance is given to the Police by all Officers and N.C.Os.

A main Guard is to be mounted in each village under the orders of the Administrative Commandant, who will detail the Guard from the troops in the village.

Town Orders will be posted at the Mairie in each village. Copies will be sent to Divisional Headquarters.

[signature] Capt.
fo
LIEUT-COLONEL,
A.A.&.Q.M.G.
14TH (LIGHT) DIVISION.

NOTICE.

LOST: On the night of the 28-2-16 at WALLHURST, one DARK BAY HORSE, (Gelding) marked "B.48" on off hind, No.114 on near Hind, with one set of Universal appointments marked "B/48th R.F.A". Clipped at the Broad arrow.

One LIGHT BAY HORSE,(Gelding) marked "B.48" on off Hind "No.29" on near hind: two white socks Hind, near Fore White, White streak down centre of face. With Head-collar, Bit, and Rein, marked "B.48th R.F.A." Clipped at the Broad arrow.

Information to O.C., B/48th Bde R. F. A.

14TH (LIGHT) DIVISION.

ROUTINE ORDERS.

8th March, 1916.

1263. HONOURS AND REWARDS.

Under authority granted by HIS MAJESTY THE KING, the following decoration has been awarded for Gallant Conduct in the Field :-

DISTINGUISHED CONDUCT MEDAL.

No.R/2988, L/Corporal R.W. Moss, 9th K.R.R.C.

The Major-General heartily congratulates L/Cpl Moss. The Army Commander and Corps Commander have also requested that their congratulations be conveyed to him.

1264. BATHS.

Baths exist at BERNEVILLE and SIMENCOURT at which about 60 men a day can bathe.
Administrative Commandants will allot the accommodation between units. All other bathing accommodation must be arranged by units.
It has not been found possible as yet, to arrange a Divisional Laundry. Until this is arranged units must make their own arrangements.

1265. DISCIPLINE.

Officers and men are forbidden to march along the railway line in this Army area, whether in formed bodies or otherwise. All ranks are warned that if this order is infringed THEY ARE LIABLE TO BE FIRED UPON.

1266. STROMBOS HORNS.

Compressed air cylinders of Strombos Horns in need of re-charging should be sent to the D.A.D.O.S.

for LIEUT-COLONEL,
A.A.&.Q.M.G.
14TH (LIGHT) DIVISION.

NOTICE.

LOST at SIMENCOURT on the morning of the 3rd inst, HORSE, Black Gelding, 14½ hands. Branded, Near Hind "5" Off hind "C/47". Wearing Headcollar and chain.
Information to O.C. 47th Brigade R.F.A.

14th (LIGHT) DIVISION.
===========================

ROUTINE ORDERS.

7th March, 1916.

1267. **FRENCH TROOPS.**

French Troops and Transport billeted in the 14th Divisional Area are not to be disturbed without reference to this office.

1268. **R.E. STORES.**

The R.E. Parks and workshop are at DAINVILLE and stores can be drawn at any hour at night.

Indents should be submitted in bulk by Infantry Brigades, Artillery Brigades and units of Divisional Troops by 9 a.m. on the day on which they are required, and they will be informed what stores are available. It will not be necessary for the transport to bring written authority but the N.C.O. in charge should know what he has to draw.

Stores which are not drawn on the same day as they are asked for, or the following day, must be re-indented for.

In the case of articles which have to be made, notification will be sent when they are ready.

The Officer i/c Park will issue small quantities of stores on demand.

Wagons must enter at the North Entrance in the WARLUS Road, but units are reminded that the WARLUS - DAINVILLE road is reserved to the 5th Division and that they must enter DAINVILLE from the South.

It is notified for information that the following are now available :-

  Sandbags,   Mining frames,
  Brushwood Hurdles, Bomb Boxes,
  Artillery Marking Boards,
  Picks and Shovels, Loopholed Plates,
  Round timber,   Barbed & plain wire.
  Knife rests, iron and wood.
  Trench Tramway.

Other stores will be obtained shortly.

1269. **FORAGE RATION.**

A Guarantee has been given by the British Authorities that Hay will not be purchased in France, even in the Area occupied by British Troops.

The purchase of Hay is, therefore, forbidden.

Unthreshed straw may not be purchased under any circumstances owing to an embargo placed by the French authorities on the sale of all grain.

1270. **LIGHTS ON MOTOR VEHICLES.**

The upper half of the glass of the headlights on all Motor vehicles and Motor bicycles are to be painted over, and a report rendered to this office by O.C. all units with motor vehicles and motor bicycles, by 10th instant that this has been done.

(over)

1271. INDENTS.

Petrol and spare parts for Motor Vehicles will, in future, be issued by Divisional Supply Column at Refilling Point.

Indents must be sent to Divisional Supply Column before 12 noon previous day.

1272. SICK WASTAGE.

The following is the Sick Wastage Return for week ended noon 6th instant :-

Unit	O.	O.R.	Unit	O.	O.R.
14th Div. Cavalry,		1.	9th K.R.R.C.		13.
14th Div. Cyclists,	1	9.	9th R.B.		24.
46th Bde R.F.A.		8.	6th Somerset L.I.		39.
47th Bde R.F.A.		8.	6th D.C.L.I.		17.
48th Bde R.F.A.		3.	6th K.O.Y.L.I.	3.	9.
49th Bde R.F.A.		1.	10th Durham L.I.		11.
14th D.A.C.		2.	11th L'pool R		21.
39th T.M.Battery,		Nil.	8th M.M.G.Battery,		Nil.
61st Field Co. R.E.		1.	14th Div. Train,		2.
62nd Field Co. R.E.		2.	14th Div. Supply Col.		1.
89th Field Co. R.E.		2.	42nd Field Amblce.	2.	6.
14th Signal Co.R.E.		Nil.	42nd Field Amb.A.S.C.Att.		1.
7th K.R.R.C.		5.	43rd Field Amb.		Nil.
8th K.R.R.C.	1.	28.	" " "A.S.C.& A.S.C.M.T.		2.
7th R.B.	1.	12.	44th Field Amblce,		2.
8th R.B.	1.	15.	" " "A.S.C.Att.		1.
5th Ox & Bucks L.I.		9.	A.O.C.		1.
5th K.S.L.I.	1.	12.			

Total Officers 10, Other Ranks 268.

1273. STEEL HELMETS.

Men to whom steel helmets have been issued are always to wear them while in the trenches. These helmets are to be carefully fitted when issued and are to remain in possession of the men to whom they are fitted.

LIEUT-COLONEL,
A.A.&.Q.M.G.
14TH (LIGHT) DIVISION.

NOTICES.

LOST: On March 4th on the BEAUMETZ - SIMENCOURT - GOUY Road, a PARCEL, about 18 in. by 11 in. by 6 in., containing Maps. If found this parcel should be returned to C.R.E., 55TH DIVISION.

LOST: On the night 29th/1st, from 7th K.R.R.C. Transport lines at DAINVILLE, a MULE (Mare), Mouse coloured, cross clipped on near side of neck.
Information to B.T.O., 41st Infantry Brigade.

14TH (LIGHT) DIVISION.

ROUTINE ORDERS.

8th March, 1916.

1274. REPORTS.

During the period when the Division was on the march to its present position, in numerous cases the orders regarding reporting the new positions of headquarters were disregarded.

Divisional War Standing Order is re-published for information.

Para.17 (h). On arrival in billeting areas, Brigade Area Commanders will send the following reports to Div'l Headquarters as early as practicable.
- (i). Protective arrangements made.
- (ii). Position of Headquarters.
- (iii). Situation of units in billets.

Failure to comply with this order leads to serious delay in the delivery of orders and messages, and may easily lead to disastrous consequences.

1275. TRANSFERS TO M.T. BRANCH, A.S.C.

Reference Corps Routine Order No. 169 dated 20th October, 1915, men for transfer to Mechanical Transport Branch of the Army Service Corps are not to be sent to the Base without reference to this office.

1276. TRAFFIC.

(1) The SAULTY - BARLY Road is closed to all Motor Traffic.

(2) The road running N.W. through U.18 to COURTURELLE is to be used one way only for traffic, i.e. from SOUTH to NORTH.   (6th Corps A/196).

1277. SPEED LIMIT.

Cases are constantly occurring of Motor Lorries exceeding the speed limit.

The maximum speed lorries may travel is :-
- On open roads,   8 M.P.H.
- In villages,   6 M.P.H.

If the above limits are exceeded the name of the Driver and the Officer or N.C.O. in charge, will be taken, and the case reported to Corps Headquarters.

This order will be read out on 3 Parades to all M.T. Units.   (6th Corps A/285.)

1278. CASUALTY RETURNS.

In future, Casualty Returns are to show whether from Shell fire, rifle fire, shock, or accidental, as formerly.

(over)

1279. DISCIPLINE.

Reference D.R.O. No.1265, the prohibition does not refer to that portion of the railway within the Divisional Area East of a line drawn North and South through DAINVILLE STATION.

1280. MEDICAL.

From today a "Garrison Medical Officer" is appointed to each of the following places :- FOSSEUX, SIMENCOURT, BERNEVILLE, and DAINVILLE. A Medical inspection room is open at each place at which will be seen the sick of units and details billeted there, who have no Medical Officer attached.

The Garrison Medical Officer will supervise the sanitation of such units and details, and assist generally the Administrative Commandant in the sanitation of the whole area for which the latter is responsible.

1281. TRAFFIC CONTROL.

With reference to D.R.O. 1248 dated 1st instant, the DOULLENS - ARRAS road from BAC DU NORD Eastwards is NOT to be used before 7 p.m.

Transport from BERNEVILLE and SIMENCOURT will not leave those villages before 6.30 p.m. All other traffic for the trenches and gun positions will remain west of SIMENCOURT till 7 p.m.

LIEUT-COLONEL,
A.A.&.Q.M.G.
14TH (LIGHT) DIVISION.

N O T I C E S.

The Field Cashier has arranged to attend at Div'l Headquarters on Mondays and Thursdays from 2-30 p.m. to 4-30 p.m.

LOST: At ARRAS, during the night of 4th/5th inst, a PONY Light Bay Gelding, about 13½ hands, white star, a black line running from Withers to Dock, signs of old ring-worm about the back and hind quarters. Two white socks on hind legs. Brushes near and off hind; wearing headcollar and chain.
Information to Transport Officer, 5th Bn. K.S.L.I.

J.O.
Офиse Please note, initial, & return by bearer

14TH (LIGHT) DIVISION.

ROUTINE ORDERS.

9th March, 1916.

1282. SANITATION.

Captain C.H. Harbinson, R.A.M.C., is appointed to act as Sanitary Officer for that part of ARRAS occupied by this Division.

1283. OAT SACKS.

Oat sacks, and Sacks used for the issue of Potatoes are to be returned to Supply Officer daily, at refilling point.

1284. COLLECTION OF MATERIAL.

Brick rubble is not to be taken from the town of ARRAS under any circumstances.

1285. ORDNANCE STORES.

14th Division Ordnance Dump will be opened at BERNEVILLE for issue of Ordnance Stores to all units of Division from the 9th instant inclusive.

LIEUT COLONEL,
A.A.&.Q.M.G.
14TH (LIGHT) DIVISION.

14TH (LIGHT) DIVISION.

ROUTINE ORDERS:

10th March, 1916.

1286. HONOURS AND REWARDS.

The undermentioned have been awarded Cards "For Gallant and Meritorious Service" by the Major-General Commanding :-

14th Div'l Artillery.

No.97952.	Bombr. W.H.Coltman,	A/48th Bde R.F.A.
89179.	A/Bombr. F. Miles,	A/48th Bde R.F.A.
21494.	" J. Ryan,	C/48th Bde R.F.A.

7th Bn. Rifle Bde.

No. B.213. Sergt. C. Rumbelow,
1818. Corpl. A. Young,

5th K.S.L.I.

No.20066. Pte V.P. Allsopp,
17470. " F.G.Prior,
16433. " G. Nicholls,

6th K.O.Y.L.I.

No. 3134. L/Cpl Perkins,

1287. WATERING HORSES.

Units of 14th Division are not to water horses at GOUY MONCHIET, or BEAUMETZ.

1288. TOWN ORDERS, ARRAS.

Provisional Town Orders, ARRAS published with C.R.O. 1st March are cancelled.
Revised Town Orders, ARRAS, are published with C.R.O. dated 9th March.
Orders 2, 4, 5, 7, 15, 17 will be read out on three consecutive parades of all units and a report rendered to Divisional Headquarters by 13th instant that this has been done.
In addition these orders will be read out to all units entering ARRAS to be billeted there on the day of move.

1289. BAGGAGE WAGON HORSES.

Baggage Wagon Horses of all units are to be sent to the Companies Divisional Train to which they belong on 11th instant.

1290. CASUALTY RETURNS.

The cause of any accidental casualty should be stated very briefly in the telegraphic daily casualty return. The casualty return is not to be delayed, however, for the insertion of the information.
A brief telegraphic report should also be made separately, stating the circumstances attending any injuries to officers and men caused by the accidental explosion of grenades.

1291. **STRENGTH**.

    Officers Commanding Infantry Units will in future, ensure that the number of men left in Transport Lines when the unit proceeds to the trenches is reduced to a minimum. Each Groom left behind will look after at least two Officers chargers.

(signed) A.M. Hamilton

LIEUT-COLONEL,
A.A.& Q.M.G.
14TH (LIGHT) DIVISION.

14TH (LIGHT) DIVISION.

ROUTINE ORDERS.

11th March, 1916.

1292. ADMINISTRATIVE.

Civilians are not allowed to move out of the commune in which they reside without a pass signed by the Maire of the Commune and countersigned by an A.P.M.

But in the case of Communes in which there is no A.P.M. a pass for one day may be accepted if countersigned by the Officer Commanding a battalion or equivalent Unit. Applications for counter-signature will be taken by civilians to Administrative Commandants of villages occupied by troops of the 14th Division, who will obtain the countersignature of the nearest Commanding Officer but will keep the register of passes countersigned in his own possession.

In the case of small villages in close proximity to the trenches the senior officer in the village is authorised to countersign one day passes.

The Town Major, ARRAS, is included in the expression A.P.M.

1293. BATHS.

Application for the use of the Baths in BERNEVILLE and SIMENCOURT should be addressed to the Administrative Commandant of the place concerned.

[signature]
LIEUT-COLONEL,
A.A.&.Q.M.G.
14TH (LIGHT) DIVISION.

NOTICE.
DIVINE SERVICE.

R.C. Mass at 10 a.m. at Church, BERNEVILLE.

14TH (LIGHT) DIVISION.

ROUTINE ORDERS.

12th March, 1916.

1294. RIFLES FOR FIRING RIFLE GRENADES.

Trials have proved that rifles are rendered unserviceable by the firing of Mills Grenades with rod attachment. Service rifles are not, therefore, to be used for firing grenades of any description. 16 rifles per battalion, preferably rifles with barrels already bulged or the rifling badly scored should be appropriated solely for the purpose of firing rifle grenades and should be used alone for this purpose.

If there are not sufficient damaged rifles with Units for this service, arrangements should be made through Divisional Ordnance Officers to obtain them through the Base.

Brigades will report to this office by noon, the 14th inst., as to whether this number has been found to be sufficient.

1295. DIVISIONAL REST STATION.

The Divisional Rest Station has been opened at FOSSEUX by the 44th Field Ambulance.

Scabies cases will also be received there, men requiring admission for this complaint should bring their blankets with them.

1296. SICK WASTAGE.

The following is the Sick Wastage Return for week ended noon 11th instant:-

Unit	O.	O.R.	Unit	O.	O.R.
14th Div. Cavalry,		3.	9th K.R.R.C.		53.
14th Div Cyclists,		2.	9th R.B.		41.
46th Bde R.F.A.		22.	6th Somerset L.I.	2.	50.
47th Bde R.F.A.		13.	6th D.C.L.I.		6.
48th Bde R.F.A.		3.	6th K.O.Y.L.I.	1.	7.
49th Bde R.F.A.		4.	10th Durham L.I.		19.
14th D.A.C.		9.	11th L'pool R.		29.
61st Field Co.R.E.		2.	8th M.M.G. Battery.		Nil.
62nd Field Co.R.E.		3.	14th Div Train.		7.
89th Field Co.R.E.		2.	42nd Field Amblce.		2.
14th Signal Co.R.E.		1.	A.O.C.		1.
7th K.R.R.C.		10.	R.A.M.C. att 46th		
8th K.R.R.C.		19.	F.A. Bde.		1.
7th R.B.		20.	R.A. H.Q.		2.
8th R.B.		38.	14th Div. H.Q.		1.
5th Ox & Bucks.L.I.		18.			
5th K.S.L.I.	1.	18.			

Total Officers 9. Other ranks 419.

LIEUT-COLONEL.
A.A. & Q.M.G.
14th (LIGHT) DIVISION.

14TH (LIGHT) DIVISION.
ROUTINE ORDERS.

13th March 1916.

1297. HONOURS AND REWARDS.

Under authority granted by HIS MAJESTY THE KING, the following decoration has been awarded for Gallant Conduct in the Field:-

DISTINGUISHED CONDUCT MEDAL.

No. 20066,	Private	V.P. Allsopp,	8th K.S.L.I.
17470,	"	F.G. Prior,	-do-
16433,	"	G. Nicholls,	-do-

The Major General Commanding heartily congratulates the recipients. The Army Commander and Corps Commander have also requested that their congratulations may be conveyed to them.

1298. STORES. (Drawing of)

All stores notified by D.A.D.O.S. as available for issue to Units must be drawn at once.
If sufficient Transport is not available to convey all the stores two journeys must be made. On no account should part be drawn and part left till next day. This is essential to prevent congestion of the Ordnance Store.

1299. GRENADES - DUMMY.

The following dummy grenades are approved for issue on a scale of 8 of each type per battalion and 150 of each type per school of instruction:-

No. 1, Percussion Hand Grenade.
" 2,   "   "   "
" 3, Rifle Grenade.
" 5, Mills   "

Indents to be forwarded to the D.A.D.O.S. through the usual channels.

1300. REFILLING.

Refilling will be at 6.30 a.m. from 14th inclusive.

1301. DISCIPLINE.

Great care must be exercised to prevent interference with growing crops. Troops are forbidden to ride across the fields. Ground required for drill purposes will be hired, application being made through Administrative Commandants who will ensure that no fields that have been sown are used.

LIEUT-COLONEL,
A.A. & Q.M.G.
14TH (LIGHT) DIVISION.

14TH (LIGHT) DIVISION.

ROUTINE ORDERS.

14th March, 1916.

1302. WINTER FOOTGEAR.

With reference to the issues which have been made during the winter months of Shoepack Boots, F.S.Boots, and Gumboots, short, Infantry Brigades and Artillery will report through the usual channels, by 18th inst., the comparative merits of these three classes
(1) The comparative merits of these three classes of footwear.
(2) Whether any improvements can be suggested in their pattern.
(3) Whether the issue of Shoepacks, and F.S.Boots, if made, should be in lieu of Ammunition Boots.

1303. BATHS.

Capt. Barr, R.AM.C., Ecole Normale, ARRAS is appointed Officer i/c Div'l Baths and Laundry.
All applications for Baths in ARRAS and AGNY are to be addressed to him.
All applications for Baths in BERNEVILLE and SIMENCOURT are to be addressed to the Administrative Commandant of these places.

1304. TRAFFIC.

Reference D.R.O.1259, Supply wagons for troops actually quartered in DAINVILLE are permitted to enter DAINVILLE by day with supplies from refilling point and to return to their Train Companies.

1305. PROMOTIONS.

The undermentioned are promoted to acting ranks as stated while doing duty with Divisional Headquarters:-

No.12031 L/Cpl. Wear, S.N. 6th D.C.L.I.
    To be Acting Sergeant (Unpaid)

No.T.2/858.Driver Gove, A., A.S.C.
    To be acting Lance-Corporal (unpaid).

LIEUT=COLONEL,
A.A.&.Q.M.G.
14TH (LIGHT) DIVISION.

NOTICES.

LOST: On night of 9th inst, CYCLE, belonging to 48th Bde Ammn.Column, taken from passage of hut occupied by above unit and replaced by a broken machine belonging to 62nd Field Co.R.E. Marked 1st Section 14th D.A.C. Number believed to be 28285.
Information to O.C., 48th Bde Ammn. Column.

HOLY COMMUNION. at 8-30 a.m. Thursday next, in the Village Schoolroom, BERNEVILLE.

14TH (LIGHT) DIVISION.

ROUTINE ORDERS.

16th March, 1916.

1306. TIME TABLE OF TRAINS:- SAULTY LARBRET - ABBEVILLE.

Following Time-table is published for the information of all concerned :-

Leave SAULTY LARBRET.		Arrive ABBEVILLE.
1. 0 p.m.) Via		5.51 p.m.
5.50 p.m.) FREVENT,		11.01 p.m.
7. 0 p.m. Via LONGPRE,		12.22 a.m.

(6th Corps A/407).

1307. GLANDERS.

Owing to cases of Glanders having occurred amongst the horses of a troop of the French 21st Chasseurs at SARS-les-BOIS, five barns belonging to the undermentioned inhabitants, which have been marked "MORVE" are put out of bounds :-

GODART JULIEN,	SALOPPE AUSTIDE,
UTHILLIER AUGUSTIN,	BRACQUART EUGENE,
LINARN JULIS.	

(6th Corps Q/200).

1308. REFILLING.

On and from tomorrow the 17th instant, refilling will take place on AVESNES - HABARCQ Road at J.23.b.1.4. Sheet 51c, at 8.30 a.m.

1309. ADMINISTRATIVE COMMANDANTS.

The undermentioned Officers are appointed Administrative Commandants as stated, from 17th inst inclusive :-

Major A.T.C. Rundle, 5th K.S.L.I. at WANQUETIN,
Major Hon. R.T. St.John, 10th D.L.I. at BERNEVILLE.

1310. RETURN.

Reference D.R.O.1232 dated 23-2-16. The Return called for therein, should be rendered so as to reach this office by noon on the 11th of each month.

C. Parsons.
Capt for Lt-Col.
A.A.&.Q.M.G.
14TH (LIGHT) DIVISION.

NOTICE.

LOST: From B/49th Wagon Lines FOSSEAUX on night of 12th:
BROWN MARE marked B/49 on off fore, 30 on near fore,
Branded lately with Broad Arrow on near flank and old
Brand of same description can be seen below new
Brand. Blaze and white stocking off hind. Top of
tail slightly rubbed. Height 15.3 hands.
Information to O.C. B/49th Bde R.F.A.

14TH (LIGHT) DIVISION.

ROUTINE ORDERS.

18th March, 1916.

1311. ORDNANCE STORES.

14th Division Ordnance Dump will open at WARLUS for issue of Ordnance Stores to all units of Division from the 19th instant inclusive.

1312. LEAVE.

Ordinary Leave for all ranks has been re-opened. The composition of Groups and the days of the week allotted to each Group respectively will for the present remain as before. Details as to number of vacancies will be issued as soon as practicable.

ROUTE VIA HAVRE.

Period of leave 8 days including day of departure from HAVRE and day of departure from ENGLAND.

Example :-
    Monday (Group E).
    Leave SAULTY LARBRET by Supply Train at 7 p.m. on Sunday;
    Leave DOULLENS at 7.44 a.m. on Monday.
    LEAVE HAVRE at 1 a.m. on Tuesday, on which day Leave
        commences.
    Arrive LONDON (Waterloo) 10 a.m. Tuesday.
    Leave LONDON (Waterloo) 4 p.m. following Tuesday.

Troops proceeding on leave will carry rations for period covering journey to England.

(It is hoped to arrange accommodation where Officers and Men can spend the night at DOULLENS on homeward journey.)

                        CAPTAIN,
                        for A.A.&Q.M.G.
                        14TH (LIGHT) DIVISION.

NOTICES.
DIVINE SERVICES.

C of E.
Holy Communion 8 a.m. and Divine Service 3 p.m. at Hut in Rue de Chateau, WARLUS.

R.C.
7 a.m. Mass at SIMENCOURT.
11 a.m. " " FOSSEUX.
5.30 p.m. Evening service at FOSSEUX.

WESLEYANS, PRESBYTERIANS, NONCONFORMISTS ETC.
9 a.m. 5th OX & Bucks, 42nd Bde Transport at Recreation Hut, SIMENCOURT.
11 a.m. Field Companies R.E. at DAINVILLE.
2.30 p.m. 9th R.B. (C & D Coys) at Recreation Room, ARRAS Billet.
5 p.m. "A" Co. 9th K.R.R.C. and "B" Co. 9th R.B. at Protestant Church, ACHICOURT.
6.30 p.m. 42nd Field Ambulance at Echole Normale, ARRAS.

FOUND. 17th inst. GELDING, light bay, height 15.1, faint star, saddle marks, little white on coronet off hind. No Broad arrow or halter.
Apply, Administrative Commandant, DAINVILLE.

FOUND. 17th inst, Chestnut MULE, gelding, 6 years, marked 171 on near fore, 3 DRE on off fore. Grey mane.
Apply O.C., 46th Brigade Ammunition Column.

14TH (LIGHT) DIVISION.

ROUTINE ORDERS.

20th March, 1916.

1316. MEDICAL.

(i) (Correction to D.R.O.1313).
 The Garrison Medical Officer appointed at HAUTEVILLE, is Captain D. Haig, R.A.M.C.

(ii)   Field Ambulances are situated as follows :-
42nd Field Ambulance at WANQUETIN.
43rd   "   "   LIGNEREUIL,
44th   "   "   FOSSEUX Chateau.
 Sick of Units will be collected as under:-
From SIMENCOURT)
 BERNEVILLE) by 42nd Field Ambulance.
 WARLUS,   )
 HAUTEVILLE   by 44th Field Ambulance.
 DAINVILLE   by Advanced Dressing Station.
 Ambulances will call at Garrison Medical Inspection Rooms only, in each place, at 10.30 a.m. daily, by which hour sick from all units must be collected there. No other calls will be made except for urgent cases.
 Units in FOSSEUX and WANQUETIN will send their sick for "Hospital" to the Field Ambulance there by 11 a.m.

1317. SANITATION.(Horse Manure)

 It is imperative that immediate steps be taken to deal with the horse manure in such a manner as to reduce to a minimum its liability to become a breeding place for flies. To attain this object the following procedure will be carried out:-
 The Manure produced at each village or camp will be carted by the units concerned to a site chosen by the Administrative Commandant after consultation with the Garrison Medical Officer and the O.C., Sanitary Section. The Manure will be dumped beside the previous day's heap. It will there be treated by a fatigue party working under a N.C.O. instructed by the O.C., Sanitary Section.

1318. COURT MARTIAL.

 A Field General Court Martial, composed as under, will assemble at Headquarters, 11th Bn. King's Liverpool Regiment (Pioneers) ARRAS, at 10 a.m. on Wednesday next, 22nd instant for the trial of:-

 ▓▓▓▓▓▓▓▓▓▓▓▓▓▓▓▓▓▓▓▓▓▓▓▓▓▓▓▓

all of 11th Bn. King's Liverpool Regiment (Pioneers) and such other accused persons as may be brought before it.
     PRESIDENT.
     Major E.W. Folson, 9th K.R.R.C.
     MEMBERS.
 One Captain to be detailed by 41st Inf.Bde.
 One Captain or Subaltern to be detailed by 42nd Inf.Bd
 All witnesses will be warned to attend.
 One Subaltern 41st and 42nd Inf.Bdes and 11th King's L'pool Regt (Pioneers) will be detailed to attend the Court under instruction.
 An Orderly will be detailed by O.C., 11th King's L'pool Regt.
 Proceedings will be forwarded to Headquarters, 14th Division.
                                              (over)

1319. ADMINISTRATIVE COMMANDANT.

The undermentioned Officers have been appointed Administrative Commandants:-

    HAUTEVILLE: Major A.I.R.Butler,R.F.A., 14th D.A.C.
    WARLUS: Capt.M.E.Yorke Eliot, B.T.O.41st Inf.Bde.

1320. BRUSHWOOD.

Brushwood has recently been cut from a patch of springs in L.32.a.
All available cover is required for the concealment of guns and no more brushwood is to be cut in the locality referred to and anywhere else without a special permit.

1321. WARNING SIGNAL FOR AEROPLANES.

The following whistle signals in force in the 3rd Army area to notify the approach and departure of aircraft will be taken into use forthwith, in substitution for the present signals.

    3 blasts - get under cover or stand still.
    1 blast - all clear.

1322. REFILLING.

On and after the 22nd instant Refilling will take place at the DECAUVILLE Railway terminus at WANQUETIN at 8 . 7.30 a.m.

                              LIEUT.COLONEL,
                              A.A.&.Q.M.G.
                          14TH (LIGHT) DIVISION.

14TH (LIGHT) DIVISION.

ROUTINE ORDERS.

21st March, 1916.

1323. LEAVE.

Reference D.R.O. No.1312, Leave Party will now leave SAULTY LABRET by 5.50 p.m. train: the 7 p.m. train has been discontinued.

1324. LEAVE.

3rd Army Circular Memo. No.15 dated 17th March, 1916, "Instructions regarding Leave" has been issued to all concerned – and will be strictly complied with. Special attention is directed to Paras 6 and 9.

With reference to para 4 thereof, an Officer will be detailed on Mondays by the D.A.A.&.Q.M.G., Tuesdays by the C.R.A. and on others days of the week by the Brigade or Brigades concerned. The Officer so detailed will be in charge of the whole Divisional party of N.C.Os and men proceeding on Leave.

1325. RETURNS (LEAVE).

Officers Commanding all Units will render through the usual channels, so as to reach this office by 6 p.m. Saturday next 25th instant, a return shewing number of all ranks now on the strength of the unit who have been in this country (a) 8 months or over (b) 6 months but not exceeding 8, (c) 4 months but not exceeding 6, and have not had leave to ENGLAND of any kind, sick or otherwise.

1326. PASSES TO ARRAS.

All civilian applicants for Passes to ARRAS should be instructed to apply in writing either to Provost Marshal, Third Army, or A.P.M. VI Corps.

On no account are Commanding Officers, Town Majors, or O.C. Troops in villages to issue such passes.

1327. REMOUNTS.

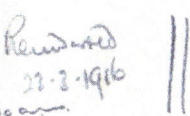

Units will render, to A.D.V.S. on 23rd, a return showing animals, by classes. Deficiencies, surpluses, and required to complete.

1328. CORRESPONDENCE.

In future Despatches, as distinct from messages, which are handed into the Signal Office for circulation, will not be entered up on the Signal Office register unless marked with the letter "R" on the top right corner.

This rule will not apply to Operation Orders or despatches sent by D.R.L.S. which will be entered up on the register as formerly.

Despatches which are important should therefore be marked "R" while those which are not should have no such mark.

(over).

1329. MEDICAL.

Attention is directed to D.R.O.1295.
Scabies cases must invariably take their Blankets with them when proceeding to Field Ambulance.

1330. APPOINTMENTS.

(i) Major W.L. Swainson, 6th Bn. D.C.L.I. is appointed Commandant, 14th Divisional School with the local rank of Lieutenant-Colonel whilst so employed: he will be retained on the strength of the 6th Bn. D.C.L.I. till further orders.

(ii) The Rev. W. Telfer, Chaplain to the Forces, has been appointed Senior Chaplain Church of England, to the 14th Division, with effect from 16th March, 1916, vice Rev. J. Kinnear, transferred to England, and is accordingly taken on the strength of the Divisional Headquarters.

1331. COURT MARTIAL.

Reference D.R.O.1318 of 20th instant, Major G.A. Delme Murray, 5th K.S.L.I. is appointed President of the Field General Court Martial therein ordered to assemble, vice Major E.W. Benson, 9th K.R.R.C.

1332. ADDRESS.

It is notified for information that the 26th Mobile Veterinary Section is at FOSSEUX.

LIEUT-COLONEL,
A.A.&.Q.M.G.
14TH (LIGHT) DIVISION.

14TH (LIGHT) DIVISION.

ROUTINE ORDERS.

22nd March, 1916.

1333. LEAVE.

Reference D.R.O. 1323, details proceeding on leave should report to R.T.O. SAULTY LARBRET one hour before the train is due to depart.

1334. BATHS.

Baths for Officers have been arranged and are now available in the Public Baths RUE D'IMPASSE of the RUE DES CAUCHIERS, ARRAS.

1335. APPOINTMENT.

No. 14859. Gunner L.E.E.Lee, 8th M.M.G. Battery is taken on the authorised establishment of Headquarters 14th (Light) Division and is appointed, clerk (A/Bombdr with pay) to the A.P.M. with effect from 13th March 1916.
(Authority, A.G., G.H.Q. A/1873 dated 12/3/16.)

Clayson Capt
LIEUT-COLONEL,
A.A. & Q.M.G.
14TH (LIGHT) DIVISION.

14TH (LIGHT) DIVISION.

ROUTINE ORDERS.

23rd March 1916.

1336. LAND - OCCUPATION OF.

Reference D.R.O. 1210 dated 15-2-16, a similar return will be rendered by all Units through the usual channels on the same pro forma to reach this office by the 31st of March, showing land occupied since arrival in Third Army Area. Land which it is desired to hire for Training purposes of resting battalions must be the subject of a separate proforma.

1337. FRENCH HUTS, STABLES, ETC.,

Stables and sheds or shelters, left by the French are not to be dismantled, or in any way interfered with.

1338. PURCHASE OF SUPPLIES.

Army Routine Order No. 345 dated 21st March 1916 is repeated for information and necessary action:-

A return of A.S.C. Supplies which are purchased by Units and paid for through their own Imprest Accounts is to be made up to and including the 7th, 14th, 21st and last day of each month, on Army Form W.3313, in duplicate, and marked with the Unit's Imprest Account number. Both copies of this form are to be sent to the Requisitioning Officer of the formation to which the Unit is attached, for endorsement, one being subsequently returned to the Unit to accompany the Imprest Account to the Paymaster, the other being retained by the Requisitioning Officer for despatch to the D.D.S. & T. Third Army.

This order to be repeated in Brigade Orders.

1339. FATIGUES.

Each Infantry Brigade will detail 1 N.C.O. and 17 men to report to the Railway Supply Officer at 3.p.m. on the 25th inst., at SAULTY LARBRET Station, where the party will be billeted, for the purpose of handling the daily Supplies and Stores arriving there for the Division. Nominal roll to be forwarded to this office.

N.C.Os and men detailed in the first instance will be relieved by others unfit for trench work as soon as the latter become available.

A Officer selected for a period of Light Duty will be detailed by the 41st Infantry Brigade to command the party. The Officer detailed will be relieved periodically by Brigades in turn: name to be submitted to this office.

LIEUT-COLONEL,
A.A. & Q.M.G.
14TH (LIGHT) DIVISION.

14TH (LIGHT) DIVISION.

ROUTINE ORDERS.

24th March, 1916.

1340. BATHS AND LAUNDRY.

Reference D.R.O. 1303 dated 14th instant:
Captain L.G. Brown, R.A.M.C. is appointed Officer i/c Div'l Baths and Laundry, vice Capt. G.F.Barr, R.A.M.C. His office is at the Public Baths, Rue d'Impasse, off the Rue des Gaugiers, ARRAS.

Apply for Baths A Coy Monday

1341. ANTI-GAS GOGGLES.

All Anti-gas goggles found to be unserviceable will be returned at once to the D.A.D.O.S.

LIEUT-COLONEL,
A.A.&.Q.M.G.
14TH (LIGHT) DIVISION.

NOTICES.

DIVINE SERVICES.

R. C.

a.m.	8.30	=	Mass at BERNEVILLE Parish Church for 10th D.L.I.
	9.0	=	" " SIMENCOURT Church.
	10.0	=	" " DAINVILLE Parish Church for R.E. & L'pool R
	11.0	=	" " FOSSEUX Church.
p.m.	4.0	=	Evening Service at HAUTEVILLE Church.
	5.30	=	" " " FOSSEUX Church.

WESLEYANS, PRESBYTERIANS, NONCONFORMISTS ETC.

a.m.	10.0	=	Divine Service, 5th K.S.L.I., SIMENCOURT.
	12.0	=	" " Fd.Coys R.E., R.G.A., R.M.A., DAINVILLE.
p.m.	3.0	=	" " 9th K.R.R.C. ARRAS.
	6.0	=	" " 42nd Field Amb. in Recreation Room.

*   *   *

14TH (LIGHT) DIVISION.

ROUTINE ORDERS.

25th March, 1916.

1342. LEAVE.

No leave is to be granted to Burnley or Fleetwood owing to an epidemic of measles at these places.

1343. TELEPHONES.

With a view to keeping the telephones on charge of Units in a good state of repair, the O.C., Battalion or other unit at rest, should notify O.C., 14th Signal Coy. when he considers that the instruments require overhauling. All minor faults will then be put right by an electrician. More serious faults will be met by the temporary issue of a fresh instrument.

1344. TRAFFIC CONTROL.

With reference to D.R.O. 1248 dated 1st instant, the DOULLENS - ARRAS road from BAC du NORD Eastwards is NOT to be used before 7.30.p.m.

Transport from Berneville and Simoncourt will not leave these villages before 7.p.m. All other traffic for the trenches and Gun positions will remain West of WARLUS till 7.30.p.m

These times will come into force from tomorrow inclusive, 26th instant.

1345. CELLS ELECTRIC.

D.R.O. 1315. is cancelled.
The Divisional Signal Coy. will deal with these as before.

1346. HAIRCUTTING.

D.R.O.1235, dated 28-2-16 is cancelled.

LIEUT-COLONEL,
A.A.&.Q.M.G.
14TH (LIGHT) DIVISION.

NOTICE.

LOST: from D/49th Bde Wagon Lines at K.31.d.1.2. Sheet 51c, TWO HORSES, on 23-3-16, description as follows :-
Dark bay blaze, 2 white socks, marked 16 on near flank, age about 10, height 16 hands.
Dark Bay, star, 1 white sock off hind, marked 13 on near hind hoof, D/49 on near flank: age about 10, height 16 hands.
Information to O.C., 49th Bde R. F. A.

DIVINE SERVICES.

C. OF E.
8.30 a.m. Holy Communion at No.8 Rue de Chateau, WARLUS.
9.30 a.m. Divine Service "   "   "   "   "   "

14TH (LIGHT) DIVISION.

ROUTINE ORDERS.

26th March, 1916.

1347. ACCIDENTAL INJURIES - COURTS OF INQUIRY.

Third Army Routine Order No. 272, as amended by C.R.O.612, is re-published :-
When Courts of Inquiry are held on accidents caused by the explosion of any kind of bombs, ammunition, etc., which are suspected to be due to a fault in the ammunition, Major STOKES, I.O.O., should, whenever possible, form one of the members of the Court. His address is :- Headquarters, Third Army.

1348. SANITATION.

Administrative Commandants, and Garrison Medical Officers will indent through the units to which they are attached for rations, for the disinfectants required from time to time.

1349. LEAVE.

Soldiers who re-engage to complete 21 years service may be granted one month's leave of absence to the United Kingdom.
(Authority A.G.,G.H.Q. B/2055, d/20-3-16.)

1350. DISCIPLINE.

Instances having been brought to notice of Commanding Officers having disposed of offences which should be reserved for superior authority, attention is again directed to Para. 487, King's Regulations.

1351. ARMY FORM B.213.

Attention is directed to General Routine Order No. 1461, regarding the compilation of Army Form B.213 in the case of Trench Mortar Batteries.

1352. R.E. STORES.

A shortage of Corrugated Iron is anticipated next month. Careful economy is therefore to be exercised in the use of this material.

[signature]
LIEUT-COLONEL,
A.A.&.Q.M.G.
14TH (LIGHT) DIVISION.

NOTICES.

FOUND. Brown MARE, about 14.2 hands, 79 stamped on near hoof, both hind fetlocks white, Government stamp on near hind quarters, Saddle, Bridle and headrope.
Apply A.P.M., 14th Division.

LOST. At WANQUETIN, on the night of 23/24th March, Brown GELDING, aged, about 15.3 hands. Marked "66" on near Fore, "D.H.C." on off fore.
Information to O.C., 48th Brigade R.F.A.

14TH (LIGHT) DIVISION.

ROUTINE ORDERS.

27th March, 1916.

1353. GAS HELMETS.

Indents are to be submitted at once to D.A.D.O.S. for "P.H." pattern helmets, at the rate of one per officer and man, to replace the "P" tube helmet now carried as second helmet.

The former are now available and should be drawn without delay.

The wooden packing cases containing the "P.H" pattern must be utilised for packing the "P" tube helmets, when returning the latter to Ordnance Stores.

1354. LEWIS GUNS.

Spade Handle Grips for Lewis Guns are urgently required at home. If any are still in possession of Units, who have had "Mark IV Mounting" replaced by "Mount, Field" Lewis Guns, they should be returned to the Base forthwith.

Reports, stating numbers returned, will reach Div'l Headquarters through the usual channels, by noon 29th inst.

1355. RETURN.

Officers Commanding all Units will render through the usual channels, so as to reach this office by 31st instant, a nominal roll of all ranks of the Jewish persuasion serving under their command.

1356. SICK WASTAGE.

The following is the Sick Wastage Return for week ended noon 25th instant :-

Unit	O.	O.R.	Unit	O.	O.R.
14th Div.Cavalry,		Nil.	9th K.R.R.C.	2	23
14th Div.Cyclists,		1.	9th R.B.	1	10
46th F.A. Bde.		3.	42nd Bde M.G. Coy,		1.
47th F.A. Bde,		2.	6th Somerset L.I.		10.
48th F.A. Bde,	1	4.	6th D.C.L.I.	1	1.
49th F.A. Bde,		4.	6th K.O.Y.L.I.		6.
14th D.A.C.		2.	10th Durham L.I.		13.
61st Field Co. R.E.	1	2.	43rd Bde M.G.Coy.		Nil.
62nd Field Co. R.E.		Nil.	11th L'pool R	1	12.
89th Field Co. R.E.		1.	8th M.M.G.Battery,		1.
14th Signal Co.R.E.		1.	14th Div. Train,		1.
7th K.R.R.C.		8.	14th Div.Supply Column,		Nil.
8th K.R.R.C.	1	19.	42nd Field Ambulance,		6.
7th R.B.	1	7.	43rd Field Ambulance,		3.
8th R.B.		4.	44th Field Ambulance,		4.
41st Bde M.G.Coy.		Nil.	26th Mob.Vet.Section,		Nil.
5th Ox & Bucks L.I.	1	9.	25th Sanitary Section,		Nil.
5th K.S.L.I.		7.	M.M.P.		Nil.
			R.A.M.C. Att.9th R.B.		1.
			14th F.A.W.U.		1.

Totals Officers 11, Other Ranks, 166.

14TH (LIGHT) DIVISION.

ROUTINE ORDERS.

28th March, 1916

1357. MISUSE OF GREEN ENVELOPES.

General Routine Order No. 1470, dated 24-3-16, is republished for information :-

The use of Green envelopes in two divisions has been suspended and the use of these envelopes by the Officers and men of those divisions has been prohibited for a month.

The general misuse of these by all ranks in the divisions concerned has led to this prohibition.

In spite of the fact that the user of each of these envelopes has to certify upon his honour, that the contents refer to nothing but private and family matters, a high percentage of the letters contain references to military movements or allusion to the location of the writer's unit, either openly or in simple dot codes and ciphers.

The contents of these envelopes will continue to be examined by the Base Censors and units and formations which abuse the privilege of their use will cease to receive them either temporarily or permanently.

This order will be republished in orders issued by all units and promulgated to all troops now serving in this country and to all troops who may arrive in this country in the future.

Nothing now published limits in any way the liability of any individual who misuses a green envelope, to be punished for his disobedience of orders.

1358. MISUSE OF GREEN ENVELOPES.

With reference to above G.R.O. No.1479, an order has been received prohibiting the use of green envelopes, A.F. W.3978, by any Officer, N.C.O. or man of this Division from this date inclusive.

The Major-General regrets that such a reflection should be cast upon the Division, owing to the Wilful abuse of a privilege by a few N.C.Os and men belonging to it.

This order is to be read out on parade in the same manner as and immediately after D.R.O.1357.

1359. TRAFFIC.

With reference to Corps Routine Order, No.1620, dated 24/3/16, the road from AVESNES via HAUTEVILLE to WANQUETIN, shown in red on the Map issued therewith, is closed to all Motor Traffic until further orders.
VI Corps A/574.

1360. ADMINISTRATIVE.

Lieut. J.A.R. Thompson, R.A.M.C., 42nd Field Ambulance, is appointed Garrison Medical Officer, WANQUETIN.

1361. CHAPLAIN.

The Rev. C.H. Meyrick, Chaplain to the Forces (C of E) is posted to the 14th Divisional Artillery for duty, and will be attached to a unit for accommodation and rations under the orders of the C.R.A.

14TH (LIGHT) DIVISION.

ROUTINE ORDERS.

29th March, 1916.

1362. APPOINTMENTS.

(i) Captain G.E.R. Prior, 1st Bn. Devonshire Regiment this day assumed the appointment of G.S.O., 3rd Grade, 14th (Light) Division, vice Major A.W. Stericker, appointed G.S.O., 3rd Grade, Third Army.

(ii) Captain G.S. Mitchell, 11th L'pool R has taken over the duties of Administrative Commandant, DAINVILLE, vice 2/Lieut. H. Brereton, 11th L'pool R.

1363. LEAVE.

Reference D.R.O.1342, leave may now be granted to Burnley and Fleetwood. Leave to Stockport is NOT to be granted for the present.

1364. MISUSE OF GREEN ENVELOPES.

Reference D.R.O. Nos.1357 and 1358, dated yesterday, Instructions have been issued for all letters posted in contravention of the above quoted orders to be returned to the Officer Commanding the Unit concerned, who will take disciplinary action.

The prohibition will remain in force until the 25th of April inclusive.

Officers Commanding all Units in the Division will take immediate steps to collect all unused Green Envelopes now in possession of Officers, N.C.Os and men and will forward the same to "Q" Office, Divisional Headquarters, by 12 noon on Saturday next April 1st, with a statement shewing numbers of envelopes so returned and a certificate to the effect that to the best of their knowledge, all have been collected.

1365. R.E. STORES.

The hours during which Stores are issued from 14th Division R.E. Parks at DAINVILLE and DAINVILLE STATION, are as follows :-

```
To R.E. & Pioneers        before 7 p.m.
 " Infantry Brigades,     7.30 p.m. to 9 p.m.
 " R.A. & Other Units,    after 9 p.m.
```

In all cases two men must be sent with each wagon for loading purposes.

1366. MISCELLANEOUS.

The O.C. Unit with which either of the undermentioned is serving is requested to communicate with this office without delay :-

J. Warrington,
Rfmn. E. Buckley,
A fuller description is not available.

Captain
for LIEUT COLONEL,
A.A.&.Q.M.G.
14TH (LIGHT) DIVISION.

NOTICE.

LOST. Strayed from stables on the night 24/25th March, BAY GELDING, Star, No.75 clipped on near side saddle patch, A/48 clipped on near hind-quarters.

Information to O.C., 48th Brigade R.F.A.

14TH (LIGHT) DIVISION.

ROUTINE ORDERS.

31st March, 1916.

1367. LOCAL PURCHASES AND REQUISITIONS OF ENGINEER STORES.

Whenever it is desired to obtain Engineer Stores locally, they should be purchased if the Owner can be found, and the price is reasonable, but if impossible to purchase they may be requisitioned.

In order to avoid subsequent correspondence with the Paymaster or Requisition Office as the case may be, the following procedure should be adopted :-

(1) In the case of intended purchases, a list of the articles required and their prices should be sent to the C.R.E. for approval. When approved it will be returned to the unit and payment can be made out of Imprest a/c.

(2) In the case of intended requisitions, a descriptive list of articles should be sent in duplicate to the C.R.E. who will assess the prices, countersign the duplicate, and return both copies. The original should be attached to the original of the requisition receipt note, and handed to the Town Major or the Maire, and the duplicate should be sent with the duplicate of requisition receipt note to the Requisition office in the ordinary way. When there is not time to obtain the approval of the C.R.E. beforehand, units may purchase or requisition at their own risk and obtain approval subsequently.

Nothing that is available from the R.E. Park should be either purchased or requisitioned by Units.

1368. RATIONS.

Vegetables (fresh or dried) will not be issued when "meat and vegetable" rations are drawn, except when the latter are issued in lieu of bacon.
(Army Routine Order No.357).

1369. CORRESPONDENCE.

Correspondence in connection with questions concerning Records, such as expiration of engagement, conditions of service, etc., should be addressed to D.A.G 3rd Echelon, and NOT to Officers in charge of Records at home.

Much time and correspondence will, in many instances, be saved by following this procedure.

1370. SCREENS FOR HORSE STANDINGS.

In view of the close approach of warm weather, screens for horse standings are considered no longer necessary.

No further issues of material will be made for this purpose.

LIEUT-COLONEL,
A.A.&.Q.M.G.
14TH (LIGHT) DIVISION.

(Over)

N O T I C E S.

SOLDIERS' CLUB.
A Divisional Soldiers' Club has been opened in the Rue Louez, Dieu, ARRAS. Billiards, games, refreshments.

DIVINE SERVICES.
C of E Chapel, at the Div'l Soldiers' Club House, Rue Louez Dieu, ARRAS. Holy Communion daily at 8.30 a.m. and by arrangement. Sunday Evensong 7.15 p.m.

DIVINE SERVICE, 2ND APRIL 1916.

C OF E.
8.30 a.m. Holy Communion,) For Div'l Headquarters, in the
9.30 a.m. Divine Service,) Hut, Rue du Chateau, WARLUS.

R.C.
7 a.m.   Mass at DAINVILLE Parish Church for R.E's, 11th L'pool R, and Pioneer Detachment.
8.30 a.m.   Mass at BERNEVILLE Parish Church for 6th K.O.Y.L.I. Transport of 10th D.L.I., 6th D.C.L.I., 6th Som.L.I. 14th Div'l Train.
9 a.m.   Mass at SIMENCOURT.
11 a.m.   "   " FOSSEUX.
4 p.m.   Evening Service HAUTEVILLE.
5.30 p.m.   "   "   FOSSEUX.

PRESBYTERIANS, WESLEYANS ETC.
8.45 a.m. Divine Service 9th R.B. at SIMENCOURT.
10 a.m.   "   "   Highland Battery R.G.A. Wagon lines at WANQUETIN.
12 noon.   "   "   R.G.A., R.E., R.H.A. at Recreation Room, DAINVILLE.
2.30 p.m.   "   "   5th Ox & Bucks L.I. ARRAS.
6 p.m.   "   "   42nd Field Ambulance, ARRAS.

==========

14TH (LIGHT) DIVISION.

ROUTINE ORDERS.

1st April, 1916.

1371. GUM BOOTS THIGH.

All Gum Boots thigh which are no longer required by units, will be returned at once to Ordnance.

1372. BOUNDS.

The Estaminet "VEUVE BLONDEL", WARLUS, is closed for 15 days from today inclusive.

1373. DIV'L AMBULANCE WORKSHOP, A.S.C.

Reference G.R.O. 1484, the F.A.W.U. will be transferred to 14th Div'l Supply Column from April 3rd, and will move to the billets occupied by 14th Divisional Supply Column on that date.

LIEUT-COLONEL,
A.A.&.Q.M.G.
14TH (LIGHT) DIVISION.

NOTICES.

LOST, on 29th ult., Dark Green BICYCLE, 2 Carriers, no bell, 1 lamp. Red tyres. Bicycle left outside a house in DAINVILLE.
Information to O.C, 13th Batt. R.F.A., or Administrative Commandant, DAINVILLE.

LOST: BICYCLE marked on rear mud-guard:- A red triangle, followed by the letters C.S.M.
Information to O.C., 89th Field Co. R.E.

DIVINE SERVICE in the great barn at the GRANDE FERME at BERNEVILLE, 11.a.m. Sunday, with Communion to follow.

14TH (LIGHT) DIVISION.

ROUTINE ORDERS.

2nd April, 1916.

1374. HONOURS & REWARDS (Investitures).

(1) Officers detailed to proceed to England to attend Investitures are not required to report at the War Office. They should proceed direct to Buckingham Palace at 10-15 a.m. on the morning of the Investiture, when the Lord Chamberlain will receive them.

The above also applies to Warrant Officers awarded the Military Cross and all ranks awarded the Victoria Cross who are detailed to attend.

(2) Every officer who proceeds to England on ordinary leave and who has not already received the decoration to which he is entitled MUST report at the War Office with a view to attending an Investiture.

1375. DISINFECTION OF BLANKETS.

Units requiring blankets disinfecting should apply to the Officer i/c Div'l Baths, Laundry Depot, WANQUETIN, who will arrange dates and times.

Units will be responsible that the blankets are conveyed to WANQUETIN at the time arranged.

1376. UNDERCLOTHING.

A large amount of underclothing has been drawn by Units during the past month and no portion of the discarded underclothing has been accounted for.

All dirty underclothing is to be sent to the Baths where it will be disinfected, repaired and washed, and prepared for re-issue to men using the Baths.

The Officer i/c Baths will arrange for the collection at all bathing establishments of dirty underclothing sent in by units, in addition to that left at the Baths by men who have bathed.

1377. DISCIPLINE.

Cases have occurred in which maps showing military information have been sent home by ordinary post.

It must be impressed on all ranks that this must never be done, as the extreme gravity of this offence is obvious.

LIEUT-COLONEL,
A.A.&.Q.M.G.
14TH (LIGHT) DIVISION.

NOTICE.

LOST. From Ordnance Yard, WARLUS, on 2/4/16, at 11 a.m. Rigid CYCLE, belonging to 14th Div'l Cyclist Co. Makers No. 21295, Enamel Plate No.7, painted on mud-guard:- White bar and No.7.
Information to D.A.D.O.S., 14th Division.

14TH (LIGHT) DIVISION.

ROUTINE ORDERS.

3rd April, 1916.

1378. STEEL HELMETS.

The Army Commander has noticed that his order on the wearing of the Steel Helmet by the troops when on duty is not invariably obeyed. Army Routine Order No.339 of the 14th March, 1916 is, therefore to be republished in Brigade and Battalion Orders, and will be read out on three successive parades.

> 339. Steel Helmets.
> "Officers and men in possession of steel helmets will invariably wear them when on duty. They are not to be carried attached to the pack when on the line of march".

[margin note: Published in Batty Orders 6th]

1379. HIRE OF LAND.

When Units make private arrangements to hire or pay for lands out of their own funds, a copy of the agreement is to be sent to Div'l Headquarters, for forwarding to the Rent Officer of the Area, to enable him to deal with any claim for rent which may be made after the departure of the unit, and so save double payment.

Whenever possible, however, the proposal to rent the land should be made beforehand to Div'l Headquarters, in order that the agreement may be made through the medium of the Rent Officer.

1380. DAMAGE TO CROPS.

Complaints continue to be received that Officers and men (principally officers) ride over growing crops.

Riding across crops is forbidden to all ranks, and officers will be particularly careful to obey the orders on the subject.

[margin note: Published in Batty Orders 6th]

1381. ADDRESSES.

The "14th Divisional School", B.E.F, and "14th Divisional Grenade School" B.E.F., are the Registered addresses of these Schools.

1382. CLAIMS OFFICER.

(1) Captain J. Bonskin, 89th Field Co.R.E. performed the duties of Division Claims Officer, 14th Division from 10th to 29th February, both dates inclusive.

(2) 2/Lieut. J. Stanning, Duke of Lancaster's Own Yeomanry is appointed Divisional Claims Officer, 14th Division, from 7th March, inclusive.

LIEUT-COLONEL,
A.A.& Q.M.G.
14TH (LIGHT) DIVISION.

14TH (LIGHT) DIVISION.

ROUTINE ORDERS.

4th April, 1916.

1383. FUEL.

The following is the scale of Fuel from this date inclusive :-

<u>For men in the trenches.</u>
½ lb coal, ½ lb coke, 1/8 lb charcoal.
<u>For men not in the trenches.</u>
1½ lbs Coal.

The allowance for officers etc., ceased on April 1st.

1384. CLOTHING.

Reference C.R.O.657, the undermentioned will be returned to D.A.D.O.S. as shown :-

Gloves, fingerless,)   Units other than Infantry
Leather Jerkins,   )   by 6 p.m. 8th instant.
Undercoats Fur,   )   Infantry by 6 p.m. 10th inst.
Mittens,   )

Drawers, woollen, will be retained for the present.

1385. FOOTBALL.

With reference to D.R.O.1260, the general prohibition against playing football is cancelled, but football will only be played on ground for which an agreement has been made with the owner. Proposals to hire ground for this purpose must be submitted to Divisional Headquarters. The ground must be out of sight from the enemy's lines and from the known positions of Observation balloons.

When football is being played an aeroplane guard must invariably be mounted.

1386. EXERCISING OF HORSES.

With reference to D.R.O.1261, horses may be exercised on roads in the Divisional Area west of BERNEVILLE and WARLUS up to 9 a.m. If <u>fallow</u> land can be hired, horses can be exercised on it in rings at any hour, an aeroplane guard being mounted and the whole parade being halted while an enemy or unidentified aeroplane is overhead.

(over)

1387. SICK WASTAGE.

The following is the Sick Wastage Return for week ended noon 1st instant:-

Unit	O.	O.R.	Unit	O.	O.R.
14th Div. Cavalry,			9th K.R.R.C.		4.
14th Div. Cyclists,		Nil	9th R.B	1.	5.
46th F.A. Bde,		2.	42nd Bde M.G. Coy,		1.
47th F.A. Bde,		3.	6th Somerset L.I.		7.
48th F.A. Bde,	1.	3.	6th D.C.L.I.	2.	5.
49th F.A. Bde,		2.	6th K.O.Y.L.I.	1.	2.
14th D.A.C.		2.	10th Durham L.I.		9.
61st Field Co. R.E.		2.	43rd Bde M.G. Coy,		Nil.
62nd Field Co. R.E.		2.	11th L'pool R		4.
89th Field Co. R.E.		1.	8th M.M.G. Battery,		Nil.
14th Signal Co. R.E.		1.	14th Div. Train,		1.
7th K.R.R.C.		3.	14th Div. Supply Col.		Nil.
8th K.R.R.C.		7.	42nd Field Ambulance,		1.
7th R.B.		7.	43rd Field Ambulance,		Nil.
8th R.B.		2.	44th Field Ambulance,		1.
41st Bde M.G. Coy.		Nil	26th Mob. Vet. Section,		Nil.
5th Ox & Bucks L.I.		2.	25th Sanitary Section,		Nil.
5th K.S.L.I.		11.	M.M.P.		Nil.
			H.Qrs, 41st Inf. Bde,		1.

Total Officers 5. Other Ranks, 91.

1388. RETURN.

Units concerned will render by 12 noon the 7th inst, through the usual channels, a return showing the numbers of "Breakers, wire No.1" in possession.

Reported
16 in possession
6/6 HS

LIEUT-COLONEL, *Captain*
A.A.&.Q.M.G. *for*
14TH (LIGHT) DIVISION.

NOTICES.

LOST. On 30th ult, the front WHEEL of a push-cycle, which was left outside office of Camp Commandant, 14th Div. H.Qrs.
Information to Camp Commandant, 14th Division.

LOST: between SAULTY and WANQUETIN on 1st inst, Chestnut GELDING, Star, No. 33 on near side saddle-patch, A/48 on near hind-quarters.
Black MARE, Blaze, No.69 on near side saddle patch, A/48 on near hind-quarters.
Both with saddles, bits and reins.
Information to O.C., 48th Brigade R.F.A.

LOST: On road between WARLUS – ARRAS, on night of 2nd instant, an "ADINFER" map.
Information to M. Bardoux, French Mission. WARLUS.

14TH (LIGHT) DIVISION.

ROUTINE ORDERS.

5th April, 1916.

1389. MISUSE OF GREEN ENVELOPES.

With reference to D.R.O.1358 dated 28-3-16:
Troops attached to the Division are not affected by the order prohibiting the use of green envelopes. Care will be taken, however, that green envelopes dispatched by troops so attached are invariably brought to Field Post Offices in a separate bag on which the name of the unit concerned is to be clearly marked.

1390. FUEL.

Reference D.R.O.1383 of 4th April.
The amount of coke for men in the trenches should read 1 lb, not ½ lb.

1391. LEAVE.

No leave is to be granted to CHORLEY or COPPULL, Lancs, owing to an epidemic of measles at these places.

LIEUT-COLONEL,
A.A.&.Q.M.G.
14TH (LIGHT) DIVISION.

NOTICE.

FOUND: On 1st inst on the LATTRE ST.QUENTIN - WANQUETIN Road, Mule, Brown, aged. Markings:- Clipped near hip and near shoulder, white mark near shoulder point and off shoulder.
Apply O.C., B/49th Bde R.F.A.

14TH (LIGHT) DIVISION.

ROUTINE ORDERS.

6th April, 1916.

1392. HONOURS AND REWARDS.

HIS MAJESTY THE KING has been graciously pleased to award the ALBERT MEDAL of the FIRST CLASS upon the Late No. 12231, Lance-Corporal G. ALDERSON, 10th Battalion, Durham Light Infantry.

1393. RATIONS.

The normal ration scale for British and Dominion troops, as shown in General Routine Order No.1235, will be amended as follows :-
JAM :- For "4 ozs" substitute "3 ozs".
MILK, CONDENSED :- For "1/16 tin" substitute "1/12 tin".
This change to take effect from 10th April, inclusive.

1394. MEAT RATION.

Until further notice the daily meat ration for all troops in France will be made up as follows :-
60% Frozen meat (at 1 lb.)
25% Preserved meat (at ¾ lb nominal).
15% (M. and V rations (3 days out of 7).
    (*Pork and beans (4 days out of 7).
The foregoing will come in operation on Sunday 2nd April, 1916.
* Issues will be made as soon as stocks are available; until then M and V Rations will be issued in lieu. The issue of the Pork and beans ration will be on the scale of 3 rations per tin.

LIEUT-COLONEL,
A.A.&.Q.M.G.
14TH (LIGHT) DIVISION.

N O T I C E.

LOST: Light BAY HORSE, about 15.3 hands high. Marked - Bald patch on crown with white face, D/49 marked on rear flank. Information to O.C., D/49 Bde, R.F.A.

14TH (LIGHT) DIVISION.

ROUTINE ORDERS.

7th April, 1916.

1395. ROAD AND RAILWAY MATERIAL.

Road metal stacked alongside roads or in road material depots is not to be removed by the troops without orders from the C.R.E. of the Division or the Chief Engineer of the Corps.

On No account will any stores or other material belonging to the French Railways Ponts et Chaussées or any other French Administration be taken by British Troops without previous permission being obtained from the French Authorities through the C.R.E., or C.E.

This order is to be repeated in Brigade and Regimental Orders.

1396. STEEL HELMETS - COVERS FOR.

The Army Commander desires that all Steel Helmets should be painted with the following special preparation :-

Middle Green	....	10 lbs.
White lead	....	5 lbs.
Common umber	....	1 lb.
Copal varnish	....	½ pint.

To this is added sufficient turpentine to produce the required consistency.

1 litre of raw linseed oil should be added to every 10 litres of turpentine and ¼ lb of "Siccatif le Revulsif"(dryers) to every 10 kilos of paint.

When the paint is nearly dry it is sprinkled with finely powdered chalk and dusted lightly with a clean wet cloth.

It is considered that the sprinkling of powdered chalk takes the shine from the paint. This point should therefore have careful attention.

(Authority Third Army O/67, d/5-4-16. VI Corps Q/246.).

1397. EXERCISING OF HORSES.

Units exercising horses on the roads should avoid passing through villages, as the passage of large numbers of horses increases the work of clearing the streets.

LIEUT-COLONEL,
A.A.&.Q.M.G.
14TH (LIGHT) DIVISION.

NOTICES.

LOST: On ARRAS - DOULLENS Road, near DAINVILLE Railway Station at about 9 p.m. on 4th inst, Officer's HAVERSACK, containing shaving outfit, Prismatic compasses, Pliers and screwdriver. Information to O.C., 47th Bde R.F.A.

LOST: At WANQUETIN, on the night of the 23/24th March, Brown GELDING, aged, about 15.3 hands, Marked "86" on near fore, "D.H.O" on off fore.
Information to O.C., 48th Bde R.F.A.

14TH (LIGHT) DIVISION.

ROUTINE ORDERS.

8th April, 1916.

1398. CLAIMS FOR DAMAGES.

The following is the procedure for payment of claims from inhabitants chargeable against units or individuals.

Where the whole claim is payable by the Unit or individuals and the claim has been investigated and accepted by the unit the amount should be paid by O.C. Unit who will recoup himself for amounts chargeable to individuals by receiving payment in Cash and if this is not possible, by entering the amount in an acquittance roll.

The O.C. Unit when paying the claim will have the receipt countersigned by the Maire and will forward the receipt with particulars of the damage paid for to the Div'l Claims Officer.

When the claim is partly chargeable to units and partly to the public, the O.C. the Unit responsible will pay over in cash to the Div'l Claims Officer the sum chargeable to his unit and to the individuals in it. The Div. Claims Officer will then settle for the full amount giving credit in his Imprest account for the sum received from the unit.

1399. FUEL.

Reference D.R.O.1383, dated 4-4-16:
The Winter scale of fuel is temporarily in force again.

1400. DISCIPLINE (Arms and Equipment).

N.C.Os and men detached from their Units are always to go fully armed and equipped.

C.L.Hamilton

LIEUT-COLONEL,
A.A.&.Q.M.G.
14TH (LIGHT) DIVISION.

NOTICES.

FOUND. MULE GELDING, mouse coloured, gall on near fore, broad arrow on near hind-quarter. No other marks. Apply O.C., 44th Field Ambulance.

LOST: Strawberry Roan GELDING, aged, about 14.1 hands. last seen with head collar.
Information to O.C., 61st Field Co. R.E.

14TH (LIGHT) DIVISION.

ROUTINE ORDERS.

10th April, 1916.

1401. DISCIPLINE.

Attention is directed to D.R.O.988 dated 3-12-15:
Heavy draught horses are never to be trotted, and Light Draught horses are not to be trotted except in cases of emergency.

This applies to all transport 1st Line, Regimental, Technical, Artillery and Train.

Horses at exercise are not to be trotted on macadam roads.

1402. COMPOSITORS.

Two compositors are required for work at Army Headquarters. O.C. Units will report through the usual channels by 6 p.m. 12th instant the names of any capable men recommended who are desirous of taking up this work.

1403. ARMY FORM B.213.

Attention is directed to G.R.O.1175 of 27-9-15, particularly to the following points :-
(i) Effective Strength should include any men detached from their Units for any purpose, a detailed note being made in the column of remarks shewing the Units and number of officers and men detached to each Unit.
(ii) Men detached to Trench Mortar Batteries & Tunnelling Companies will be shewn on the Effective Strength of their Units, and a note will be made in the column of remarks.
(iii) O's C Tunnelling Companies will not shew these men on the Effective Strength of the Company but will include them in the Total Rationed, and make a note in the Remarks Column that so many men are attached for rations only.

1404. SANITATION.

The villages in occupation by the Division are to be thoroughly cleaned. All old dung and refuse is to be moved outside the village. New Stable refuse is to be treated as laid down in D.R.O.1317.

All Barns are to be cleaned out and made sweet ready for occupation, if necessary, by men.

The R.E. will provide bunks in all Barns as labour and material may be available.

No Building which is capable of being converted into accommodation for men is to be used for stabling horses. Places which have been used as stabling by French Troops may be retained as such until all other accommodation in the village has been prepared as accommodation for men. If any buildings have been recently taken into use as stables, the horses are to be turned out at once and the place cleaned up.

Town Commandants will make all arrangements, drawing fatigue parties from troops in their villages.

(over).

1405. REPORTS (Occupation of land).

O.C. Units will furnish reports by 15th instant to Town Commandants of villages occupied by troops under their command, as to the condition of the land occupied by them, and the condition of buildings, and trees, on it.

The Town Commandants will verify these reports and get them countersigned by the Maires of the villages.

When the reports of villages are complete, they will be forwarded to Divisional Headquarters for safe custody.

1406. MEDICAL COMFORTS.

Medical Comforts required by Medical Officers attached to units will be obtained by them from the Field Ambulance nearest them. These supplies will not be issued by Supply Officers to units other than Medical Units.

1407. MISCELLANEOUS.

Information is required as to the whereabouts of the undermentioned men. Any Unit having this information will report to this office:
No.18279. Pte A.J. Boggis, 9th Bn. Norfolk Regt.
No.18280. " E.W. Bowman, 9th Bn. Norfolk Regt.
No. 8009. " A.C. Bowdery, 9th Bn. Norfolk Regt.

1408. TEMPORARY PROMOTION - OFFICERS.

All applications for temporary promotion under M.S.3522/1 should, in future, state whether the Officer causing the vacancy has been previously temporarily promoted to fill the Establishment of his Unit, or has been granted temporary rank under Sec.III, C.D.S.384.

1409. FIRES:

Corps Routine Order No.686 is republished for information. It is to be repeated in Brigade and Battalion Orders and the order and appended Circular "Precautions against fire" are to be read out on three parades. A copy of the circular is also to be posted in every barn or billet occupied by British Troops. A supply will be sent to Town Commandants and for use in front line villages to Infantry Brigades.

686. FIRES.

Several instances of fires in billets have recently occurred in the VI Corps area owing to the lack of ordinary precautions.

To minimise the chances of similar outbreaks in future, a list of steps to be taken to prevent the outbreak of fire is circulated with these orders.

Courts of Enquiry on fires will in future ascertain whether these instructions have been complied with. Failure to carry out these orders will render the unit or individual liable to bear the cost of the damage caused by the fire.

This order will be published in the Routine Orders of all units in the VI Corps area, and read out on three parades.

(Continued).

1410. **SICK WASTAGE.**

The following is the Sick Wastage Return for week ended noon 8th instant :-

	O.R.R.		O.O.
			1 7
	Nil.	9th K.R.R.C.	6
14th Div.Cavalry	1.	9th R.B.	Nil
14th Div.Cyclists,		42nd Bde M.G. Coy,	4
46th F.A.Bde,	1.	6th Somerset L.I.	3
47th F.A. Bde,	2.	6th D.C.L.I.	
48th F.A. Bde,	4.	6th K.O.Y.L.I.	1 3
49th F.A. Bde,	3.	10th Durham L.I.	9
14th D.A.C.	7.	43rd Bde M.G. Coy	Nil
61st Field Co. R.E.	1.	11th L'pool R	
62nd Field Co. R.E.	2.	8th M.M.G.Battery	Ni
89th Field Co. R.E.	Nil.	14th Div.Train,	
14th Signal Co. R.E.	1.	14th Supply Column,	
7th K.R.R.C.	5.	42nd Field Ambulance,	
8th K.R.R.C.	4.	43rd Field Ambulance,	
7th R.B.	7.	44th Field Ambulance,	
8th R.B.		26th Mob.Vet.Section,	N
41st Bde M.G. Coy,	Nil.	25th Sanitary Section,	N
5th Ox & Bucks L.I.	7.	M.M.P.	N
5th K.S.L.I.	13.		

Total Officers 3 Other Ranks 105.

(signed) B.L. Hamilton
LEIUT-COLONEL,
A.A.&.Q.M.G.
14TH (LIGHT) DIVISION.

NOTICES.

LOST: Bay GELDING, on morning of 5th instant. Marks :- Stamped on near hind No.92, on off hind D/48. Information to O.C. D/48 Bde R.F.A.

LOST: On the evening of 9th inst, between WARLUS and WANQUET SPARE WHEEL, fitted with 820 X 135 tyres, belonging to a Sunbeam Motor Ambulance, 42nd Field Ambulance. Information to O.C., 42nd Field Ambulance.

FOUND: Bay Mare, light draught, 5 years, 59 near fore, 55 off fore. Three arrow marks near hind quarter, off hind coronet white. Clipped except legs. Undocked. Prominent sternum. 15 hands. Old kicks on both stifles. Apply 119th Battery R.G.A.,

14TH (LIGHT) DIVISION.

ROUTINE ORDERS.

12th April, 1916.

1411. HONOURS AND REWARDS.

The undermentioned have been awarded Cards "For Gallant and Meritorious Service" by the Major-General Commanding:-

28th Siege Battery, R.G.A.

No. 45488, Gunner H. Brown,
51492, Gunner J. Cleeton.

1412. LEAVE.

Return Leave trains (BOULOGNE ROUTE) leave VICTORIA for FOLKESTONE, at 7.50 a.m. 8.5 a.m. 8.30 a.m. and 8.45 a.m. throughout April.

1413. SHOEMAKERS.

4 practical shoemakers are required for work in boot repairing shop under D.A.D.O.S., 14th Division.
Units will submit through the usual channels names of any capable men desirous and recommended for such employment.

1414. BILLETS.

Before Units or Detachments billetted in villages in the Divisional area relinquish their billets, the Officer Commanding unit or detachment concerned will report the fact to the Administrative Commandant of the village.

1415. CONCEALMENT FROM AIRCRAFT.

With reference to D.R.O. 1321 dated 20-3-16:
Working parties are not to cease work when the presence of aeroplanes is signified by 3 blasts on a whistle.
The orders as to transport halting and as to troops other than working parties halting or taking cover will remain as before.

LIEUT-COLONEL,
A.A.& Q.M.G.
14TH (LIGHT) DIVISION.

14TH (LIGHT) DIVISION.

ROUTINE ORDERS.

13th April, 1916.

1416. LEAVE - DISCIPLINE.

Commanding Officers are responsible that leave parties are inspected before departure, to ensure that no man is in possession of S.A.A. or Grenades.
Cases are still occurring of ammunition or grenades being taken by men proceeding on leave.

1417. APPOINTMENT.

2/Lieut. J.H. Cupper, 5th Ox & Bucks L.I. is appointed Commandant, 14th Div'l Grenade School, with the local rank of Captain whilst so employed.
He will be retained on the strength of his Battalion.

1418. POTATO SACKS.

In future all Potato Sacks received from Bases will be returned as early as possible, so that they may be sent back to England in accordance with War Office instructions.
(Third Army DDS & T S/339, d/10-4-16, VI Corps Q/371).

1419. LANTERNS, LAMPS & STOVES.

All Lanterns, Lamps and Stoves issued to troops in connection with their winter accommodation, which are not required during the summer months, will be returned to the D.A.D.O.S.

1420. LEAVE.

No leave will be granted until further orders.

A.H. Hamilton
LIEUT-COLONEL,
A.A.&.Q.M.G.
14TH (LIGHT) DIVISION.

14TH (LIGHT) DIVISION.

ROUTINE ORDERS.

15th April, 1916.

1425. CORRESPONDENCE WITH STRANGERS.

All ranks are forbidden :-

(i) To insert advertisements, or to have letters inserted, in any publication, inviting strangers to communicate with them.
(ii) To answer the advertisements of strangers who offer to write letters to the troops.
(iii) To advertise or to have letters inserted in any publication asking for gifts or loans of articles of personal equipment for themselves and for gifts of clothing and necessaries and medical comforts for the use of the troops.

When acknowledging gifts received the greatest care must be taken to avoid giving information of military value.

It has come to knowledge that hostile agents (especially females) are making use of the means indicated above to collect information of value to the enemy, and that in corresponding with them officers and men are playing into the hands of the enemy spy system.

This order is to be republished in orders issued by all units and is to be promulgated to all troops now serving in this country and to troops who may arrive in the future.

1426. AEROPLANE PRECAUTIONS.

With reference to D.R.O.1260, the posting of aeroplane sentries at such frequent intervals is no longer necessary.

Only such sentries as are considered necessary by Town Commandants will be posted in future.

1427. ACCELERATED MAIL SERVICE.

Commencing on the 16th April, and continuing as long as the service is found to be practicable, there will be an afternoon despatch of LETTERS from the Field Post Offices attached to 14th Div'l H.Qrs and the Train. The latest hour of posting at these offices and at the F.P.O. attached to 41st Infantry Brigade will be 4.30 p.m.

Correspondence so posted will be conveyed to BOULOGNE by special postal lorries, and should normally connect with the next morning's packet boat.

If Units served by the F.P.Os attached to the 42nd and 43rd Infantry Brigades desire to avail themselves of this facility, it will be necessary for the Brigades to provide transport for the conveyance of the mails to the Div.H.Qr Field Post Office. The latest hour of posting at these offices will be 3.30 p.m.

The arrangements for posting and despatch of Parcels will remain unchanged.

LIEUT-COLONEL,
A.A.&.Q.M.G.
14TH (LIGHT) DIVISION.

(over)

NOTICES.

DIVINE SERVICES.
C of E.
9.30 a.m. Divine Service, followed by Holy Communion, in the barn in Chateau Grounds, WARLUS, inside white iron gates opposite new wooden shed, at the top of Rue de CHATEAU.

R.C.
7 a.m.   Mass at DAINVILLE Parish Church for L'pool R, 47th & 49th Btt.R.F.A. and 89th Field Co.R.E.
8 a.m.   Mass at Simencourt.
8.30 a.m. Mass at BERNEVILLE Parish Church for 46th & 48th B.A.C. Div.Train, Transport of 10th D.L.I., 6th K.O.Y.L.I. 6th Som.L.I. 6th D.C.L.I. and 8th Bde R.G.A.
11.a.m. Mass at FOSSEUX.
5 p.m.   Evening service at SIMENCOURT.
6 p.m.   "   "   "   HAUTEVILLE.

LOST: Two wheels belonging to a cooks' cart of the 62nd Field Coy.R.E. under repair in the Foundry in Rue Adam de la Halle, ARRAS, were removed by persons unknown on night of 9/10th inst.
They should be returned forthwith to Town Major, ARRAS.

14TH (LIGHT) DIVISION.

ROUTINE ORDERS.

16th April, 1916.

1428. MEDICAL.

(1) It is notified for information of all Medical Officers that a limited supply of T.A.B. VACCINE is now available at 42nd and 43rd Field Ambulances.

(2) The attention of all concerned is directed to D.R.O. 1316, Part II, which is republished for information :-

Field Ambulances are situated as follows :-
42nd Field Ambulance at WANQUETIN.
43rd   "   "   " LIGNEREUIL.
44th   "   "   " FOSSEUX Chateau.

Sick of Units will be collected as under :-
From SIMENCOURT)
     BERNEVILLE) by 42nd Field Ambulance.
     WARLUS   )
     HAUTEVILLE   by 44th Field Ambulance.
     DAINVILLE   by Advanced Dressing Station.

Ambulances will call at Garrison Medical Inspection Rooms only, in each place, at 10.30 a.m. daily, by which hour sick from all units must be collected there. No other calls will be made except for urgent cases.

Units in FOSSEUX and WANQUETIN will send their sick for "Hospital" to the Field Ambulance there by 11 a.m.

1429. CONCEALMENT FROM AIRCRAFT.

D.R.O. No.1415 dated April 12th is cancelled and the following substituted :-

"With reference to D.R.O.1321 dated March 20th, attention has been drawn to the time wasted on defence and other work by working parties taking cover on hearing the 3 blasts on a whistle denoting the presence of aeroplanes, more often than not when the aeroplane in question turns out to be a friendly one. As men working in trenches are invisible from a reconnaissance height, there is no reason for work to cease in their case. In the case of working parties in the open not under direct observation from the German Lines, work should only cease when the party is a large one and the spot very exposed.

The orders as to transport halting and as to troops other than working parties halting or taking cover will remain as before".

1430. LAND :- OCCUPATION OF.

Reference D.R.O.1210 dated 15th February, 1916,
A new pro-forma for report of occupation of land is circulated for future guidance. A return on this form showing all land occupied during the month is to be rendered to this office on the last day but one of each month.

for LIEUT-COLONEL,
A.A.&.Q.M.G.
14TH (LIGHT) DIVISION.

DIVINE SERVICES FOR EASTER.

CHURCH OF ENGLAND.

EASTER COMMUNION.

AVESNES:	C.C.S. 7.30 a.m.
	Cinema Hall 12 noon.
HAUTEVILLE:	8.30 a.m. in Guard Room, Chateau.
FOSSEUX:	6.30 a.m. Chateau.
	10.30 a.m. 14th Div'l Cavalry Sergeants' Mess.
	11.30 a.m. 14th Div'l Cyclist Coy's billet.
SIMENCOURT:	School (behind Baths) at 8 a.m, 10 a.m, & 11.30 a.m.
WANQUETIN:	Reformed Church, 8.30 a.m, 10 a.m. & 12 noon.
BERNEVILLE:	School 11.45 a.m.
WARLUS:	Barn at top of Rue de Chateau, 8.30, & 10.15 a.m.
DAINVILLE:	2 Rue de Charron 7.30 a.m., Town Major's Office 8 a.m.
FAUBOURG d'AMIENS:	School 9 a.m., opposite Villa des Cerisethers at 12 noon.
ARRAS:	Soldiers' Club 7 a.m., 9 a.m. (Choral) & 11.30 a.m.
	Ursuline College 10.15 a.m.
	6 Rue Pasteur 11.15 a.m.
ACHICOURT:	Reformed Church (Easter Monday) 9 a.m.
RONVILLE:	(Easter Monday) 8 a.m.
AGNY:	Brigade Dump 8 a.m.

Commanding Officers are requested to grant facilities for men to be present at Easter Communion and to inform them accordingly.

DIVINE SERVICES.

WANQUETIN:	Reformed Church 6 p.m. Open to all.
DAINVILLE:	2 Rue de Charron 6.30 p.m. do.
ARRAS:	Soldiers' Club 7.15 p.m. do.
HAUTEVILLE:	at 3.p.m. in Chateau Grounds (if wet in No.45, – wheeler's shop).

ROMAN CATHOLIC.

MASS	9 a.m. WANQUETIN.	MASS at BERNEVILLE Parish
	11 a.m. FOSSEUX.	Church for all Units
EVENING	5 p.m. FOSSEUX.	in BERNEVILLE, at
SERVICE.	5.30 p.m. WANQUETIN.	8.30 a.m.
	6 p.m. HAUTEVILLE.	at DAINVILLE Parish
MASS.	7 p.m. SIMENCOURT Church.	Church for all units
	9 a.m. do.	in DAINVILLE at 7 a.m.
EVENING	5.30 p.m. do.	
SERVICE.		

WESLEYANS, PRESBYTERIANS, NONCONFORMISTS ETC.

8.45 a.m.	5th K.S.L.I. and Communion Service at SIMENCOURT.
10.0 a.m.	R.G.A. Wagon Lines & Communion service at WANQUETIN.
12 noon.	R.G.A., R.M.A., at DAINVILLE.
2.30 p.m.	9th K.R.R.C. at ARRAS.
6.0 p.m.	42nd Field Ambulance, 8th R.B., 49th Bde Wagon Lines, at WANQUETIN.

****

14TH (LIGHT) DIVISION.

ROUTINE ORDERS.

17th April, 1916.

1431. WASHING BOWLS.

Washing bowls are not available in sufficient quantity to supply all the needs of units in the trenches and in billets. A distribution of those available is made immediately on receipt at Div. Ordnance Stores, but these must be supplemented by improvised basins made of biscuit tins and other waste material.

1432. SICK WASTAGE.

The following is the Sick Wastage Return for week ended noon 15th instant :-

Unit	O.	O.R.	Unit	O.	O.R.
14th Div.Cavalry,		Nil.	9th K.R.R.C.		5.
14th Div.Cyclists,		Nil.	9th R.B.		10.
46th F.A. Bde,		4.	42nd Bde M.G. Coy.		Nil.
47th F.A. Bde,		2.	6th Somerset L.I.		8.
48th F.A. Bde,	1.	4.	6th D.C.L.I.		3.
49th F.A. Bde,		3.	6th K.O.Y.L.I.		2.
14th D.A.C.		Nil.	10th Durham L.I.		2.
61st Field Co. R.E.		1.	43rd Bde M.G. Coy,		Nil.
62nd Field Co. R.E.		1.	11th L'pool R		5.
89th Field Co. R.E.		2.	8th M.M.G.Battery,		Nil.
14th Signal Co.R.E.		1.	14th Div. Train,		2.
7th K.R.R.C. x		4.	14th Supply Column,		2.
8th K.R.R.C.		16.	42nd Field Amblce,		1.
7th R.B.		1.	43rd Field Amblce,		Nil.
8th R.B.		1.	44th Field Amblce,		1.
41st Bde M.G. Coy,		Nil.	14th Ammn.Sub-Park,		1.
5th Ox & Bucks L.I.		6.	26th Mob.Vet.Section,		Nil.
5th K.S.L.I.		5.	25th Sanitary Sec.		Nil.

Totals, Officer 1, O.R. 93.

LIEUT-COLONEL,
A.A.& Q.M.G.
14TH (LIGHT) DIVISION.

14TH (LIGHT) DIVISION.

ROUTINE ORDERS.   19th April, 1916.

1433. LEAVE - COMBINED LEAVE AND RAILWAY TICKETS.

Notification has been received from the General Manager, South Eastern and Chatham Railway, that a new form of combined leave and Rail Ticket comes into issue from 1st June next, and will be available to all destinations, Ireland inclusive, via BOUDOGNE.

These tickets will be issued to various divisions by the O.C., Base Stationery Depot, BOULOGNE. The present stock of tickets will not be used after 31st May, 1916.

Steps are to be taken to impress on all concerned the necessity for completing the Warrants and Tickets more carefully than has hitherto been the case.

1434. ADVANCES OF CASH - OFFICERS.

G.R.O. No.1493 is published for information :-
"With reference to General Routine Order No.1326, dated 20th December, 1915, a new form of advance book (A.F. W.3241) to be issued to individual officers, has been approved, and is now ready for issue. On and after 15th April, 1916, no other form for advances of cash will be accepted by Field Cashiers. The Books, each containing 25 forms, will be demanded by Officers Commanding Units from the Field Cashier of the formation in which the unit is serving, the number of officers of the unit in payment of each Agent being furnished. The Officer Commanding the unit will be responsible that the name of the officer to whom the book is issued, is entered on the cover, and that the serial number of the book, the name of the officer and the latter's receipt, are secured on the receipt form issued with the books. This receipt, when completed, will be returned to the Field Cashier.

The instructions printed on the cover of the book are always to be observed."

1435. STROMBOS HORNS.

Compressed air cylinders of Strombos Horns, which require recharging, should be forwarded through Ordnance Officers concerned to Heavy Mobile Workshops, where plant has now been established for carrying out this work.
(Authority Third Army 0/103/113 d/17-4-16. VI Corps Q/8/10).

1436. HONOURS AND REWARDS, (Investitures).

D.R.O.1374 is cancelled and the following substituted.
In future, no officer, whether on ordinary leave or otherwise will attend an Investiture unless detailed from this office to do so. It is to be clearly understood that Officers attending Investitures should NOT report at the War Office or to the Lord Chamberlain for further instructions. They will attend at Buckingham Palace at 10.15 a.m. on the day named.

                       A.C.Hamilton
                       LIEUT-COLONEL,
                       A.A.&Q.M.G.
                       14TH (LIGHT) DIVISION.

NOTICE.

GOOD FRIDAY. DIVINE SERVICE:
C of E at 9.30 a.m. in the barn just below the Church in the Rue de Chateau, WARLUS.

14TH (LIGHT) DIVISION.

ROUTINE ORDERS.

20th April, 1916.

1437. APPOINTMENT.

No.7929, Sergeant G. Owen, 6th Bn. Somerset L.I. is granted the local and temporary rank of Bandmaster whilst employed in charge of the 14th Div'l. Band.

1438. REMOUNTS - Officers' Chargers.

When demanding Officers' Chargers to complete establishment, the name of the officer and his walking weight should be given.

LIEUT-COLONEL,
A.A.&.Q.M.G.
14TH (LIGHT) DIVISION.

N O T I C E S.

A Divisional CANTEEN has been opened at BERNEVILLE. Prices are the same as at the Expeditionary Force Canteen.
Discount of 5% will be allowed on bulk orders from Presidents of Regimental Institutes or Officers' Messes, signed by the P.R.I. or P.M.C.
Such orders should be sent in 2 days in advance whenever possible.

******

LOST: MULE, Dark Dun Colour, about 14 hands, Jennet, Prominent markings across shoulders and along back. Very nervous, sensitive round ears. Strayed from AGNIEZ on night April 14/15th. Information to 165th Brigade Machine Gun Co., 55th Divn.

14TH (LIGHT) DIVISION.

ROUTINE ORDERS.

21st April, 1916.

1439. **TRAFFIC INSTRUCTIONS AND ROAD CONTROL.**

The following Army Routine Orders are revised and republished for information :-
  210. **Traffic Instructions.**

In order to save the roads as much as possible, the following orders are to be strictly complied with :-

(i) As far as possible lorries will only move in convoys under a responsible officer or N.C.O.

(ii) Ambulance Motor cars will only be used for the carriage of sick and wounded, and will, whenever possible, move in convoys.

(iii) No lorry will be used for any service which can be carried out by horse transport.

(iv) Small Units which are only provided with lorry transport and which are billeted close together will endeavour to combine and use one vehicle for drawing and delivering their supplies.

(v) The following speed limits will be strictly adhered to and are not to be exceeded except by the written order of an officer :-

    In the open Country
    (Motor Cars & Motor Cycles, 20 M.P.H.
    (Motor Ambulances & R.F.C.
    (light motor tenders,   12 M.P.H.
    (Motor lorries,   8 M.P.H.

    When passing through (Motor Ambulances,   6 M.P.H.
    villages or over bad (Motor Lorries.   6 M.P.H.
        roads,   (

Army Routine Order 31 (c) is cancelled.

(vi) Vehicles travelling in convoys in charge of an officer will not require passes.

All vehicles, single or in convoys, which are not in charge of an officer will require a pass (specimen below) which will be signed by the O.C. Unit to which the vehicle is attached.

The Officer signing the pass will be responsible that the journey is necessary and is made on duty; that the number of vehicles is not in excess of that required to perform the duty; and that the duty cannot be performed by horse transport or by combining it with some other duty thereby reducing the amount of motor traffic on the roads.

(vii) To assist in controlling and checking the speed of Motor lorries and other motor vehicles, Corps will arrange for additional men (mounted or cyclists) to be placed at the disposal of A.P.Ms.

SPECIMEN OF PASS.

Motor Transport Pass.

Unit .... Rank and Name .... i/c Motor......No.......
is to proceed from..........to..........Route..........Load.......
Speed limit..............
Date................   Pass issued by ....

NOTE: Copies will be issued in due course for distribution.

(over)

236. **Road Control.**

When passing stationary mechanical transport Units and lorry parks, motor vehicles will reduce their speed as under:-

Motor cars and cycles are not to exceed 10 miles per hour; lorries, ambulances, and tenders are not to exceed 6 miles per hour.

261. **Road Control.**

The arrows on the traffic routes apply to all motor vehicles except cars, box-cars and motor cycles. Where the word "lorries" is used on road notices, it will include also motor ambulances, R.F.C. Light tenders and busses.

(Army Routine Order 376).

1440. **TOWN OF ARRAS.**

Army Routine Order No. 375 d/19-4-16 is republished :-

The Town of ARRAS is out of bounds to all ranks unless on duty.

Officers and other ranks entering the town on duty must be provided with a written pass signed by a Commanding or Staff Officer specifying the nature of the duty on which employed.

This does not apply to :-

    Staff Officers,
    Despatch riders,
    Orderlies with messages.

1441. **FUEL WOOD.**

Reference C.R.O.744 dated 20-4-16:
Units which have formed agreements for supply of Fuel-wood which are now in force will forward copies of agreements to this office by 12 noon 23rd inst.

Nil returns are not required.

C.H. Hamilton
LIEUT-COLONEL,
A.A.&.Q.M.G.
14th (LIGHT) DIVISION.

14TH (LIGHT) DIVISION.

ROUTINE ORDERS.

24th April, 1916.

1442. ARRAS - TOWN ORDERS.

The following amen[dments to the following or]ders,
ARRAS", all copies bein[g ...]

Para. 1 add :-
The FAUBOURG D'AMIENS up to the Road Junction G.25.b. will be included in the Town of ARRAS, and will come under the administration of the Town Major.

Para. 12, delete the words "or horses", and add at end of para:-
By day horses may be ridden by officers into ARRAS as far as the Riding School in Rue Ste. Claire, if the rider is on duty.

In all these cases these officers must be in possession of a pass signed by their Commanding Officer, stating the specific duty on which they are employed.

Horses billeted in ARRAS may be allowed to proceed from their billets to the western boundary and return, when the rider in charge is in possession of a pass as mentioned above.

In no case may any one party exceed five in number. Mounted orderlies should be as limited as possible.

1443. LEAVE.

N.C.Os and men on short leave to United Kingdom are forbidden to apply to War Office or Officer i/c Records for an extension on account of delay in travelling to destination.

Men delayed in departure from FRANCE must have their passes endorsed before embarkation, those delayed in cross-channel passage must apply on arrival to the Embarkation Commandant at FOLKESTONE or SOUTHAMPTON,

Men returning from leave who are delayed owing to exceptional circumstances (such as stoppage of trains) should apply to Railway Transport Officer for their passes to be endorsed on arrival at the station at which the part of the journey is completed during which the delay occurred.

1444. COMPENSATION CLAIMS - COLLECTION OF.

It is notified by G.H.Q. that cases are continually occurring in which G.R.O.1146 (republished in 14th Div.R.O.1203 dated 11th February) is not complied with and that unnecessary trouble and very often hardship to the inhabitants is caused in consequence.

The O.C. any Unit leaving its billets is to leave an officer behind in each commune concerned, who will communicate with the Maire and inform him of the hour up to which he will receive claims. In Towns and villages where there is a Town Major or Town Commdt. the officer left behind will communicate with the Maire through him.

Units leaving billets to take their turns in the trenches etc., are not exempt from this order.

(over)

1445. COURT MARTIAL.

A Field General Court Martial composed as under, will assemble at Headquarters, 11th Bn. King's Liverpool Regiment, ARRAS, at 10 a.m. on Wednesday next, for the trial of:-

[redacted]

all of 11th Bn. King's Liverpool Regiment, and such other accused persons as may be brought before it.

PRESIDENT.
Temp.Lieut-Col. G.A.P. Rennie, D.S.O.   7th K.R.R.C.

MEMBERS.
A Field Officer to be detailed by G.O.C., 42nd Infantry Bde.
Capt. F.S.A. Baker, 2nd Battn. Seaforth Highlanders.
A Captain or Subaltern to be detailed by G.O.C., 41st Inf.Bde.

UNDER INSTRUCTION.
One Subaltern to be detailed by from each Infantry Brigade.

A French Interpreter will be detailed by 41st Infantry Bde to attend the Court.

The accused will be warned and all witnesses required to attend.

O.C., 11th Bn. King's Liverpool Regiment will arrange suitable accommodation for the Court and detail an Orderly.

Proceedings to be forwarded to Headquarters, 14th Division.

1446. SICK WASTAGE.

The following is the Sick Wastage Return for week ended noon 22nd instant :-

Unit	O.	O.R.	Unit	O.	O.R.
14th Div.Cavalry,		Nil.	9th K.R.R.C.	1	2.
14th Div.Cylist Coy.		Nil.	9th R.B.		12.
46th Bde R.F.A.	1.	4.	42nd Bde M.G.Coy,		1.
47th Bde R.F.A.		2.	6th Som.L.I.	1.	21.
48th Bde R.F.A.		4.	6th D.C.L.I.	1.	6.
49th Bde R.F.A.		1.	6th K.O.Y.L.I.		1.
14th D.A.C.		Nil.	10th Durham L.I.	1.	5.
61st Field Co. R.E.		1.	43rd Bde M.G.Coy,		Nil.
62nd Field Co. R.E.		2.	43/2 T.M.Bty,	1	
89th Field Co. R.E.		1.	11th L'pool R		10.
14th Signal Co.R.E.		Nil.	8th M.M.G.Battery		Nil.
7th K.R.R.C.		7.	14th Div. Train,		1.
8th K.R.R.C.		6.	14th Div.Supply Col.		Nil.
7th R.B.		2.	42nd Field Ambulance,		1.
8th R.B.		1.	43rd Field Ambulance,		Nil.
41st Bde M.G.Coy,		Nil.	44th Field Ambulance,		Nil.
5th Ox & Bucks L.I.		6.	14th Ammn.Sub-Park,		1.
5th K.S.L.I.		7.	26th Mob.Vet.Section,		Nil.
			25th Sanitary Section,		Nil.

Totals Officers 6 Other Ranks:- 105.

(Continued).

-3-

1447. SENTENCES BY FIELD GENERAL COURTS MARTIAL. Weeded

The following sentences awarded by Field General Courts Martial have, among others, been ordered by the Army Commander to be put into execution :-

LIEUT-COLONEL,
A.A.&.Q.M.G.
14TH (LIGHT) DIVISION.

14TH (LIGHT) DIVISION.

ROUTINE ORDERS.

25th April, 1916.

1448. HONOURS AND AWARDS.

The undermentioned have been awarded cards "For Gallant and Meritorious Service" by the Major-General Commanding :-

14TH DIV. CYCLIST CO.

No. 3259, L/Sergt. C.H. Shock,

14TH DIVISIONAL ARTILLERY.

No. 95791.	Bombr. N.J. Margetts,	A/46th R.F.A.
94715.	Corpl. E. Ashley,	D/46th R.F.A.
89303.	Sergt. F.G. Sawyer,	A/47th R.F.A.
96437.	" F. Coggan,	47th B.A.C.
99392.	Bombr. E.G. Strickland,	48th Bde R.F.A.
97854.	Corpl. R.W. Frith,	B/48th R.F.A.
96269.	Fitter F.J. Pell,	B/48th R.F.A.
83939.	Gunner J. Chamberlain,	B/48th R.F.A.
99981.	Corpl. C. Robinson,	D/48th R.F.A.
38810.	Sergt. A.C. Mousley,	49th Bde R.F.A.
10072.	A/Bombr. S. Bailey,	D/49th R.F.A.
45538.	Bombr. A. Copsey,	14th D.A.C.

14TH DIVISIONAL ENGINEERS.

41866.	Sergt. W. Duckett,	61st Field Co. R.E.
41851.	A/Cpl. E.J. Sharp,	do.
40044.	Sapper A. Thompson,	do.
52852.	C.S.M. Lockwood,	89th Field Co. R.E.
49000.	Sergt. P.M. Elton.	do.

14TH SIGNAL CO. R.E.

47842.	Sergt. L. Sharp,
40209.	L/Cpl. C. Harris,
58789.	Sapper H. Orchard.

7th K.R.R.C.

2851.	C.S.M. J. Jones,
3324.	L/Cpl. R. Mayles,

8th K.R.R.C.

1587. C.S.M. A. Webb,

7th R.B.

B. 53.	Sergt. A. Beckingham,
2635.	A/Cpl. R. Perry,
B.1509.	Rfmn. H. Thomas,
B.1510.	" W. Hanson,

8th R.B.

580.	Sergt. N. Haywood,	
S.3057.	"	J. Buck,
B. 176.	"	C. Cowen,
B.3199.	"	A.W. Kimberley,
377.	A/Cpl. W. Ward.	

5th OX & BUCKS L.I.

No.10514.	Sergt. T. Maycock,
7570.	" G. Bignoll,

5th K.S.L.I.

No.11495.	Sergt. A. King,	
20157.	"	E.J. Davies,
10830.	L/Cpl. W.R. Chorley,	
15391.	Pte. S. Butterworth,	
10931.	" J. Lloyd,	
17003.	" C. Herring.	

9th K.R.R.C.

11709.	Sergt. H. Elderfield,
10439.	L/Cpl. S. Moorley,
A.2007.	Rfmn. H. Blackwell.

9th R.B.

B. 937.	A/Sergt. E. Angel,
S.5935.	Rfmn. J. Phillips.

(over)

1448. HONOURS AND AWARDS (Continued).

    6TH SOMERSET L.I.

        No. 5346. R.S.M. Buss,
           10160. Sergt. T. Summerhayes,
            8015. " A. J. Baker,
           11990. L/Sergt. S.W. Smith,
            9909. Pte. F. Heal,
           11542. " W.H. Elliott,
           12088. " C. Gwynn.

    6th D.C.L.I.

        7383. C.S.M. P. Fuller,
       10904. Sergt. C.H. Pullen-Burry.

    6TH K.O.Y.L.I.

        8796. R.S.M. G.E.E. Howes,
       11368. Sergt. T. Joyner,
        8634. " W. Bertoft,
       23629. Corpl. F. Summers,
        3134. L/Cpl. J.C. Perkins.

    10TH DURHAM L.I.

       14006. C.S.M. J.H.A. Slater.

    11TH KING'S LIVERPOOL REGT (PIONEERS).

       20502. A/Sergt. E. Walker,
       12408. L/Corpl. W. Heald.

    8TH M.M.G. BATTERY.   43RD FIELD AMBULANCE.

       15162. Sergt. S. Hall,   30581. S.M. J.W. Lockwood.
         543. Gunner J. Wholan,

    5TH K.S.L.I.   14TH SIGNAL CO. R.E.

    No. 8078. Corpl. F. Pope,   44004. Sapper L.J. Sutton,
      5486. Pte. J. Goulding.   48048. Pioneer C. Ramsey,
                              48019. " A. Hepburn.

1449. HORSES.

    Government animals are constantly left in charge of civilian boys outside shops and houses in towns and villages in the Third Army Area.
    This practice is forbidden.
    Commanding Officers are directed to take disciplinary action in all cases where it is proved that Government animals have been left, by those responsible for them, in charge of civilians.

                                                        (Contd).

1450. CIVILIANS.

Circulation of civilians in the "Zone Reserves" of Armies will now be forbidden only between 9-0 p.m. and 4-0 a.m. instead of 8-0 p.m. and 5-0 a.m.

1451. STORES TAKEN OVER FROM THE FRENCH.

All stores taken over from the French, which are not required, should be collected at the R.E. Park, DAINVILLE, and an inventory sent in to Div'l Headquarters as early as possible. (Authority Third Army Q.C/2480 d/23-4-16. VI Corps Q/126).

1452. EXPLOSIVES - INSTRUCTIONS RE.

With reference to Army Routine Order No. 380:
Blind shells will be dealt with by R.A. and Bombs and grenades which have failed to explode by Infantry Brigades. R.E. will supply the necessary explosives and the party to fire them.

The C.R.E. will select sites for the exploding of blind shell and of bombs and grenades which have failed to explode for each Sector and will notify the Infantry Brigadier and Artillery Brigade Commander concerned of the site selected.

An Officer R.A. is to superintend the removal of blind shell and an Infantry Bombing Officer the removal of bombs and grenades to the place selected for their destruction, and will be responsible for informing Div'l Headquarters at once if he considers the blind shell or bomb, or grenade, too dangerous to move.

If the shell, bomb or grenade cannot them be destroyed in situ, a decision will be given from Div'l Headquarters as to whether the risk of removal must be undertaken.

On no account will any blind shell or any bomb or grenade that has failed to explode be moved except under the superintendance of an officer of the arm of the service detailed above.

add dump.
Achicourt. G 33 c.o.9.

LIEUT-COLONEL,
A.A.&.Q.M.G.
14TH (LIGHT) DIVISION.

N O T I C E.

LOST: HORSE, No.124, Bay Gelding, Aged, Height about 15.2 hands, Branded:- B.167 Off Hind hoof, 124 Near Hind hoof: Cut in;- 124 Near Hind Quarter; Number on Hind quarter may be taken for 121. Probably same markings fore hoofs. Peculiar action Stringhalt off hind.
Information to O.C.,"R" Batty. 2/4 London How.Bde,R.F.A.

LOST: On the night of 23/24th April, MULE, Brown,Gelding,about 15 hands, gall off fore (old) trace marks on body, headcollar.
Information to O.C., 11th L'pool R (Pioneers).

14TH (LIGHT) DIVISION.

ROUTINE ORDERS.

26th April, 1916.

1453. LEAVE.

Owing to the occurrence of cases of smallpox in the following centres, leave to these areas is not to be granted until further orders :-

LANCASHIRE. Leigh, Hindley, Atherton, Radcliffe, Whitefield, Swinton and Pendlebury Urban Districts.
Manchester, Salford & Bury County Boroughs and Heywood Borough.

DURHAM. South Shields County Borough and Willington Urban District.

1454. COURT MARTIAL PRISONERS.

No Court Martial Prisoners are to be dispatched to the Base until authority is received from this office. On receipt of authority the prisoner should be sent to the A.P.M. by escort, accompanied by Committal Warrant, (duly filled in and signed) A.F., C.385 in cases of Imprisonment or A.F., C.384 in cases of Penal Servitude.

1455. REPLACEMENT OF TOOL RESERVES.

Indents should now be sent to C.R.E., for any picks or shovels still required to complete Regimental or Brigade Reserves.

1456. ISSUE OF CARD PASSES.

All out of date passes are to be returned, or accounted for, to the A.P.M., 14th Division by May 3rd in order that they may be cancelled.

1457. LEAVE.

The names of N.C.Os and men who become entitled to one month's leave on re-engagement should be forwarded to this office. A specific date on which they can proceed on leave will then be notified and an extra leave vacancy allotted for the purpose.

LIEUT-COLONEL,
A.A.&.Q.M.G.
14TH (LIGHT) DIVISION.

14TH (LIGHT) DIVISION.

ROUTINE ORDERS.

27th April, 1916.

1458. FUEL.

The Summer scale of fuel as under will come into force from 27th instant inclusive :-

For men in the trenches.

½ lb coal, 1 lb coke, 1/8 lb charcoal.

For men not in the trenches.

1½ lbs coal.

There is no allowance for offices.

1459. DOGS.

Owing to cases of Hydrophobia having recently occurred in Third Army area, until further orders dogs in the possession of troops are to wear a muzzle, constructed and adjusted in such a manner as to render it impossible for the dog to bite.

Stray dogs found without a muzzle will be handed over by the Military Police to the Civil Authorities to be destroyed after an interval of 48 hours if the owner is unknown.

1460. SUPPLIES (A.B.55 - France).

When supplies demanded on an A.B.55 (Indent for Rations) are issued, in addition to the Certificate at the foot being completed, it is necessary that the date the supplies were issued or received should be distinctly stated by the person completing the Certificate, under his signature.

1461. FLIES - Precautions against.

Improvised safes for the protection of food from Flies should be provided everywhere where food is stored, in or out of the trenches, as soon as possible.

Below is a sketch of a Fly proof Food safe which can be made from an ordinary packing case :-

[Sketch: Suggested Fly Proof Food Safe made of Packing Case and Canvas. Labels: Canvas nailed along top; edges curved; Canvas front; piece of wood; Stones as weights; Packing Case.]

Canvas, or sacking, curtain should be at least two inches wider than the opening so as to overlap on either side.

1462. ROAD TRAFFIC.

The following road traffic orders of 55th Division are published for information and compliance by troops of 14th Division :-

(1) <u>Roads to be used by Horse Transport in one direction only.</u>

    SAULTY - BAVINCOURT (West to East).
    GOUY   - SIMENCOURT   " " "

(2) <u>Roads closed to all traffic</u> :-

    V.6.b.   to   GOUY.
    V.13.b.5.4. to V.7.b.8.(loads from main DOULLENS
                               road to SAULTY).

(3) <u>Road closed to LORRIES and MOTOR AMBULANCES</u>:-

    GOUY - SIMENCOURT.

(4) <u>Road closed to LORRIES</u>:-

    GOUY - MONCHIET.

(5) <u>Road closed except for movement of Troops</u> :-

    SOLERNEAU (U.18.d.) to SAULTY.

(6) <u>The Controls shown on Third Army Traffic Map is temporarily altered as follows</u> :-

    SAULTY - BARLY will be used for LORRY TRAFFIC from SOUTH to NORTH instead of NORTH to SOUTH.

1463. MOTOR TRAFFIC (Speed Limits).

With reference to A.R.O.376, republished in D.R.O.1439: Officers Commanding Units which have motor vehicles in their possession will render a certificate to Div.H.Qrs that the speed limits have been made known to each driver individually.

Officers travelling in Motor cars are responsible that the speed limit is not exceeded.

                                       LIEUT-COLONEL,
                                        A.A.&Q.M.G.
                                      14TH (LIGHT) DIVISION.

NOTICE.

BERNEVILLE CANTEEN.

HOURS OF OPENING: 10-0 a.m.   to 12.45 p.m.
                               1.15 p.m.   to 2-0 p.m.
                               4-0 p.m.   to 8-0 p.m.

14TH (LIGHT) DIVISION.

ROUTINE ORDERS.

27th April, 1916.

1464. TRAFFIC CONTROL.

On and after May 1st the following traffic orders will be substituted for those in D.R.O.1344:-

The DOULLENS - ARRAS road from BAC du NORD Eastwards is closed to all traffic from Sunrise to 8 p.m.

Vehicular traffic for the trenches and gun positions will not pass the undermentioned places before the hours in the following table :-

```
BAC DU NORD.              8 p.m.
RAILWAY BRIDGE DAINVILLE, 8 p.m.
WARLUS      )
BERNEVILLE, )
SIMENCOURT, )             7.45 p.m.
WANQUETIN,  )
```

A.L. Hamilton
LIEUT-COLONEL,
A.A.&.Q.M.G.
14TH (LIGHT) DIVISION.

(over).

NOTICES.

The Baths at ECOLE DES JEUNES FILLES have been transferred to the ECOLE COMMUNALE.

FOUND: Heavy Draught HORSE, Dark Bay, 15 hands, White face and nose, aged, Hoof Off fore 37, near fore 39. Hindquarters Broad arrow & F near, W.N.(painted) off.
Apply Camp Commandant, 14th Division.

DIVINE SERVICES.
(30 - 4 - 16)

CHURCH OF ENGLAND.

7 a.m.   Holy Communion, at Soldiers Club, ARRAS,
8.30 a.m.   "   "   "   "   "   "
9.30 a.m. Divine Service in Barn at top of Rue de Chateau, WARLUS.
7.15 p.m.   "   "   at Soldiers Club, ARRAS.

ROMAN CATHOLIC.

9 a.m.   Mass at WANQUETIN.
10 a.m.   "   " DAINVILLE Parish Church for all troops in DAINVILLE.
10 a.m.   "   " BERNEVILLE Parish Church "   "   "   " BERNEVILLE.
11 a.m.   "   " FOSSEUX.

WESLEYANS, PRESBYTERIANS, ETC.

DAINVILLE.
9.30 a.m. For Trench Mortar Batteries, R.E., Pioneer Detachment;
10. a.m.   " R.G.A. and R.M.A.
6.0 p.m.   " 43rd Field Ambulance.

BERNEVILLE.(In field at the back of Church).
11.30 a.m. For 6th K.O.Y.L.I., 43rd Bde Transport, 46th Bde R.F.A.,
           Ammn. Column, Div'l Train, and Troops in WARLUS.

FOSSEUX.

2.30 p.m. For Div'l Cavalry, Div'l Cyclists, 44th Field Ambulance,
          Mob.Vet.Section, M.M.G.Battery.

ARRAS.

10.30 a.m. For 7th K.R.R.C., 11th L'pool R, M.G.Coys, T.M.Btys.
           at H.Q., 7th K.R.R.C.
11.30 a.m. " 5th Ox & Bucks L.I.
6-0 p.m.   " 42nd Field Ambulance at Advanced Dressing Station.

SIMENCOURT.

6.30 p.m. For 9th R.B., R.F.A., in Y.M.C.A. Hut.

WANQUETIN.

3 p.m. For 42nd Field Ambulance.
5 p.m.   " R.G.A. Horse Lines.

14TH (LIGHT) DIVISION.

ROUTINE ORDERS.

29th April, 1916.

1465. SENTENCES BY FIELD GENERAL COURTS MARTIAL.

The following sentences awarded by Field General Courts Martial, have been ordered by the Army Commander to be put into execution :-

1466. PROFICIENCY PAY FOR GRENADIERS.

It is notified that the Army Council has approved of the issue of a grenadier badge to Cavalry and Infantry soldiers who reach the required standard of proficiency in bomb throwing and also of the admission of efficiency in bomb throwing as an addition to the special technical qualifications for Class 1 Proficiency Pay laid down in para 683 King's Regulations for those arms. The Two years service condition for the grant of proficiency pay of course applies.

LIEUT-COLONEL,
A.A. & Q.M.G.
14TH (LIGHT) DIVISION.

NOTICE.

Reference second notice of yesterday, for "HORSE" read "MARE".

14TH (LIGHT) DIVISION.

ROUTINE ORDERS.

30th April, 1916.

1467. R.E. STORES.

D.R.O.1365 is cancelled and the following substituted:-
The hours during which stores are issued from 14th Divn R.E. Parks at DAINVILLE and DAINVILLE STATION will be as follows on and after May 1st :-

R.E. and Pioneers,	before 8 p.m.
Infantry Brigades,	8.30 p.m. to 10 p.m.
R.A. and other units,	after 10 p.m.

In all cases two men per vehicle must be sent for loading.

1468. INDENTS.

Third Army Routine Order 238 dated 1-1-16 authorised the issue of 16 suits cooks' clothing per Infantry Battalion, 8 suits per Labour battalion, and 8 suits per Entrenching Battn.
Indents should be submitted in the usual way.

1469. PAYMENT OF POSTAL ORDERS.

The last para. of Army Routine Order No.329 of 4th March is republished for information :-
"Arrangements may be made by Officers Commanding Units for the Post Orderly of the unit to cash Postal Orders for the men of the unit at the Field Post Office, provided that a proper system of receipt is maintained, and that the Order so cashed is signed by the payee and countersigned on the back by the Post Orderly who cashed the order".

1470. SICK WASTAGE.

The following is the Sick Wastage Return for week ended noon 29th instant :-

	O.	O.R.		O.	O.R.
14th Div.Cavalry,		Nil.	9th K.R.R.C.		4.
14th Div.Cyclist Co.		1.	9th R.B.		11.
46th Bde, R.F.A.	2.	3.	42nd Bde M.G.Coy,		Nil.
47th Bde, R.F.A.		4.	6th Som.L.I.		2.
48th Bde, R.F.A.		3.	6th D.C.L.I.	1.	7.
49th Bde, R.F.A.		6.	6th K.O.Y.L.I.		6.
14th D.A.C.		Nil.	10th Durham L.I.		4.
61st Field Co. R.E.		1.	43rd Bde M.G.Coy,		1.
62nd Field Co. R.E.		Nil.	11th L'pool R		2.
89th Field Co. R.E.		Nil.	8th M.M.G.Battery,		Nil.
14th Signal Co.R.E.		Nil.	14th Div.Train,	1.	3.
7th K.R.R.C.		1.	14th Div.Supply Column,		Nil.
8th K.R.R.C.		6.	42nd Field Ambulance,		1.
7th R.B.		9.	43rd Field Ambulance,		1.
8th R.B.		6.	44th Field Ambulance,		2.
41st Bde M.G.Coy,		Nil.	A.S.C.Att.44th Field Amb.		1.
5th Ox & Bucks L.I.		5.	14th Ammn.Sub-Park,		Nil.
5th K.S.L.I.		12.	26th Mobile Vet.Section,		Nil.
			25th Sanitary Section,		Nil.

Total Officers 4, Other Ranks 102.

LIEUT-COLONEL,
A.A.&.Q.M.G.
14TH (LIGHT) DIVISION.

14TH (LIGHT) DIVISION.

ROUTINE ORDERS.

1st May, 1916.

1471. WARRANT OFFICERS - CLASS II.

Army Order 129, 1916, is re-published for information:-
WARRANT OFFICERS, CLASS II - With reference to Army Order 70 of 1915, it is notified that the words "Warrant Officers" in Royal Warrants and Regulations refer only to Warrant Officers, Class 1, except in paragraphs 284 and 1791, King's Regulations, which apply to Warrant Officers, Classes I and II. Warrant Officers, Class II come under the provisions of Royal Warrants and Regulations in all respects as if they were non-commissioned officers, unless otherwise expressly provided for, e.g. as in the case of colonial and field allowances provided for in Army Order 108 of 1915.

1472. FIRES-COMMANDING OFFICER'S RESPONSIBILITY.

Attention is called to the financial liability which may be incurred under Section 137 of the Army Act by an officer for any loss, damage, or destruction of public property caused by wrongful negligence on his part.

The Army Council has recently directed that three Commanding Officers shall pay £50 each towards the cost of damage done by fires which occurred in buildings occupied by their units. In these cases the fires were due to Commanding Officers failing to take steps to ensure the observance of orders and of elementary precautions which they should have known were being neglected.
(G.R.O.1535, dated 29th April, 1916).

1473. BILLETING.

Paragraph 15 of the instructions contained in Army Book 397 is cancelled as from May 1st, 1916).
(G.R.O.1544 dated 29th April, 1916).

1474. COMPENSATION CLAIMS.

Officers investigating claims which cannot be settled under G.R.O.No.763, will on no account express an opinion, either as to the validity of the claim or as to the sum which will be paid in settlement of the claim unless such an opinion is expressed officially for the information of superior military authority. Such claims are assessed by the Claims Commission as representing the British Government..
(G.R.O.1545 dated 29th April, 1916).

(over)

- 2 -

1475. PURCHASES OF SUPPLIES.

Except in exceptional cases, purchases of A.S.C. supplies must be made only by Requisitioning Officers, and payment made through their own Imprest Account and not through the Imprest Account of the Unit Commander, but if, in some emergency, A.S.C. supplies are purchased by Units and paid for through their own Imprest Accounts, a return is to be made, up to and including the 7th, 14th, 21st and last day of each month, on Army Form W,3313 (in duplicate) and marked with the title of the account and the Units Imprest Account number, if any. Both copies of this form are to be sent for endorsement to the Requisitioning Officer of the formation to which the unit is attached, one being subsequently returned to the unit to accompany the Imprest Account to the Paymaster, the other being retained by the Requisitioning Officer for despatch to the D.D.S.&T. of the Army concerned.

In this connection, it is pointed out that Grazing is an A.S.C. service, and must be reported on Army Form W.3313.
(G.R.O.1548 dated 29th April, 1916).

1476. ORDERS FOR WATERING ANIMALS.

Owing to the lack of system which prevails in many units in the watering arrangements, the following routine will be observed.

Animals will be paraded for watering not less than 3 times daily. One man will not be in charge of more than two animals.

An Officer is to be present all the time; only in the event of no officer being available may a Senior N.C.O. be in charge.

When watering at troughs, a pumping party will be detailed to clean and fill the troughs before the first batch arrives and keep them full until the parade is finished.

The Officer or N.C.O. in charge is responsible that the troughs are properly filled and kept full.

Animals are not to be crowded while drinking. They must not be closer together than one horse or mule to each four feet run of trough.

Girths will be loosened and bits removed. Each batch will be kept at the water until all animals in the batch have finished drinking.
(A.R.O. No.390 dated 29-4-16).

1477. BRANCH REQUISITION OFFICES.

Reference Army Routine Order 321, the present organisation of a Branch Requisition Office at each Corps H.Q. is being discontinued. From May 1st 1916 inclusive, there will only be one Branch Requisition Office for each Army. On and after May 1st all duplicate billeting certificates will accordingly be sent in weekly to the Officer i/c B.R.O., Headquarters, Third Army.
(A.R.O. 399 dated 29-4-16).

1478. FLIES.

Reference C.R.O.792, reports will reach Div'l Headquarters by noon 3rd May.

1479. ANTI-GAS GOGGLES.

Reference C.R.O.794, Certificates will be sent to Div'l H.Q. by noon 3rd May.

1480. HIRE OF LAND.

D.R.O.1379 dated 3rd April, 1916, is cancelled.

1481. SOYERS STOVES & FOOD CONTAINERS.

All Soyers Stoves and all Food Containers which are not actually in use are to be returned to D.A.D.O.S. at once.

(Continued)

1482. LIME JUICE.

The A.D.M.S. has recommended that Lime Juice be issued to the troops twice weekly on the days on which fresh vegetables are not supplied.

Units will indent for Lime Juice accordingly on A.B.55 supporting their indents by a certificate from a Medical Officer.

(VI Corps Q/341/3).

for LIEUT-COLONEL,
A.A.&.Q.M.G.
14TH (LIGHT) DIVISION.

N O T I C E S.

LOST: On Night of 29/30th April, MULE, Dark Bay, wearing set of wheel harness complete. Breast collar & saddle marked No.10, Traces marked No.14. All harness marked 62nd Fd.Coy.R.E.
Information to C.R.E., 14th Division.

The DIVISIONAL BAND will play at SIMENCOURT tomorrow from 4 p.m. to 6 p.m.

14TH (LIGHT) DIVISION.

ROUTINE ORDERS.

3rd May, 1916.

1483. HONOURS AND REWARDS.

Under authority granted by His Majesty The King, the following decoration has been awarded for Gallant Conduct in the Field :-

MILITARY MEDAL.

97982. Bombardier	W.H. Coltman,	48th Bde, R.F.A.
25251. Sapper	F. Morris,	62nd Field Co. R.E.
1912. Corporal	A. Young,	7th Bn. Rifle Bde.

The Major-General Commanding congratulates the recipients. The Army Commander and the Corps Commander have also requested that their congratulations may be conveyed to them.

1484. TEMPORARY COMMISSIONS.

In future when submitting applications for Temporary Commissions on A.F.,M.T.393, the College, School or University at which the Candidate was educated and his profession or occupation in Civil Life must be stated.

1485. CLAIMS OFFICER.

Lieut. F.H. Bateman-Champain is appointed Divisional Claims Officer, 14th (Light) Division, from April 29th inclusive.
The Office of the Div'l Claims Officer is in WARLUS.

1486. POSTAL REFILLING.

Postal Refilling on and after 5th instant will be at the eastern exit of WANQUETIN, on the WANQUETIN-WARLUS road, at 10a.m.

1487. ADDRESS.

Mobile Veterinary Section will be at FME FILESCAMP in J.5.c., Sheet 51c, from noon 5th instant.

1488. SENTENCES BY FIELD GENERAL COURTS MARTIAL.

The following sentences awarded by Field General Court Martial have been ordered by the Army Commander to be put into execution :-

"COMMITTING AN OFFENCE AGAINST THE PROPERTY OF AN INHABITANT" namely Attempting to remove wine from a cellar in ARRAS.

12292. Sergt.	W.H. Cairns,	11th L'pool Regt.	3 Years Penal Servitude
12343. "	W. Smith,	do.	3 Years Penal Servitude
11369. Corpl.	J. Chapman,	do.	3 Years Penal Servitude
9013. Pte.	J. Dwyer,	do.	6 Mths Impt. H.L.
13101. "	W. Davies,	do.	6 Mths Impt. H.L.

(over)

1489. **LIME JUICE.**

Reference D.R.O.1482, the recommendation of A.D.M.S. in possession of S.S.O., 14th Division is sufficient to cover the issue of Lime Juice therein authorised, and no other medical certificates are necessary.

1490. **DEMANDS FOR STORES.**

Care should be taken by Units to demand stores allowed as soon as they become deficient. An accumulation of requirements, involving a consequent heavy demand at one time, causes undue strain at the Base.

C.L. Hamilton

LIEUT-COLONEL,
A.A.&.Q.M.G.
14TH (LIGHT) DIVISION.

NOTICE.

FOUND: In the Horse lines of 14th D.A.C., BAY MARE, Heavy draught, age 7 years, 15.2 hands high. No.962 on near fore hoof.

LIGHT BAY MARE, Heavy Draught, age 8 years, 16 hands high, no marks on hoofs.

Apply Officer Commanding, 14th Div'l Ammunition Column.

14TH (LIGHT) DIVISION.

ROUTINE ORDERS.

5th May, 1916.

1491. LEAVE.

Until further orders, no leave will be granted to MANCHESTER, owing to an outbreak of measles.

1492. APPOINTMENT.

Major C.G. Mansfield Clarke, M.V.O., 9th R.B. will be transferred from SIMENCOURT to HAUTEVILLE on 6th May as Town Commandant, relieving Major R.G. Brooksbank, R.F.A., 14th D.A.C.

1493. HORSE SHOES.

Horse shoes that are not completely worn out when horses require re-shoeing, are to be "removed" only. New shoes will be fitted when required. It is realised that this entails extra work for Shoeing Smiths, but under existing conditions this must be accepted. D.A.D.O.S. will report to Div'l Headquarters any consignment of shoes returned to him of which any but a small proportion are capable of further wear.

1494. PURCHASE OR REQUISITION OF STORES & CLOTHING.

Attention is called to G.R.O.683, para 4.
"Purchases and requisitions for current requirements should as a rule be carried out under Divisional arrangements by Officers of the Administrative service concerned".
Covering authority will not be given in future for any purchase or requisition subsequent to the purchase or requisition unless the urgency of the case is clearly shown.
C.R.E., O.C. Train, and D.A.D.O.S. deal with Engineer, Supply and Ordnance services respectively and are alone authorised to sanction purchases and requisitions for their respective services.

1495. LEAVE.

All officers and men proceeding on leave will now travel via BOULOGNE. The instructions for this route given on the reverse of the Leave Allotment hold good.
The lorries will call en route at HABARCQ at 5.30 p.m.

C. Parsons Capt
for LIEUT COLONEL,
A.A. & Q.M.G.
14TH (LIGHT) DIVISION.

NOTICES.
DIVINE SERVICES, SUNDAY MAY 7TH.

C OF E.
8.a.m. Holy Communion, WARLUS.
9.30 a.m. Divine Service, WARLUS.
8.30 a.m. Holy Communion, Soldiers' Club, ARRAS.
7.15 p.m. Evensong, " " "
8 a.m. Holy Communion, Church Hut, HABARCQ.
11 a.m. Morning Service " " "
6 p.m. Evensong, " " "

R.C.
Mass at 7 a.m. at DAINVILLE,
 " " 7.30 a.m. BERNEVILLE.
 " " 9 a.m. WANQUETIN.
 " " 9.30 a.m. Hopital St.Jean, ARRAS.
 " " 11 a.m. AVESNES LE COMTE.
Evening Service at 5.30 p.m. WANQUETIN.
 " " " 6.p.m. BERNEVILLE. & DAINVILLE.

14TH (LIGHT) DIVISION.

ROUTINE ORDERS.

6th May, 1916.

1496. GRENADES.

It is forbidden under any circumstances to return to store, or to hand over to other troops, any hand grenades with detonators fixed in them; all grenades must be properly packed in boxes as they are sent up to the trenches, without detonators; and detonators must be carefully wrapped up in cotton wool, sawdust, or some other soft material, and separately packed in tins or boxes.

Each box, whether containing grenades or detonators must be examined by an officer, who must sign a certificate to that effect and insert it in the box.

Any infringement of the above order will be treated with the utmost severity.

see B.R.O. 7³ of 8/5/16

C.E. Hamilton
LIEUT-COLONEL,
A.A.&.Q.M.G.
14TH (LIGHT) DIVISION.

NOTICES.

STRAYED: On 5th May, from Wagon Lines of S.Q.Q. Cable detachment, c/o 111th Bde, 37th Division, at BAILLEULEMONT, THREE MULES.

Description
- Black Gelding,   6368.
- Brown Mare,   8413.
- Brown Mare,   2417.

Information to S.Q.Q. Cable Detachment, c/o 111th Bde, 37th Division.

FOUND: HORSE, Light Draught, on the WARLUS - WANQUETIN road on the morning of the 1st May.
Description - Light Draught Gelding about 14 hands, aged - No.593 on near fore. White and Bay pickall - white star and race on face - white bottom lip - white stocking off fore.

Apply 165th Infantry Bde M.G.Company, 55th Division.

14TH (LIGHT) DIVISION.

ROUTINE ORDERS.

7th May, 1916.

1497. HONOURS AND REWARDS.

Under authority granted by HIS MAJESTY THE KING, the following decoration has been awarded for Gallant Conduct in the Field :-

MILITARY MEDAL.

1676. Corpl. Charles Saysell,	8th Bn. K.R.R.C.	
6023. L/Cpl. John Lang,	-do-	
10214. L/Cpl. Ernest Mason,	-do-	

The Major General Commanding congratulates the recipients. The Army Commander and the Corps Commander have also requested that their congratulations may be conveyed to them.

1498. SICK WASTAGE.

The following is the Sick Wastage Return for week ended noon 6th instant :-

O.	O.R.		O.	O.R.
	14th Div. Cavalry,	Nil. 42nd Bde M.G. Coy,		1.
	14th Div. Cyclist Co.	1. 42nd T.M. Batteries,		1.
	46th F.A. Bde,	6. 6th Somerset L.I.	1.	11.
	47th F.A. Bde,	3. 6th D.C.L.I.		5.
	48th F.A. Bde,	10. 6th K.O.Y.L.I.		6.
	49th F.A. Bde,	3. 10th D.L.I.		15.
	14th D.A.C.	3. 11th King's L'pool Regt.		2.
	61st Field Co. R.E.	3. 8th M.M.G. Battery,		Nil.
	62nd Field Co. R.E.	4. 14th Div. Train,		3.
	89th Field Co. R.E.	1. 14th Div. Supply Column,		1.
	14th Signal Co. R.E.	1. 42nd Field Amblce,	1	1.
	7th K.R.R.C.	7. do. A.S.C.(M.T)att.		1.
	8th K.R.R.C.	1. 14. 43rd Field Amblce,		1.
	7th R.B.	4. do. A.S.C. attd.		1.
	8th R.B.	3. 44th Field Amblce,		1.
	5th Ox & Bucks L.I.	10. do. A.S.C. attd.		1.
	5th K.S.L.I.	13. 14th Ammn. Sub-Park,		Nil.
	9th K.R.R.C.	9. 26th Mobile Vet. Sec.		Nil.
	9th R.B.	11. 25th Sanitary Section,		1.

Totals Officers 3, Other Ranks 158.

1499. REFILLING POINT.

Refilling Point from 8th instant inclusive will be on the AVESNES LE COMTE - HABARCQ road near NOYELLETTE, at 9 a.m.

C.L.Hamilton
LIEUT-COLONEL.
A.A.&.Q.M.G.
14TH (LIGHT) DIVISION.

NOTICES.

LOST: On the night of the 4th May, dark chestnut MARE, 15.3 hands, and mark on off hind 46 H.Q. near hind No.9. Information to 46th Bde R.F.A.

On 5th May, Black MARE, No.48, clipped trace high, 44 on near hind.
Information to O.C. Section, 1/4 London Ammn. Col.

14TH (LIGHT) DIVISION.

ROUTINE ORDERS.

9th May, 1916.

1500. **REFILLING.**

Reference D.R.O.1499, Refilling will be at 8.30 a.m. in future.

1501. **TOBACCO.**

Reference C.R.O. 826, the reports called for therein should reach this office through the usual channels by 12 noon 11th instant.

1502. **RETURNS.**

All Units will render through the usual channels so as to reach this office not later than 6 p.m. 12th instant, a nominal roll of all men (not employed as Artificers in their Units) who in Civil life have drawn skilled rates of pay as Engineers, Engine Erectors, Fitters, Fitters' skilled labourers, Motor Fitters who can use a file, and Wheelwrights, the trade in which skilled to be stated against each name.

LIEUT-COLONEL,
A.A.&.Q.M.G.
14TH (LIGHT) DIVISION.

NOTICE.

LOST: On 6-5-16 between AUXI-le-Chateau and GOUY via FREVENT AND AVESNES-le-Comte, an Infantryman's valise the property of Lieut-Colonel G.Hesketh, 1/5th N.Lan.R.marked "G.H." containing the following articles :-
Letters, Compass, Toilet Requisites, Towels, Silver Hair Brush and Comb, Mirror, Mess Tin, Books, Sundry articles of Clothing etc.
Any information regarding same should be addressed to Lieut-Colonel. G. Hesketh, 1/5th N.Lan. R.

FOUND: At WANQUETIN on the 6th inst, MULE (Mare), Dark Brown, 14¼ hands, near Fore Shoulder T, Near Hind H, off Shoulder, White patch.
Information apply O.C., 42nd Field Ambulance.

14TH (LIGHT) DIVISION.

ROUTINE ORDERS.

11th May, 1916.

1503. RETURNS.

All Units, including Headquarters of Formations, will render through the usual channels so as to reach this office by 12 noon on the 2nd of each month, a Nominal roll of all officers on the Strength of the unit.

Rolls to be rendered in duplicate on foolscap paper, made up to 12 noon on the last day of the preceding month.

The Column of remarks should show the location and employment of any officer not available for Regimental duty.

1504. STEEL HELMETS.

When men, wearing steel helmets, are wounded in the head, the helmets should accompany the patient to the Field Ambulance, where they will be labelled with the patients name, number, and unit, and sent to the Base with him.

1505. LEAVE - DISCIPLINE.

Cases are still occurring of men proceeding on leave in possession of S.A.A. and Grenades.

Commanding Officers are held responsible that leave parties are inspected before departure.

N.C.Os and men will be again inspected at Railhead by the Officer in charge of the leave party and if any man is found in possession of Ammunition, Grenades, or explosives of any kind, his leave will be cancelled on the spot and he will be ordered to return to his unit forthwith.

Disciplinary action will be taken in all such cases.

This order to be republished in Brigade and Regimental Orders.

LIEUT-COLONEL,
A.A.&.Q.M.G.
14TH (LIGHT) DIVISION.

NOTICE.

LOST: On night of 6/7th May, Dark Chestnut GELDING, 14 hands, White Stockings behind, Slight Star, Fan tail, showy action. Marks A.36 near hind and 17 B R.G.A. off hind.

Light Chestnut GELDING, 15.1 hands, weedy looking, Bang tail, Marks:- 0.24 near hind and 17 B R.G.A. off hind.

Information to O.C., 17th Heavy Bde, R.G.A.

14TH (LIGHT) DIVISION.

ROUTINE ORDERS.

12th May, 1916.

1506. BOUNDS.

1. It is notified that the town of AMIENS is placed out of bounds for all British Troops, Officers and men, from 11th May, 1916, until further orders. Officers and men will only be permitted to enter AMIENS during that period if in possession of a special pass which will only be granted for urgent reasons.

2. The above orders do not apply to persons travelling by rail and passing through AMIENS station in transit, not leaving the same.

3. The following may enter AMIENS without special passes :-
   (a) Cars containing Staff Officers flying the Union Jack or G.H.Q. flag.
   (b) Officers of, or above the rank of Major-General.

4. All persons found in AMIENS not having complied with the above rules will be arrested.
   (G.R.O.1557).

This order is to be republished in the orders of Brigades.

1507. TELEGRAMS - LEAVE.

Many telegrams have recently been sent recalling officers and men from leave which were unnecessarily verbose, thereby causing an excessive strain to fall on the Signal Service.

If time admits, an order for recall will be sent by post. If orders have to be sent by wire, the following standard message will be used for this purpose :- "Rejoin (day of month in letters") Sender's designation and address not to be telegraphed.

It should be explained to all ranks before proceeding on leave, that on receipt of this wire, it is their duty to cross to France on the date mentioned. (G.R.O.1558).

This order is to be republished in the orders of Brigades.

1508. STRENGTH.

Men who have been sentenced to terms of imprisonment and whose sentences have not been suspended, should be struck off the strength of their units and reinforcements demanded in their place.
(Authority:- A.G., G.H.Q., A/12932 d/- 9/5/16).

LIEUT-COLONEL,
A.A.&.Q.M.G.
14TH (LIGHT) DIVISION.

NOTICES.

LOST: Bicycle, at ARRAS on 4/5/16, belonging to 61st Field Co.R.E., Service pattern, marked with red triangle, and No.18 on rear mud-guard.
Information to O.C., 61st Field Co. R.E.

LOST: White fox terrier DOG - black markings on head, thick tail - last seen wearing a collar marked Captain Gardner, Norfolk Regiment.
Information to Major Payntor "Q" Battery, R.H.A., 5th Division.

(Over)

DIVINE SERVICES FOR

SUNDAY - 14TH MAY, 1916.
****

CHURCH OF ENGLAND.

8.30 a.m. Holy Communion at DIVISIONAL CLUB, ARRAS.
9.30 a.m. Morning Service at WARLUS.
11 a.m.   "   "   " BERNEVILLE (Battn. Football Ground).
11.30 a.m. Holy Communion   at BERNEVILLE.
7.15 p.m. Evensong at Divisional Club, ARRAS.

ROMAN CATHOLIC.

7 a.m.   Mass at DAINVILLE Parish Church for all troops in DAINVILLE.
7.30 a.m.   "   " Parish Church, WANQUETIN.
8 a.m.   "   " BERNEVILLE.
9.30 a.m.   "   " WARLUS.
9.30 a.m.   "   " Parish Church, LIENCOURT.
11.15 a.m. "   " AVESNES-Le-COMTE.
5.30 p.m. Evening Service at Parish Church, LIENCOURT.

WESLEYANS, PRESBYTERIANS, ETC.

9.30 a.m. at BERNEVILLE for 9th K.R.R., 2 B.A.Cs, 18th Bn. Cheshire
              Regt (Labour Bn) 56th Siege Bty, 47th &
              49th R.F.A.
10 a.m.   at ARRAS for 11th Bn. The King's L'pool Regt.
11.15 a.m. In Barn behind Town Major's office, DAINVILLE, for 10th D.L.I
              T.M.Bty, Field Coys RE, detachment 11th Bn.
              The King's.
12 noon. for R.G.A. and R.M.A. at DAINVILLE.
2.15 p.m. in Y.M.C.A. Barn, HAUTEVILLE, for D.A.C., A.S.C., Div'l Schools.
2.30 p.m. for 5th K.S.L.I. at ARRAS.
3.45 p.m. in Canteen Hut, AVESNES, for Supply Column, and Sub-Park.
5.30 p.m. R.G.A. Horse lines, WANQUETIN.
6.30 p.m. 42nd Field Ambulance, WANQUETIN.
6.30 p.m. In Barn 19 Rue d'Agnez, WARLUS.

****

14TH (LIGHT) DIVISION.

ROUTINE ORDERS.

15th May, 1916.

1509. DISCIPLINE.

Attention is called to D.R.O.686 dated 15-10-15:

N.C.O's and men are forbidden to carry away Wine, Beer, Stout, or other liquor from Estaminets or Canteens for consumption elsewhere. All drinks supplied to them at Estaminets or Canteens must be consumed on the premises except when supplied for officers' messes.

Officers requiring Wine, Beer or Stout from Estaminets will obtain an order from the Town Commandant, without whose signature estaminet keepers are not allowed to sell any liquor for consumption off the premises. The Divisional Canteen will supply such liquors as it is allowed to stock on the order of Mess Presidents and Commanding Officers.

1510. LAND - HIRE OF.

Attention is called to Corps Routine Order No.836 of 14th May, 1916.

This order does not cancel this office circular A.R/3/1 dated 3rd April, which lays down the procedure to be adopted in 14th Division and embodies the principles contained in the Corps Order now published. Communications with the Rents Officer will continue to be made through Div'l Headquarters and agreements for private hirings will be submitted to Div'l Headquarters as has been done hitherto.

1511. SICK WASTAGE.

The following is the Sick Wastage Return for week ended noon 13th instant:-

Unit	O.O.R.	Unit	O.O.R.
14th Div. Cavalry,	Nil.	42nd Bde M.G. Coy,	Nil.
14th Div. Cyclist Co.	2.	42nd Bde T.M. Batteries,	Nil.
46th F.A. Bde,	2.	6th Somerset L.I.	8.
47th F.A. Bde,	4.	6th D.C.L.I.	5.
48th F.A. Bde,	4.	6th K.O.Y.L.I.	6.
49th F.A. Bde,	Nil.	10th Durham L.I.	8.
14th D.A.C.	1.	43rd Bde M.G. Coy,	1.
Y 14 T.M. Battery,	1.	43rd Bde T.M. Batteries,	1.
61st Field Co. R.E.	2.	11th L'pool R	3.
62nd Field Co. R.E.	3.	8th M.M.G. Battery,	Nil.
69th Field Co. R.E.	Nil.	14th Div. Train,	2.
14th Signal Co. R.E.	1.	14th Div. Supply Column,	Nil.
7th K.R.R.C.	2.	42nd Field Ambulance,	Nil.
8th K.R.R.C.	9.	43rd Field Ambulance,	1.
7th R.B.	4.	43rd Field Amb. A.S.C. Att.	1.
8th R.B.	3.	14th Ammn. Sub-Park,	Nil.
41st Bde M.G. Company,	Nil.	26th Mob. Vet. Section,	1.
41st Bde T.M. Batteries,	Nil.	25th Sanitary Section,	Nil.
5th Ox & Bucks L.I.	6.	Army Chaplains Dept.	1
5th K.S.L.I.	4.	A.O.C.	Nil.
9th K.R.R.C.	3.	M.M.P.	Nil.
9th R.B.	12.		

Totals- Officers 1, Other Ranks 99.

LIEUT-COLONEL,
A.A.&.Q.M.G.
14TH (LIGHT) DIVISION.

(over)

NOTICES.

FOUND: Jenny MULE, coming from direction of WANQUETIN, on WANQUETIN-WARLUS Road, at 11 a.m. 14th inst: height about 14 hands, in good condition. No head-collar or rope.
Information apply A.P.M., 14th Division.

LOST: Bay GELDING, 16 hands, 9 years, very faint star, N.H.coronet O.H.Pastern, saddle marks, L.K.brand N thigh F.42, white paint marks on near side of neck.
Information to A.P.M., 5th Division.

LOST: On the night of the 12/13th inst. from horse lines of B/49 at WANQUETIN Bay Mare, height 15.2 hands, age about 8 years, star race and snip, Off hind partly white - near hind coronet white. B/49 marked on near hind-quarter. No.82 marked on near fore hoof. B/49 marked on off fore hoof.
Information to B/49 Brigade R.F.A.

14TH (LIGHT) DIVISION.

ROUTINE ORDERS.

16th May, 1916.

1512. COURT MARTIAL. wudul

1513. SALE OF ALCOHOL.

With reference to G.R.O.1252, soldiers are forbidden either to buy or accept as gifts from inhabitants any alcohol or alcoholic drinks, whether such are offered for sale or acceptance in Cafes, Cabarets, Estaminets, Wine Shops, Farms or Private Houses.
(G.R.B. 1567).

1514. TRENCH MORTAR BATTERIES - A.F. B.158.

Heavy Medium and Light Trench Mortar Batteries will render A.F. B.158 on the last day of each month to the Deputy Adjutant General, A.G's office at the Base. Any casualties that may affect Officers of Trench Mortar Batteries during the month will be at once reported to the above-mentioned Officer.
(G.R.O.1568)

1515. COMPENSATION TO OFFICERS FOR LOSS OF KIT ON ACTIVE SERVICE.

Compasses magnetic pocket (or prismatic) lost on Active Service will in future be replaced from store, and monetary compensation will not be admissible in respect of the loss of these articles.

Indents for the replacement of articles so lost will be submitted in accordance with the instructions laid down in General Routine Order No.990.

Any grants of monetary compensation already made to officers in respect of the loss of compasses may be allowed to stand, and in cases where officers whose claims are still awaiting settlement have, prior to the receipt of these instructions, re-equipped themselves privately with compasses, monetary compensation may be granted under the usual conditions.

The above applies to officers both of the British and Indian Armies in France.

Care is to be taken to ensure that these instructions are communicated to sick and wounded officers undergoing treatment in Military Hospitals.
(G.R.O. 1570).

1516. RATIONS.

Attention is again directed to Army Routine Order 45.
When units or detachments or individuals are transferred from one formation to another within the Third Army they must take with them rations for the day following the day of joining.

LIEUT-COLONEL,
A.A.&.Q.M.G.
14TH (LIGHT) DIVISION.

14TH (LIGHT) DIVISION.

ROUTINE ORDERS.

17th May, 1916.

1517. LEAVE.

    (1) Reference D.R.O.1453, leave may now be granted to South Shields County Borough and Willington Urban District.
    (2) No leave is to be granted to CARDIFF and PENARTH until further orders, owing to Small-pox.

1518. INDENTS.

    Indents for Remounts rendered on 13th and 28th of each month by units will show the reason for demanding each animal, e.g. to replace .... Died or destroyed, evacuated through Mobile Veterinary Section, cast for vice, lost, increase of establishment, etc.

LIEUT-COLONEL,
A.A.&.Q.M.G.
14TH (LIGHT) DIVISION.

14TH (LIGHT) DIVISION.

18th May, 1916.

1519. SENTENCES BY FIELD GENERAL COURTS MARTIAL.

1520. LEAVE.

(1) Leave may now be granted to CHORLEY, but not to COPPULL.

(2) Leave may not be granted to STOCKPORT until further orders, owing to an outbreak of Measles.

1521. BOMBING GROUNDS.

An accident having occurred to some French children through playing with a live grenade found on a bombing ground, such measures are to be taken as will exclude civilians, and especially children, from all localities used as bombing grounds.

LIEUT-COLONEL,
A.A. & Q.M.G.
14TH (LIGHT) DIVISION.

14TH (LIGHT) DIVISION.

ROUTINE ORDERS.

19th May, 1916.

1522. LEAVE.

Leave to BLACKPOOL is not to be granted until further orders owing to an outbreak of Smallpox.

1523. CASUALTIES.

Attention is directed to Field Service Regulations Part II, Sec.133 "Units will report by letter at the earliest possible moment direct to D.A.G., 3rd Echelon, by D.R.L.S. post the Regimental Number, Rank and Name of dead and missing".
This order will be strictly complied with.

1524. DISCIPLINE.

Officers and men are reminded that it is their duty to give no information of a military nature to anyone whilst they are on leave in England. Information which is widely known in England soon reaches the enemy, and the success of military operations may be endangered thereby. Non-observance of the above will lead to cancellation of any present leave granted to the offender and the stoppage of all future leave.
(G.R.O.1583).

LIEUT-COLONEL,
A.A.&.Q.M.G.
14TH (LIGHT) DIVISION.

NOTICES.

FOUND: Brown GELDING, 15.2 hands, black points, Hog mane, star on forehead. Long tail.
Apply A.P.M., 14th Division.

DIVINE SERVICES.

C. OF E.
WARLUS: 8.30 a.m. Holy Communion.
9.30 a.m. Morning Service.
ARRAS: (Div'l Club) 8.30 a.m. Holy Communion.
10.0 a.m. Morning Service.
8.0 p.m. Evening Service.

R. C.
DAINVILLE (Parish Church) 7 a.m. Mass.
" " " 6 p.m. Benediction.
BERNEVILLE. " " 8.30 a.m. Mass.
WARLUS, " " 8.30 a.m. Mass.
ARRAS (Hospital St.Jean) 10.30 a.m. Mass.
" (Orphelinat Faubourg d'Amiens) 8.30 a.m. Mass.
LIENCOURT. (Parish Church) 9.30 a.m. Mass.
AVESNES-LE-COMTE (Parish Church) 11.30 a.m. Mass.
LIENCOURT (Parish Church) 5.30 p.m. Benediction.

WESLEYANS, PRESBYTERIANS ETC.
9.30 a.m. 5th Ox & Bucks L.I.,46th/49th B.A.C.,56 Siege Bty, at BERNEVILLE.
11.15 a.m. 6th K.O.Y.L.I.,43/Bde M.G.Coy,43rd Fd.Amb. L'pool R, T.M.Battery,R.Es, at DAINVILLE.
12 noon. R.G.A., R.M.A. at DAINVILLE.
2.15 p.m. A.S.C. at HAUTEVILLE, and 14th D.A.C.
3.45 p.m. Supply Column & Sub-Park in Canteen, AVESNES.
5.30 p.m. R.G.A.Horse lines at WANQUETIN.
6.30 p.m. 42nd Fd.Amb. at WANQUETIN.

14TH (LIGHT) DIVISION.

ROUTINE ORDERS.

21st May, 1916.

1525. FORAGE RATION.

Purchases for green forage and hire of grazing will be arranged through Supply Officer and not by any Unit.

1526. FIRES.

Commanding Officers are reminded that their own orders as to precautions against fire and the orders issued by VI Corps as to general precautions to be taken are to be posted up in every billet.

Should a fire take place a report is to be sent at once by wire to Div'l Headquarters.

1527. BILLETING.

Attention is directed to A.R.Os 307, 170, 231 and 247 republished in Extracts from Third Army Routine Orders.

Billeting certificates will be given for the following services :-

Billets for Officers & men,	by O.C. Unit,
Drying rooms authorised by G.O.C.Division,	by O.C. Unit.
Baths,	by O i/c Baths.
Workshops,	by O.C. Unit.
Offices,	by O.C. Unit.

Cash will be paid for the following :-

Officers' Messes,	
Dining Rooms,	
Regimental Canteens & Recreation Rooms,	by O.C. Unit.
Brigade Canteens and Recreation Rooms,	by Bde H.Qrs.
Div'l Canteen,	by Div'l H.Qrs.

Commanding Officers are responsible that all expenses incurred with owners of houses occupied as Officers' Messes, Mens' Dining Rooms, or as Regimental Canteen and Recreation rooms are properly adjusted before the premises are vacated.

They are also responsible that copies of Billeting certificates are given to the Mayor and sent to O i/c Branch Requisition Office, H.Qrs, 3rd Army, as laid down.

LIEUT-COLONEL,
A.A.&.Q.M.G.
14TH (LIGHT) DIVISION.

NOTICES.

LOST: Black Gelding MULE, strayed from Horse Lines on 18th inst, 44 on off hind, 76 on near hind.
Information to O.C., 44th Field Ambulance.

FOUND: On morning of 18th instant, Bay Gelding HORSE, Broad arrow 124 on near hip, B.167 on off hind, 124 on near hind.
Apply O.C., 46th Bde, R.F.A.

FOUND: Black MULE, marks T on left breast, square with 4 below on left hind quarters.
Apply Town Commandant, WANQUETIN.

14TH (LIGHT) DIVISION.

ROUTINE ORDERS.

22nd May, 1916.

1528. LEAVE.

Leave may not be granted to WARRINGTON until further orders, owing to an outbreak of Smallpox.

1529. RETURNS - LEWIS MAGAZINES.

Reference Corps Routine Order No.859 dated 21st May, 1916, Return to reach Div'l Headquarters by 12 noon 12th and 27th of each month.

1530. SICK WASTAGE.

The following is the Sick Wastage Return for week ended noon 20th instant :-

	O.	O.R.		O.	O.R.
14th Div.Cyclist Co.		1.	9th K.R.R.C.		3.
46th F.A. Bde.		3.	9th R.B.		3.
47th F.A. Bde.		5.	6th Somerset L.I.		4.
48th F.A. Bde.		6.	6th D.C.L.I.		12.
49th F.A. Bde.		1.	6th K.O.Y.L.I.		5.
14th D.A.C.		2.	10th Durham L.I.		2.
Y.14 T.M. Battery,		1.	11th L'pool R.		3.
H.Q., 14th Div.R.E.	1.	-	8th M.M.G.Bty,		Nil.
61st Field Co. R.E.		1.	14th Div. Train,		2.
62nd Field Co. R.E.		Nil.	14th Supply Column,		Nil.
89th Field Co. R.E.		Nil.	42nd Field Ambulance,		Nil.
14th Signal Co.R.E.		Nil.	43rd Field Ambulance,		Nil.
7th K.R.R.C.		1. 9.	44th Field Ambulance,		2.
8th K.R.R.C.		2. 5.	14th Ammn. Sub-Park,		Nil.
7th R.B.		9.	26th Mobile Vet.Sec.		-
8th R.B.		2.	25th Sanitary Section;		Nil.
5th Ox & Bucks L.I.		6.			
5th K.S.L.I.	1	6.			

Total Officers 6, Other Ranks 93.

Captain
for.
LIEUT-COLONEL,
A.A.&.Q.M.G.
14TH (LIGHT) DIVISION.

14TH (LIGHT) DIVISION

ROUTINE ORDERS.

23rd May, 1916.

1531. OCCUPATION OF PREMISES OTHER THAN BILLETS.

Premises other than billets required by units and authorised to be occupied by them, e.g. Offices, Storerooms, and workshops, must be occupied by arrangement and a suitable agreement concluded. A copy of the agreement must be sent to the Director of Requisition Services accompanied by sufficient explanation to permit of the terms of the agreement being considered and approved. These agreements should be endorsed "Payable by Billeting Certificate through Branch Requisition Office".

When the Billeting Certificates are issued for the occupation of such premises, the duplicate should contain a reference to the agreement for those premises for the information of the O i/c Branch Requisition Office.

Premises for bath houses, laundries, for hospital accommodation, will be the subject of agreements concluded by O i/c Baths or O.C. Field Ambulance concerned. The agreements and billeting certificates will be endorsed and disposed of as above.

1532. SALVAGE COMPANY.

The 14th Divisional Salvage Company forms, from this date, an organization separate from Div'l Headquarters.

Lieut. F.H. Bateman Champain is appointed O.C., 14th Div. Salvage Coy.

The Headquarters of the Company will be billeted near Divisional Headquarters but all N.C.Os and men employed in Divisional Employments are included in the Salvage Company and men for all such employments will be detailed in future by O.C., Div'l Salvage Company, and their position and duties will be recorded by him.

N.C.Os and men will be examined medically under arrangements made by A.D.M.S. and when fit will be returned to their own units with the exception of certain N.C.Os in responsible positions.

O.C. Salvage Company will arrange such Salvage Collecting parties in front areas as may be necessary and will also collect Salvage from the various villages into his dump at Div'l Headquarters.

N.C.Os and men employed under Town Commandants will search the billets in their villages whenever they are vacated by troops. Any Salvage found will be kept in the Town Commandants store until called for by Salvage transport. A record of items collected by the detachment Salvage Coy in each village will be kept up by the Garrison Sergeant Major or other Senior N.C.O.

A rough general list of salvage collected is to be sent by this N.C.O. to O.C. Salvage Coy on the day following the departure of any troops to enable him to decide whether special transport arrangements are necessary.

All units will send any Salvage that comes into their possession to this dump where it will be taken charge of by O.C., Salvage Company.

Salvage will be sorted and disposed of at the Salvage Dump at Div'l Headquarters.

1533. APPOINTMENT.- Claims Officer.

9th R.B.
Major C.G. Mansfield-Clarke, M.V.O., is appointed Divisional Claims Officer from this date, vice Lieut. F.H. Bateman-Champain. 9th R.B.

1534. ADDRESS.

The Claims Office is temporarily in HAUTEVILLE.

C.C. Hamilton
LIEUT-COLONEL,
A.A.&.Q.M.G.
14TH (LIGHT) DIVISION.

NOTICE.

LOST: On night of 21/22nd May, Black MARE, about 14.3 hands, slit on right ear, Last seen heading towards left of BEAUMETZ from BERNEVILLE.
Information to Capt. Thornewill, A.V.C., No.1 Sec. D.A.C.

14TH (LIGHT) DIVISION.

ROUTINE ORDERS.

May 24th 1916.

1535. The following message has been received from General JOFFRE, by the Commander-in-Chief :-
"I am happy to express to you the sentiments of high esteem and cordial comradeship which the French Armies feel for the valiant troops of the Dominions and Colonies and their admiration for their fine conduct and brilliant feats of arms on all the Battlefields where they have fought. I beg you to transmit these sentiments to the Officers, Non-Commissioned Officers and men of the Dominions, India and The Colonies with whom the French Troops are happy to fight side by side and for the same ideal".

Commander-in-Chief's reply to General JOFFRE:-
"On behalf of all ranks of the forces of the British Empire now serving in France, I beg to express our warmest appreciation of the generous sentiments contained in your message to the forces of the Overseas Dominions, India and the Colonies. It is their pride and their privilege to share with you the dangers of our common battlefield and to defend the same noble cause of freedom. This close union intensifying as it has done the great esteem and admiration with which they have always regarded your countrymen cannot fail to achieve victory."

These messages are to be communicated to the Troops.

1536. HORSES LOST.

A report is to be sent to Div'l Headquarters when any animals which are reported to Div'l Headquarters as Lost are subsequently found.

Officers Commanding Units are held responsible that all animals found straying or handed over to their units by French Police or inhabitants are reported at once through the usual channels to Div'l Headquarters, with a statement as to how they have been disposed of. The report called for in Army Routine Orders No.423 will be forwarded to D.D.R., 3rd Army by Div'l Headquarters.

1537. OATS.

Attention is called to A.R.O.424.
Oats are to be carefully inspected under arrangements made by Officers Commanding Units.
Dirty samples are to be screened to remove any beans that may be present.

[signature]

LIEUT-COLONEL,
A.A.&.Q.M.G.
14TH (LIGHT) DIVISION.

NOTICE.

FOUND: on 21st, MULE, Dark Bay, about 15 hands. Marked No.44 on near fore.
Apply O.C., 62nd Field Co. R.E.

At the Sports to be held on the Football Ground, BERNEVILLE, by 5th K.S.L.I. on Friday and Saturday next, 26th and 27th, commencing at 2 p.m. each day, the following events are open to all ranks of the Division.

220 Yards: 1st Prize 20fr. 2nd Prize 15fr. 3rd Prize 10fr.
Half Mile: 1st " 25fr. 2nd " 15fr. 3rd " 10fr.

Entries to Transport Officer 5th K.S.L.I. by 12 noon Thursday 25th.

14TH (LIGHT) DIVISION.

ROUTINE ORDERS.

26th May, 1916.

1538. HORSES - Loss of.

It is observed that a large number of horses are lost from horse lines. Officers Commanding units will report to Div'l H.Qrs through the usual channels the disciplinary action which they take in each case that occurs from this date.

1539. ACCUMULATION OF STORES.

The accumulation of stores by units, above the proportions laid down, is forbidden.
This applies whether the articles are included in the Mobilization Store Tables, G.R.Os, A.R.Os, or any other authority, and is equally applicable to articles of clothing, necessaries, and general stores.
(A.R.O.428)

LIEUT-COLONEL,
A.A.&.Q.M.G.
14TH (LIGHT) DIVISION.

NOTICES.
DIVINE SERVICES.
SUNDAY - MAY 28TH, 1916.

CHURCH OF ENGLAND.
WARLUS: Holy Communion 7.30 a.m.
        Divine Service 9.30 a.m.
WANQUETIN: Reformed Church, Evening Service 6 p.m.
        Holy Communion, Church Army Hut (Monday) 7.30 a.m.
ARRAS: Soldiers' Club, Holy Communion 8.30 a.m.
        Evening Service 8 p.m.

ROMAN CATHOLIC.
DAINVILLE: Parish Church. Holy Mass at 7 a.m.
WARLUS: "   "   "   "   " 8 a.m.
BERNEVILLE "   "   "   "   " 8 a.m.
AVESNES LE COMTE "   "   "   "   " 8.15 a.m.
LIENCOURT "   "   "   "   " 9.30 a.m.
   "   "   " Evening Service 5.30 p.m.
ARRAS: (Hopital St.Jean) Holy Mass at 9.30 a.m.
   " (Orphelinat Faubourg d'Amiens) Mass at 8.30 a.m.
ECOIRRES: Parish Church 11.30 a.m.
DAINVILLE: "   " Benediction 6 p.m.

14TH (LIGHT) DIVISION.

ROUTINE ORDERS.

27th May, 1916.

1540. G.S. WAGONS.

In future the G.S. Wagons shown in War Establishments in italics as "for extra forage" for certain units will no longer be considered as earmarked for those individual units but will be treated as a pool at the disposal of the Division to assist the Divisional Train in delivering hay to all units located within the Divisional area, including Heavy Artillery.

1541. BICYCLE TYRES.

Reference C.R.O.884, the report called for will be sent to Div'l Headquarters by noon 29th inst.

C.L. Hamilton
LIEUT-COLONEL,
A.A.&.Q.M.G.
14TH (LIGHT) DIVISION.

NOTICES.

FOUND: On Horse lines No.4 Coy.14th Div'l Train, 25-5-16:
Heavy Draught HORSE, marked on Off Fore No.5, near foot D.A.C. near hind 199.
Apply O.C., No.4 Coy, 14th Div'l Train.

LOST: Removed from Signal Office, 43rd Infantry Bde, 25th inst.
BICYCLE, Service Pattern, Makers No.28130. No.12 painted on frame. Marked with white and blue on Top Tube and on front and rear mudguards. Tail end of rear mudguard marked with three white lines.
Information to O.C., 14th Signal Co. R.E.

14TH (LIGHT) DIVISION.

ROUTINE ORDERS.

28th May, 1916.

1542. SENTENCES BY FIELD GENERAL COURTS MARTIAL.

The following sentences awarded by Field General Courts Martial, have been ordered by the Army Commander to be put into execution :-

1543. TRENCH MORTARS.

Reference the "Handbook for Stokes Trench Mortar 3" Mark I" which has been issued to all concerned, the detachment for each gun consists of 1 N.C.O. and 4 men, not 1 N.C.O. and 5 men as stated in the Handbook.

1544. RATIONS - FORAGE.

The question of increasing the supply of linseed has been referred to higher authority and it has been decided that no increase will be made.

It is considered that the condition of horses is a matter of stable management within the unit, careful watering and feeding: the ration is ample and sufficiently varied.

No application for increasing or varying the forage ration will be entertained at present.

1545. EXERCISING OF HORSES.

Attention is called to D.R.O.1397 dated 7-4-16:
Horses exercising are to avoid villages as much as possible.

1546. SICK WASTAGE.

The following is the Sick Wastage Return for week ended noon 27th instant :-

	O.	O.R.		O.	O.R.
46th Bde R.F.A.	1.		7. 9th K.R.R.C.		6.
47th Bde R.F.A.			2. 9th R.B.		3.
48th Bde R.F.A.		Nil.	42nd Bde M.G.Coy,		1.
49th Bde R.F.A.	1		2. 6th Somerset L.I.		6.
14th D.A.C.			4. 6th D.C.L.I.		8.
RAMC att.49th Bde,RFA,	1	-	6th K.O.Y.L.I.		4.
61st Coy, R.E.			2. 10th Durham L.I.		7.
62nd Coy, R.E.			1. 11th L'pool R		5.
89th Coy, R.E.		Nil.	8th M.M.G.Bty,		Nil.
14th Signal Co.R.E.		Nil.	14th Div. Train,		1.
7th K.R.R.C.			10. 14th Div.Supply Column,		Nil.
8th K.R.R.C.	1		8. 42nd Field Amb.		1.
7th R.B.			15. 43rd Field Amb,		Nil.
8th R.B.			11. 43rd Field Amb,ASC Att.		1.
5th Ox & Bucks L.I.	1		6. 44th Field Amb.		Nil.
5th K.S.L.I.	1		6. 26th Mob.Vety.Section,	1	-
			25th Sanitary Section,		Nil.

Total Officers 7, Other Ranks, 117.

LIEUT COLONEL,
A.A.&.Q.M.G.
14TH (LIGHT) DIVISION.

14TH (LIGHT) DIVISION.

ROUTINE ORDERS.

29th May, 1916.

1547. MISUSE OF GREEN ENVELOPES.

It has again been brought to notice that Green Envelopes are still being misused. In consequence the use of these envelopes has been withdrawn from one Unit in the Division for one month from this date. If any further cases occur the privilege will be withdrawn from the whole Division and the Offender will be tried by Court Martial. In some few instances no doubt ignorance exists as to what constitutes "misuse". Officers Commanding all Units are therefore directed to take immediate steps to explain to all ranks now present and all reinforcements which may join hereafter the precise meaning of the Certificate on A.F. W.3078, which is signed by the writer on his honour.

1548. TRAFFIC CONTROL.

On and after June 1st the following traffic order will be substituted for those issued in D.R.O.1464.

The DOULLENS - ARRAS road from BAC DU NORD Eastwards is closed to all traffic from Sunrise to 8.30 p.m.

Vehicular traffic for the trenches and gun positions will not pass the undermentioned places before the hours in the following table :-

BAC DU NORD	8.30 p.m.
Railway Bridge, DAINVILLE,	8.35 p.m.
WARLUS	
BERNEVILLE	8.15 p.m.
WANQUETIN	

C.L. Hamilton
LIEUT-COLONEL.
A.A.&.Q.M.G.
14TH (LIGHT) DIVISION.

NOTICE.

FOUND: at WARLUS end of WANQUETIN Road, at 5.15 a.m. 25th, Government pattern TELEPHONE in Brown leathercase. Description:- D. Mk III, Siemens, No.3721, minus cells and one receiver. No other marks.
Apply to A.P.M., 14th Division.

14TH (LIGHT) DIVISION.

ROUTINE ORDERS.

30th May, 1916.

1549. CLOTHING.

It is observed that men are still wearing Boots F.S. All Boots F.S. will be returned to D.A.D.O.S. at once and a report rendered through the usual channels to this office by 12 noon the 5th prox, stating numbers returned.

1550. MEDICAL.

It is notified for information that under the existing Medical arrangements, calls for ambulances to collect Sick or wounded are NOT to be sent to the 44th Field Ambulance.

1551. DIVISIONAL BATHS - CLOTHING.

Men attending the Divisional Baths will receive equivalent garments to those which they leave. If an extra garment is for any reason necessary, the Officer or N.C.O. in charge of the party will be required to sign a receipt for it and under no other circumstances will the N.C.O. in charge of the clothing store at the Baths issue a garment in exchange for which he has not a garment of the same nature.

1552. TOWN ORDERS, ARRAS.

Attention is directed to Para 17, Town Orders, ARRAS:-
"17. During the hours of daylight, no officers, or other ranks are permitted to leave their billets until 7.45 p.m.** unless in possession of a pass signed by their Commanding Officer.
These passes are only to be issued for some specific "DUTY" which must invariably be stated on the pass.
Orderlies, Officers and Other Ranks, on duty, fatigue parties and civilians are to walk down the pavement close to the houses, and on no account to use the Roads or open or exposed places".

N.B. ** These hours will be amnded from time to time, and units will be informed by the Town Major.

LIEUT COLONEL,
A.A.&.Q.M.G.
14TH (LIGHT) DIVISION.

14TH (LIGHT) DIVISION.

ROUTINE ORDERS.

31st May, 1916.

1553. WATER SUPPLY - MEDICAL.

A water cart containing Chlorinated water is to be available at all times in each Transport Camp from which all drinking water for use by the troops is to be drawn. Disciplinary action will be taken against any man found filling his water-bottle at a local well or elsewhere.

1554. FOOD SAFES.

Every cook-house and every place where food is stored is to be provided with an improvised safe, by June 7th.
A simple pattern was described in D.R.O.1461, dated 27th April.

LIEUT-COLONEL,
A.A.&.Q.M.G.
14TH (LIGHT) DIVISION.

NOTICE.

DIVINE SERVICES - ASCENSION DAY.
Thursday June 1st.

HOLY COMMUNION: WARLUS, Barn next Church. 7.30 a.m.
                 ARRAS. Soldier Club, 8.30 a.m. & 11 a.m.
Elsewhere as in Unit orders.

14TH (LIGHT) DIVISION.

ROUTINE ORDERS.

June 1st, 1916.

1555. BOX RESPIRATORS & P.H.G. HELMETS.

Box Respirators and P.H.G. Helmets have been received for issue in accordance with this office letter Q.347/6 dated 21-4-16.

P.H. Helmets will be withdrawn in exchange for P.H.G. Helmets and box respirators.

1556. LEAVE WARRANTS.

No additional orders or instructions are to be added to the Combined Leave and Railway Warrant forms, or to A.F. W.3337 without authority from Third Army.

1557. MACKINTOSH CAPES.

All mackintosh capes in possession will be returned to D.A.D.O.S. by June 6th.

This applies equally to mounted men and Labour Battalions.

1558. BOUNDS - TIME AT WHICH TROOPS MUST BE IN BILLETS.

With reference to G.R.O.1247 of 6th November, 1915, the hour by which all Warrant Officers, non-commissioned officers, and men, except those on duty and others with special passes, must be in their billets, is extended to 9 p.m. nightly from the 1st June 1916, until further orders.
(G.R.O.1599)

1559. WITHDRAWAL OF ENGLISH SILVER.

From the 1st of June inclusive, the purchase of English silver from individuals, by Field and Base Cashiers, will cease. The purchase from institutions which exchange money for the soldiers will continue, the rate, which will be given to the soldiers, being fixed from time to time, in accordance with the market value.

G.R.O.1417 dated 20th February, 1916 is cancelled.
(G.R.O.1603).

LIEUT COLONEL,
A.A.&Q.M.G.
14TH (LIGHT) DIVISION.

14TH (LIGHT) DIVISION.

ROUTINE ORDERS.

2nd June, 1916.

1560. HONOURS AND REWARDS.

The undermentioned have been awarded cards "For Gallant and Meritorious Service" by the Major-General Commanding:-

14TH DIVISIONAL ARTILLERY.

No.27259, Gnr. A.J. Brocklesby, A Battery, 40th Bde.

14TH DIVISIONAL ENGINEERS.

No.61173, L/Cpl. C. Ward, 89th Field Coy, R.E.

7TH K.R.R.C.

No.A.509, Sergt. J. Ellis,

R.10788. L/Cpl. W. Anderson,
11447. " Coombes,

7TH R.B.

S.961, Sergt. L. Pope,

8TH R.B.

B.724. Sergt. B. Driver.

6TH K.O.Y.L.I.

No. 8404. Sergt. E. Crow.

10th DURHAM L.I.

24312. Pte S. Russell.

44TH FIELD AMBULANCE.

32143. Pte H. Ayre,
32791. " A. O'Hara.

1561. CLOTHING.

With reference to C.R.O.905:
All uniform is to be returned when unserviceable to D.AD.O.S. direct by units.
All unserviceable underclothing is to be handed over by units to the nearest Bath establishment.
Receipts are to be taken in both cases.
O i/c Baths will return unserviceable underclothing to D.A.D.O.S. after washing and disinfecting, but will retain repairable underclothing and arrange for its repair and re-issue at the Baths.
O.C. Units and O i/c Baths will arrange as far as possible to send the various items in separate packages, e.g. jackets, trousers, shirts, socks etc.
D.A.D.O.S. will arrange with O.C. Salvage Company as regards the sorting and baling of the clothing for despatch to the Base etc.

1562. POSTAL REFILLING.

Postal refilling is now at 10 a.m.

LIEUT COLONEL,
A.A.&.Q.M.G.
14TH (LIGHT) DIVISION.

(over)

DIVINE SERVICES.

SUNDAY - JUNE 4TH, 1916.

C OF E.
WARLUS: Rue du Chateau, Divine Service 9.30 a.m.
ARRAS: Soldiers' Club, Holy Communion 8.30 a.m.
        Evening Service 8 p.m.
WANQUETIN: Reformed Church, Evening Service 6 p.m.
BERNEVILLE: Church Army Hut, Holy Communion 7.30 a.m.
        Evening Service, 6.30 p.m.
Other services by arrangement with units.

R.C.
DAINVILLE Parish Church, Holy Mass & Sermon, 7 a.m.
AGNY (L'pool R Orderly Room) 10.30 a.m.
ARRAS (Hopital St.Joan) Holy Mass & Sermon 9.30 a.m.
MAROEUIL Parish Church, Holy Mass & Sermon, 10 a.m.
ECOIRRES Parish Church, Holy Mass & Sermon, 10.30 a.m.
BERNEVILLE Parish Church, Holy Mass & Sermon, 8 a.m.
DAINVILLE Parish Church, Benediction 6 p.m.
WARLUS Parish Church, Holy Mass 8 a.m.

14TH (LIGHT) DIVISION.

ROUTINE ORDERS.

June 4th, 1916.

1563. VERMOREL SPRAYERS.

In consequence of the frequent loss of round covers or complete lids No.12 of Vermorel Sprayers, it has been decided to attach the lids with a small chain.

Sprayers with lids complete are to be sent to D.A.D.O.S. for the fixing of the chain, as many as can be spared being sent at a time. Sprayers of which the lids are missing should not be sent, but D.A.D.O.S. will be informed by each Brigade of the number of lids or round covers which are required to complete. D.A.D.O.S. will inform Brigades of the arrival from the Base of the lids to complete their Vermorel Sprayers and the latter will then be sent to him to affix the chains.

1564. FILING OF FEED BLOCKS FOR VICKERS GUN.

Reference C.R.O.No.916:
The Report called for therein should reach this office by noon 8th instant.

1565. HONOURS AND REWARDS.

His Majesty the King has been graciously pleased to approve of the undermentioned rewards for Distinguished Service in the Field to Officers, N.C.O's and men who are serving or have served in the 14th (Light) Division. The notification appeared in the London Gazette of June 2nd.

To be a Companion of the Most Honourable Order of the Bath.

Colonel Thomas A.H. Biggs.

To be a Companion of the Most Distinguished Order of Saint Michael and Saint George.
Colonel George C. Dowell.
Lt-Colonel William B. Browell R.A.
Lt-Colonel James D. Heriot-Maitland. D.S.O. Rifle Bde
Major (Temporary Lt-Col, C.G. Rawling, C.I.E.
Somerset Light Infantry.

To be Brevet Colonel.
Lieut-Col,(Temp,Brig-Genl) P.R.Wood,C.M.G.
Royal Irish Fusiliers.

To be Brevet Lieut-Colonel.
Major Tempy(Lieut-Col,) O.C.Borrett, D.S.O.
Royal Lancaster Regt,
Commanding 5th K.S.L.I.

To be Brevet Majors.
Capt, (Tempy Lt-Colonel) T.H.P. Morris,
Commanding 9th Rifle Brigade.
Capt, (Tempy Lt-Colonel) W.F.R. Webb. Indian Army,
Commanding 5th Oxf & Bucks L.I.

To be Companions of the Distinguished Service Order.

STAFF
Lt-Col, C.L.C. Hamilton. R.A.
Major C.C. Armitage, R.A.
Major F.H. Lister, R.A.
Capt, H.M.J. Alves. R.A.
Major, A.G. Bayley, Ox & Bucks L.I.
Major J.L. Buxton, Rifle Brigade.

Royal Artillery.

        Major A.E. Erskine.

Royal Engineers.

        Captain. C.H.R. Chesney.
        Captain. J. Benskin.

Duke of Cornwalls Light Infantry.

        Major J. L. Swainson

King's Royal Rifle Corps.

        Major (Temp. Lt. Col.) H.C.R. Green 8th Batn.
        Lieut. Colonel C.J. Davis (22nd Punjab's) 7th Batn.

Rifle Brigade.

        Lieut. Colonel R.C. Maclachlan 8th Batn.

Awarded Military Cross.

STAFF.

        Capt. G.F. Plowden Ox. & Bucks L.I.
        Capt. C.R. Shield H.L.I. (Special Reserve)
        Capt. R.B. Stewart Rifle Brigade.
        Capt. P.H.N.N. Vyvyan A.S.C.

Royal Artillery.

        Capt. B.F. Rhodes (B. Battery 46th Brigade)

Royal Engineers.

        Temp. Lieut. S.G. Anderson (14th Div. Signal Coy.)
        Temp. 2nd Lieut. B. Llewellyn.

King's (Liverpool) Regiment.

        Temp. Capt. H. Johnson 11th Batn.

King's Own Yorkshire Light Infantry.

        Temp. Capt. C.B. Leatham 6th Batn.

King's Shropshire Light Infantry.

        Temp. 2nd Lieut. A. Gittins 5th Batn.

Durham Light Infantry.

        Temp. Capt. B. G. Bryant 10th Batn.

Rifle Brigade.

        Temp. Capt. H.B. Moore 9th Batn.
        Temp. Capt. J. Maxwell 7th Batn.

Motor Machine Gun Service.

Temp. Capt. S.A. Westropp 8th M.M.G. Battery.

R. A. M. C.

Temp. Capt. C. R. Dudgeon.

Army Chaplain Department.

4th Class Chaplain Rev. W. Telfer.

Awarded Distinguished Conduct Medal.

Royal Artillery.

No. 89179 A/Bombr. F. Mills (A Battery 48th Bde.)

Royal Engineers.

No. 52852 C.S.M., E. Lockwood (89th Field Coy.)
" 47842 Sergt. L.H. Sharp (14th Signal Coy.)

Somerset Light Infantry.

No. 5346 S.M. Buss 6th Bn.

King's Own Yorkshire Light Infantry.

No. 8796 Actg. S.M. G.E.E. Howes 6th Bn.
" 23629 Corpl. F. Summers 6th Bn.

King's Royal Rifle Corps.

No. 6547 C.S.M., H. Oxley 7th Bn.

Durham Light Infantry.

No. 14006 C.S.M., J.H.A. Slater 10th Bn.

Rifle Brigade.

No. B. 213 Sergt. A. Rumbelow 7th Bn.

Awarded Clasp to D. C. M.

King's Royal Rifle Corps.

No. 1143 C.S.M., Macintyre 8th Bn.

Awarded Military Medal.

Royal Artillery.

No. 89303 Sergt. F.G. Sawyer (A Batt. 47th Bde.)
" 38810 Sergt. A.C. Mousley (H.Q. 49th Bde.)
" 97984 Bombr. R.W. Firth (B Batt. 48th Bde.)
" 95874 Sergt. E. Ashley (D Batt. 48th Bde.)
" 21484 A/Bombr. J.W. Ryan (C Batt. 48th Bde.)

-4-

Royal Engineers.

        No. 41866   Sergt. W. Duckett (61st Field Coy.)
        "   49000   Sergt. R.M. Elton (99th Field Coy.)
        "   40209   L/Cpl. C. Harris (14th Signal Coy.)

Somerset Light Infantry.

        No. 10160   Sergt. T.R. Summerhayes 6th Bn.

Oxford & Buckinghamshire Light Infantry.

        No. 7570   Sergt. C. Bignell 5th Bn.

King's Shropshire Light Infantry.

        No. 11495   A/Sergt. A. King
        "   8078   Corpl. F. Pope
        "   17003   Pte. C. Herring
        "   5486   Pte. J. Goulding

King's Royal Rifle Corps.

        No. A 2007   Rifleman H. Blackwell 9th Bn.

Rifle Brigade.

        No. 6-377   A/Cpl. W. Ward 9th Bn.

R.A.M.C.

        No. 31667   Sergt. R. Eastham (44th Field Ambulance)

566. AUDIT.

    A Board of Officers as under will audit the accounts of the following institutions made up to May 31st:-
        Divisional Canteen
        Divisional Beer Supply
        Divisional School Officers Mess
        Divisional School Canteen
        Soldiers Club, Arras
        Church Army Hut, Wanquetin
        Church Army Hut, Berneville.
    The President will arrange with the Officer in charge as regards the date of inspection of their accounts.
        President.   Lt-Col. Richards. A.S.C.
        Member.   Major C.G. Mansfield-Clarke R.B.
The proceedings will be sent to Divisional Head Quarters.

                                    LIEUT. COLONEL.
                                    A.A.&Q.M.G.
                                14th (Light) Division.

14TH (LIGHT) DIVISION.

ROUTINE ORDERS.

5th June 1916.

1567. MULES.

In future the number and class of mules on the strength of each unit will be shown separately on the weekly Army Form "B.213" thus :-

MULES.
Large. Small.
4   4

Mules of 15 hands and upwards are large, under 15 hands small.

1568. CART AND WAGON COMPONENTS.

Units will forward a list, through the usual channel, to reach this office by noon 9th instant, showing the average monthly requirements of cart and wagon components.
(Authority : Third Army O/14/11, dated 2/6/16. VI Corps Q/513.)

1569. SICK WASTAGE.

The following is the Sick Wastage Return for week ended noon 3rd instant :-

	O.	O.R.		O.	O.R.
46th Bde R.F.A.		3	9th K.R.R.C.		2
47th Bde R.F.A.		1	9th R.B.		6
48th Bde R.F.A.		Nil	42nd Bde M.G.Coy.		1
49th Bde R.F.A.		2	42nd T.M.Batteries		2
14th D.A.C.		1	6th Somerset L.I.		6
61st Field Co.R.E.		2	6th D.C.L.I.	1	5
62nd Field Co.R.E.		Nil	6th K.O.Y.L.I.		5
89th Field Co.R.E.		Nil	10th D.L.I.		10
14th Signal Co.R.E.		1	43rd T.M. Battery.		1
7th K.R.R.C.		9	11th L'pool Regt.		1
8th K.R.R.C.		5	8th M.M.G. Battery.	1	-
7th R.B.		7	14th Div'l Train		1
8th R.B.		3	42nd Field Ambulance		1
5th Ox. & Bucks L.I.		6	43rd Field Ambulance		1
5th K.S.L.I.		6	44th Field Ambulance	1	-
			25th Sanitary Section		1

Total Officers 3, Other ranks, 89.

LIEUT COLONEL
A.A.& Q.M.G.
14th (LIGHT) DIVISION,

14TH (LIGHT) DIVISION.

ROUTINE ORDERS.

6th June 1916.

1570. REQUISITIONS.

The French Mission at G.H.Q., have drawn attention to the necessity for strict compliance with the laws and regulations in respect to requisitioning in all cases in which it becomes necessary to requisition landed property for Military use. Such property will only be requisitioned when it is impossible to arrange terms by agreement.

The actual agreements are made by Rent Officers. Land occupied by leave of the Maire and duly reported to Divisional Headquarters for the information of the Rent Officers is to be considered as occupied by agreement, but in the case of Railway property the consent of an Officer of the French Railway Service is also necessary. Railway property is not to be occupied either by agreement or by requisition in any but the most exceptional circumstances.

The procedure to be followed when requisitioning land will be that laid down for the requisitioning of buildings on page 9. of the Instructions as to Requisitions, Billeting and Quartering in France and Belgium, dated April 1916.

1571. WORKING PAY.

Attention is directed to G.R.O. 1288. reprinted in Extracts from G.R.Os Part II, dated 1st April 1916. Advantage should be taken of the order by all Units as far as is possible in order to reduce the demands for horse shoes on the Base.

1572. STRAY ANIMALS.

Stray animals caught by Units and reported, should if not claimed in 3 days of the notice of finding appearing in C.R.O, be again reported to Divisional Headquarters as unclaimed.

1573. LEAVE.

Restrictions regarding leave to certain places mentioned in previous D.R.Os are removed with the exception of HINDLEY, BLACKPOOL, and CARDIFF.

Those places should only be considered infected towns for soldiers not recently vaccinated or re-vaccinated.

LIEUT COLONEL
A.A. & Q.M.G.
14TH (LIGHT) DIVISION.

14th. (LIGHT) DIVISION.

ROUTINE ORDERS.

8th June, 1916.

1574. WATER CARTS.

Units are reminded that they are entirely responsible for the water carts on their charge. The whole apparatus must be kept complete and clean, and any deficiency of cleaning materials such as brushes, etc. should be made good at once.

1575. APPOINTMENT.

Captain E. J. TYRRELL, R.A.M.C., is appointed Garrison Medical Officer, WANQUETIN, vice Lieut. E. D. LINDOW, R.A.M.C.

1576. REPORTS.

Reference C.R.Os. 931, 932, 933. The reports called for therein must reach this office through the usual channel by 12 noon, 10th instant.

C Parson s/Capt
for Lieut. Colonel,
A.A. & Q.M.G.
14th (Light) Division.

14th (Light) Division.
****

ROUTINE ORDERS.

10th June, 1916.

1577. SENTENCE BY FIELD GENERAL COURT MARTIAL.

The following sentence awarded by Field General Court Martial, has been ordered by the Army Commander to be put into execution:-

[redacted]

1578. "P" HELMETS.

Some "P" helmets have recently been found in the possession of units. Attention is directed to the importance of replacing them by P.H. Helmets on account of the inferior protection given by the 'P' helmet against gas.

1579. RETURN.

The weekly return of Casualties to Animals rendered to the A.D.V.S. is cancelled from this date.

1580. POTATO SACKS.

In future all Potato sacks received from Bases will be returned as early as possible, so that they may be sent back to England in accordance with War Office instructions. (Third Army DDS & T S/339, d/10-4-16, VI Corps Q/371).

1581 LIME JUICE -ISSUE OF.

Until further orders lime juice may be issued twice weekly as per General Routine Order No. 1235 when neither green vegetables nor onions are part of the daily ration.

1582. RIFLES FITTED WITH TELESCOPIC SIGHTS.

Attention is drawn to Army Routine Order No. 120.

"When telescopic sights, or the rifles to which they are fitted, are damaged, both are invariably to be returned to the Base for transmission to the Chief Inspector of Small Arms."

1583. CLINOMETERS.

Clinometers Field, not being necessary for use with Lewis Guns, all those at present in possession of Infantry Battalions will be returned at once to D.A.D.O.S. for transmission to Base.
(Authority G.R.O. 1616)

for A.A. & Q.M.G.
14th (Light) Division.

NOTICES.
******

FOUND. In the Rue de SIMENCOURT, BERNEVILLE, at 8-30 p.m. on June 5th, 1916.
   1 Fuze Indicator Q.F. 18 Pdr.
   1 Bar Testing Rocking Bar Q.F. 18 Pdr with box.
   Apply to O.C., No. 1 Section, 14th. Div 1 Ammn. Column, BERNEVILLE.

FOUND. In DAINVILLE. A bay mare. Marks and descriptions Off hind R.F.A.T., Near hind A 129, Near fore 828. A white stocking off hind. White blaze on face. Apply Town Commdt. Dainville.

FOUND. SERVICE CYCLE No. 28537. Red triangle with white triangle ...ainville.

SUNDAY – 11th June, 1916.

CHURCH of ENGLAND.
   WARLUS: Rue du Chateau.
      Holy Communion 8-30 a.m.
      Morning Service 9-30 a.m.
   BERNEVILLE: Church Army Hut.
      Holy Communion 7-30 a.m.
      Evening Service 6-30 p.m.
   WANQUETIN: Church Army Hut.
      Holy Communion 7-30 a.m.
      Morning Service 11 a.m.
         Reformed Church.
      Evening Service 6 p.m.
   ARRAS: Holy Communion 8-30 a.m. Short Evening Service 9 p.m.

WESLEYANS, PRESBYTERIANS, NONCONFORMISTS, etc.
   BERNEVILLE: 9-30 a.m. 9th K.R.R.C., 1 & 3 Sections D.A.C. with Communion Service.
   DAINVILLE: 12 noon Highland R.G.A..
   ARRAS: 2-15 p.m. 5th K.S.L.I.
   WANQUETIN: 5-30 p.m. Horselines R.G.A.
   6-15 p.m. 42nd Field Ambulance.

ROMAN CATHOLIC.
   DAINVILLE Parish Church, Holy Mass at 7 a.m.
   WARLUS   "   "   "   "   " 8 a.m.
   BERNEVILLE   "   "   "   "   " 8 a.m.
   ARRAS Hospital S. Jean   "   "   " 9-30 a.m.
      Faubourg d'Amiens Orphanage " 8-30 a.m.
   AGNY Orderly Room, King's L'pool Rgt. at 10-30 a.m.
   ECOIVRES Parish Church Holy Mass at 9-0 a.m.
   ACQ Parish Church Holy Mass at 9-0 a.m.
   DAINVILLE Parish Church Benediction at 6 p.m.

14th (LIGHT) DIVISION.

ROUTINE ORDERS.

11th June 1916.

1584. BLANKETS.

Reference C.R.O. 940. Blankets not already returned may be returned up to a maximum of 25% of the strength of the unit, if desired, for men sleeping in huts or in the open.

Units who have returned their blankets should submit indents to D.A.D.O.S. on the same scale.

1585. SPONGE GOGGLES.

Issue is approved for the use of drivers on a scale of one pair per lorry carrying ammunition to Siege Batteries (6 inch Howitzer and upwards), one pair per Motor Ambulance car of Field Ambulances and Cavalry Field Ambulances and one pair per Motor car of Army Corps, Divisional and Cavalry Divisional Staffs.

These goggles should always be kept on the lorry or car ready for immediate use in case of necessity.

Indents should be submitted through the usual channel.
(Authority: Q.O.S./317/4/2/A, dated 8/6/16. VI Corps Q/8/26.)
(C.R.O. No. 944.)

1586. SICK WASTAGE.

The following is the Sick Wastage Return for week ended noon 10th instant:-

Unit	O.	O.R.	Unit	O.	O.R.
46th Bde. R.F.A.	1	2	9th K.R.R.C.		2.
47th Bde. R.F.A.		1	9th R.B.		5.
48th Bde. R.F.A.		Nil	42nd T.M.Batty.		1.
49th Bde. R.F.A.		1	6th Somerset L.I.	1	6.
14th D.A.C.		2	6th D.C.L.I.		2.
61st Coy. R.E.		Nil	6th K.O.Y.L.I.		6.
62nd Coy R.E.		Nil	10th Durham L.I.	1	7.
89th Coy R.E.		2.	42rd T.M. Batty.		1.
7th K.R.R.C.		5	11th L'pool Regt.		4.
8th K.R.R.C.		9	8th M.M.G. Batty.		Nil,
7th R.B.		5	14th Div. Train.		1.
8th R.B.		2	42nd Field Amb.		1.
5th Ox & Bucks L.I.	1	QQ	43rd Field Amb.		1.
5th K.S.L.I.		4	44th Field Amb.		1.
			R.A.M.C. ASC Att.	1.	-

Total Officers, 5. Other Ranks 82.

LIEUT COLOEL
A.A. & Q.M.G.
14th (Light) Division.

14th (Light) DIVISION.

ROUTINE ORDERS.

12th June, 1916.

1587. BLANKETS.

Reference D.R.O. 1584. For RETURNED in second line read RETAINED.

1588. STEEL HELMETS.

Units will report through the usual channels to reach this office by 12 noon, 16th June, the number of STEEL HELMETS in possession.
Nil returns are not required.

1589. BOUNDS.

The undermentioned Estaminets have been put out of bounds for an indefinite period:-

Mme. BRIDOUX, 58 Rue de LATTRE, HAUTEVILLE,
Mme. BAILLEUL, 2 Rue de MOULIN, HAUTEVILLE,
Mme. VOISIN TIERON, 7 Rue de MOULIN, HAUTEVILLE,
Farm of LEON BRIMONT, 18 Rue d'AVESNES, HAUTEVILLE,

at the request of the proprietors.

for C. Sassoon Captn
A.A. & Q.M.G.,
14th (Light) Division.

NOTICE.

A Memorial Service for the late Field Marshal EARL KITCHENER, K.G., will be held at Divisional Headquarters at 12 noon, tomorrow, 13th instant.
Officers able to do so are invited to attend.

14th (Light) DIVISION.

ROUTINE ORDERS.

13th June, 1916.

1590. ARRAS.

Complaints having been received that the instructions regarding Requisitioning in the Town of ARRAS are not being complied with, para. 8 of the Town Orders - ARRAS, is republished for the information of all concerned:-

8. Requisitions.
It is absolutely forbidden to take anything in the town of ARRAS, even for tactical purposes, without a requisition order. No requisition order may be given unless signed by the Town Major and counter-signed by the French Authorities. If it is impossible to hand this requisition to the owner, it will be given to the Town Major, who will pass to the Maire or French Authorities.

The attention of all units should be drawn to the above instructions.

1591. STROMBOS HORNS.

As it is impossible to obtain replacements of Strombos Horns at present, every care must be taken to protect those in possession from damage.

1592. HORSES - PICKED UP NAILS.

A number of cases have occurred of lameness in horses due to punctured feet by nails strewn on the ground.
Care must be exercised, at refilling points and all places where boxes are opened, and where work involving the use of nails is carried out, to ensure that no nails are left on the ground.

for A.A. & Q.M.G.,
14th (Light) Division.

14TH (LIGHT) DIVISION.

ROUTINE ORDERS.

1593. RETURNS - ANIMALS. 14th June 1916.

Units will render through the usual channels to reach this office by 8 pm 16th inst a return showing number of animals of each class in possession.

1594. ANIMALS - DESCRIPTIVE ROLLS.

From this date all units will keep a descriptive roll showing all animals held on their strength.
All animals lost or found should be shown on this roll as such, the date lost or found and how disposed of to be shown in column of remarks.

1595. HAIRCUTTING CHARGES.

Paragraph 1 of G.R.O. 1410 which relates to Haircutting is hereby cancelled.
Regimental arrangements should be made for haircutting. Charges (calculated on the strength at the end of each month) will be made at the rate of 1d per man per month.
Commanding Officers may use their discretion in arranging details of expenditure, provided that no portion of the fund is applied to purposes other than those connected with haircutting.
(G.R.O. 1629)

Captain, for
A.A.&.Q.M.G.
14th (Light) Division.

14th (LIGHT) DIVISION.

ROUTINE ORDERS.

15th June, 1916.

1596. RETURNS - TENTAGE.

Trench Shelters, paulins, marquees, tents C.S.L., and Tent Bottoms, which are held under Mobilization Store Table, will <u>not</u> be included in future returns.
(VI Corps Routine Order 955)

1597. FLIES.

The issue of fly-traps and butter-muslin is approved for all units, not exceeding the following scale :-
Fly-traps, 1 per 30 Officers and men.
Muslin,   1 sq.yard per 20 officers and men.
Indents will be submitted through the usual channel, and will be certified by the Administrative Medical Officer concerned that the quantities demanded are not in excess of actual requirements.
Officers Commanding units to whom issues are made will be held responsible for the proper care of these stores.
(Authority O.S.R/3668, d/13-6-16. VI Corps Q/424/1)
(VI Corps Routine Order No.956).

1598. PERISCOPES.

With reference to G.R.O.No.861, approval has been given for the scale of issue of No.18 (Vigilant) Periscopes to be increased from 40 to 80 per battalion.
Indents to complete to this scale will be submitted through the usual channel.
(Authority.QMG Letter unnumbered,dated 11-6-16 & 9/115/6, dated 13-6-16. VI Corps Q/532).
(VI Corps Routine Order No. 957).

1599. STEEL HELMETS.

Attention is drawn to VI Corps Routine Orders Nos. 947 dated 11th June, and 959 dated 14th June, 1916.

1600. ORDNANCE - RECEIPTS FOR STORES.

In future one copy of the Voucher for "Detail Stores" will be handed over to the units representative for Signature by the Officer Commanding and immediate return to the D.A.D.O.S.
This will enable the unit to mark up its indents correctly.

1601. TRAFFIC CONTROL.

On and after this date the following traffic order will be substituted for those issued in D.R.O.1548.
The DOULLENS - ARRAS Road from BAC DU NORD Eastwards is closed to all traffic from Sunrise to 9.30 p.m.
Vehicular traffic for the trenches and gun positions will not pass the undermentioned places before the hours in the following table :-

BAC DU NORD   9.30 p.m.
Railway Bridge, DAINVILLE, 9.30 p.m.
WARLUS   )
BERNEVILLE)   9.15 p.m.
WANQUETIN   )

CAPTAIN, for
A.A.&.Q.M.G.
14TH (LIGHT) DIVISION.

14th (LIGHT) DIVISION.

ROUTINE ORDERS.

16th June, 1916.

1602. SENTENCE BY FIELD GENERAL COURT MARTIAL. Duties

The following sentence awarded by Field General Court Martial, has been ordered by the Army Commander to be put into execution :-

[redacted]

LIEUT.COLONEL,
A.A.&Q.M.G.
14th (LIGHT) DIVISION.

NOTICES.

LOST: MULE, 16½ hands, Dark Brown, 1/D.A.C. on off fore, 102 on near fore. Brushes slightly with hind legs. Last seen near SIMENCOURT 14-6-16.
Information to O.C., No.1 Section, 14th D.A.C.

CHURCH SERVICES, 18-6-16.

C OF E.
WARLUS: Rue du Chateau, Holy Communion 7 a.m.
                                 Morning Service 9.30 a.m.
                                 Voluntary Evening Service 6 p.m.
ARRAS: Soldiers' Club. Holy Communion 8.30 a.m.
                                 Morning Service 10 a.m. & 11.30 a.m.
                                 Evening Service 9 p.m.
WANQUETIN: Church Army Hut. Holy Communion 7 a.m. & 11.30 a.m.
                                 Morning Service 11 am.
                                 Evening Service 7 p.m.
BERNEVILLE: Church Army Hut. Holy Communion 8 a.m.
                                 Evening Service 6.30 p.m.
Elsewhere by arrangement with Units.

R.Cs.
Holy Mass & Sermon DAINVILLE Parish Church 7 a.m.
   "   "   "   BERNEVILLE   "   8 a.m.
   "   "   "   AGNY (L'poolR)   10.30 a.m.
   "   "   "   WARLUS Parish Church, 8 a.m.
   "   "   "   ARRAS (Orphanage Faubourg d'Amiens) 8.30 a.m.
   "   "   "   ARRAS (Hospital St.Jean) 9.30 a.m.
   "   "   "   ECOIRRES Parish Church 9 a.m.
   "   "   "   MAROEUIL   "   "   10 a.m.
Benediction at DAINVILLE Parish Church 6 p.m.

WESLEYANS, PRESBYTERIANS, NONCONFORMISTS ETC.
10.30 a.m. 9th K.R.R.C. followed by Communion at ARRAS.
11.30 a.m. 5th K.S.L.I., & 42nd Bde M.G.Co.followed by
                                Communion at ARRAS.
2.30 p.m. R.G.A. with Communion, at DAINVILLE.
5.30 p.m. Horse lines R.G.A. & 2/1 Midlands, at WANQUETIN.
6.15 p.m. 42nd Field Ambulance, at WANQUETIN.

14TH (LIGHT) DIVISION.

ROUTINE ORDERS.

17th June, 1916.

1603. R.E. STORES.

Reference D.R.O.1467 dated 30th April, the times of drawing R.E. Stores laid down therein are amended to read as follows :-
- R.E. and Pioneers, before 9.30 p.m.
- Infantry Brigades, 9.30 p.m. to 11 p.m.
- R.A. & Other units, after 11 p.m.

In all cases 2 men per vehicle must be sent for loading.

1604. 3" STOKES MORTAR.

In order to prevent the safety button being hung up on the lever by friction, later supplies of pistols have the end of the lever turned over to form a ledge to butt against the set back pellet, instead of being perforated by the "Button" on the end of the pellet.

This should be more sensitive, but care should be taken, while screwing the pistol into the bomb, that the end of the lever is not displaced sideways from the pellet, and allowed to rise so as to release the striker.

In future levers will be provided with ledges to prevent such sideways movement taking place.
(Authority Third Army O/50/24, d/14-6-16. VI Corps Q/2/34).

1605. FIELD FORGES.

Attention is drawn to C.R.O.963 dated 15-6-16.

C. Parsons

Captain, for
A.A.&.Q.M.G.
14TH (LIGHT) DIVISION.

14TH (LIGHT) DIVISION.

ROUTINE ORDERS.

1606. LEAVE.

Owing to outbreak of Smallpox in SWINTON, PENDLEBURY, and MOORSIDE, County Lancashire, leave should not be granted to soldiers to proceed to those places until further orders.

1607. BATHS.

Capt M.J. Kelly, R.A.M.C. is appointed Officer in charge Divisional Baths, vice Capt. W. Brown.

1608. MEDICAL.

Capt. D. Reid King, R.A.M.C. is appointed Garrison Medical Officer, WARLUS, vice Capt. M.J. Kelly, R.A.M.C.

1609. SICK WASTAGE.

The following is the Sick Wastage Return for week ended noon 17th instant :-

	O.	O.R.		O.	O.R.
46th Bde R.F.A.		6.	9th K.R.R.C.		5.
47th Bde R.F.A.		5.	9th R.B.		8.
48th Bde R.F.A.		3.	42nd Bde M.G.Coy,		2.
49th Bde R.F.A.		3.	42nd Bde T.M.Bty.		1.
14th D.A.C.		7.	6th Somerset L.I.		7.
61st Field Co. R.E.		Nil.	6th D.C.L.I.		6.
62nd Field Co. R.E.		Nil.	6th K.O.Y.L.I.		8.
89th Field Co. R.E.		Nil.	10th Durham L.I.		9.
14th Signal Co. R.E.		1.	43rd Bde M.G. Co.		1.
7th K.R.R.C.		5.	43rd Bde T.M. Bty.		Nil.
8th K.R.R.C.		6.	11th Bn.The King's,L'pool R		5.
7th Bn. R.B.	1	2.	14th Div. Train,		Nil.
8th Bn. R.B.	1	-	42nd Field Ambulance,		1.
41st Bde M.G.Coy,		Nil.	43rd Field Ambulance,	1	-
41st Bde T.M.Bty,		Nil.	44th Field Ambulance,	1	-
5th Ox & Bucks L.I.		3.	A.O.C.		2.
5th K.S.L.I.		10.			

Totals **Officers 4, Other Ranks 106.**

1610. LEAVE OF ABSENCE TO N.C.Os AND MEN CONTINUING TO SERVE FOR THE DURATION OF THE WAR.

Attention is drawn to G.R.O. 1637 dated 17-6-16.

Lieut-Colonel,
A.A.& Q.M.G.
14th (Light) Division.

14TH (LIGHT) DIVISION.

ROUTINE ORDERS.

20th June, 1916.

1611. LEAVE.

D.R.O. 1606 of yesterday is cancelled.

1612. CAMPS AND BIVOUACS.

It is notified for information that woods and forests are not to be used in future for camps and bivouacs to a greater extent than may be rendered necessary by the Military situation. When necessity exists for concealing troops they may on that account be bivouaced or camped in woods and forests.

1613. RETURN.

Units will render to this office, through the usual channels, as early as possible, a return shewing number of N.C.Os and men who signed A.F. W.3125 or A.F. W.3126 (re-engagement) before 30th May 1916, who have not been granted one months leave of absence.

1614. PASSES.

The Blue Card Pass now in force will not be accepted after the 25TH JUNE.
A new Card Pass will be issued for use from the 25th JUNE to the 31ST AUGUST, 1916.
Old Card Passes should invariably be returned to the issuing officer.

LIEUT-COLONEL,
A.A.&.Q.M.G.
14TH (LIGHT) DIVISION.

14TH (LIGHT) DIVISION.

ROUTINE ORDERS.

22nd June, 1916.

1615. RETURNS.

Units will render through the usual channels by 12 noon Monday, 26th instant, nominal rolls of all men extra-regimentally employed, showing in each case the nature of their employment.

1616. HORSES.

All Units will report their deficiencies in horses to Div'l Headquarters by noon 24th instant.

1617. R.A.M.C. PERSONNEL FOR WATER DUTIES.

Units entitled to R.A.M.C. personnel for water duties who have not been furnished with them should apply for regimental personnel in lieu, such personnel to be in addition to the regimental War Establishment of the Unit.
R.A.M.C. are no longer available to replace casualties for water duties of units, vide A.O.446 of 1915.

1618. MEDICAL.

Cases can be taken for Dental Treatment at 42nd Field Ambulance on Mondays and Thursdays. This is in addition to those sent to 44th Field Ambulance on Tuesdays & Fridays.

1619. HEADLIGHTS ON MOTOR VEHICLES.

Attention is called to D.R.O.1270 dated 7th March, 1916.
O.C. all units with Motor vehicles will inspect the headlights and ensure that the upper half of the glasses are properly painted over.

1620. REFILLING.

Refilling will be at 7.30 a.m. from 27th inst. inclusive.

LIEUT-COLONEL,
A.A.&.Q.M.G.
14TH (LIGHT) DIVISION.

NOTICES.

LOST: On morning of 18th inst., at WARLUS, Brown MARE, 15 hands. Marks :- White spot on near wither under saddle, old scar inside off stifle, three quarter tail, Clipped fore legs, hindlegs not clipped.
Information to A.P.M., 14th Division.

LOST: At Horse Show of 55th Division, BRITISH WARM, Dark Green, leather buttons. Left hanging up on the post at No.3 Paddock, at start of jumps.
Information to A.P.M., 14th Division.

14TH (LIGHT) DIVISION.

ROUTINE ORDERS.

24th ~~May~~ June, 1916.

1621. LEAVE.

The 0.35 leave train from ST.POL to BOULOGNE will run for the last time on the 24th inst; Third Army leave service via BOULOGNE will then be as follows :-
```
          AUBIGNY    depart  15.30
          TINCQUES,    "     15.50
          ST.POL,      "     18.30
          BOULOGNE (via ETAPLES) arrive 22.45.
```
Service via HAVRE remains unchanged.

From Sunday 25th instant, inclusive, leave lorry will leave cross-roads WARLUS for ST.POL at 4 p.m., going and returning via DUISANS.

                                    [signature]
                                    LIEUT COLONEL,
                                      A.A.&.Q.M.G.
                                    14TH (LIGHT) DIVISION.

DIVINE SERVICES
Sunday, 25th June, 1916.

C OF E.
WARLUS-Rue de Chateau: Holy Communion 7 a.m.
                       Morning Service 9.30 a.m.
                       Evening Service 6 p.m.
BERNEVILLE. Church Army Hut: Holy Communion 8 a.m.
                             Evening Service 6.30 p.m.
ARRAS: Soldiers' Club: Holy Communion 8.30 a.m.
                       Evening Service 9.30 p.m.
Elsewhere by arrangement with Units.

R.C.
Mass at 7 a.m. DAINVILLE Parish Church.
  "   " 8 a.m. LIENCOURT   "   "
  "   " 8 a.m. DUISANS   "   " for 8th K.R.R.C.
Morning Service 9.30 a.m. Hospital St.Jean, ARRAS.
   "   "   10 a.m.   BERNEVILLE Parish Church.
   "   "   10.30 a.m. St.Catherines Parish Church.ARRAS
Evening Service 5.30 p.m. DUISANS Parish Church.
   "   "   6 p.m.   DAINVILLE Parish Church.

14TH (LIGHT) DIVISION.

ROUTINE ORDERS.

25th June, 1916.

1622. HONOURS AND REWARDS.

When recommendations for honours and rewards are submitted to Divisional Headquarters, one copy only is to be forwarded. The quadruplicate copies required by Corps Headquarters are prepared at Div'l Headquarters.

1623. STEEL HELMETS.

Steel Helmets of men evacuated from Field Ambulances sick and wounded, will be withdrawn from them and returned to D.A.D.O.S., Caps being issued in lieu at the Field Ambulances.

1624. IRON RATIONS.

With reference to C.R.O.No.812 dated 5-5-16, in addition to the reason for the demand of the Iron Rations being stated on the A.B.55 (Indent for Rations) and repeated by the Supply Officer concerned on A.F's W.3316 and W.3317, a certificate signed by the Officer Commanding the Unit requiring the Iron Rations will be obtained and endorsed by the Senior Supply Officer, who will thus make himself responsible that Iron Rations are not irregularly issued. This certificate will be subsequently handed to the R.S.O. or Officer i/c Depot from which the Iron Rations are drawn. (Authority Third Army B.D.S.&.T. I.D/1/41 dated 22-6-16, VI Corps Q/443.)

1625. MILLS RIFLE GRENADES.

Under instructions from War Office, Mills Grenades with aluminium plugs will not be fired from rifles.
(VI Corps Q/18/37).

1626. LEAVE.

The restrictions placed on HINDLEY in D.R.O.1373 are now removed.

LIEUT-COLONEL,
A.A.&.Q.M.G.
14TH (LIGHT) DIVISION.

NOTICE.

An Officers "Rest House" has been opened at ST.POL adjacent to the Station.

The house has a large comfortable combined sitting, reading and writing room; also dining room and bedroom accommodation for 20 officers.

Light refreshments may be obtained from E.F.O. close by.
The "Rest House" is for the accommodation of :-
(a) Officers passing through ST.POL, who have to spend the night there,
(b) Officers who have to spend a few hours in ST.POL en route.

Officers desirous of being accommodated for the night should apply to R.T.O. ST.POL Station.

14TH (LIGHT) DIVISION.

ROUTINE ORDERS.

27th June, 1916.

1627. LEAVE.

The attention of all units is drawn to the following extract from D.R.O.1621, which is republished:-
"From SUNDAY, 25TH INST, inclusive, the leave lorry will leave cross-roads WARLUS, for ST.POL daily at 4 p.m., going and returning via DUISANS".

1628. RETURNS.

The return called for in D.R.O.1186 is no longer required.

1629. SICK WASTAGE.

The following is the Sick Wastage return for week ended noon 24th instant :-

Unit	O.	O.R.	Unit	O.	O.R.
46th Bde R.F.A.		6.	9th K.R.R.C.	1	16.
47th Bde R.F.A.		4.	9th R.B.		9.
48th Bde R.F.A.		3.	42nd Bde M.G. Coy,		1.
49th Bde R.F.A.		3.	42nd Bde T.M.Bty,		1.
14th D.A.C.		2.	6th Somerset L.I.		14.
Y.14 T.M. Battery,	1	1.	6th D.C.L.I.	1	11
Z.14 T.M. Battery,		1.	6th K.O.Y.L.I.		13.
61st Field Co. R.E.		2.	10th D.L.I.	1	7.
62nd Field Co. R.E.		5.	43rd Bde M.G. Coy,		1.
89th Field Co. R.E.		2.	43rd Bde T.M. Battery,		Nil.
14th Signal Co.R.E.		Nil.	11th The King's,L'pool R,		4.
7th K.R.R.C.		5	14th Div'l Train,		5.
8th K.R.R.C.		3.	42nd Field Amb.		Nil.
7th R.B.		15.	42nd Field Amb.ASC att.		1.
8th R.B.		7.	43rd Field Amb.		1.
41st Bde M.G.Coy,	1	-	44th Field Amb.		2.
41st T.M.Battery,		Nil.	A.O.C.		Nil.
5th Ox & Bucks L.I.		6.	M.M.P.		1.
5th K.S L.I.		13.	25th Sanitary Section,		Nil.

Total Officers 5, Other Ranks 165.

LIEUT-COLONEL,
A.A.&.Q.M.G.
14TH (LIGHT) DIVISION.

NOTICES.

LOST: Believed removed from Hall of Soldiers' Club, ARRAS, on the night of June 24th, green Service BICYCLE, marked C.F.43 in white on back mudguard, and lower bar of frame. Mended saddle, with copper rivets Red tyres.
Information to Senior Chaplain, c/o 11th L'pool R.

FOUND: On 25th instant at BAC DU NORD, Black MARE, 16 hands, several white spots on saddle mark. Cut on near hind between hock and fetlock.
Information apply A.P.M.,14th Division.

14TH (LIGHT) DIVISION.

ROUTINE ORDERS.

28th June, 1916.

1630. REFILLING.

Refilling for all units except 41st Infantry Brigade Group will be at K.10 on the HABARCQ - ARRAS Road at 8.30 a.m. from 29th instant, inclusive.

1631. LEAVE.

D.R.O.1621 is cancelled and the following substituted:-
From Thursday 29th inst., inclusive, a leave bus will run as follows :-

AVESNES	depart	1.45 p.m.
HABARCQ	"	2.15 p.m.
AGNEZ	"	2.30 p.m.
WARLUS	"	2.50 p.m.
WANQUETIN,	"	3.10 p.m.
HAUTEVILLE,	"	3.25 p.m.
AVESNES,	"	3.40 p.m.
IZEL,	"	4.10 p.m.
LE HAMEAU,	"	4.15 p.m.
TILLOY,	"	4.20 p.m.
Road junction D.12.c.4.0	"	4.30 p.m.
ST.POL,	arrive	5.30 p.m.

Men proceeding on leave via HAVRE will leave the bus at Road junction D.12.c.4.0.(51.c.) for AUBIGNY.
On the return journey from ST.POL, the bus passes AGNEZ, WARLUS, WANQUETIN, HAUTEVILLE, in that order.

1632. SADDLE BLANKETS.

Reference C.R.O.995, Mounted Units will report by 12 noon 30th instant whether a second saddle blanket was brought overseas. If so, whether it is still in possession, and if not still in possession how it has been disposed of.

1633. ABSENTEES.

General Routine Order No.1379 dated 26-1-16 is again republished :-
"General Routine Orders Nos.679 and 1071 are cancelled. Commanding Officers will in future transmit Absentee Reports concerning men absent in the United Kingdom direct to the Officer i/c Records of the unit at home, who will also be informed direct of the return of any soldiers who have previously been reported as absent.
Reports of Absentees in this Country will, as heretofore, be sent to the A.P.M. of the formation concerned".

LIEUT-COLONEL,
A.A.&.Q.M.G.
14TH (LIGHT) DIVISION.

NOTICE.

FOUND: Dark Bay MARE, unbranded, height 15.2 hands.
Apply O.C.,278th Bde,R.F.A., 55th Divn.

14TH (LIGHT) DIVISION

ROUTINE ORDERS.

30th June, 1916.

1634. SENTENCES BY FIELD GENERAL COURT MARTIAL.

The following sentences awarded by Field General Court Martial have been ordered by the Army Commander to be put into execution :-

LIEUT-COLONEL,
A.A.&.Q.M.G.
14TH (LIGHT) DIVISION.

NOTICES.

LOST: On 26th inst, on road between ARRAS and WANQUETIN, Brown WATERPROOF, made by Pope & Bradley.
Information to A.P.M., 14th Division.

FOUND: In Officers' Latrine, near A.P.M's office on 29th inst: Officers Brown WATERPROOF (Short size) No initials or maker.
Information apply A.P.M., 14th Division.

DIVINE SERVICES
Sunday 2nd July, 1916.

C. OF E.
WARLUS: Rue du Chateau. Holy Communion 7 a.m.
              Morning Service 9.30 a.m.
              Evening Service 6 p.m.
BERNEVILLE: Church Army Hut. Holy Communion 8 a.m.
ARRAS: Soldiers' Club. Holy Communion 7 and 8.30 a.m.
              Evening Service 9.30 p.m.

R.C.
DUISANS: Parish Church: Mass at 9 a.m.
ARRAS: Hopital St.Jean, Mass at 9.30 a.m.
              Evening Service 5.15 p.m.
   "   St.Catherines. Mass at 11 a.m.
   "   St.Nicholas, Mass at 11 a.m.
   "   Notre Dame des Ardents, Mass at 10.30 a.m.
RONVILLE: Mass 9 a.m.
ACHICOURT: Evening service 5 p.m.
WARLUS: Mass 8 a.m.
BERNEVILLE: Mass 10.30 am.
DAINVILLE: Mass at 7 a.m.

14TH (LIGHT) DIVISION.

ROUTINE ORDERS.

1st July, 1916.

1635. MILLS GRENADES.

It is of great importance that the ends of the split safety pins of No.5 Grenades should be splayed out before the igniter is inserted, and instructions must be issued to all concerned to ensure that this is done.

If the ends of the pin are not splayed out there is a risk of the pin coming out when the grenade is being handled or transported, and this has already been the cause of serious accidents.
(Authority: Third Army O/60/6, dated 29-6-16, VI Corps Q/18/7).
    (C.R.O.1008 dated 30th June, 1916).

1636. STEEL HELMETS.

Attention is draw to Army Routine Order No.339, which is re-published :-
"Officers and men in possession of steel helmets will invariably wear them when on duty. They are not to be carried attached to the pack when on the line of march."

Disciplinary action will be taken in all cases where this order is disregarded.

1637. TRAFFIC CONTROL.

(a) No troops or transport will halt on the ST.POL – ARRAS road east of the road junction in G.13.d.

Parties of troops not exceeding a platoon may march along the road into ARRAS in case of necessity. Single lorries may pass along the road at 200 yards distance. Horsed vehicles may use the road as far as the road junction G.20.b.2.8. where they must turn off except in case of emergency. Motor cars and Motor Ambulance Wagons may use the road as required. Otherwise the road is not to be used by any traffic at all.

(b) The following alterations have been made to Third Army Traffic Control Map, and all copies are to be amended accordingly :-
    AGNEZ to DUISANS Rd can be used in both directions for
        Motor Transport.
(Authority Third Army QA/483 dated 30/6/16. VI Corps A/303.

LIEUT-COLONEL,
A.A.&.Q.M.G.
14TH (LIGHT) DIVISION.

NOTICE.
Church Services (Corrections).

C.E.
BERNEVILLE: Church Army Hut, Holy Communion 7 a.m. & 8.30 a.m.
WARLUS: Rue de Chateau,   Holy Communion 7.30 a.m.

R.C.
For "ARRAS, Notre Dame des Ardents, Mass at 10.30 a.m." read
    "ARRAS, Hopital St.Jean, Mass at 8 a.m."

14TH (LIGHT) DIVISION.

ROUTINE ORDERS.

2nd July, 1916.

1638. COURTS MARTIAL.

Attention is directed to Third Army Circular Memo. No.20 dated 29th June, 1916, circulated with D.R.Os of the 1st instant. A copy is to be laid before the Court which tries all cases of Self Inflicted injuries.

1639. DISCIPLINE.

Before cleaning any part of a rifle, the magazine will invariably be removed and the bolt opened.
This order is to be republished in the Regimental Orders of all units.
(Army Routine Order No.457 dated 1-7-16).

1640. FIRES.

General Routine Order 1295 and 1436 will be read out on parade to every unit at least once a month. Officers Commanding Unit are held responsible that all officers and men under their command are acquainted with these orders.

1641. VEHICLES.

Attention is drawn to General Routine Order No.981.
During the hot weather the spokes and felloe of wheels are liable to shrink, with the result that the tyres get loose and the wheels become unserviceable.
A simple method of preventing shrinkage consists in winding round the spokes, close up to the nave, a rope made of plaited hay or straw, which should be kept wetted. The rope is passed in and out through the spokes, half a dozen or so turns being generally used, and the coils secured in position by tying.
Indents for straw should be submitted to Supply Officers. Straw will be purchased by Requisitioning Officers and NOT by the troops.

LIEUT-COLONEL,
A.A.&.Q.M.G.
14TH (LIGHT) DIVISION.

14TH (LIGHT) DIVISION.

ROUTINE ORDERS.

4th July, 1916.

1642. BADGES.

Attention is drawn to G.R.O.55, which forbids the practice of soldiers disposing of their regimental badges.

1643. WASTE-PAPER.

Units in the Field are reminded that it is their duty to see that all waste-paper in offices, billets.,etc., is burnt. Failure to observe this rule may result in leakage of information to the enemy.

This order does not apply to offices from which waste-paper is collected under arrangements made by the Stationery Services.

(G.R.O.1653, dated 30-6-16).

1644. LEAVE.

When leave trains are available, no officer or man proceeding to or returning from leave is permitted to travel at the public expense on a French passenger train.

1645. LEAVE BUS.

The bus referred to in D.R.O.1631 dated 28th June, is cancelled.

1646. BAYONET FIGHTING -Sacks for.

Units will indent on D.A.D.O.S. for Sacks for Bayonet Training, scale 100 per Battalion, quoting as authority, O.S.R/4012 dated 22-6-16.

LIEUT-COLONEL,
A.A.&.Q.M.G.
14TH (LIGHT) DIVISION.

NOTICE.

FOUND: ON WARLUS-BERNEVILLE Road, in afternoon of 3rd inst: fold-up LANTERN in tin case, with leather strap. Brass plate on side of case marked "Jas.Hinks & Sons, Birmingham".
Apply A.P.M., 14th Division.

14TH (LIGHT) DIVISION.

ROUTINE ORDERS.

5th July, 1916.

1647. BICYCLE SADDLES.

    n Reference C.R.O.1017, reports should reach this office by 12 noon the 7th instant. Nil returns are not required.

1648. APPOINTMENT.

    Capt. J. Benskin, D.S.O., R.E. is appointed Commandant, Divisional School and is granted the temporary and local rank of Major whilst so employed.

C.L.C. Hamilton
LIEUT-COLONEL,
A.A.&.Q.M.G.
14TH (LIGHT) DIVISION.

14TH (LIGHT) DIVISION.

ROUTINE ORDERS.

6th July, 1916.

1649. IRON RATIONS.

All Units will render a certificate through the usual channels, to reach this office by July 9th, that every officer and man is in possession of an Iron Ration.

1650. SICK WASTAGE.

Sick wastage Return for week ended noon 1st instant is as follows :-

Unit	O.	O.R.	Unit	O.	O.R.
46th Bde R.F.A.	2	6	9th K.R.R.C.		28.
47th Bde R.F.A.		3.	9th R.B.		18.
48th Bde R.F.A.		Nil.	42nd Bde M.G.Coy,		4.
49th Bde R.F.A.		5.	42nd T.M.Battery,		Nil.
14th D.A.C.		9.	6th Somerset L.I.	1	10.
X.14 T.M.Battery,		Nil.	6th D.C.L.I.	1	19.
Y.14 T.M.Battery,		Nil.	6th K.O.Y.L.I.		4.
Z.14 T.M. Battery,		1.	10th Durham L.I.		12.
61st Field Co. R.E.		2.	43rd Bde M.G.Coy,		1.
62nd Field Co. R.E.		1.	43rd T.M.Battery,		Nil.
89th Field Co. R.E.		1.	11th L'pool R		12.
14th Signal Co.R.E.		1.	14th Div.Train.		2.
7th K.R.R.C.		9.	42nd Field Ambulance,		Nil.
8th K.R.R.C.	1	9.	43rd Field Ambulance,		2.
7th R.B.		22.	44th Field Ambulance,		2.
8th R.B.	1	21.	25th Sanitary Section,		Nil.
41st Bde M.G. Coy,		1.	M.M.P.		Nil.
41st T.M. Battery,		2.	A.O.C.		Nil.
5th Ox & Bucks L.I.		14.			
5th K.S.L.I.		10.			

Total Officers 6, Other Ranks 231.

LIEUT-COLONEL,
A.A.&.Q.M.G.
14TH (LIGHT) DIVISION.

NOTICES.

LOST: Bicycle, from Barracks in Rue des Quartre Crosses, ARRAS, marked on rear mud guard with white dot in centre of red triangle and letter No.3 Section,5, in white. Last seen 21-6-16.
Information to C.R.E., 14th Division.

LOST: Bicycle (new) No.B.1917 from doorway on Faubourg d'Amiens - ARRAS road, on night of 16-6-16 between 11 p.m. and midnight.
Information to A.P.M., 14th Division.

FOUND: Chesnut MARE, about 14 hands, white blaze, No.392 on near fore, 32 on off fore. T.56 off hind, Shoe off near fore, A.C. on near shoulder. Found galloping on DAINVILLE - ARRAS Road.
Apply A/49 Bde R.F.A.

14TH (LIGHT) DIVISION.

ROUTINE ORDERS.

7th July, 1916.

1651. The following message from HIS MAJESTY THE KING has been received by the Commander-in-Chief :-
"   Please convey to the Army under your Command my sincere congratulations on the results achieved in the recent fighting. I am proud of my troops, none could have fought more bravely,
                                                GEORGE, R.I.   "
To be republished in Regimental Orders.

1652. WAR DIARIES.

Reference Field Service Regulations, Part II, Section 140, para 2:
The following procedure will in future be adopted with regard to the transmission of War Diaries (Original copy). The C.R.A., C.R.E., G.O.C. Infantry Brigades, A.D.M.S. and O.C., 14th Divisional Train will collect the War Diaries of Units under their Command and forward them to Divisional H.Qrs on the 1st of each month, accompanied by a Roll of Units showing the number of the Volume and the period covered by each Diary enclosed.
War Diaries of other Units will be forwarded direct to Divisional Headquarters by the date stated.
Each Diary will be enclosed in a special cover as laid down in F.S. Regs, Part II, Section 140, para 4.

1653. OFFICERS' SURPLUS KITS.

Instructions for disposal of Officers' Surplus kits are contained in G.R.O.1435.
The instructions for securing the packages are the same as those for securing kits of Officers deceased, missing, sick, or wounded. They are contained in G.R.O.~~1484~~ 1387
Attention is drawn to the following points :-
(1) Every package, whether kit bag, box, or bale, must be secured by string and the ends of the string must be secured on the back of a label by a wax seal.
(2) The wax-seal must be sealed with a numbered seal supplied to the unit by A.O.D. Every unit should be in possession of such a seal for use with kits of killed and wounded officers. Any unit which has not got such a seal is to demand one at once.
(3) The label will bear a Censor stamp, and officer's signature. This guarantees that no explosives, trophies or military information is contained in the package, and if such articles or information are found there by the Censor, the officer is liable to heavy penalties on conviction by Court Martial.
(4) Surplus kits must be addressed to the place to which it is intended that they should be sent. They are handed over by Military Forwarding Officer to Messrs Cox & Co., who will forward them as addressed.
(5) The special labels issued for kits of deceased, etc., officers are NOT TO BE USED for surplus kits.
(6) *General nature of contents of each package must be stated on label thus "Officers Surplus clothing".*

See D.R.O. 1654

                                                LIEUT-COLONEL,
                                                A.A.& Q.M.G.
                                                14TH (LIGHT) DIVISION.

Church Services on reverse.

CHURCH SERVICES FOR SUNDAY
9TH JULY, 1916.
****

C. OF E.
<u>WARLUS</u>: Rue du Chateau, Holy Communion 8.am.
                        Morning Service 9.30 a.m.
                        Evening Service, 6 p.m.
<u>BERNEVILLE</u>: Church Army Hut: Holy Communion 7 a.m.
                        Morning Service 11 a.m.
<u>ARRAS</u>. Soldiers' Club Chapel: Holy Communion 8.30 a.m. & 10 a.m.
                        Evening Service 9.30 p.m.
<u>WANQUETIN</u>. Church Army Hut: Evening Service 7 p.m.

    Elsewhere by arrangement with units.

R.C.
<u>DAINVILLE</u>, Mass in Parish Church at 7 a.m.
<u>DUISANS</u>.   "   "   "   "   9 a.m.
         Evening Service at 5.30 p.m.
<u>ARRAS</u>: Mass at Hopital St.Jean at 9.30 a.m.
       "   " St.Nicholas at 11.30 a.m.
        Evening Service at Hospital St.Jean, 5.15 p.m.
<u>RONVILLE</u>. Mass at 9.30 a.m.
<u>ACHICOURT</u>. Mass at 10.30 a.m.
Mass for "B" Coy, 11th King's L'pool Regt. at 10.30 a.m.

14TH (LIGHT) DIVISION.

ROUTINE ORDERS.

8th July, 1916.

1654. OFFICERS' SURPLUS KITS.

(a) Reference D.R.O.1653 of yesterday, the instructions for securing packages are contained in G.R.O.1387 and not in G.R.O.1484 as therein stated. All copies of yesterday's Divisional Routine Orders are to be amended accordingly.

(b) In addition to the points brought to notice in D.R.O.1653, the general nature of the contents of each package must be stated on the label thus "Officer's Surplus Clothing".

1655. TRAFFIC CONTROL.

The road BAC DU NORD - BEAUMETZ is closed by day to all traffic, including motor cars.
A barrier will be placed at BAC DU NORD.

LIEUT-COLONEL,
A.A.&.Q.M.G.
14TH (LIGHT) DIVISION.

NOTICE.

LOST: On road between DAINVILLE RAILWAY BRIDGE and ARRAS, about 11 a.m. 8th instant, Plain CANVAS BAG, with ring round neck. Contents:- Uncensored letters and parcel in tin tobacco box.
Information to A.P.M., 14th Division.

14TH (LIGHT) DIVISION.

ROUTINE ORDERS.

9th July, 1916.

1656. MEDICAL.

Reference D.R.O.1618, cases for dental treatment are no longer to be sent to 42nd Field Ambulance, but treatment will still be given at 44th Field Ambulance, (D.R.S.) on Tuesdays and Fridays.

1657. SICK WASTAGE.

The following is the Sick Wastage Return for week ended noon 8th instant :-

	O.	O.R.		O.	O.R.
46th F.A. Bde,		3	5th Ox & Bucks L.I.		11.
47th F.A. Bde,		3	5th K.S.L.I.		7.
48th F.A. Bde,		1	9th K.R.R.C.		17.
49th F.A. Bde,		2	9th R.B.		6.
14th D.A.C.		3.	42nd Bde M.G. Coy,		Nil.
X.14 T.M. Battery,		Nil.	42nd T.M. Battery,		Nil.
Y.14 T.M. Battery,		Nil.	6th Somerset L.I.		3.
Z.14 T.M. Battery,		Nil.	6th D.C.L.I.		10.
61st Field Co. R.E.		2.	6th K.O.Y.L.I.		5.
62nd Field Co. R.E.		3.	10th Durham L.I.		10.
89th Field Co. R.E.		2.	43rd Bde M.G.Coy,		1.
14th Signal Co.R.E.		1.	43rd T.M. Battery,		Nil.
7th K.R.R.C.		9.	11th L'pool R		4.
8th K.R.R.C.		14.	14th Div'l Train,		1.
7th R.B.		4.	A.S.C. att.Div'l H.Qrs,		1.
8th R.B.		6.	42nd F.Amb,		2
41st Bde M.G. Coy,		2.	43rd F.Amb,		1
41st Bde T.M. Battery,		Nil.	44th F.Amb,		2.
			25th Sanitary Section,		Nil.

Total: Officers NIL, Other Ranks 136.

1658. PURCHASE OF BREAD.

The purchase of bread from civilian bakeries and shops before the hour of 11-0 a.m. is prohibited in any Commune where the Maire may require it, on his representing the matter to the Officer Commanding the troops billeted there. (Authority Q.M.G. Q/5055, dated 6/7/16, VI Corps Q/593.)

1659. BATHS.

The baths at AGNEZ are open and available for all troops at AGNEZ and DUISANS.
Town Commandant, AGNEZ will allot hours of bathing and all applications for baths will be addressed to him.
150 men can bath per hour.

A.H. Hamilton

LIEUT-COLONEL,
A.A.&.Q.M.G.
14TH (LIGHT) DIVISION.

NOTICE.

LOST: Brown WATERPROOF, Ordnance make, on road between BRIQUETERIE and WARLUS, on afternoon 6th inst. Information to A.P.M., 14th Division.

14TH (LIGHT) DIVISION.

ROUTINE ORDERS.

11th June, 1916.

1660. ACCOUNTING FOR SUPPLIES.

Attention is drawn to G.R.O.1673.
Rations overdrawn on any day owing to casualties are to be underdrawn within 3 days.
A.F. F.773 is checked in the Division Office with A.F. B.213 and the numbers must correspond exactly.

1661. CLOSING OF ESTAMINETS

With reference to General Routine Order No.1107, Estaminets will, until further notice, be closed to British Troops except between the hours of 12 noon to 2 p.m., and 6 p.m. to 8 p.m.
(G.R.O.1681 dated 7-7-16).

C.H. Hamilton
LIEUT-COLONEL,
A.A.&.Q.M.G.
14TH (LIGHT) DIVISION.

14TH (LIGHT) DIVISION.

ROUTINE ORDERS.

12th July, 1916.

1662. TRANSPORT.

The normal method by which Officers, N.C.Os and men are transported to railhead is by empty supply lorry from refilling point. The Supply lorries leave refilling point half an hour before the hour of refilling.

Special arrangements made for transporting classes of instruction and other large parties, will be notified when special arrangements are made.

All other Officers, N.C.Os and men will use the normal means of transportation as above.

[signature]
LIEUT-COLONEL,
A.A.&.Q.M.G.
14TH (LIGHT) DIVISION.

NOTICES.

LOST: From H.Q.15th Bde R.F.A., BICYCLE, No.H.956. Information to O.C., 15th Bde R.F.A.

LOST: Since night of 10th/11th July, from 2/2nd West Lancs Field Co. R.E.(T.F) Orderly Room, Government BICYCLE, marked on back mudguard 2/2nd W.L.Fld.Co.R.E. No.33. Green Machine with rim brakes: red tyres.
Information to 2/2nd West Lancs Field Co.R.E.(T.F), 55th Division.

14TH (LIGHT) DIVISION.

ROUTINE ORDERS.

13th July, 1916.

1663. IDENTITY DISCS.

It has been brought to notice that many men lately received into Field Ambulances and Casualty Clearing Stations were not wearing an identity disc. Great difficulty has consequently been experienced in establishing the identity of those who were unconscious when admitted.

The attention of Commanding Officers is directed to Section 90 (i) Field Service Regulations, Part II. Weekly inspection is to be made in all units to ensure that the provisions of this paragraph are carried out.

(A.R.O.461).

1664. PRISONERS' ARMS AND EQUIPMENT.

General Routine Order 595 of 31st January, 1915 is re-published :-

"Prisoners sentenced to penal servitude or imprisonment will not take their arms and equipment to prison with them. Their arms, etc., will be handed over to the Divisional Ordnance Officer for return to the Base".

1665. HIRE OF LAND.

Copies of all agreements made by the Rent Officer of the Area are deposited with the Maires of the Communes.

Town Commandants will compile lists of fields which are hired from the information in possession of the Maires.

They will not allow troops to occupy unnecessarily any fields which are not already hired.

1666. CLOSING OF ESTAMINETS.

D.R.O.1661 dated 11th inst referring to the hours during which Estaminets may be open, does not refer to ARRAS, in which Town there are special orders in force.

1667. MARKS ON VEHICLES.

Divisional and Unit marks on vehicles are to be maintained at all times in such condition as to be easily recognisable.

The marking of all vehicles is to be examined and the marks repainted where necessary, by July 25th.

Captain
for
LIEUT-COLONEL,
A.A.&.Q.M.G.
14TH (LIGHT) DIVISION.

14TH (LIGHT) DIVISION.

ROUTINE ORDERS.

14th July, 1916.

1668. SENTENCES BY FIELD GENERAL COURT MARTIAL. Deleted

The following sentences awarded by F.G.C.M. have been ordered by the Army Commander to be put into execution :-

1669. LORRIES.

Lorries detailed for special duties are not to be called upon to do any journeys in addition to those for which they have been sent out, unless the additional duty is a matter of urgency. Drivers have orders not to deviate from the instructions given to them by their Commanding Officers without a written order from an officer. Officers giving such orders must immediately inform the Column or Park to which the lorry belongs by telegraph or telephone that the lorry is carrying out further duties and will be late returning to its own unit. Whenever possible a Staff Officer should be consulted before such orders are given to a lorry and the officer giving the order is to bear in mind that lorries are often required for other important duties as soon as they reach their own unit and that any delay in their return may interfere with other movements of troops or ammunition.

Captain
for
LIEUT-COLONEL,
A.A.&.Q.M.G.
14TH (LIGHT) DIVISION.

CHURCH SERVICES, 16TH JUNE, 1916.

C OF E.

WARLUS: Rue du Chateau, Holy Communion 8 a.m.
　　　　　　　　　　　　 Morning Service 9.30 a.m.
　　　　　　　　　　　　 Evening Service 6 p.m.
BERNEVILLE: Church Army Hut)
WANQUETIN:　　　"　　"　　") Holy Communion, 8 a.m.
AGNEZ;　　　　　"　　"　　") Evening Service 7 p.m.
ARRAS: Soldiers' Club: Holy Communion 8.30 a.m.
　　　　　　　　　　　　 Evening Service 9.30 p.m.
Elsewhere by arrangement with units.

R.C.

ARRAS: Mass at St.Nicholas for 8th R.B. in R.C.Chapel, Bn.H.Q. 9 am
　"　　"　" Hopital St.Jean, 9.30 a.m.
　"　　"　" St.Nicholas at 11 a.m.
　"　　Evening Service, Hopital St.Jean 5.15 p.m.
　"　　"　　"　　8th R.B. 5.30 p.m.
ACHICOURT: Mass at 8.30 a.m.
ST.SAVEUR:　"　" 10.30 a.m. for troops in St.SAVEUR & RONVILLE.
DUISANS: Mass at 11.30 a.m.

(Contd)

WESLEYANS, PRESBYTERIANS AND NONCONFORMISTS.

ARRAS: 10 a.m. for "B" Coy.6th D.C.L.I. in Billets.

2 p.m. at 19 Rue de trois fillores for 8th R.B., L'pool R, M.G.Corps, and T.M. Battery.
3 p.m. at Main Dressing Station for 44th & 42nd F.Amb.
5.30 p.m. at School Room for 8th K.R.R. & transport lines.
7 p.m. at Barrocks Reading Room for N.Z.E.Tun.Co. & 14th Div.
　　　　　　　　　　　　　　Pioneer Detachment.

14TH (LIGHT) DIVISION.

ROUTINE ORDERS.

15th July, 1916.

1670. DESIGNATIONS - OFFICERS.

"Battalion Machine Gun Officers" will in future be known as "Battalion Lewis Gun Officers".

1671. CAMP KETTLES.

With reference to Army Routine Order No.463 dated 12/7/16:
Approval is given for 40 extra Camp Kettles per Battalion to be demanded where necessary.
Authority to be quoted on indents is Third Army M.B/1249 dated 14/7/16.

LIEUT-COLONEL,
A.A.&.Q.M.G.
14TH (LIGHT) DIVISION.

14TH (LIGHT) DIVISION.

ROUTINE ORDERS.

16th June, 1916.

1672. WINTER HUTTING - STOVES.

All stoves issued during the winter months for heating billets, huts, and offices, will be returned to the C.R.E. at the BRIQUETERIE, K.28.d. Sheet 51.c. not later than the 19th instant.

1673. SICK WASTAGE.

The following is the Sick Wastage return for week ended noon 15th instant :-

	O.	O.R.		O.	O.R.
46th F.A.Bde,		4.	5th Ox & Bucks L.I.	1	6
47th F.A. Bde,		2.	5th K.S.L.I.		8.
48th F.A. Bde,		1.	9th K.R.R.C.		3.
49th F.A. Bde,		1.	9th R.B.		7.
14th D.A.C.		3.	42nd Bde M.G. Coy,		Nil.
X.14 T.M. Battery,		Nil.	42nd Bde T.M. Battery,		Nil.
Y.14 T.M. Battery,		Nil.	6th Somerset L.I.		2.
Z.14 T.M. Battery,		Nil.	6th D.C.L.I.		3.
61st Field Co. R.E.		2.	6th K.O.Y.L.I.		9.
62nd Field Co. R.E.		1.	10th Durham L.I.		6.
89th Field Co. R.E.		3.	43rd Bde M.G. Coy,		Nil.
14th Signal Co.R.E.		1.	43rd Bde T.M. Battery,		Nil.
7th K.R.R.C.		1.	11th L'pool R		4.
8th K.R.R.C.	1	4.	14th Div'l Train,		Nil.
7th R.B.		6.	14th Supply Column	1	-
8th R.B.		6.	RAMC, att Div'l H.Qrs,		1.
41st Bde M.G. Coy.		1.	42nd F.Amb,		1.
41st Bde T.M.Bty.		2.	43rd F.Amb,		3.
K.R.R.C. attd. 7th R.B.		1.	43rd F.Amb, ASC att.		1.
			44th F.Amb.		Nil.

Totals: Officers 3, Other Ranks 93.

1674. THE RESPONSIBILITIES OF REGIMENTAL OFFICERS WITH REGARD TO PREVENTION OF MANGE AMONG ARMY HORSES.

Attention is drawn to G.R.O.1685 and to the memorandum issued with G.R.Os, on the responsibilities of regimental officers with regard to prevention of mange.

1675. WAGONS LIMBERED G.S.

In future supplies, the tailboards of the fore and hind portions of limbered G.S.Wagons will differ.
To ensure the correct pattern being obtained, units must state clearly on their indents whether tailboards for hind or fore portions are required. (G.R.O.1686).

1676. CHANGE IN NOMENCLATURE.

With reference to G.R.O.1210.
The nomenclature of "Rimers" for use with Lewis guns has now been changed to "Cleaners gas regulator".
G.R.O.1210 will be amended accordingly.
(List of Changes 17741). (G.R.O.1687).

LIEUT-COLONEL.
A.A.&Q.M.G.
14TH (LIGHT) DIVISION.

14TH (LIGHT) DIVISION.

ROUTINE ORDERS.

17th July, 1916.

1677. HONOURS AND REWARDS.

The General Officer Commanding-in-Chief has, under special authority of HIS MAJESTY THE KING, awarded the Military Cross, dated 1st July, 1916, to the undermentioned Warrant Officers :-

Coy.Sergt.Major T. Peppin,   6th Somerset L.I.
Coy.Sergt.Major (A/R.S.M) W.Harris,   9th K.R.R.C.
Coy.Sergt.Major S. Mound,   5th Bn. K.S.L.I.

LIEUT-COLONEL,
A.A.&.Q.M.G.
14TH (LIGHT) DIVISION.

NOTICE.

LOST: On evening of 14th instant, in APPAS, a Grey PONY, 14.2 hands, Hog mane, very long tail, No.7 on off fore, Government mark on hindquarters. Saddle, and blanket attached. Information to O.C., 6th Somerset L.I.

14th (Light) Division
Routine Orders

19th July, 1916.

1678 Ration - Pork & Beans

Reference CRO 1062. Units wishing to report on the Pork & Beans ration will do so through the usual channels to reach this office by 12 noon 23rd inst. In the absence of a report it will be concluded that the unit concerned has no complaints and agree with CRO. 1047.

1679 Traffic Map

The following alterations should be made to Third Army Traffic Control Map

Gouy - Monchiet — West to East
Monchiet - Simencourt — South to North
Simencourt - Gouy — East to West

(Third Army Routine Order No 468).

14TH (LIGHT) DIVISION.

ROUTINE ORDERS.

20th July, 1916.

1680. **BICYCLES - Loss of.**

Several losses of bicycles have recently been reported. In some cases they are alleged to have been stolen while their riders went into billets or offices on duty. In others they have become deficient from the place in which the bicycles of the unit were stored.

It is apparent that bicycle thieving is prevalent. Greater care is to be taken by Commanding Officers as regards the storage of bicycles, and by Officers and men using bicycles, as to where they leave them.

The cost of replacing a lost bicycle falls on the unit or individual who lost it unless the circumstances are of a most exceptional nature.

LIEUT-COLONEL,
A.A.&.Q.M.G.
14TH (LIGHT) DIVISION.

NOTICE.

STRAYED: On 14th instant, BAY GELDING, marked near hind 13/63. Branded 88 on near quarter, with appointments marked :- Saddle B.G.5, Bit A.10, W.D. mark and B.64 on Buckling pieces: Head chain, stable head collar.
Information to O.C. B/277 Bde R.F.A.

14TH (LIGHT) DIVISION.

ROUTINE ORDERS.

21st July, 1916.

1681. STORES.

All stores in possession of Brigade Machine Gun Companies, which are not shewn on the revised Mobilization Store Table for a Machine Gun Company (A.F. G.1098-203, dated June 1916) will be returned to Ordnance Officers, and a report rendered to Divisional Headquarters through the usual channel of any such stores returned.

Indents should be put forward for any additional stores allowed by the revised table.

VI Corps Q/50.

A.L. Hamilton
LIEUT-COLONEL,
A.A.&.Q.M.G.
14TH (LIGHT) DIVISION.

DIVINE SERVICES,
Sunday – 23rd July, 1916.

C OF E.

```
WARLUS: Rue de Chateau:   Holy Communion, 8 a.m.
                          Morning Service 9.30 a.m.
                          Evening Service 7 p.m.
ARRAS: Soldiers' Club:    Holy Communion 8.30 a.m.
                          Morning Service 10 a.m.
                          Evening Service 9.30 p.m.
AGNEZ: Church Army Hut:   Holy Communion 8 a.m.
                          Morning Service 11 a.m.
                          Evening Service 7 p.m.
```
Elsewhere by arrangement with units.

R.C.

MASS at DAINVILLE Parish Church at 8 a.m.
  " " ST. NICOLAS in Chapel at Bn.H.Qrs at 9 a.m.
  " " Hopital St.Jean 9.30 and 11 a.m.
  " " St.Sauveur at 10 a.m.
  " " DUISANS Parish Church at 11.30 a.m.
Service for "A" Co. D.L.I. 10.30 a.m.
Evening Service at DUISANS Parish Church 5.30 p.m.
    "   "   " DAINVILLE "   " 6 p.m.

14TH (LIGHT) DIVISION.

ROUTINE ORDERS.

22nd July, 1916.

1682. HONOURS AND REWARDS.

Under authority granted by HIS MAJESTY THE KING, Military Medals have been awarded to the undermentioned N.C.Os and men :-

8th K.R.R.C.

No. 4782, Sergeant R. Hughes,
A/1349, Corporal G. Hannas,
6707, L/Corpl. J. Barnett,
14048,   "   R. Whitehouse,
A/3526, Rfmn. F. Edwards.

9th K.R.R.C.

No. R/11561, L/Corpl. W. Bowcock.

42nd Bde M.G.Company.

No. 19955. Private J. Davis.

1683. LEAVE.

Reference G.R.O.1679.
The names of Warrant Officers, N.C.Os and men who become eligible for one month's leave under the terms of above order will be submitted to Divisional Headquarters for a special leave vacancy to be allotted.

Applications will be accompanied by a statement (a) That the terms of Enlistment have been verified by O.C., Records, (b) That the necessary A.Fs have been signed by the Applicant, (c) giving date discharge would have become due.

LIEUT-COLONEL,
A.A.&.Q.M.G.
14TH (LIGHT) DIVISION.

NOTICE.

FOUND: Bay MARE, aged, about 15 hands, hog mane, two white hind fetlocks, white heel near fore, old scar off stifle. Apply Transport Officer, 9th Rifle Brigade.

14TH (LIGHT) DIVISION.

ROUTINE ORDERS.

23rd July, 1916.

1684. REFILLING.

Refilling from 25th instant onwards will be at 7.30 a.m.

1685. STANDARD HOSE COUPLINGS.

It is required to collect all standard hose couplings available from damaged hose.

Any spare or damaged hose couplins in possession of units or that may be found derelict are to be returned to R.E. Park, DAINVILLE, or to the Salvage Company, WARLUS, with the least possible delay.

1686. TENT BOTTOMS.

Units will report through the usual channel, to reach Divisional Headquarters by noon 26th instant, as to the number of tent bottoms C.S.L. and wood marquee bottoms in possession which is estimated will be available towards next winters requirements.

(Authority Third Army O/49/7, dated 21-7-16, VI Corps Q/26/381).

1687. CLOTHING.

The following extract from Army Council Instruction No. 1321 of 1916, is published for information and guidance :-

ARMY COUNCIL INSTRUCTION.
No. 1321 of 1916.

1321. Utilization of part worn clothing *** &c.

* * * *

"This is an emergency measure to meet existing conditions, and though the standard of the renovated part-worn clothing may be much below that of ordinary peace issues, it must be accepted without question and continued in wear to the utmost possible extent. So long as wearable no objection to its re-issue can be entertained."

(Authority Third Army O/28/21, dated 18-7-16. VI Corps Q/83).

1688. SENTENCES BY FIELD GENERAL COURTS MARTIAL.

The following sentences awarded by F.G.C.M. have been ordered by the Army Commander to be put into execution :-

14TH (LIGHT) DIVISION.
ROUTINE ORDERS.

24th July, 1916.

1689. ARRAS - TOWN ORDERS.

Attention is drawn to C.R.O.1076 dated 23-7-16.

1690. CARRIERS FOR LEWIS GUN AMMUNITION.

The report called for in C.R.O.1077 of the 23rd inst should reach this office by noon 27th instant.

1691. REVOLVER AMMUNITION.

Reference C.R.O.1078 dated 23-7-16, the report called for in (iii) should reach this office by noon 26th inst.

1692. SACKS.

Attention is drawn to C.R.O.1079 dated 23-7-16.

1693. IRON RATIONS.

It is notified for information that it is impossible to issue the grocery portion of the Iron Ration separately from the complete Iron Ration.
(Authority Third Army S/357 d/- 22-7-16. VI Corps Q/341/16)

1694. IGNITERS, No.5 Grenades, Fitting of.

The operation of putting igniters into No.5 Grenades is not free from danger, and, in view of the serious accidents which have recently occurred in the process, the following instructions will be observed :-
(a) As far as possible, the work should be done in the open and NOT in a cellar, dug-out or other confined space, and men should not be permitted to crowd around.
(b) Good light, so that the grenades can be carefully inspected, is important.
(c) Igniters are not to be inserted in, or removed from, grenades within five yards of any stack of grenades unless a substantial splinter-proof traverse intervenes.
(d) A pit three feet deep, or failing this, a large tub of water, to be within close reach of all men fitting igniters to grenades, so that if a grenade ignites it can be at once dropped into the pit, or tub, where the explosion will be confined.
(e) A responsible officer is to be present whilst grenades are being fitted with igniters, and he will exercise the closest supervision over the work.
(A.R.O.470 dated 23-7-16).

1695. OVERLOADING OF VEHICLES.

Army Routine Order No.309 of 19-2-16 is republished for information :-
"The practice of adding super-structures to vehicles, so as to enable them to carry extra loads is forbidden.
The axletree and wheels of each class of vehicle are only designed for a definite load, which can be contained in the existing body. To add to this load causes an undue strain on all parts of the vehicle, which results in a breakdown."

(Continued)

-2-

1896. **SICK WASTAGE.**

The following is the Sick Wastage Return for week ended noon 22nd instant :-

Unit	O.	O.R.	Unit	O.	O.R.
46th F.A. Bde,		Nil.	5th Ox & Bucks L.I.		9.
47th F.A. Bde,		Nil.	5th K.S.L.I.		7.
48th F.A. Bde,		1.	9th K.R.R.C.		6.
49th F.A. Bde,	1	3.	9th R.B.		7.
14th D.A.C.		3.	42nd Bde M.G. Coy,		1.
X.14 T.M. Battery,		Nil.	42nd Bde T.M. Battery,		Nil.
Y.14 T.M. Battery,		Nil.	6th Som.L.I.		5.
Z.14 T.M. Battery,		Nil.	6th D.C.L.I.		5.
8th M.M.G.Battery,		1.	6th K.O.Y.L.I.		5.
61st Field Co. R.E.		Nil.	10th Durham L.I.		4.
62nd Field Co. R.E.		2.	43rd Bde M.G. Coy,		Nil.
89th Field Co. R.E.		2.	43rd Bde T.M. Bty,		Nil.
14th Signal Co.R.E.		1.	11th L'pool R	1	5.
7th K.R.R.C.		6.	14th Div'l Train,		Nil.
8th K.R.R.C.		7.	14th Div'l Supply Column,		Nil.
7th R.B.					
8th R.B.	1	6.	42nd F.Amb,		1.
41st Bde M.G. Coy,	1	1.	43rd F.Amb,		1.
41st Bde T.M. Bty,		Nil.	44th F.Amb,		Nil.
			44th F.Amb, ASC att		1.

Totals Officers 5 Other Ranks, 88.

LIEUT-COLONEL,
A.A.&Q.M.G.
14TH (LIGHT) DIVISION.

NOTICE.

A Y.M.C.A. Institution will be opened in ARRAS at 4 Rue du Tripot, from Thursday inclusive.

14TH (LIGHT) DIVISION.

ROUTINE ORDERS.

25th July, 1916.

1697. POSTAL REFILLING.

There will be no special postal refilling on or after 27th instant.

Mails will be delivered to units at Supply Refilling Points.

Post Orderlies will be attached to Train Companies and accompany the Supply wagons.

1698. TRAFFIC.

Wagons and other vehicles must not be parked in streets and open places, including barrack enclosures in ARRAS.

They must be drawn up under cover or close to buildings.

They must not move by daylight.

LIEUT-COLONEL,
A.A.&Q.M.G.
14TH (LIGHT) DIVISION.

NOTICE.

LOST: BAY MULE, (Gelding) about 15.2 hands, natural tail, Scar near fore coronary band.
Information to 42nd Infantry Bde Headquarters.

14TH (LIGHT) DIVISION.

ROUTINE ORDERS.

27th July, 1916.

1699. HONOURS AND REWARDS.

Under authority of HIS MAJESTY THE KING, The Commander-in-Chief has awarded the Military Cross to :-

Captain T.M. RIXON,	8th K.R.R.C.
2/Lieut. P.A. COOKE,	8th K.R.R.C.
2/Lieut. M.C. MOWBRAY,	89th Field Co. R.E.

1700. POSTAL.

Letters and parcels for despatch will be taken to refilling point daily by empty supply wagon.
Special arrangements for collection will cease from today.

1701. ANIMALS SICK ON THE LINE OF MARCH.

Attention is drawn to D.R.O.1049 dated 25-12-15;
Units leaving animals behind will forward full details as to name of person and place where the animal is left, and also furnish description of animal and unit to which it belongs, to A.D.V.S., 14th Division.

1702. 2" TRENCH MORTAR - FAULTY IGNITION.

Attention is drawn to C.R.O.1087 dated 25-7-16.

1703. 2" TRENCH MORTAR - RIFLE MECHANISM.

Attention is drawn to C.R.O.1088 dated 25-7-16.

[signature]
LIEUT-COLONEL,
A.A.&Q.M.G.
14TH (LIGHT) DIVISION.

NOTICES.

MISSING: Green bicycle, No.10569, B.S.A.Fittings, from near Wood 105, Nr. DAINVILLE.
Any information to Capt. Lawrence, c/o Town Major, ARRAS.

LOST: In ARRAS on night of 26/27th, TWO brown Baym CHARGERS, 15 hands high, 6 lon hoofs, VI on left flanks.
Officers saddle on one horse.
Information to O.C., 6th Native Cavalry Regiment.

14TH (LIGHT) DIVISION.

ROUTINE ORDERS.

2nd August, 1916

1706. ANTI-GAS HELMETS.

All Anti-gas helmets are to be examined and indents submitted to D.A.D.O.S. by 4th instant for those required for exchange.

1707. RIFLES - Revised Scale.

Attention is drawn to VI Corps Routine Order No.1105 dated 30th July, 1916.

LIEUT-COLONEL,
A.A.&.Q.M.G.
14TH (LIGHT) DIVISION.

14TH (LIGHT) DIVISION.

ROUTINE ORDERS.

7th August 1916.

1708. IDENTITY DISCS.

Identity discs of the official pattern are to be worn by all officers, N.C.Os and men in the manner laid down in F.S.Regs, Part II, para 90, sub-para 1, that is by a string round the neck.

There is no objection to identity discs of other kinds being worn in addition to the official pattern but no other pattern or other method of wearing may be substituted for the official pattern and method of wearing.

1709. INDENTS - Shirts and Socks.

Units will forward indents as usual for shirts and socks required to keep up the current establishment. These articles will be issued whenever the supply of new or washed clothing permits.

1710. PROMOTION.

No. P.961, A/Sergeant I.C. Sims, H.M.P., attached 14th Division is promoted to the acting rank of Squadron Sergeant Major, without extra pay, pension, or other allowances of that rank.

(Authority Third Army No. AC/1377, VI Corps A/1640, 14th Divn. A.661).

1711. ENEMY DOCUMENTS.

All documents captured from the enemy, or found in places occupied by the enemy, or which may contain information about the enemy, must be forwarded without delay to the nearest General Staff Officer.

Neglect to obey the instructions on this point not only endangers the safety and lives of comrades, but may also have a grave effect on the success of operations. Such negligence must therefore be treated as a most serious offence. Those who connive at the suppression of documents will be held equally responsible with those who actually suppress them.

This order is to be re-published in orders issued by all formations and units and is to be promulgated to all troops now serving in this country and to all troops who may arrive in this country in the future.

(G.R.O.1711 dated 3rd August, 1916).

LIEUT-COLONEL,
A.A.&.Q.M.G.
14TH (LIGHT) DIVISION.

14TH (LIGHT) DIVISION.

ROUTINE ORDERS.

8th August, 1916.

1712. ORDNANCE STORES.

Units will draw daily from D.A.D.O.S. the stores due to them on indent which have arrived from the Base.

The whole of the stores available must be cleared daily. D.A.D.O.S. will not hold them over. The present accumulation is to be cleared at once.

D.A.D.O.S. store is at the Western end of BUIRE.

1713. FIELD CASHIER.

The Field Cashier, attends at HEILLY daily from 9.30 a.m. to 12.30 p.m. and 2.30 p.m. to 4.30 p.m. He will also attend at Div'l Headquarters the 10th inst., from 2 p.m. to 3.30 p.m.

LIEUT-COLONEL,
A.A.&.Q.M.G.
14TH (LIGHT) DIVISION.

14TH (LIGHT) DIVISION.

ROUTINE ORDERS.

9th August, 1916.

1714. REFILLING POINT.

Refilling will be from 9.30 a.m. from tomorrow, 10th instant inclusive.

1715. FRENCH OR BELGIAN AREAS, VISITING.

Attention is directed to G.R.O.589 wherein it is ordered that no officer or man, except in performance of his duty, will visit the area occupied by the French or Belgian armies without the permission of General Headquarters.

Parsons, Capt for.
LIEUT-COLONEL,
A.A.&.Q.M.G.
14TH (LIGHT) DIVISION.

NOTICE.

LOST: On night of 5th/6th on the road between DOULLENS and GEZAINCOURT, BAY PONY, with military saddle and snaffle bit, white off-hind. Five white patches in withers. Short tail. About 14.1 hands.
Information to 7th K.R.R.C.

14TH (LIGHT) DIVISION.

ROUTINE ORDERS.

10th August, 1916.

1716. HONOURS AND REWARDS.

Under authority of H.M. THE KING, Military Medals have been awarded to the undermentioned N.C.O. and men :-

```
No.18178, Sergt. J.W. Sharpe, 6th Bn. K.O.Y.L.I.
   17010, Pte   J. Cogan,           -do-
   11374,  "    E.W. Poole,         -do-
```

1717. MEAT RATION.

Reference G.R.O.1716:
It is notified for information that the Pork and Beans rations issued to 15% of the troops on 4 days out of 7 consists:-

1/3rd tin Pork & Beans + 5/6th Lb Frozen Meat.
or
1/3rd tin Pork & Beans + 2/3rds tin Preserved Meat.

(Authority D of S. No.85/15).

C.L. Hamilton
LIEUT-COLONEL,
A.A.&.Q.M.G.
14TH (LIGHT) DIVISION.

NOTICE.

LOST: Bicycle, No.2137 from Wagon Lines of C/49 Bde R.F.A. at WANQUETIN, between the hours of noon 3rd inst and 5 a.m. 4th instant.
Information to O.C., C/49th Bde R.F.A.

14TH (LIGHT) DIVISION.

ROUTINE ORDERS.

12th August, 1916.

1718. REFILLING.

Refilling tomorrow, 13th instant and until further orders will take place on the road from ALBERT through E.10.Central, and E.16.Central, Sheet 62,d. at 9 a.m.

1719. PRISONERS OF WAR.

Prisoners of War are not to be deprived of their Water bottles, haversacks or cups.

1720. VETERINARY.

Advanced Collecting Station for Mobile Veterinary Section will be at E.12.c.2.2. from 9 a.m. 13th inst.

C.L. Hamilton
LIEUT-COLONEL,
A.A.&.Q.M.G.
14TH (LIGHT) DIVISION.

NOTICE.

FOUND: Dark Bay Mare, Star on forehead, both hind fetlocks white, 113 on near hind quarter and 90 on off hind quarter.
Apply A.P.M., 17th Division.

14TH (LIGHT) DIVISION.

ROUTINE ORDERS.

14th August, 1918.

1721. RETURNS - LEWIS MAGAZINES.

The return called for in D.R.O.1529 is no longer required.

1722. SICK WASTAGE.

The following is the Sick Wastage Return for week ended noon 12th inst:-

	O.	O.R.		O.	O.R.
46th Bde R.F.A.		3.	5th Ox & Bucks L.I.		5.
47th Bde R.F.A.		Nil.	5th K.S.L.I.		12.
48th Bde R.F.A.		1.	9th K.R.R.C.	2	12.
49th Bde R.F.A.		Nil.	9th R.B.		23.
14th D.A.C.		1.	42nd M.G.Company,		9.
X.14 T.M.Battery,		Nil.	42nd T.M.Battery,		3.
Y.14 T.M.Battery,		Nil.	6th Som.L.I.	1	11.
Z.14 T.M.Battery,		Nil.	6th D.C.L.I.		5.
8th M.M.G.Battery,		1.	6th K.O.Y.L.I.		7.
61st Field Co. R.E.		Nil.	10th Durham L.I.		13.
62nd Field Co. R.E.		4.	43rd M.G.Company,		1.
89th Field Co. R.E.		Nil.	43rd T.M.Battery,		1.
14th Signal Co.R.E.		1.	11th L'pool R	1	34.
7th K.R.R.C.	1	3.	14th Div'l Train,		1.
8th K.R.R.C.		6.	14th Supply Column,		Nil.
7th R.B.		10.	42nd F.Amb,		4.
8th R.B.		8.	43rd F.Amb,		1.
41st M.G.Company,		2.	44th F.Amb,		1.
41st T.M.Battery,		1.	25th Sanitary Section		1.

Total Officers 5, Other Ranks 185.

[signature]
for LIEUT-COLONEL,
A.A.&.Q.M.G.
14TH (LIGHT) DIVISION.

NOTICES.

LOST: From 124th Battery, RFA Wagon Lines, on night of 9/10th, a Dark Bay GELDING, Star, two white stockings both hinds, Height 15½, Age 10 years, Branded 124 on near hind and 91 on off hind.
Information to 5th Div'l Artillery.

LOST: From 52nd Battery RFA Wagon Lines, during night of 8/9th inst, a Light Bay MARE, Height about 15.3, Branded 52 near hind quarters, 57 off hind quarters.
Information to 5th Div'l Artillery.

LOST: From R.T.Os Office at ABBEVILLE on 3rd inst: Small dark brown WATERPROOF VALISE. No name outside: containing 2 Prismatic Compasses, 2 Protractors, number of Geometric scales, books, papers etc., and a Bank Pass Book (Holt & Co) with the name of Capt.Berisford, 10th D.L.I. on the outside cover.
Information to O.C., 10th Durham L.I.

DIVINE SERVICES, C of E.

Holy Communion 7.30 a.m.) on Tuesday and Thursday, in
Evening Prayer 6.30 p.m.) Chaplain's tent.
Div. H.Q.

14TH (LIGHT) DIVISION.

ROUTINE ORDERS.

16th August, 1916.

1723. LOCAL AND TEMPORARY EMOLUMENTS OF WARRANT OFFICERS AND SOLDIERS.

Reference G.R.O.1532, cases have occurred where additional Pay, especially the 6d Accountants Pay, admissable under Art.898, P.W., has been issued, and no claim rendered to the Command Paymaster, Base. Consequently the corresponding credit has not been given to the soldier's accounts, and he gets into debt.

It is important that claims should be rendered to Command Paymaster, Base, for any additional pay it is proposed to issue.

1724. CANTEENS - IMPORTATION OF SUPPLIES FOR.

Reference G.R.O.1730, Units which have been in the habit of importing goods direct for their Canteens will communicate direct with E.F.C. H.Qrs, BOULOGNE.

1725. FIRE APPLIANCES.

Reference G.R.O.1733, a return of fire extinguishers and fire first-aid appliances in possession of units will be rendered to Div'l H.Q. on the 1st of each month.

1726. SPARE COMPONENTS FOR VEHICLES OF 1ST LINE TRANSPORT AND TRAIN TRANSPORT.

Reference G.R.O.1734, indents will be submitted forthwith. Reports will be rendered by each unit through the usual channels when the new scale is complete.

1727. CUPS FOR FIRING No.23 RIFLE GRENADES.

Reference G.R.O.1727, indents will be submitted at once by all battalions.

1728. WATER FOR HORSES.

All G.S. Wagons are to have fittings made to enable them to carry 2 four gallon petrol tins with water for horses.

Four gallon petrol tins will be collected as soon as possible and issued to units, but the latter should obtain as many as they can by Salvage.

The fittings must be such as will give good support to the tins as they are otherwise liable to break.

1729. MARKING POSTS.

  Posts, upper half painted white, lower half tarred, have been placed in position to mark the track leading from ALBERT to BECORDEL and must not be removed.
  Any infringement of this order will be severely dealt with.

           LIEUT-COLONEL,
            A.A.&.Q.M.G.
           14TH (LIGHT) DIVISION.

NOTICE.

REMOVED: From Smith's Shop of 40 Siege Battery, on road at W.10.c.9.1. during night 14th/15th, ANVIL - 1 cwt. Information to A.P.M. XVth Corps.

14TH (LIGHT) DIVISION.

ROUTINE ORDERS.

18th August, 1916.

1730. HORSES - BRANDING OF.

Any horses not branded on the quarter with ↑ should have this done at once.

In some cases, where the branding has been badly done, and has become faint and not easily seen, it should be done again.

(Authority Fourth Army No.62, dated 12-8-16).

1731. SMOKE HELMETS.

One P.H.G.helmet per Officer and man not equipped with a box respirator will be issued when available in substitution for one of the P.H.Helmets now in possession.

The scale of issue arrived at is One P.H.G.Helmet and one P.H.Helmet per officer and man not equipped with box respirators. Officers and men equipped with one box respirator and one P.H.Helmet each will retain the P.H.Helmet.

Indents for the number of P.H.G.Helmets required to complete are to be forwarded to D.A.D.O.S. by 21st instant.

LIEUT-COLONEL,
A.A.&.Q.M.G.
14TH (LIGHT) DIVISION.

NOTICE

DIVINE SERVICE.
C.of E. Holy Communion at 7.30 a.m. in Chaplain's Tent, Div.H.Q.
   Morning Service, 9.30 a.m. in field opposite "Q" Office,
   Evening Service 5 p.m. in Chaplain's Tent.

FOUND: Bay GELDING, about 16 hands. Star off hind pastern, Brand ⊕ near quarter, Foot marks 26 NF, 106 NH. Apply 26th Mobile Vety Section.

LOST: On night of 14th from D/48th Bde Wagon Lines, BLACK GELDING, 15 hands, marked D/49 off hind, 2 on near hind. Information to 48th Bde R.F.A.

LOST: at BECORDEL CAMP on night of 14th inst: Bay MARE, No.45 on near hind, B/48 on off hind, Off hind white coronet, Saddle patch on back. Height 15 hands. Broke loose from Water trough with a Universal bit and head collar, marked B/48, No.45.
Information to 48th Bde R.F.A.

14TH (LIGHT) DIVISION.

ROUTINE ORDERS.

20th August, 1916.

1738. CUPS FOR FIRING NO.23 RIFLE GRENADES.

(i) Cups for attachment to rifles for firing Mills Grenades with rod attachment with shortly be issued.

(ii) These Grenades are known as No.23 Rifle Grenade, they are packed in the same design of box as the Hand Grenade but the letter "R" is stencilled at either end of the box.

(iii) The 16 rifles per battalion set aside for firing rifle grenades are to be increased to 34 as soon as the cup attachments are received.

No rifle other than those specially set aside is to be used for firing a Mills or any other Rifle Grenade.

Commanding Officers are responsible that this order is observed.

LIEUT-COLONEL,
A.A.&.Q.M.G.
14TH (LIGHT) DIVISION.

NOTICE.

STRAYED: From lines of No.4 Section 5th D.A.C. on the evening of the 15th inst: BROWN MARE, Aged, Height 15.2, Star, Branded 65 ⋀ Near side hind-quarter, H.4 off side hind-quarter, Markings on hoof off fore 5, near fore D.A.C., off hind H.4, near hind 91.

Information to 5th Div'l Artillery.

14TH (LIGHT) DIVISION.
ROUTINE ORDERS.

22nd August, 1916.

2. DISCIPLINE:

The slackness in saluting referred to in G.R.O.81 is still noticeable.

A practice appears to have arisen of one soldier only saluting when more than one are passing an officer. This practice is to cease.

When several soldiers pass an officer, unless they are being marched as a party, they will all salute, whether there are N.C.Os. among them or not. All will take time from the man nearest to the officer.

When a party of men is being marched by an N.C.O. or older soldier, the N.C.O. or man in charge of the party will give the order "Eyes right" or "Left" and himself salute.

When two or more men are sitting or standing about, and an officer passes them, the senior N.C.O. or oldest soldier will face the officer, call the rest to attention and alone salute.

Soldiers will salute in the manner laid down in the training manuals.

Officers must return the salutes of their subordinates with a definite motion of the hand and not perfunctorily: if more than one officer is present the senior alone will return the salute.

Officers will check lack of discipline in saluting and will report to the unit concerned the names of men who fail to salute them.

Officers Commanding Units will deal severely with men whose names are reported to them on this account.

G.R.O.3 dated 18th August 1914, is republished :-
"(3) Salutes - The strictest attention of all officers and soldiers should be directed to studying the uniforms and rank distinctions of our Allies and to the necessity of observing the obvious courtesy of saluting and returning salutes.

Quite irrespective of rank, it should be an accepted rule that no officer or soldier passes or is passed by any officer or soldier of the allied army without some act of recognition.

When foreign officers or soldiers salute British Officers all the officers so saluted will acknowledge the compliment, irrespective of who is the senior.
(G.R.O.1756 dated 18-8-16)

1733. **SICK WASTAGE.**

The following is the Sick Wastage Return for week ending noon 10th inst :-

	O.	O.R.		O.	O.R.
46th Bde R.F.A.		Nil	5th Ox & Bucks L.I.	2	8.
47th Bde R.F.A.		3.	5th K.S.L.I.	1	6
48th Bde R.F.A.		7.	9th K.R.R.C.		8.
49th Bde R.F.A.		2.	9th R.B.		5.
14th D.A.C.		2.	42nd M.G.Coy,		1.
X.14 T.M.Battery,		1.	42nd T.M.Bty,		5.
Y.14 T.M.Battery,	1	-	6th Som.L.I.		4.
Z.14 T.M.Battery,		Nil	5th DC.L.I.		4.
8th H.M.C.Battery,		Nil	6th K.O.Y.L.I.		8.
61st Field Co. R.E.		Nil	10th Durham L.I.	1	6.
62nd Field Co. R.E.		1.	43rd M.G. Coy,		Nil.
89th Field Co. R.E.		2.	43rd T.M. Bty,		3.
14th Signal Co.R.E.		1.	11th L'pool R.		8.
7th K.R.R.C.		8.	14th Div'l Train,		5.
8th K.R.R.C.		11.	14th Div'l Supply Column		Nil
7th R.B.		5.	42nd F.Amb,		2.
RAMC Att 7th R.B.	1	-	42nd F.Amb, ASC.MT Att.		1.
8th R.B.		1.	43rd Field Amb.		1.
41st M.G.Coy,		1.	44th F.Amb,		1.
41st T.M. Battery,		3.	25th Sanitary Section,		1.
			26th Mobile Vety Section,		1.

Total Officers 6, Other Ranks 124.

[signature]
for LIEUT-COLONEL,
A.A.&Q.M.G.
14TH (LIGHT) DIVISION.

NOTICE.

LOST: BAY MARE from "X" Battery, R.H.A. Height about 15 hands, small white star on forehead, small scar on near shoulder, branded "H.107" on near hind quarter.
Information to O.C., "X" Battery, Royal Horse Artillery.

LOST: BAY HORSE from "X" Battery R.H.A., Height 14½, White blaze on forehead, Thick Bushy tail, white fetlock near hind, Branded "X" on off hind hoof, "148" on near hind hoof.
Information to O.C. "X" Battery, Royal Horse Artillery.

14TH (LIGHT) DIVISION.

ROUTINE ORDERS.

23rd August, 1916.

1735. RATIONS.

Owing to a shortage of butter a proportion of margarine will be substituted in the near future. The proportion of each commodity issued will depend on the quantities received from England.

1736. HORSES.

Led horses being exercised or taken to water will invariably wear bits.
(Fourth Army Routine Order 180).

1737. TRESPASS ON RAILWAYS.

It has been brought to notice that individuals and small parties of troops are in the habit of walking along the main railway line CORBIE - MERICOURT - DERNANCOURT - ALBERT.
This practice is forbidden and must cease forthwith.
(Fourth Army Routine Order 183).

1738. STEEL HELMETS.

Units will report by 27th inst, through the usual channels, the number of Steel Helmets actually required to complete them to establishment.

LIEUT-COLONEL,
A.A.&.Q.M.G.
14TH (LIGHT) DIVISION.

NOTICES.

CHURCH SERVICES, C OF E.

Holy Communion on Thursday (S.Bartholomew) in the Chaplain's Tent, Div.H.Qrs. at 7.30 a.m., and
Evening Service at 6.30 p.m.

FOUND: Brown JENNY MULE, 14 hands, 7.B.4 and U.D. branded on off side. Government mark on near side.
Apply A.P.M., 14th Division.

LOST: From No.4 Section, 5th D.A.C. whilst grazing on 17th inst, BAY GELDING, Star, B.H.Pasterns. Branded "5" on off fore, "D.A.C." near fore, "1" near hind, "H.4" off hind.
Information to O.C., 5th Div'l Ammunition Column.

14TH (LIGHT) DIVISION.

ROUTINE ORDERS.

1st Sept: 1916.

1739. ARRIVAL OF REINFORCEMENTS.

The arrival of reinforcements during the preceding 24 hours ending 9 a.m. will be reported to Div'l Headquarters by all units through the usual channels.
Reports to reach this office by 6 p.m.
Rank, Name and initials of Officers to be stated: number of Other Ranks.
No Officer or man returning from Field Ambulances or elsewhere who is already on the strength is to be included in this return.

1740. FIELD POST OFFICES.

Field Post Offices whilst the Division is in present billets will be accommodated at their Brigade Headquarters: accommodation and rations will be arranged by Brigade H.Qrs.
The incoming mail will be delivered by lorry direct to Field Post Offices daily and the outgoing mail collected and removed by the same lorry.
Post Orderlies with Transport will be at Field Post Offices at 10 a.m.

1741. WATER CARTS.

Units will indent at once on D.A.D.O.S. to complete any deficiencies in the equipment of their Water Carts
A report will be rendered through the usual channels to reach this office by 12 noon the 10th inst, showing what items are still deficient and if indented for date of indent.

1742. FIELD CASHIER.

The Field Cashier will attend at Div'l Headquarters tomorrow, September 2nd, from 10.15 a.m. to 12.15 p.m.

1743. REFILLING.

Refilling will take place tomorrow at 9 a.m. as follows:-

41st Inf.Bde Group. 2½ Miles South of AIRAINES on the main AIRAINES - CAMPS Road.
42nd Inf.Bde Group. 3 Miles South of AIRAINES on the same road.
43rd Inf.Bde Group. 3½ Miles South of AIRAINES on the same road.

Groups are made up as follows:-

41st Inf.Bde Group. H.Q., 4 Bns, Bde M.G.Coy, 11th King's L'pool Regt, 62nd Field Co.R.E., 44th Field Ambulance Div'l H.Q. R.E. H.Q., Train H.Q., Signals, No.2 Coy, Train.
42nd Inf.Bde Group. H.Q., 4 Bns, Bde M.G.Coy, 89th Field Co.R.E. 42nd Field Ambulance, 8th M.M.G.Bty, No.3 Coy Train.
43rd Inf.Bde Group. H.Q., 4 Bns, Bde M.G.Coy, 43rd Field Ambulance 61st Field Co.R.E., Mobile Vety Section, No.4 Coy Train.

LIEUT-COLONEL,
A.A.& Q.M.G.
14TH (LIGHT) DIVISION.

14TH (LIGHT) DIVISION.

ROUTINE ORDERS.

2nd Sept: 1916.

1744. HONOURS AND REWARDS.

Under authority granted by H.M. THE KING, Military Medals have been awarded to the following N.C.Os and men:-

"A" Battery, 46th Bde R.F.A. 27132, Gn. Ralph Briggs,
                       8120. Gr. Percival Spencer,
"D" Battery, 46th Bde R.F.A. 83521. A/Bombr. George Spalding.

11th King's (L'pool) Regt. (Pioneers).

    12755, Sergeant Albert Gilliver,
    12231. Sergeant Herbert Fardoe.

6th Bn. Somerset L.I.

    10771. L/Corpl. Ernest Jouxson,
    10192. Sergt. George Collins,
    10273. Sergt. Albert E. Crow,
    3/6836. L/Corpl. Wilfred T. Hucker,
    9909. Pte Frederick C. Heal,
    10629. L/Corpl. Charles Coggins,
    17645. Pte Albert Ferguson,
    7300. " Thomas Buttle,
    9177. " Leonard Moore,
    10403. Sergt. Walter E. Arnold,
    26495. Pte Walter Curley,
    11919. Sergt. John Dowie Harcombe.

6th Bn. D.C.L.I.

    13675. Sergt. Arthur T. Cook,
    11909. L/Corpl. Walter T. Robbins.

6th K.O.Y.L.I. (att 43rd M.G. Coy).

    18209. Pte Harold E. Grant.

7th K.R.R.C.

    A.1064. A/C.S.M. Eric Townley,
    R/11819. Rfn. John Luckin,
    R/14253. " Edward Barker.

7th Bn. Rifle Brigade.

    B/3013. Rfn. Andrew Murphy,
    B/461. " Alan Joseph,
    B/699. " Louis Silver,
    B/7394. " Lewis Harris,
    S/11192. Cpl. George Harle.

1745. EMPTY GRENADE BOXES.

Units will return to Ammunition Railheads, through the usual channel, all empty Mills No.5 Grenade Boxes, Stokes Mortar boxes and Nos. 3 and 23 Rifle Grenade Boxes.

(Continued)

1746. **REFILLING.**

Refilling tomorrow 3rd instant will take place as follows:-

<u>41st Bde Group</u>: At the same place as to-day at 8 a.m. and again at 4 p.m.
<u>42nd Bde Group</u>. On the EPAUMESNIL - METIGNY - AIRAINES Road just East of EPAUMESNIL at 8 a.m. and again at 4 p.m.
<u>43rd Bde Group</u>. On the HORNOY - CAMPS-EN-AMIENOIS Road just N.E. of HORNOY at 8 a.m. and again at 4 p.m.

The Train wagons will remain loaded with the Supplies drawn at the second Refilling and will deliver them to units early on the morning of the 4th inst.

Refilling on the 4th and onwards will be at those points at 9.30 a.m.

(signed)
for LIEUT-COLONEL,
A.A.&.Q.M.G.
14TH (LIGHT) DIVISION.

<u>NOTICES.</u>

<u>DIVINE SERVICE (C of E.)</u> - 3rd September, 1916.

MORNING SERVICE at 9.30 a.m. in paddock at main gate of Chateau Grounds, Div. H.Q.

<u>LOST</u>:- On night 31-8-16 at HEUCOURT, BAY PONY, 14 hands, star, stamped near fore No.19, hind 14 Sig.

Also BROWN MARE, 14.3 hands, stamped near fore No.87, hind 14 Sig.
Information to H.Q., 41st Infantry Bde.

14TH (LIGHT) DIVISION.

ROUTINE ORDERS.

3rd September, 1916.

1747. HONOURS AND REWARDS.

Under Authority of H.M. THE KING, Military Medals have been awarded to the undermentioned N.C.Os and men :-

6th Bn. D.C.L.I.

10428, Pte Herbert Brackenbury,

K.R.R.C. attached 7th R.B.

C/1656, Rfn. Charles Walker,

7th Bn. R.B.

S/7189, Rfn. Amos Steptoe.
S/ 504. Cpl. Alfred Rout,
S/12759, Rfn. William Church,
B/ 456. Cpl. Harry Forbes.

1748. SICK WASTAGE.

The following is the Sick Wastage Return for week ended noon 31-8-16:-

	O.	O.R.		O.	O.R.
46th Bde R.F.A.		2.	5th Ox & Bucks L.I.		2.
47th Bde R.F.A.		1.	5th K.S.L.I.		2.
48th Bde R.F.A.		Nil.	9th K.R.R.C.		3.
49th Bde R.F.A.		1.	9th R.B.		1.
14th D.A.C.		1.	RAMC Att 9th R.B.		1.
X.14 T.M.Battery,		Nil.	42nd M.G. Coy.		Nil.
Y.14 T.M. Battery,		Nil.	42nd T.M. Bty.		Nil.
Z.14 T.M. Battery,		Nil.	6th Som.L.I.		3.
8th M.M.G.Battery,		Nil.	6th D.C.L.I.	2	2
61st Field Co. R.E.		1.	6th K.O.Y.L.I.		6.
62nd Field Co. R.E.		1.	10th Durham L.I.		8.
89th Field Co. R.E.		Nil.	43rd M.G. Coy.		3.
14th Signal Co.R.E.		Nil.	43rd T.M. Bty.		Nil.
7th K.R.R.C.	1	5	11th L'pool R	1	7.
8th K.R.R.C.	2	4	14th Div'l Train.	2	2.
7th R.B.		1.	14th Div'l Supply Col.		Nil.
8th R.B.	3	6.	42nd F.Amb.		1.
RAMC Att 8th RRR.	1.		43rd F. Amb,		2.
41st M.G. Coy.		1.	44th F.Amb,		Nil.
41st T.M. Bty.		Nil.	25th Sanitary Section,		Nil.
			A.V.C.		1.

[signature] Captain

LIEUT-COLONEL, for
A.A.&.Q.M.G.
14TH (LIGHT) DIVISION.

NOTICE.

LOST - On morning of 31st August, 1916, in vicinity of ALBERT a BLACK GELDING, height 14.3 hands, aged, white face, wearing night holder with bit and curb chain. Broke loose from Water Trough. Information to C.R.E., 14th Division.

14TH (LIGHT) DIVISION.

ROUTINE ORDERS.

5th September, 1916.

1749. FIELD CASHIER.

The Field Cashier will attend at Div'l Headquarters from 9.40 a.m. to 11.10 a.m. and at Headquarters 43rd Inf. Brigade from 11.45 a.m. to 12.30 p.m. tomorrow 6th inst.

1750. BOUNDS.

The Town of AIRAINES is placed out of bounds for all Troops 14th Division unless in possession of Special pass signed by a Commanding Officer.
Formed parties proceeding there on duty excepted.

LIEUT-COLONEL,
A.A.&Q.M.G.
14TH (LIGHT) DIVISION.

NOTICES.

Divine Service.
Wednesday 10 a.m. (Choral) Thursday 7.30 a.m., in house at corner of AUMONT ROAD, adjoining Ordnance Stores, Div'l H.Qrs.

LOST: In INNER TRENCH, DELVILLE WOOD, on the 24th August, a Leather POCKET BOOK, containing Photographs, private papers, and 500 francs (200 in 20-frs and 300 in 5 frs notes)
Information to O.C., 5th K.S.L.I.

LOST: Between Station AIRAINES and VERGIES, FIELD CONDUCT Case containing A.Fs B.122 marked I to Z.
Information to O.C., 5th K.S.L.I.

14TH (LIGHT) DIVISION.

ROUTINE ORDERS.

7th September, 1916.

1751. HORSES - WATERING OF.

Attention is drawn to Army Routine Order No.76. All parties of horses of 25 or more being taken to water will invariably be in charge of an officer who will be responsible that they do not march on roads except when it is unavoidable.

1752. RATIONS.

The following will be added to G.R.O.1235, para 2, under "Extras" :-
"Two Oxo Cubes to men who are employed at Railheads or Ammunition Dumps for four hours and over on night duty between the hours of 9 p.m. and 6 a.m."
(G.R.O.1777)

1753. GLOVES FOR LIGHT T.M. BATTERIES.

Approval is given for the issue of Gloves, Machine Gunners, to Light Trench Mortar (3-inch Stokes) Batteries on a scale of two pairs per Mortar for use in handling the mortar when hot.
Indents should be submitted to Ordnance Officers and issue will be made when supplies become available.
(G.R.O.1778)

LIEUT COLONEL,
A.A.&.Q.M.G.
14TH (LIGHT) DIVISION.

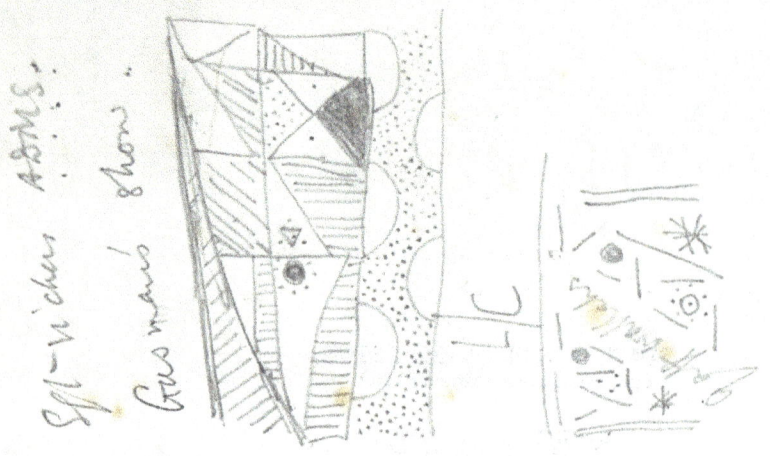

Sgt Vickers ADMS. Gas mans show.

Sgt Vickers ADMS Gas Mac Saturday

File

14TH (LIGHT) DIVISION.

ROUTINE ORDERS.

8th September, 1916.

1754. ROAD DISCIPLINE.

It has been noticed that the Road discipline of Troops and Transport of the Division leaves much to be desired. The strictest March Discipline is imperative in congested areas. Officers Commanding Columns and Transport Officers are held personally responsible that Fourth Army Traffic Orders are rigidly adhered to, non-compliance therewith may have far reaching effects on the general situation and this important point is to be impressed on all ranks.

The following points require special attention :-

(a) Led horses must be kept off roads as far as possible and must be properly under control.

(b) Gaps to be left at intervals in transport.

(c) Troops and transport to keep well to the right of the road, and when halted to move clear of the road if this is possible.

(d) Look-out men in lorries are not sufficiently alert.

Commanders of Brigade Groups and other Divisional Units are directed to deal severely with any breaches of March Discipline which may be brought to their notice.

The Major-General trusts that he will not again have to call attention to this matter.

1755. POSTAL.

Letters arriving for N.C.Os and men at AULT Camp will not be sent on to them, but will be kept with their units until the return of the detachments.

LIEUT-COLONEL,
A.A.&.Q.M.G.
14TH (LIGHT) DIVISION.

NOTICES.
DIVINE SERVICES.

R.C. 10-9-16.
Holy Mass at HORNOY Parish Church 8.30 a.m.
" " " SELINCOURT Parish Church at 9.30 a.m.
Benediction HORNOY Parish Church 7.30 p.m.

WESLEYAN & PRESBYTERIAN ETC.
10 a.m. for 9th K.R.R., 5th Ox & Bucks, at ST.MAULVIS. Communion to follow.
11.30 a.m. for 9th R.B., 5th K.S.L.I., 89th Field Co.R.E. No.3 Coy.A.S.C. at LE FAY. Communion to follow.
5.30 p.m. for 42nd F.Amb, 42nd M.G.Co & T.M.Bty at ETREJUST. Communion to follow.

14TH (LIGH^T) DIVISION.

ROUTINE ORDERS.

9th September, 1916.

1756. HONOURS AND REWARDS.

The General Officer Commanding-in-Chief has under authority granted by HIS MAJESTY THE KING, awarded decorations as detailed below, to the undermentioned Officers, N.C.Os and men of the 14th (Light) Division:-

THE DISTINGUISHED SERVICE ORDER.

T/2nd Lieut. W.H.G. JESSUP,
   6th Battn Duke of Cornwall's L.I.

THE MILITARY CROSS.

T/Captain G.P. MANSON,
   6th Battn Somerset Light Infantry,
T/2nd Lieut. G.E. CLARKE,
   6th Battn. Duke of Cornwall's L.I.
2/Lieut. F.V. KIBBEY,
No.B/157 C.S.M. A.J. SMITH,
   7th Battn Rifle Brigade.

THE DISTINGUISHED CONDUCT MEDAL.

No.10272 Sergeant W.H. BRYANT,
  20154 L/Sergt. T. BARTLETT,
   6th Battn. Somerset L.I.
No. A/517 Sergeant W. KNIGHT,
  A/3264 L/Sergt. R. LONGLEY,
   7th Battn. K.R.R.Corps.
No. 6053, A/Corpl. W.J. JEFFREY,
   7th Battn. Rifle Brigade.

BAR TO DISTINGUISHED CONDUCT MEDAL.

No. A/412 Sergeant E. WOOD,
   7th Battn. K.R.R.Corps.

THE MILITARY CROSS.

T/2nd Lieut. A.C. MEREDITH,
   41st Co. Machine Gun Corps.

1757. SANITATION.

i. On leaving a camp, bivouac or billeting area, every unit must provide a party whose duty it will be to clear up thoroughly the area vacated, burn all refuse not disposed of etc., and leave the area in a tidy and sanitary condition.
ii. If the area is likely to be occupied by other troops afterwards, all permanent and semi-permanent sanitary works such as flyproof latrines, incinerators, soakage pits, grease traps, ablution places etc., must be left in good working order and not destroyed or removed.

                            LIEUT-COLONEL,
                            A.A.&.Q.M.G.
                    14TH (LIGHT) DIVISION.

NOTICE.
DIVINE SERVICE - 10 : 9 : 16.

C OF E.
Morning Service 9.30 a.m. in Paddock beside the gate of the
    Chateau Grounds, Div. H.Q.

14TH (LIGHT) DIVISION.

ROUTINE ORDERS.

12th September, 1916.

1758. LEWIS GUN COURSES.

All ammunition and grenades will be withdrawn from N.C.Os and men proceeding to the Lewis Gun School prior to their departure from their units.

1759. SACKS.

Attention is directed to VI Corps Routine Order No.888 of May 27th 1916. It is imperative that all sacks not required for use at the front should be sent back to Base where there is always a demand for them.

1760. HONOURS AND REWARDS.

The General Officer Commanding-in-Chief has under authority granted by HIS MAJESTY THE KING, awarded decorations as detailed below, to the undermentioned Officer and N.C.O. of the 14th (Light) Division :-

THE MILITARY CROSS.

2/Lieut. J.G. WALSER, R.F.A, att. X/14 T.M.Battery.

THE DISTINGUISHED CONDUCT MEDAL.

2nd Corpl (A/Corpl) W.J. RICHARDS, 61st Field Co.R.E.

1761. SICK WASTAGE.

The following is the Sick Wastage Return for week ended noon 9th inst:

Unit	O.	O.R.	Unit	O.	O.R.
H.Q,14th Division,	1	-	5th Ox & Bucks L.I.		9.
46th Bde R.F.A.		3.	5th K.S.L.I.		8.
47th Bde R.F.A.		2.	9th K.R.R.C.		3.
48th Bde R.F.A.	1	3.	9th R.B.		4.
49th Bde R.F.A.		6.	42nd M.G. Coy.		1.
14th D.A.C.		4.	42nd M.G. Coy.		3.
W.14 T.M. Battery,		2.	6th Som.L.I.		8.
X.14 T.M. Battery,		-	6th D.C.L.I.	1	10.
Y.14 T.M. Battery,		1.	6th K.O.Y.L.I.	1	10.
Z.14 T.M. Battery,		-	10th Durham L.I.	3	16.
8th M.M.G.Battery,		-	43rd M.G. Coy.		5.
61st Field Co. R.E.		3.	43rd T.M. Bty.		4.
62nd Field Co. R.E.		-	11th L'pool R		21.
89th Field Co. R.E.	1	5	14th Div'l Train,		2.
14th Signal Co.R.E.		2.	14th Div.Supply Column,		4.
7th K.R.R.C.	1	7.	42nd F. Amb,		2.
8th K.R.R.C.		8.	43rd F. Amb,		2.
7th R.B.	2	21.	44th F. Amb,		1.
8th R.B.		5.	25th Sanitary Section,		-
41st M.G. Coy.		2.	A.V.C.		-
41st T.M. Bty.	1	3.			

Total Officers 12, Other Ranks 190.

LIEUT-COLONEL,
A.A.& Q.M.G.
14TH (LIGHT) DIVISION.

14TH (LIGHT) DIVISION.

ROUTINE ORDERS.

14th September, 1916.

1762. TUNNELLING COMPANIES - A.F. B.213.

Infantry personnel which is permanently attached to a Tunnelling Company will be struck off the Strength of the Unit from which it is detached and will be shown in the Effective Strength on A.F. B.213 of the Tunnelling Company to which it is permanently attached, with a note in the column of remarks stating "Includes so many Infantry personnel permanently attached".

The number of permanently attached Infantry must not exceed 216 per Tunnelling Company.
(G.R.O.1783).

1763. PROFICIENCY PAY.

Reference Army Order 368/15, the Classification of all men who will complete their service qualification before 1st May next, and the review of the qualification of all men already in receipt of Class 1 rate, should be completed before 30th September.

Nominal rolls on A.F. O.1614 should be forwarded to the appropriate Regimental Paymaster, of all men certified as fit to be granted, or to retain Class 1 rate.

For soldiers of the Territorial Force, A.F. O.1614a will be used.
(G.R.O.1784).

1764. LEAVE.

G.R.O.911 is re-published for information :-
"Officers and other ranks proceeding on leave of absence will invariably take with them, for production when demanded, the written authority for granting such leave.
(G.R.O.1788)

1765. HORSES - PICKED UP NAILS.

Owing to the large number of horses injured by nails picked up on the roads, attention is directed to G.R.O.1135.

O.C. Div'l Train will arrange for boxes, plainly marked;- "NAILS" to be placed at refilling points used by the Division, into which loose nails can be thrown, and similar measures will be taken by all Units at dumps used by them.

Much can be done to avoid this evil if all men in charge of horses are instructed to examine more frequently, their horses feet at halts and on returning to Transport Camps.

1766. EMPTY AMMUNITION BOXES.

Empty Ammunition Boxes must not be left in vacated billets.

All such boxes must be returned to railheads, where they are urgently required.

1767. ORDNANCE DUMP.

The Ordnance Dump is at E.18.a.5.6.

LIEUT-COLONEL,
A.A.&.Q.M.G.
14TH (LIGHT) DIVISION.

NOTICE.

FOUND: On morning of 10th inst, BAY MARE, 16.2 - D.14 over S S Near Rump, Near fore and hind socks. Wearing a repaired head-collar.
Apply A.P.M., 14th Division.

14TH (LIGHT) DIVISION.

ROUTINE ORDERS.

15th September, 1916.

1768. POSTAL.

Mails of all Units will be delivered with Supplies until further orders.

1769. PUTTEES - REPAIR OF.

With reference to C.R.O.112, Puttees that are repairable are to be sent to D.A.D.O.S. when the repair cannot be carried out regimentally.

1770. DISCIPLINE.

Cases of charges against drivers of mechanically propelled vehicles including motor bicycles for accidents to their machines through negligence, are not to be disposed of without reference to Div'l Headquarters.

1771. PASSES FOR MOTOR VEHICLES.

Officers, N.C.Os and men who are not issued with Card Passes must, whenever they travel by motor car or motor cycle, be in possession of a one day pass signed by their Commanding Officers.

Drivers of mechanically propelled vehicles when not travelling in convoys under charge of officers must be in possession of orders signed by their Commanding Officers or by a Staff Officer, showing the duty on which they are engaged and the places to which they have been ordered to go.

On and after September 21st, mechanically propelled vehicles whose drivers and passengers are not provided with passes or orders as above will be stopped at Police and examining Posts, and will not be allowed to proceed further.

C.M. Hamilton

LIEUT-COLONEL,
A.A.&.Q.M.G.
14TH (LIGHT) DIVISION.

14TH (LIGHT) DIVISION.

ROUTINE ORDERS.

16th September, 1916.

1772. HONOURS AND REWARDS.

The following awards of RUSSIAN decorations have been made:-

CROSS OF ST. GEORGE 4TH CLASS.

    No.10272, Sergeant W. Bryant,   6th Somerset L.I.

MEDAL OF ST. GEORGE, 1ST CLASS.

    No. 4928, Sergeant E.J. Vranch, 6th Somerset L.I.

Under authority granted by H.M. THE KING, Military Medals have been awarded to the undermentioned N.C.Os and men :-

ROAYL ARTILLERY.

    No.95931, Bombr. N.J. Margetts,   A/46 Bde R.F.A.
    96214. Gnr.   C.J. Moss,   A/48 Bde R.F.A.
    97969. Gnr.   W. Edwards,   A/48 Bde R.F.A.

ROYAL ENGINEERS.

    No.48526, Sapper G.V. Gibson,   89th Field Co.R.E.

8TH BN. THE RIFLE BRIGADE.

    No. 176, Sergeant C. Cowan,
    603. A/Corpl. G. Snow,

9TH BN. K.R.R.C.

    No. 6573.Sergt.(A/C.S.M.) R. Kidd,
    7669.Rifleman W. Smith,
    9392.   "   A. Hanford,
    2805.   "   J.C. Lapworth,
    6554.   "   W.E. Jones,
    1029.   "   A. Bradley,

5TH OX & BUCKS L.I.

    No.20896.Sergeant A.W. Lewendon,
    6346.L/Corpl. G. Kenyon.

5TH BN. K.S.L.I.

    No. 9444.Corporal D. Jones,
    18046.L/Corpl. E. Parry,
    20056.Private W. Buckley,
    20025.   "   E. Barber,
    11648.Sergeant V. Malt,
    10685.Private W.H. Ashton,
    17707.   "   W. Longworth,
    18183.   "   F. Stephenson,
    17229.Sergeant H. Bufton.

(Continued).

Honours and Rewards (continued).

9TH BN. K.R.R.C.

No. 3060. A/Sergeant R. Gill,
8396. L/Corporal W.H. Danbury,
13135. Rifleman F. Plum,
1907. Rifleman F. Evans,
11681. Corporal C. Garnett,
8496. Rifleman T. Fletcher,
1529. " A. Barnett,
2096. Sergeant S. Martin,
8049. " E. Vickers,
9706. L/Corporal W. Williamson,
15141. L/Corporal C. Jordan,
7213. L/Corporal J. Jones,
13279. Rifleman J.W. Derbyshire,
8500. " H.S. Besant,
2521. " H. Ougham,

9TH RIFLE BRIGADE.

No. 2020. A/Lce-Corpl. C. Storer,

6TH K.O.Y.L.I.

No. 3091. Sergeant S. Gollick,
10272. Private A. Hill,
9526. Corporal T. McDonough,

10TH DURHAM L.I.

No. 25306. Private W. Jordan,
12707. Sergeant E.W. Chicken,
11872. L/Corporal J.W. Hepworth,
12398. " W. Laverick,
11986. Private H. Drummond,
12897. " E. Clayton,
12135. " J. Taylor,
8542. " P. Swales,
21351. " B. Burns,
21358. " T. Dawson,
9440. " J. Carr.

1773. **AREA STORES.**

It has come to notice that Corps, Divisions and Units when transferred from one area, or from one Formation, to another, have taken with them Machinery, Plant, Buildings and other R.E. Stores, and in some cases, transport specially allotted for area purposes.

This practice causes great inconvenience to the incoming troops and hampers the progress of works.

No Machinery, plant, buildings, tents or R.E. Stores of any description, which are not included in the regimental equipment of units, are to be removed by Units or formations when they are transferred.

C.L. Hamilton

LIEUT-COLONLE.
A.A.&.Q.M.G.
14TH (LIGHT) DIVISION.

14TH (LIGHT) DIVISION.

ROUTINE ORDERS.

18th Sept: 1916.

1774. The following gracious telegram has been received from HIS MAJESTY THE KING by the Commander in Chief :-

" I congratulate you and my brave troops on the"
"brilliant success just achieved. AAA I have never"
"doubted that complete victory will ultimately   "
"crown our efforts and the splended results of the"
"fighting yesterday confirmed this view. AAA

GEORGE, R.I.   "

1775. FIELD CASHIER.

The Field Cashier will attend at Div'l Headquarters, BUIRE CAMP, at 10.30 a.m. to 12.30 p.m. tomorrow 19th inst.

LIEUT-COLONEL,
A.A.&.Q.M.
14TH (LIGHT) DIVISION.

14TH (LIGHT) DIVISION.

ROUTINE ORDERS.

20th September, 1916.

1776. HONOURS AND REWARDS.

Under Authority of H.M. THE KING, the following decorations have been awarded :-

THE MILITARY CROSS.

ROYAL ARTILLERY.

2/Lieut. A.W. Tredinnick,   A Bty, 46th Bde R.F.A.
2/Lt (T/Lieut) C.J. Tyndale-Biscoe, A Bty. 48th Bde R.F.A.

5TH OX & BUCKS L.I.

2/Lieut. B.A. Anderson,
2/Lieut. D.L. Jacks,
No.10908, C.S.M. C.A. Hill.

7TH K.R.R.C.

Lieut. G.H. Williamson,
2/Lt. C. Whitley,
No.A.692, C.S.M. J. Lever.

5TH BN. K.S.L.I.

2/Lieut. G.P. Bulmer,
2/Lieut. J.C. Jinks,

9TH K.R.R.C.

2/Lieut. A. Cook,
Lieut. H. Dowson.

10TH DURHAM L.I.

Lieut. A. Todd,
Capt. J.G. Parr,
2/Lieut. E.E. Canney,
2/Lieut. J.R. Paris.

9TH RIFLE BDE.

Lieut. J.P. Day.

MACHINE GUN CORPS.

2/Lt. N.W. Clayton, 42nd M.G.Co.

DISTINGUISHED CONDUCT MEDAL.

5TH K.S.L.I.

No.10598, Sergt. J. Burnham,
No. 8198. Sergt. B.B. Lloyd.

8TH K.R.R.C.

No.3186. Sergt. J. Orchard,
No.8042. Pte. E.G. Hayward.

10TH DURHAM L.I.

No. 7335. C.S.M. W. Cooper,
No.16364. L/Cpl. W. Hoole,

9TH K.R.R.C.

No.R.2989. L/Cpl. G.H. Morley.

MILITARY MEDAL.

ROYAL ARTILLERY.

No.14037, Gnr. J.S. Martin,   B Bty. 47th Bde R.F.A.
No.93809. Gnr. P. Marsden,   -do-
No.89311. Gnr. E. Tilling,   B Bty. 48th Bde R.F.A.
No.97998. Gnr. A.W. Walters   -do-

6TH D.C.L.I.

No.15686, Pte S. Ward.

MACHINE GUN CORPS.

No.20017, Pte J. Baron,) 43rd
No.20024. Pte B. Perry,) M.G. Coy.

LIEUT-COLONEL,
A.A.& Q.M.G.
14TH (Light) Division.

NOTICE.
HOLY COMMUNION, Div.H.Qrs, tomorrow 21st (St.Matthew's Day) at 7.30 a.m. Chaplain's Tent.

14TH (LIGHT) DIVISION.

ROUTINE ORDERS.

24th September, 1916.

1777. HONOURS AND REWARDS.

Under authority of H.M. THE KING, Military Medals are awarded to the undermentioned N.C.Os and Men :-

ROYAL ARTILLERY.

No.10772, Bombr. S. Bailey,   D Battery, 48th Bde R.F.A.

7TH BN. K.R.R.C.

No. 1606, L/Corpl. A. Potter,
14817. L/Corpl. J. Vasey,

8TH BN. K.R.R.C.

No.1092. Rfmn. H. Pound,

9TH BN. K.R.R.C.

No. 2273, L/Corpl W. Penistone,
1276. L/Corpl. A. Johnson,

9TH BN. RIFLE BDE.

No.7813, Rfmn. H. Richardson.

42ND MACHINE GUN COY.

No. 19952, Pte C. Burcombe,
19878, " H. Samuels.

1778. ORDNANCE DUMP.

The Ordnance Dump is at LE CAUROY.

1779. HORSES, MULES ETC. FOUND STRAYING OR CAPTURED.

All British horses and mules which may be found straying or in the possession of civilians, and all horses, mules and donkeys captured from the enemy, or brought in by deserters, are to be handed over at once to the nearest Mobile Veterinary Section. The retention of such animals in the unit which finds or captures them is strictly prohibited.

1780. CASUALTY REPORTS.

Casualty reports will be made up from mid-night to mid-night, and must reach Div'l Headquarters by wire by 9 a.m. the following morning. Wires to be worded in the usual way.
Nil reports to be rendered.

LIEUT COLONEL,
A.A.&.Q.M.G.
14TH (LIGHT) DIVISION.

14TH (LIGHT) DIVISION.

ROUTINE ORDERS.

25th September 1916.

1781. **BROKEN HANDLES, LEWIS GUN HANDCARTS.**

    Broken handles of Lewis Gun Handcarts should be sent to D.A.D.O.S. to be repaired at Vl Corps Workshop.

1782. **TOWN ORDERS, ARRAS.**

    Copies of Town Orders, ARRAS are being circulated.
    Orders Nos 2.4.5.10.11.12.15.17.19 and 20. will be read out on three consecutive parades to all Units of the Division and to all Drafts on arrival.

1783 **STEEL HELMETS.**

    All demands for steel helmets should be sent to D.A.D.O.S. at once.

LIEUT COLONEL,
A.A.& Q.M.G.
14th (Light) Division.

14th (Light) Division.

27th September 1916.

1784. HONOURS AND REWARDS.

Under authority of H.M. THE KING decorations have been awarded as follows :-

The Military Cross.

ROYAL ARTILLERY.

Lieut. J.D. Brooksmith   B battery 47th Brigade R.F.A.
2/Lt. B.P. Tallyour   A battery 48th Brigade R.F.A.

5th D.C.L.I.

Capt. G.D. Brookes.
Lieut. E.C. Codyre
2/Lt. A.W. Turner.

The Distinguished Conduct Medal.

5th Bn. D.C.L.I.   **6th Bn. K.O.Y.L.I.**

No.18699 Pte. A. Warren.   No.20959 Pte. D.E. Lancashire

1785. ORDNANCE DUMP.

The Ordnance Dump is located at WARLUS.

1786. STOVES FOR WINTER USE.

Empty oil drums and large petrol tins are to be collected and handed over to Divl. Salvage Company for transfer to Corps R.E. Park where they will be converted into "Canadian" pattern stoves for winter use.

1787. WINTER CLOTHING.

In view of the approaching winter and the issue of additional underclothing, care must be taken to fit service dress clothing loose enough to admit of the extra articles being worn without inconvenience.

1788. JAMS - 3-inch Stokes Mortar Shells.

If a 3-inch Stokes Mortar Shell should jam in the bore, no attempt to remove it should be made, but the services of the A.D.O.S., Corps, should be asked for.
(VI Corps R.O. 1501)

A.M. Hamilton
LIEUT-COL.
A.A.& Q.M.G.
14th (Light) Division.

TRAFFIC ORDERS, 14TH DIVISION.
(Issued with D.R.Os dated 29th September, 1916).

No formed bodies of troops or traffic, except single Motor Cars and ambulances may proceed East of the MANOEUIL - DAINVILLE Railway during the hours of daylight, unless the driver is in possession of a pass issued by the A.P.M., 14th Division.

A.P.M., 14th Division will only issue these <u>special</u> passes <u>on requisition by an officer of the Staff</u> of the VI Corps or of a Division.

The Control Posts at WARLUS and BERNEVILLE have orders to stop all formed bodies of troops and traffic at the outlets of those villages leading to ARRAS or DAINVILLE, unless they have the necessary pass.

(2) Vehicular traffic for trenches or gun positions and large parties of troops will not pass the undermentioned places before the following hours :-

    WARLUS   7 p.m.
    BERNEVILLE   7 p.m.
    BEAUMETZ   7.15 p.m.

These hours also apply to all traffic for DAINVILLE and ARRAS.

(3) No Motor, Lorry, wagon, horseman, bicycle or foot passenger is allowed to go along the ARRAS - DOULLENS road, during the hours of daylight.

(4) The road leading from BEAUMETZ cross-roads to GROSVILLE and RIVIERE is closed to all traffic during daylight.

Exceptions are made for despatch riders with urgent messages

(5) The road from the Sugar factory at DAINVILLE to ACHICOURT is closed to all vehicles by daylight.

14TH (LIGHT) DIVISION.

ROUTINE ORDERS.

29th September, 1916.

1789. FIELD CASHIER.

The Field Cashier will attend at Div'l Headquarters on Mondays and Thursdays from 2.30 to 4 p.m.

1790. TRAFFIC ORDERS.

Traffic Orders are issued herewith.

1791. DISCIPLINE - IMPROPER DISPOSAL OF GOVERNMENT PROPERTY.

Attention is drawn to G.R.O. Nos 388, 689, and 1156.
In all cases where arms, equipment, clothing or stores the property of the British Government, are discovered to be in possession of civilians, immediate steps will be taken to trace and bring to trial the soldier or soldiers implicated. The proceedings of such trials will be forwarded to G.H.Q. (G.R.O.1817).

1792. DISPOSAL OF KIT AND EFFECTS OF DECEASED OFFICERS.

The attention of all Officers Commanding Units, and Medical Officers in charge of Hospitals, is drawn to pages 10 to 14 of Extracts from General Routine Orders, and especially to the proforma mentioned in pages 13 and 14 headed Regulations under the Regimental Debts Act 1893.

[signature]

LIEUT COLONEL,
A.A.&.Q.M.G.
14TH (LIGHT) DIVISION.

NOTICE.

Church Services, Sunday October 1st, 1916.

WARLUS = Holy Communion 7.30 a.m.
             Evensong 7 p.m.
  in the C.E. Chapel, Rue d'Agnez.
BERNEVILLE = Holy Communion 7.30 a.m.
             Div.H.Q.Morning Service 9.30 a.m.
             Evensong 6 p.m.
  in the Church Army Hut.
  Elsewhere as by local arrangement.

14TH (LIGHT) DIVISION.

ROUTINE ORDERS.

30th September, 1916.

1783. HIRE OF GROUND.

If it is desired to take up any ground for training, ground suitable also for purposes of recreation should be selected as long as the requirements of training are fully met.

Rent agreements will be made by Rents Officer on application through Div'l Headquarters.

1784. WINTER HEATING.

Town Commandants will forward to Div'l H.Qrs by October 3rd an estimate of the number of stoves required for their area for winter heating, on the following form :-

Description of building.	Number of Buildings	Stoves each	Total Stoves.
Huts holding less than 10 men,			
" " 10 to 25 men,			
" " 25 to 50 "			
" " 50 to 100 "			
Barns holding less than 10 men			
" " 10 to 25 men			
" " 25 to 50 "			
Rooms holding less than 10 men			
" " 10 to 25 men			
" " more than 25 men			
Huts holding One Officer,			
" " 2 to 5 Officers,			
Rooms holding one officer,			
" " 2 to 5 Officers			
Mess rooms less than 100 sq feet			
" " over 100 sq feet			
Offices,			
Drying Rooms,			

(2) Div.R.A. and Infantry Brigades will forward by the same date an estimate of the number of braziers and stoves required for the areas occupied by them outside the jurisdiction of Town Commandants. Estimates of stoves required within the jurisdiction of the Town Major, ARRAS, will be rendered by R.A. and Infantry Brigades concerned on the form in para 1.

1785. WINTER TIME.

Winter time will come into force on the 1st October. At 1 a.m. (Summer Time) on that date the clocks will be put back one hour.
(G.R.O.1828).

(Continued)

-2-

1786. **BICYCLES.**

It has been brought to notice that a considerable number of bicycles have recently been lost owing to their having been removed when left unattended by their riders.

It is to be distinctly under that any individual who removes a motor bicycle or pedal bicycle, even though it has been abandoned, is responsible for reporting the matter to his Commanding Officer at once, with a view to a notice being published in Division, Corps and Army Routine Orders.

Any bicycle so found is to be returned at once to the Supply Column through which the unit draws its supplies.

Disciplinary action will be taken in all cases of persons being found in improper possession of bicycles.
(G.R.O.1829).

1787. **TRENCH MORTAR AMMUNITION.**

An effort is to be made to collect spare parts of Trench Mortar Ammunition of which a large quantity is believed to be lying about in the trenches and forward area.

LIEUT COLONEL,
A.A.&.Q.M.G.
14TH (LIGHT) DIVISION.

CHURCH SERVICES.
R.C. = 1-10-16.

Holy Mass at DAINVILLE Parish Church 8.30 a.m.
Benediction   "   "   "   6 p.m.
Holy Mass at WARLUS Parish Church 8 a.m.
   "   "   " ARRAS (Hopital St.Jean) 9.30 a.m.
Holy Mass at ACHICOURT (Mairie) 7.30 a.m.

14TH (LIGHT) DIVISION.

ROUTINE ORDERS.

1st October, 1916.

1788. HONOURS AND REWARDS.

Under authority of H.M. THE KING, Military Medals are awarded to the undermentioned N.C.Os and men :-

5TH OX & BUCKS L.I.

23824. Pte E. Horton,
10243. " A.E. White,
11764. L/Corpl.H. Smith,
10921. Pte E.G. Danks,
11543. Cpl R.S. Angell,
24424. Pte E. Halloran,
23834. " F.J. Salisbury,
18784. " J.H. Endicott,
10896. Sgt.A.W. Lewendon,
16596. Pte H. Jones
   (att.42nd Bde H.Qrs).

5TH K.S.L.I.

11512. Pte.W.Thomas (att.42ndBde H.
10773. Sergt.J. Maddox,
11083. " T. Tomkins,
10677. Corpl. J. Rogers,
16350. Pte J. Challinor,
18170. " T. Bithell,
11508. " J. Lawley,
17469. " W. Lewis,
17488. " J. Hopwood,
7133. Sergt.F. Langford,
6843. Pte. J. McKeon,
11084. " C. James.

7TH K.R.R.C.

1504. Rfmn. A. Shaw,
8008. " J. Millward,
9726. " W. Charity,
3274. " H. Batson,
8277. Sergt.R. Morris,
5421. Rfmn. R. Lee,
8225. L/Cpl.T. Taylor,
12045. Rfmn. W. Woodhouse,
   (att.41st Bde H.Qrs).

9th K.R.R.C.

6986. Corpl.W. Barker,
2507. Rfmn. R.F. Ames,
12353. L/Cpl.W. Peyto,
11697. Rfmn. S. Styants,
99. Rfmn. A. Ellis,
13411. L/Cpl.C.A. Russell,
10452. Corpl.E. Rutty,
11517. Rfmn. W. Seddon,
5/5064. " D. Savage,
10900. " A. Tyler,
8216. L/Cpl.L. Pendleton,
2773. " W.R. Peniston,-
   (Bar to Military Medal).

7TH RIFLE BDE.

14543. Rfmn. A.E. Ward,
3459. Sergt. C. Blunt,
10128. Corpl. A. Miles,
2055. Rfmn. T. Pugh,
2421. Rfmn. H. Duncan,
707. Rfmn. C. Fincham,
13386. Rfmn. R. Tyreman,
   (att.41st Inf.Bde H.Qrs).

9TH RIFLE BDE.

203129. Rfmn. H. Walters,
47. L/Cpl.G. Gullifer,
2020. " C. Storer,
   (bar to Military Medal).
1561. Rfmn. C. Hadley,
9833. Corpl.J. Hathaway,
3278. Sergt.H. Joyce,
8689. Rfmn. G.F. Linton,
   (att.42nd Inf.Bde H.Qrs).

1789. REPORT - Issue of Paillasses.

It has been proposed that the issue of paillasses to troops out of the line would tend to economy in straw and cleanliness, and would be much appreciated by the troops.

It is proposed to sanction the issue on condition that :-

(a) The Paillasses are kept in the areas for which they are issued and not removed by troops when moving, nor taken into the trenches.

(b) The paillasses are not used in tents.

The covers for the paillasses will be issued from Ordnance Base Depots ready made up.

Units will report by noon 3rd instant through the usual channels the number of paillasses required by them in the location they occupy on 2nd instant.

(Continued)

1790. ARRAS - TOWN ORDERS.

In consequence of the alteration of the time, the following amendments will be made to Town Orders, ARRAS:-

                    Alter to read:-
Para.	6.	6-0 p.m. to 9-0 p.m.
"	5.	7.45 p.m. to 9-0 p.m.
"	13e.	4-0 p.m.
"	15.	8-45 p.m. to 9-0 p.m.
"	19a.	6-0 p.m.
"	19c.	10-0 p.m.

All copies to be amended accordingly.
    (VI Corps A.269/1.)

1791. TRAFFIC ORDERS.

Reference Traffic Orders issued with D.R.Os dated 29th September, 1916:
The hours therein mentioned are altered to read as follows :-

        WARLUS   6 p.m.
        BERNEVILLE 6 p.m.
        BEAUMETZ.   6.15 p.m.

                        LIEUT-COLONEL,
                        A.A.&.Q.M.G.
               14TH (LIGHT) DIVISION.

NOTICE.

Div'l Canteen will be open at BERNEVILLE daily from 10 am to 12 noon, 12.45 to 2 p.m. and 4 to 8 p.m. beginning on Monday October 2nd.

Div. Beer Supply is open at Train Headquarters, BARLY; Price of French Beer 75 francs per 100 litres, Deposit on barrels 10 francs per 100 litres. Terms Cash.

LOST: Service Bicycle, No.24974 - Mark on Frame No.103 Coy. Red club on rear Mudguard.
    Missed from yard in WANQUETIN on 27th September, 1916.
    Information to O.C. No.4 Coy, 14th Div'l Train.

14TH (LIGHT) DIVISION.

ROUTINE ORDERS.

rd October, 1916.

1792. R.E. MATERIAL.- Waste of.

A certain amount of R.E. material is wastefully employed throughout the area owing to men having built themselves bivouacs holding 2 or 3 men only.

The construction of further bivouacs of this kind is forbidden.

The occupation of existing bivouacs is also forbidden in all localities where there is sufficient accommodation in huts or barns.

Town Commandants will salve all possible R.E. material especially corrugated iron and will report what they have on hand to C.R.E.

C.R.E. has placed his Regimental Sergeant Major at the disposal of Div'l Headquarters, to advise Town Commandants on the question of Salvage of R.E. material and this W.O. will visit all Villages in turn. C.R.E. will wire to each Town Commandant the day before the W.O. is due to visit his village and the Town Commandant will arrange to meet him.

1793. TRANSPORT.

No transport vehicles are to move at a faster pace than a walk. Guns and ammunition wagons will only trot when necessary for tactical reasons.

1794. DIVINE SERVICE.

Requested that every facility may be given to soldiers of the Jewish Faith to attend a Special Service to be held at ACQ by the Senior Jewish Chaplain to the Forces at 10 a.m. on Saturday next, the 7th inst. Soldiers wishing to attend should be directed to report at Cross-roads WARLUS at 9 a.m. that day, when conveyances to and from ACQ will be in waiting.

C.L. Hamilton

LIEUT-COLONEL,
A.A.&.Q.M.G.
14TH (LIGHT) DIVISION.

NOTICE.

CHURCH OF ENGLAND CHAPEL, WARLUS.

A furnished Chapel has been established opposite the French Mission, Rue d'Agnez:

Holy Communion Sundays, Tuesdays, Thursdays 7.30 a.m.
                 Wednesdays 10.30 a.m. (Choral).
Evensong   Sundays (Choral) 7 p.m.
                 Wednesdays 6.30 p.m.

14TH (LIGHT) DIVISION.

ROUTINE ORDERS.

1795. LIGHTS.

C.R.O.854 dated 21-5-16 as amended by C.R.O.901 dated 1-6-16, is republished for information :-

(a) Between the hours of dusk and dawn, all Motor vehicles will, except as specified below, have both side lamps lighted in area where lights are allowed. If in possession of headlights, these will be used in addition.

(b) Headlights may not be used East of the following line :- AGNEZ-LES-DUISANS - GOUVES - MONTENESCOURT - WANQUETIN - GOUY-EN-ARTOIS - all exclusive.

(c) East of the MAROEUIL - DAINVILLE Railway, and South of the DAINVILLE - BERNEVILLE - SIMENCOURT - GOUY-EN-ARTOIS road, exclusive, no lights may be used.

(d) Bicycles and Motor bicycles will be exempt from the above regulations and will use their lights up to ARRAS, except on the DOULLENS - ARRAS Road east of LE BAC DU SUD, or on any of the roads running east from the above road, when no lights are permitted.

1796. CHALK PITS.

Chalk pits are allotted as follows:-

POSITION.	For troops at.	Officer in charge
BARLY, P.15.c.5.5.	BARLY, FOSSEUX.	Town Major, BARLY.
SIMENCOURT, Q.16.d.8.9.	BEAUMETZ, SIMENCOURT, MONCHIET.	" " SIMENCOURT.
BERNEVILLE, Q.12.a.8.5.	BERNEVILLE, WARLUS.	" " BERNEVILLE.

All wagons requiring chalk will call at the office of the Town Major in charge of the chalk pit before going to the chalk pit.

Instructions as to the correct way of working chalk pits have been issued to Town Majors concerned.

1797. BRICKS.

Bricks are available near AGNY Chateau, M.8.a.8.9. and will be issued by 62nd Field Co. R.E. nightly between 7.30 and 10.30 p.m.

Indents must be sent to the C.R.E. who will given written authority for 62nd Field Co.R.E. to issue the bricks. The transport fetching the bricks must produce this written authority.

1798. VERMOREL SPRAYERS.

The allowance of Vermorel Sprayers is as follows:-

41st Infantry Brigade,	32.
42nd Infantry Brigade,	24.
43rd Infantry Brigade,	24.
Div'l Artillery,	11.
Field Ambulance Dressing Stations,	9.
Divisional Anti-Gas School,	6.

All in excess of this number are to be sent to D.A.D.O.S. by October 7th.

LIEUT-COLONEL,
A.A.&.Q.M.G.
14TH (LIGHT) DIVISION.

14TH (LIGHT) DIVISION.

ROUTINE ORDERS.

5th October, 1916.

1799. R.E. STORES.

Units other than Infantry, R.E. and Pioneers drawing stores from R.E. Parks must send 2 men per vehicle for loading.

1800. USE OF LIVE GRENADES NEAR TELEGRAPH AND TELEPHONE LINES.

Attention is called to VI Corps Routine Order No. 1263 dated 9-9-16, forbidding practice with live grenades within 100 yards of Poled telegraph lines.

C.A. Hamilton
LIEUT-COLONEL,
A.A.&.Q.M.G.
14TH (LIGHT) DIVISION.

14TH (LIGHT) DIVISION.

ROUTINE ORDERS.

6th October, 1916.

1801. HONOURS AND REWARDS.

Under authority granted by H.M. THE KING, Military Medals are awarded to the undermentioned N.C.Os and men :-

ROYAL ARTILLERY.

No.83677.	Sergeant F. Greening,	A/49th Bde R.F.A.
72718.	Bombr. J.J. Clark,	B/49th Bde R.F.A.
72758.	Gunner A. Ward,	B/49th Bde R.F.A.

14TH SIGNAL CO. R.E.

No.48044. Sergt. R.G. Thompson,
48070. Sapper F. Lydiate,
48069. 2/Cpl. R. Dickinson,
40483. Sapper L.N. Lewis,
48027. Pioneer W.T. Smith.

[signature]

LIEUT-COLONEL,
A.A.&.Q.M.G.
14TH (LIGHT) DIVISION.

DIVINE SERVICES - OCT.8TH 1916.

C OF E.

WARLUS:- H.Q.Chapel, opposite French Mission, Rue d'Agnez,
   Holy Communion 7.30 a.m.
   Evening Service 7 p.m.

BERNEVILLE: Church Army Hut.
   Holy Communion 8.15 p.m.
   Div.H.Q.service 9.30 a.m.
   Evening Service 6 p.m.

ARRAS: Cavalry Barracks Chapel.
   Holy Communion 7.15 p.m.
   Morning Service 6.30 p.m.
   Elsewhere as by local arrangement.

R.C.
Mass at Parish Church, BERNEVILLE 8 a.m.
 "   "   "   "   DAINVILLE, 8 a.m.
 "   " Hospital St.Jean, ARRAS, 9.30 a.m.
 "   " RIVIERE 9.30 a.m.
 "   " AGNY 10 a.m.
 "   " BERNEVILLE 10 a.m.
Evening Service at RIVIERE 5.30 p.m.
 "   "   " DAINVILLE 6 p.m.

ROUTINE ORDERS.   7th October, 1916.

1802. HONOURS AND REWARDS.

Under authority granted by H.M. THE KING, the following decorations have been awarded :-

THE MILITARY CROSS.

ROYAL ARTILLERY.

T/Lieut. E.A.E. Hart,   A/49th Bde R.F.A.
2/Lieut. G.W. Jones,   C/49th Bde R.F.A.
2/Lieut. S.L. McIvor,   D/48th Bde R.F.A.

14TH SIGNAL CO. R.E.

T/Lieut. A.H. Douglas.

5th OX & BUCKS L.I.

T/Captain E.W. Maude,
T/Lieut. C.H. Walter.

5th BN. K.S.L.I.

T/Capt. G. Turner,
No. 9406, Coy.Sergt.Major G.C. Furber.

9TH K.R.R.C.

T/2nd Lieut. G.B.deC. Ireland,
T/2nd Lieut. M. Summerfield.

9th RIFLE BDE.

T/Lieut. R.O. Brown.

9TH RIFLE BDE.

2/Lieut. H.C. Round.

R.A.M.C. Attached 5th Bn. K.S.L.I.

Capt. J.T. Smeall, R.A.M.C.

THE DISTINGUSIHED CONDUCT MEDAL.

5TH OX & BUCKS L.I.

No. 8614, Corpl. V.M. Mills.

5th BN. K.S.L.I.

No. 9714. Sergt. H. Beeston,
11089. "   J. Morgan.

9TH BN. K.R.R.C.

No. 21709. Sergt. L. Elderfield,
A.425. Pte. F. Gristwood.

7TH BN. RIFLE BDE.

No. S/6207. Pte A. Jessup.

9TH BN. RIFLE BDE.

No. 5328, Sergt. H. Gerrard,
1372. Pte. M.P. McMorrow,

THE MILITARY MEDAL.

9TH BN. RIFLE BDE.

No. S/8174. Pte. L. Sandretch.

1803. BANDS.

No band is permitted to play in ARRAS.

14TH (LIGHT) DIVISION.

ROUTINE ORDERS.

8th October, 1916.

1804. HONOURS AND REWARDS.

Reference D.R.O.1788 dated 1st October, the award of a MILITARY MEDAL to No.10896, Sergeant A.W. Lewendon, 5th Ox & Bucks L.I. should read BAR to MILITARY MEDAL, a Military Medal having been awarded to him on 14th September.

1805. FUEL.

The following are the days allotted to units for drawing Fuel :-

MONDAY.	WEDNESDAY.
H.Q. 43rd Inf.Bde.	H.Q. 42nd Inf. Bde.
43rd M.G. Coy.	42nd M.G. Coy.
4 Bns, 43rd Inf.Bde.	4 Bns 42nd Inf.Bde.
47th Bde R.F.A.	14th D.A.C.
62nd Field Co. R.E.	14th T.M.Batteries.
	26th Mob.Vet.Section.

TUESDAY.	THURSDAY.
H.Q.41st Inf.Bde.	
41st M.G. Coy.	4 Bns 43rd Inf.Bde.
4 Bns 41st Inf.Bde.	H.Q.49th Bde R.F.A.
48th Bde R.F.A.	8th M.M.G.Bty.
H.Q.14th Division.	Units attached for rations:-
H.Q.14th Div.Train.	4th Kite Sqdn. R.F.C.
11th L'pool R	3rd Field Survey Co.
89th Field Co.R.E.	14th Div'l School.
1,2,3,& 4 Coys.Div.Train.	

FRIDAY.
4 Bns.41st Inf.Bde.
11th L'pool R
R.A.,H.Q.,14th Divn.
R.E.,H.Q.,14th Divn.
61st Field Co.R.E.
46th Bde R.F.A.

SATURDAY.
4 Bns.42nd Inf.Bde.
Div.Supply Column.
14th Div.Signal Co.R.E.
M.M.P.
25th Sanitary Section.

Field Ambulances to draw daily, if required.
Fuel will be issued between the hours of 9 a.m. and 4 p.m. on production of an order signed by the Supply Officer from whom the unit draws rations.

1806. RETURNS.

The fortnightly return of deficiencies of Lewis Gun Magazines is no longer required.
The normal procedure of indenting will be followed.

(Continued)

1807. SALVAGE.

The following is a list of articles salved by 14th Div'l Salvage Coy:-

WEEK ENDED 7-10-16.

No. Collected.	Description of Articles	Serviceable (S) or Unserviceable (US)	How Disposed of.
7	Wheels, G.S.	U.S.	DADOS for Railhead.
13 Bxs.	Horse Shoes,	U.S.	Railhead.
1 Bag	Brake Blocks,	U.S.	-do-
5	Boilers, T.K.	U.S.	-do-
10 Sacks	Clothing,	S.	D.A.D.O.S
8 "	Clothing,	U.S.	DADOS for railhead.
4 "	Underclothing,	U.S.	railhead.
4 "	Boots,	U.S.	-do-
1	Wheel (cycle)	S.	remaining at dump.
15	Oil drums,	S.	
1 Bag	Equipment,	S.	
6	Shrapnel Helmets,	S.	D.A.D.O.S
3 Bags	Smoke Helmets, P.H.	U.S.	Remaining at dump
5 Reels	Wire Cable,	S.	
1	Pole Bar No.7	U.S.	

1808. SICK WASTAGE.

The following is the Sick Wastage Return for week ended Noon 7th October, 1916:-

Unit	O.	O.R.	Unit	O.	O.R
46th Bde R.F.A.		4.	5th Ox & Bucks L.I.		1.
47th Bde R.F.A.		1.	5th K.S.L.I.	1.	5.
48th Bde R.F.A.		2.	9th K.R.R.C.		3.
49th Bde R.F.A.		9.	9th R.B.		2.
14th D.A.C.		Nil.	42nd M.G. Coy.		Nil
V.14 T.M. Battery,		Nil.	42nd T.M. Bty.		Nil
X.14 T.M. Battery		Nil.	6th Som.L.I.		1.
Y.14 T.M. Battery,		Nil.	6th D.C.L.I.		4.
Z.14 T.M. Battery,		Nil.	6th K.O.Y.L.I.		5.
8th M.M.G.Battery,		Nil.	10th Durham L.I.		8.
61st Field Co. R.E.		1.	43rd M.G. Coy.		1.
62nd Field Co. R.E.		2.	43rd T.M. Bty.		Nil
89th Field Co. R.E.		3.	11th L'pool R		5.
14th Signal Co.R.E.		2.	14th Div'l Train.		2.
7th K.R.R.C.		4.	14th Div.Supply Col.		Nil
8th K.R.R.C.		7.	42nd F.Amb.		Nil
7th R.B.		7.	43rd F.Amb.		Nil
8th R.B.		Nil.	44th F.Amb.		2.
41st M.G. Coy.		1.	25th Sanitary Section		Nil
41st T.M. Bty.		Nil.	26th Mob.Vet.Section,		1.

Totals Officers 1, Other Ranks 83.

Lieut-Colonel,
A.A.& Q.M.G.
14th (Light) Division.

14TH (LIGHT) DIVISION.

ROUTINE ORDERS.

9th October, 1916

1809. **HONOURS AND REWARDS.**

Under authority granted by H.M. THE KING, Military Medals have been awarded as under :-

ROYAL ARTILLERY.

No. 38.	Corpl. W. Belding,	C/46th Bde R.F.A.
3896.	Gunner G.H. Holliday,	D/46th Bde R.F.A.
84810.	Bombr. W. Holmes,	H.Q., 46th Bde R.F.A.
27422.	Driver R. Cherry.	
83935.	Bombr. (now Corpl) W.H. Fripp,	B/48th Bde R.F.A.
89329.	Sergt. T. White,	B/48th Bde R.F.A.
83738.	Gunner, Frank A. Vincent,	C/48th Bde R.F.A.
98047.	Gunner C.H. Woolford.	

8TH BN. K.R.R.C.

No. 650.	Rfmn. H. Booker,
No. 157.	Sergt. W.E. Crew,
10845.	Rfmn. T. Green,
112.	L/Cpl. B. Creswick,
156.	Sergt. R. Greig,
631.	Rfmn. G.F. Wicketts,
12921.	Rfmn. E.G. Thackwell,
130.	Sergt. A.E. Remington,
2958.	Rfmn. H.J. Barr,
16196.	Rfmn. V. Stokes,
8099.	Corpl. S. Johnson,
3528.	L/Cpl. F. Edwards
	(Bar to Military Medal.)
8405.	Rfmn. J. Hill,
10698.	Rfmn. S. Cottee,
9460.	Rfmn. T. Smith,

8TH BN. RIFLE BDE.

No. 7205.	Corpl. J.R. Aspden,	
683.	Rfmn. H. Warden,	
6/621.	"	F. Smith,
9482.	"	F. Eckman,
11346.	"	H. Meech,
688.	"	J.W. Bennett,
1113.	A/Cpl. S. Mather,	
526.	Rfmn. G. Parsons,	
6600.	"	C. Parker,

41ST MACHINE GUN CO.

19805.	Sergt. A.M. McColl,
19776.	L/Cpl. R.C. Stephens,
19774.	Sergt. L.V. Shepherd,
19775.	Corpl. E.W. Osborne,
19777.	Corpl. V.L.H. Smith,
19781.	L/Cpl. F.A. Lee,

7TH K.R.R.C. attd 41st Machine Gun Co.

No. 6432.	Rfmn. W.E. Pidgeon,
12129.	Pte. A.E. May.

1810. **RIFLE GRENADES.**

To eliminate a slight risk of prematures all detonators for No.3 and No.20 Rifle Grenades in possession will, wherever possible, be varnished at the cap end.

If it is found impracticable to do this, the danger of accidents from prematures may be minimised by firing the grenades from behind cover by means of a string attached to the trigger.

No.3 and No.20 Rifle Grenades of later date than 14th June 1916, will have altered caps, but none of these have yet been issued to VI Corps. No more manufactured prior to the date mentioned will be issued from Railhead unvarnished.

A suitable varnish is the following :-
    1 lb. Gum shellac.
    2 lbs. Methylated spirit.

Any No.3 and No.20 Rifle Grenades prior to June 14th 1916 will be evacuated to D.A.C. and treated there.

Captain for
Lieut-Colonel,

14TH (LIGHT) DIVISION

ROUTINE ORDERS.

10th October, 1916.

1811. **HONOURS AND REWARDS.**

Under authority granted by H.M. THE KING, Military Medals have been awarded as under:-

ROYAL ARTILLERY.

No.51827, Sergt. (A/B.Q.M.S) F.H. Lee, 'A' Echelon,
14th D.A.C.

ROYAL ENGINEERS.

No.46898, Sapper E. Tomlinson, 89th Field Co. R.E.

43RD MACHINE GUN COMPANY.

No.22053, Pte A. McPheely,
20101. A.L/Cpl. R. Craig,
43834. Pte G.N.F. Kent.

1/4TH SUFFOLK REGT attd 43RD M.G. COY.

No. 3127. Pte.E. Shephard,
3694. " W. Ward.

11TH BN. KING'S (L'POOL) REGT (PIONEERS).

No.1/7003.A/Cpl. W. Roberts.

6th SOMERSET L.I.

No.14657. Sergt. L. Phippen,
7256. Corpl. H.G. Symington,
7372. Bugler W.H. Phillips,
14878. Sergt. A. Bolwell.

6TH D.C.L.I.

No.10665. Sergt. A. Humphries
12363. A/Cpl. F. Dobsen,
12125. Sergt. G.F. Dowsett,
11275. Pte A. Flynn,
11972. " E.W. Fellows,
12297. " C.A. Blake,
11408. A/Cpl. L.J. Broadway,
10708. Cpl. H.H. Martin,
19680. Pte. R. Smith,
11675. " F.A.V. Atkins.

21104. Pte J.A. Baker.
Attd.43rd Bde H.Qrs :-
19660. Pte A.J. Vernon.

10TH DURHAM L.I.

No.13053. Cpl. R. Gordon,
23082. L/Cpl. W. Beale,
8516. Pte H. Grier,
(attd.43rd Bde H.Qrs).

6TH BN. K.O.Y.L.I.

No.11327. Pte M. Murray,
21758. Sgt. T. Cooke,
15573. " A. Vaughan,
10378. " A. Norcliffe,
1123. Cpl. T. Guite,
11473. Pte. J.W. Howell,
3117. " T. Benson,
9249. Sgt. G. Whatmore.
attd.43rd Bde H.Qrs.,:-
18081. Pte B. Cave.

ROYAL ARMY MEDICAL CORPS.

42nd Field Ambulance.

No. 1223. Pte A. Suckling.

44th Field Ambulance,

No.31658. Sergt. J. Corbishley,
32142. L/Cpl. J.G. Atkinson,
30818. Pte. J. Rimmer.

43rd Field Ambulance.

No.31822. Pte R. Gill,
36420. Sgt. B. Pearce,
34871. Cpl. P. Hannigan,
32983. Pte A. Stockburn,
33393. " L. Tingle.

(Over)

1812. **CARRIAGE OF WATER TO THE TRENCHES.**

In future all 2-gallon tins issued for the purpose of carrying water to the trenches will be taken on as Trench Stores, and included in the weekly return.

1813. **PUMPS, FIRE, HAND.**

Attention is directed to C.R.O.1339.
Pumps, hand, fire, Mark II, will be included on the weekly return of Trench and Area Stores.

CAPTAIN FOR
LIEUT-COLONEL,
A.A.&Q.M.G.
14TH (LIGHT) DIVISION.

14TH (LIGHT) DIVISION.

ROUTINE ORDERS.

12th October, 1916.

1814. VERY PISTOLS.

Attention is directed to C.R.O.1347.

1815. BILLETS IN ARRAS.

Attention of all units is directed to para 7(a) of Town Orders, ARRAS, which must be strictly complied with in every detail.

1816. ROADS.

Town Commandants and Officers Commanding troops billeted in towns and villages are responsible that the roads are kept clean.

The mud on the surface and at the sides of the road must be removed to some convenient place outside the town or village.

Ditches alongside the roads must be kept clean and special attention given to the portion of the ground between the ditches and the road so that the surface water from the road may drain into the ditches.

Mud must not be allowed to remain in heaps at the side of the road as this lessens the width of the road. Such heaps also interfere with the drainage of the road surface.

Indents for road scrapers and road brooms should be sent in to C.R.E.

Capt
LIEUT-COLONEL,
A.A.&.Q.M.G.
14TH (LIGHT) DIVISION.

ROUTINE ORDERS.

14th October, 1916.

1817. RAILWAY WARRANTS.

Attention of all concerned is drawn to G.R.O. No.1859, dated 10-10-16.

1818. REVOLVERS: SPANISH MANUFACTURE.

All revolvers in possession of troops marked on top of barrel :-
"Manafactura Especial de Revolvers Garate Anitua Y Cia., Eibar, (Espana) "
will be replaced, and demands for the number required in replacement will be submitted through the usual channels.
The revolvers of this pattern should be inspected and those found faulty should be considered first: The remainder will be dealt with directly the position of supply enables exchange to be carried out: It should be stated on indents whether those in exchange are required to replace revolvers actually found to be defective.
(Authority: Q.O.S./141/40/A, dated 10-10-16. VI Corps Q/663.).

1819. LEAVE.

The names of any N.C.Os and men who become entitled to ONE MONTHS leave under G.R.O.1679 during October and November should be forwarded to this office without delay.

1820. ARRIVAL OF REINFORCEMENTS.

D.R.O. No.1739 is re-published :-
"The arrival of reinforcements during the preceding 24 hours ending 9 a.m. will be reported to Div'l Headquarters by all units through the usual channels.
Reports to reach this office by 6 p.m.
Rank, Name and Initials of Officers to be stated: number of Other Ranks.
No Officer or man returning from Field Ambulances or elsewhere who is already on the strength is to be included in this return.

CAPTAIN, for
LIEUT-COLONEL,
A.A.&.Q.M.G.
14TH (LIGHT) DIVISION.

14/10/16.

DIVINE SERVICES.
SUNDAY, OCT. 19th 1916.

C of E.
WARLUS. Chapel, Rue d'Agnez. Holy Communion 7 a.m.
                                Evensong, 7 p.m.
BERNEVILLE. Church Army Hut. Holy Communion 8 a.m.
                    D.H.Q. Morning Service 9.30 a.m.
                            Evening Service, 6. p.m.
ARRAS. Cavalry Barrack Chapel. Holy Communion 7.30 a.m.
                           Morning Service 10 a.m.
                           Sung Celebration 11.45 a.m.
                           Evening Service 6.30 p.m.
RONVILLE. Canteen. Holy Communion 11 a.m.
ACHICOURT. Reformed Chapel. Holy Communion 8.30 a.m.
DAINVILLE) Church of England Chapels are established in each place,
RIVIERE.) with regular services. See local notices.

R.C.
 8.30 a.m:- Mass at DAINVILLE Parish Church: BERNEVILLE Parish Chu
 9.30 a.m:-   "   " RIVIERE.
10.30 a.m.   "   " AGNY.
11 a.m.   "   " WAILLY.
Evening Services at RIVIERE at 5.30 p.m. and DAINVILLE 6.30 p.m

14TH (LIGHT) DIVISION.

ROUTINE ORDERS.

15th October, 1916.

1821. HONOURS AND REWARDS.

Under authority granted by H.M. THE KING, Military Medals have been awarded as under :-

ROYAL ARTILLERY.

B/48th Bde R.F.A.	30054	Gunner D. Edwards,
" " "	8013.	" W.O. Harding,
" " "	97973.	" G.W. Thear.
C/47th Bde R.F.A.	83971.	Corporal W. Gibbs,
B/48th Bde R.F.A.	23817.	Driver F. Feeney,
B/47th Bde R.F.A.	83727.	Gunner G. Ray,
C/47th Bde R.F.A.	96256.	Sergeant W.J. Merryweather,
C/46th Bde R.F.A.	33421.	Bombr. J. Boyle,
D/46th Bde R.F.A.	95525.	Gunner T. Ragan,
" " "	93613.	" J. McIntosh,
C/47th Bde R.F.A.	97797.	Sergeant A. Latimer,
D/47th Bde R.F.A.	99767.	Gunner J. Noonan,
No.1 Sect. "A" Ech.		
14th D.A.C.	27134.	Sergeant H.G. Bailey,
-do-	1805.	" S.D. Pearce,
-do-	123124.	Wheeler J.S. Tremayne,
-do-	62607.	Driver W.J. Restrick.

41ST INFANTRY BDE.
7th K.R.R.C. attd.
41st T.M. Bty.   Y/1059.   Sergeant H.C. Wheeler.

1822. PRISONERS OF WAR - INTERCOURSE AND COMMERCE WITH PROHIBITED.

G.R.O. No.1839 dated 5/10/16 is republished for information.
"No communication, except on official matters, and in the performance of duty: and no sale or barter of articles whatsoever is allowed between officers, soldiers and civilians on the one hand, and Prisoners of War on the other. This does not refer to the authorised purchase of articles from the Canteen by Prisoners of War.

Any breach of this order will entail severe punishment.
This order is to be read out on three consecutive parades and promulgated to all ranks.
A copy of this order is to be posted in all Prisoners of War Camps".

1823. DOGS.

Attention is directed to General Routine Orders 1808 and 1843 re Dogs. Cases have occurred where these orders have not been enforced. Steps will immediately be taken to ensure that the above mentioned General Routine Orders are complied with forthwith.
This order is to be re-published in Brigade Orders.

1824. STEEL HELMETS.

With reference to General Routine Order No. 1847, Indents to complete to the authorised scale of Steel Helmets should be forwarded to Base as early as possible, and a report furnished by wire to this office through the usual channels by noon 19th inst that this has been done.

(Continued)

1825. **MAXIMUM PRICES OF FOODSTUFFS.**

The maximum prices to be paid for dried vegetables, potatoes and eggs, have been fixed under French Law as follows :-

```
                          Beans
Dried Vegetables,/(Lingots)              0.90 per Kg.
                                         0.30  "    "
Dry Onions,                             15.00 per 100 Kgs.
Potatoes, Yellow (at the farmer)        20.00  "   "    "
          do.    (market and retail)    12.00  "   "    "
          White  (at the farmer)        17.00  "   "    "
          do.    (market and retail)    10.00  "   "    "
          Bigblue(at the farmer)        15.00  "   "    "
          do.    (market and retail)
The same quality taken at wholesale merchants by 1,000 Kgs.
          Yellow                        16.25
          White                         13.25
          Bigblue                       11.25
Eggs (newly laid)                    {   5.85 for 26.
                                     {   0.45 for 2.
   do. (fresh)                       {   3.90 for 26.
                                     {   0.30 for 2.
```

Purchasing Officers should take note of these prices.
(Authority Third Army (D.D.S.&.T.) IDI/69 dated 13-10-16.
VI Corps Q/140).

1826. **SALVAGE.**

The following is a list of articles salved by 14th Div'l Salvage Company :-

WEEK ENDED 14 - 10 - 16.

No. Collected	Description of articles	Serviceable (S) or Unserviceable (US)	How disposed of
12 Sacks	Boots,	U.S.	DADOS for railhead.
21 "	Clothing, S.D.	U.S.	do.
11 "	Underclothes, woollen	U.S.	do.
9. "	Smoke Helmets,	U.S.	do.
10	Shovels,	US.	do.
1 "	Gas Goggles,	U.S.	do.
1	Boiler, T.K.	U.S.	do.
4 Boxes	Horse Shoes,	S.	D.A.D.O.S.
15	Rifles,	S.	D.A.D.O.S.
12	Steel Helmets,	S.	D.A.D.O.S.
48 Pairs	Boots, ankle,	S.	D.A.D.O.S.
1	Bayonet	S.	11th L'pool
1 Reel,	Wire cable,	S.	Remaining at Dump.
2 Sacks	Equipment,	U.S.	-do-
20	Mess tins,	S.	-do-
12	Water Bottles,	U.S.	-do-
5 Sacks	Clothing,	U.S.	-do-
4 "	Boots,	S.	-do-
2	Rifles,	S.	-do-
4.	Bayonets,	S.	-do-
4.	Steel Helmets,	U.S.	-do-
2 Boxes	Smoke Helmets,	S.	-do-
4 Reels	Cable wire,	S.	-do-
22 Boxes	S.A.A. (empty)	U.S.	-do-
4 Sacks	Horse Shoes	S.	-do-
5 Bags	S.A.A.	U.S.	-do-
2	Sheets, ground,		

CAPTAIN, for
A.A.&.Q.M.G.
14TH (LIGHT) DIVISION

14TH (LIGHT) DIVISION.

ROUTINE ORDERS.

16th October, 1916.

1827. BICYCLES - "Tyreoid" Solution.

Reports will be rendered to this office through the usual channels by noon 19th inst, as to whether any complaints have been received regarding the "Tyreoid" solution for Bicycles, authorised under G.R.O.1639.
(Authority Third Army O/210 dated 12-10-16. VI Corps G/754).

1828. FUEL.

G.R.O. 1242 is republished for information :-
"Attention is drawn to the danger of using braziers burning coke and charcoal, or stoves without chimneys, in covered places where there is no proper ventilation.
In view of the number of dug-outs, cellars and other closed shelters which will be occupied by the troops this winter, it is important that the attention of all concerned should be drawn to the risk involved.
Stoves with piping will be provided by the R.E. where Medical Officers consider the use of braziers undesirable".

1829. SICK WASTAGE.

The following is the Sick Wastage Return for week ended Noon 14th October, 1916 :-

	O.	O.R.		O.	O.R.
46th Bde R.F.A.	1	8	5th Ox & Bucks L.I.	1	10.
47th Bde R.F.A.	1	-	5th K.S.L.I.		8.
48th Bde R.F.A.	1	4	9th K.R.R.C.		8.
49th Bde R.F.A.		Nil.	9th R.B.		7.
14th D.A.C.		4.	42nd M.G. Company,		2.
V.14 T.M. Battery,		Nil.	42nd T.M. Battery,		1.
X.14 T.M. Battery,		Nil.	6th Somerset L.I.		4.
Y.14 T.M. Battery,		Nil.	6th D.C.L.I.		4.
Z.14 T.M. Battery,		Nil.	6th K.O.Y.L.I.		6.
8th M.M.G.Battery,		Nil.	10th Durham L. .	1	4.
61st Field Co. R.E.		3.	43rd M.G. Company,		1.
62nd Field Co. R.E.		2.	43rd T.M. Battery,		Nil.
89th Field Co. R.E.		3.	11th L'pool R		10.
14th Signal Co.R.E.		1.	14th Div'l Train.		3.
7th K.R.R.C.		9.	No.14 Div. Supply Column		2.
8th K.R.R.C.	1	5.	42nd F. Amb.		1.
7th Rifle Bde.		2.	43rd F. Amb.		3.
8th Rifle Bde.		1.	44th Field Amb.		Nil.
41st M.G. Company,		Nil.	25th Sanitary Section,		Nil.
42nd T.M. Battery,		Nil.	26th Mob. Vet. Section,		Nil.

Totals Officers 6, Other Ranks 115.

LIEUT-COLONEL,
A.A.&.Q.M.G.
14TH (LIGHT) DIVISION.

14TH (LIGHT) DIVISION.

ROUTINE ORDERS.

17th October, 1916.

1830. HONOURS AND REWARDS.

Under authority granted by H.M. THE KING, The Military Medal has been awarded to the under-named Non-Commissioned Officer:-

Corporal C. LAWRENCE, 7th Bn. The Rifle Brigade.

1831. BANDS.

D.R.O. No.1803 dated 7-10-16, is cancelled, but discretion is to be observed when selecting the place for a Band to play in ARRAS.

1832. DUMMY DETONATORS.

Reference C.R.O. 1366, dated 16-10-16:
Certificates will be rendered so as to reach this office, through the usual channels, by Noon 29th instant.

1833. ABSENTEES.

Officers Commanding Units should at once notify the A.P.M. of the Return to their Units of any men who have previously been reported to him as absentees.

CAPTAIN, FOR
LIEUT-COLONEL,
A.A.&.Q.M.G.
14TH (LIGHT) DIVISION.

CHURCH SERVICES.
ST.LUKE'S DAY - WEDNESDAY OCTOBER 18TH '16.

Sung Eucharist in the Chapel, WARLUS   10.30 a.m.
Holy Communion, " " " " 19th at   7.30 a.m.

14TH (LIGHT) DIVISION.

ROUTINE ORDERS.

18th October, 1916.

1834. HONOURS AND REWARDS.

Under authority granted by H.M. THE KING, the General Officer Commanding-in-Chief has awarded Decorations as follows :-

DISTINGUISHED SERVICE ORDER

T/Lieut. F.W. Rhodes,	5th Shropshire L.I.

MILITARY CROSS.

Lieut. C.G. Duffin,	B/48th Bde R.F.A.
2/Lt. W.E. Dunnett,	D/46th Bde R.F.A.
2/Lt. C.C. Rowlands,	A/46th Bde R.F.A.
T/Lieut. M.McK. Hughes,	14th D.A.C., R.F.A.
T/Capt. J.W. Lesley,	8th K.R.R.C.
T/Lieut. T.L. Bourdillon,	8th K.R.R.C.
Capt. C.E. Winter,	7th Rifle Bde.
T/Lieut. F.J. Strachan,	RAMC attd. 8th Rifle Bde.
7603. C.S.M. A. Baldock,	8th Rifle Bde.
3469. C.S.M. G.H. Jackson,	8th Rifle Bde.
T/Lieut. L.P.B. Merriam,	41st M.G.Coy, M.G.Corps.
5907. C.S.M. W. Giles,	6th Somerset L.I.
T/Capt. G.H. Forty,	6th D.C.L.I.
T/2nd Lt. V.C. Beckerleg,	-do-
T/2nd Lt. W.J. Bell,	-do-
T/2nd Lt. R.J.O. Adams,	-do-
T/2nd Lt. W.T. Sawyer,	-do-
T/2nd Lt. R. Foulkes,	6th K.O.Y.L.I.
7755. C.S.M. E. Jacobs,	-do-
T/2nd Lt. A.E. Turner,	10th Durham L.I.
24258. C.S.M. C. Wakeham,	-do-.

DISTINGUISHED CONDUCT MEDAL.

6306 C.S.M.(A/R.S.M) J. Bonham,	6th D.C.L.I.
18558. Sergt. C. Coates,	6th K.O.Y.L.I.
20916. " J. Donelly,	10th Durham L.I.

MILITARY MEDAL.

41982. Sapper R. Read,	14th Signal Co. R.E.
12903. Pte. D.L. Hatton,	11th King's L'pools. (Pioneers).
19840. Sergt. F.H. Morris,	42nd M.G. Co. M.G.Corps.

1835. MOTOR VEHICLES.

Attention is directed to Third Army Routine Order No. 530 dated 16th October, 1916.

1836. RIFLE GRENADES.

C.R.O. 1369 dated 17-10-16 is re-published for information:-
It has come to notice that in some cases the safety pins of Rifle Grenades are withdrawn before the grenade has been inserted in the rifle.
This is forbidden, and disciplinary action will be taken in any case where this order is proved to have been disregarded.

(Continued)

183. THIRD ARMY ROUTINE ORDERS.

The following Third Army Routine Orders which have not been otherwise published to 14th Division are inserted for general information :-

475 - Bicycles.
Owing to the large number of bicycles which are reported as lost or stolen, Officers Commanding Units which have bicycles on their charge as part of their equipment will take steps to ensure that these articles are frequently checked, and never less than once a month. Any deficiency will be at once enquired into and dealt with, and the date when this was last done will invariably be stated in the proceedings of any enquiry or report which may arise out of the loss of a bicycle.

478 - Traffic Instructions.
Reference Army Routine Order 376, Motor Transport Movement Orders (S.S.Press No.P.447) are now issued in books of 50. Units should apply direct for future requirements to the Stationery Depot, HAVRE.

480 - Steel Helmets.

Men have been noticed wearing the lining of their steel helmets as a cap. This practice is to cease forthwith. It is forbidden to remove the lining from the steel helmet.

481 - Discipline - Rum, issue of.
The following instructions will be observed regarding the issue of rum :-
(a) Rum may be made a daily issue to Tunnelling Companies, at the discretion of the Corps Commander. Otherwise, rum will not be issued in summer, unless under exceptional circumstances: it will then only be supplied on the authority of the Corps Commander, who will specify the units by whom it may be drawn.
(b) Rum will be issued to the troops in the trenches in the early morning: to troops not in the trenches not later than 8 a.m.
(c) An Officer must be present the whole time the rum is being issued in detail. It is not sufficient for him to see it issued in bulk to squads or platoons. Any surplus will be returned to battalion or other store as soon as possible, and not kept in billets or dug-outs.
(d) All rum will be kept in charge of an officer. In the trenches this officer will be the Company Commander.
(e) Men undergoing punishment for drunkenness will receive no rum for 14 days, unless it is considered necessary, for medical reasons, by a Medical Officer.

(Continued)

1837.
(Contd) **490 - Civilian Furniture.**

Cases have occurred in which civilian furniture has been removed by troops from unoccupied houses and retained for use in messes. etc.

Civilian furniture may only be obtained by purchase. Receipts for the purchase are to be kept, and will be produced on demand when necessary in order to prove ownership.

Units and individuals are forbidden to hold any civilian furniture for which the receipt cannot be immediately produced.

It is to be understood that in the event of a move, it is forbidden to transfer civilian furniture by means of Government transport.

495 - Courts-Martial.

Several cases have occurred recently where men who are under arrest in Field Ambulances of Casualty Clearing Stations in connection with self-inflicted wounds have been tried by Court-Martial and found "Not Guilty" but the finding of the Court has not been intimated to the Medical Authorities concerned.

In such cases, the Medical Authorities should always be informed immediately by the Officer Commanding the man's unit of the finding of "Not Guilty" in order that he may be released from arrest.

507 - Cresol.

Cresol should be used for ordinary disinfecting purposes at a strength of 1½ ozs to the gallon of water except for the spraying of manure, in which case it should be used at a strength of 7½ ozs to the gallon.

Cresol from drums marked "Co-efficiency 3" should be used at a strength of 4½ ozs and 22½ ozs to the gallon of water for above purposes.

The above strength should not be exceeded, except by order of the Medical Officer for special reasons.

LIEUT-COLONEL.
A.A.&.Q.M.G.
14TH (LIGHT) DIVISION.

14TH (LIGHT) DIVISION.

ROUTINE ORDERS.

1838. HORSES.

D.R.O.1736 dated 23-8-16 is republished for information:-
Led Horses being exercised or taken to water will invariably wear bits.

1839. BURIAL GROUNDS.

(i) The following are the authorised burial grounds in the Divisional Area. Reference Sheet 51.b.
- FAUBOURG D'AMIENS, ARRAS,   G.26.b.8.7.
- AGNY Chateau,   H.2.c.9.3.
- WAILLY New Cemetery,   R.22.b.5.9.
- LE FERMONT   R.21.d.3.3.

Graves are kept ready dug at the first-named burial ground. If notification is sent to the cemetery caretaker, ECOLE NORMALE, ARRAS, units need send no one but the actual funeral party.

(ii) No other burial grounds than those specified above are to be used in rear of the trench system.

(iii) The Cemetery in the Rue de Bapaume, RONVILLE, G.34.b.2.6. is closed. No more burials must take place in it.

R. Barrington-Ward Capt
for LIEUT-COLONEL,
A.A.&.Q.M.G.
14TH (LIGHT) DIVISION.

NOTICE.

FOUND: Unmarked Universal SADDLE.
Apply O.C., 54th H.A. Group, R.4.a.50.30.

14TH (LIGHT) DIVISION.

ROUTINE ORDERS.

20th October, 1916.

1840. HONOURS AND REWARDS.

Under authority granted by HIS MAJESTY THE KING, The General Officer Commanding-in-Chief has awarded the following decoration :-

DISTINGUISHED SERVICE ORDER.

Major H.C.M. Porter,   9th Bn. K.R.R.C.

1841. CENSORSHIP.

All ranks are forbidden to disclose in any letter the Brigade, Division or other formation to which their own or any other unit belongs, unless it forms a necessary part of that unit's address. This applies equally to the address on the envelope and the contents of the letter. Holders of Censor stamps will refuse to pass any letters addressed in a manner contravening this order to officers and men serving in this country.

Commanding Officers will ensure that all ranks are aware of this order which will be read in connection with Censorship Orders para 16.

(G.R.O.1869).

1842. CORRESPONDENCE RELATING TO OFFICERS.

Considerable difficulty is experienced in dealing with letters relating to Officers owing to the failure in many cases to state their initials and regiments. Names are, moreover, often wrongly spelt and designations, when given, are incorrect.

Great care is to be taken in correspondence to state accurately the names, ranks and regiments or departments of Officers referred to.

(G.R.O.1873).

1843. DISPOSAL OF CAPTURED STORES.

(a) Attention is called to Field Service Regulations, Part II, Section 118-2. All ranks are reminded that captured guns, mortars, arms, ammunition (including fired cases) equipment of all kinds, clothing, vehicles and other stores, are the property of the Government and should be handed in to the Army Ordnance Department.

Ammunition should be sent in to the nearest Ammunition Railhead, other stores to the nearest Supply Railhead, and handed over to the Ordnance Officer at that Railhead for transmission to the Base.

Should units desire to claim any captured article as a Trophy of War, application should be made to superior authority.

Any person found in possession of, or sending home, property of this nature, except such articles as are mentioned below, and who, having had an opportunity to do so, has failed to report his possession of such property to a superior officer, will be arrested and his conduct in the matter investigated, with a view to bringing him to trial on a charge of theft, or other suitable charge.

(Continued)

DISPOSAL OF CAPTURED STORES (Ctd).

The following articles, not being required by the Government, may be retained and either taken or sent home without special authority:-
- German helmets,
- German caps.
- German badges.
- German numerals.
- German buttons.

(b) Hostile Aircraft. When a hostile aircraft is brought down within our lines, the Officer Commanding the troops on the spot will report its capture and situation to the nearest Royal Flying Corps Wing or Squadron Commander and arrange for the safeguarding of the material until it is taken over by the Royal Flying Corps.

The aircraft and material will be disposed of under the orders of the G.O.C., Royal Flying Corps, who will arrange for such articles as are not required for use or experiment to be handed over to the nearest Ordnance Officer, in accordance with (a) above.

General Routine Orders 549, 1269 and 1448 which are embodied in the above instructions are cancelled.
(G.R.O. 1879).

1844. HORSES - PICKED UP NAILS.

The loss of efficiency in horses attributable to "Picked up Nail" has greatly increased. (700 cases per week have been reported from Veterinary Hospitals alone).

General Routine Order 1135, dated 3-9-15, is cancelled, and the following substituted :-
"(1) All nails must be extracted from wood of boxes before this is issued as fuel.
(2) Ashes from Field Kitchens are not to be raked out near roads, but are to be buried.
(3) Ground in the vicinity of refilling points, both ammunition and supply, or which has been used as such, is to be swept or otherwise cleared of nails.
(4) Care is to be taken in building operations that nails are not left lying about.
(5) Red boxes, with the word 'Nails' painted on them, are to be put up at refilling points, and in lorry parks, villages, and camps, as receptacles for loose nails. These will be cleared periodically under Divisional arrangements."
(G.R.O.1882).

LIEUT-COLONEL,
A.A.&.Q.M.G.
14TH (LIGHT) DIVISION.

C OF E.   CHURCH SERVICES.   Oct.22nd 1916.
WARLUS - Chapel Holy Communion 7 a.m.   Evensong 7 p.m.
BERNEVILLE - C.A.Hut. Holy Communion 8 a.m. F.Q.Morning service 9.30
   Evening Service 6 p.m.
ARRAS - Cavalry Barrack Chapel. Holy Communion 7.30 and 11.45 a.m.
   Evening Service 6.30 p.m.   (Choral)
RIVIERE.English Church.Morning Service & Holy Communion 11.15 a.m.
   Evening Service 7 p.m.

Elsewhere by local arrangement.
At Morning services the monthly authorised collection will be made. Object - the Army Missionary Association.

R.C.
8 a.m. Mass at Hospital St.Jean,ARRAS, DAINVILLE Parish Church and RIVIERE.
8.30 am   "   "   BERNEVILLE.
10.30 am   "   "   AGNY.
11 a.m.   "   "   WAILLY.
5.30 p.m.Evening Service DAINVILLE, and RIVIERE.

14TH (LIGHT) DIVISION.

ROUTINE ORDERS.

21st October, 1916.

1845. HAND PUMPS, - Damage to.

It has been brought to notice that numerous hand pumps scattered over the VI Corps area are frequently out of repair through ill-usage.

Each hand pump will be placed in charge of a unit which uses it, the unit being detailed by the Town Commandant in whose area it lies. The unit will detail attendants who will be in charge of the pump and see that it is properly cared for and used.

Report of any damage giving the name of the unit which caused it is to be sent within 24 hours to Div. H.Qrs by the Town Commandant concerned.

1846. POSTAL REFILLING.

From tomorrow (22nd instant) inclusive until further orders, Postal Refilling will take place at 11 a.m. instead of 12 noon.

R M Barrington Ward Capt.
for LIEUT-COLONEL,
A.A.&.Q.M.G.
14TH (LIGHT) DIVISION.

14TH (LIGHT) DIVISION.

ROUTINE ORDERS.

22nd October, 1916.

1847. PETROL TINS.

Units will report through the usual channels to reach Divisional Headquarters by noon 24th instant the number of petrol tins in use at the present time for carrying water.

1848. FUEL.

The winter scale of fuel in force from October 1st is that laid down in G.R.O.1170, republished in extracts from G.R.Os Part II, dated 1-4-16.

1849. S.A.A. CARTS.

Any Unit in possession of a S.A.A. cart will report the fact to Div'l Headquarters by noon 24th instant.

1850. RETURN AND SALVAGE OF CLOTHING.

In view of the value of worn out clothing the instructions on the subject have been consolidated and are published for general information.
Every effort will be made to comply with them, as much extra work is caused by want of attention to detail.

SERVICE DRESS CLOTHING.

Bonnets, Balmoral, Tam O'Shanters, Jackets, Trousers, Pantaloons, Knickerbockers, Kilts, Puttees, Greatcoats.

Unserviceable articles of the above nature will be returned to the D.A.D.O.S. 14th (Light) Division as soon as possible after receipt of the new articles demanded in replacement.

Before return, each description will be tied in separate bundles of ten.

A receipt for the numbers of each article will be given. The number of each description returned should normally approximate to the numbers issued, and where this is not possible, an explanation should be given when handing in.

Very lousy or bloodstained garments will be burnt regimentally, but a certificate as to the numbers destroyed should be sent by the Commanding Officer of the Unit to the Ordnance Officer

RECORDS.

Every quarter, a comparative statement, showing the numbers of each article returned, will be prepared by the Ordnance Officer and will accompany his report of issues.

RETURN TO BE STOPPED IN CASE OF INFECTIOUS DISEASE.

In the event of any infectious disease breaking out among the troops, the return of all clothing from such troops is to be at once suspended, and a telegram to that effect will be sent by the Officer Commanding the Formation to Div'l Headquarters for the information of Army Headquarters.

UNDERCLOTHING.

Vests, Cotton Drawers, Woollen Drawers, Socks, Hosetops, Cotton Shirts, Flannel Shirts, Cholera Belts, Gloves, Mittens, Scarves, Balaclava Helmets, Cardigan Waistcoats.

To be washed and disinfected before dispatch, when possible. Unserviceable and worn out woollen, flannel and cotton articles of the above natures, will be sent by units, whenever possible, to the Div'l Baths.

(Continued)

SALVAGE.

1851.

The following is a list of articles of articles salved by the 14th Div'l Salvage Company :-

WEEK ENDED 21 - 10 - 16.

No Collected	Description of articles	Serviceable (S) or Unserviceable (US)	How disposed of.
4.	Cycle tyres,	U.S.	25th San.Sec
6.	Valises,	S.	6th DCLI.
4.Reels	Cable wire,	S.	14th Signals
49 pairs	Boots,	U.S.	D.A.D.O.S.
19	Helmets, Steel,	S.	D.A.D.O.S.
4	Rifles,	S.	D.A.D.O.S.
2	Bayonets,	S.	D.A.D.O.S.
4	Scabbards,	S.	D.A.D.O.S.
1	Saddle,	U.S.	DADOS for railhead.
2 bags	Underclothing,	U.S.	railhead.
5 "	Clothing, S.D.	U.S.	-do-
2 "	Boots,	U.S.	-do-
1 bag.	Gas Helmets,	U.S.	-do-
4 bags	Horse Shoes,	U.S.	-do-
21 bags	Clothing,	U.S.	Remaining at Dump.
5 boxes	Horse shoes,	U.S.	Dump.
2 bags	" "	U.S.	-do-
6 bags	Underclothing,	U.S.	-do-
3 bags	Boots,	U.S.	-do-
1	Bicycle,	U.S.	-do-
6	Lamps hurricane,	U.S.	-do-
2	Rifles,	U.S.	-do-
20	Headropes,	U.S.	-do-
1	Saddle,	U.S.	-do-
1	Outer Cover,	U.S.	-do-
4	Periscopes Box,	U.S.	-do-

LIEUT-COLONEL,
A.A.&.Q.M.G.
14TH (LIGHT) DIVISION.

ROUTINE ORDERS.

23rd October, 1916.

1852. HONOURS AND REWARDS.

THE KING has been graciously pleased to award the Meritorious Service Medal to the undermentioned N.C.Os :-

    No. 40230, Sergeant R.H. Banks, R.E.
    No. S/4/091248, Staff-Sergeant G.Checkley, A.S.C.
    No. SS/1546, Sergeant F. Stead, A.S.C.

1853. BATHS.

Baths at BERNEVILLE and SIMENCOURT will not be available for 14th Division from 12 noon today until further orders.

1854. TRAFFIC ORDERS.

Reference Traffic Orders issued with D.R.Os dated 29th September, 1916:
The hours therein mentioned are altered to read as follows :-

    WARLUS   5.30 p.m.
    BERNEVILLE   5.30 p.m.
    BEAUMETZ   5.45 p.m.

1855. TRENCH MORTAR BATTERIES - PERSONNEL.

Commanding Officers are responsible that a report is rendered to Brigade Headquarters when N.C.Os and men who have been detached to T.M.Batteries and have become casualties while so detached, rejoin their battalions from Hospital etc.

Infantry Brigades will issue orders to ensure that these men's services are not lost to Trench Mortar Batteries.

1856. SICK WASTAGE.

The following is the Sick Wastage Return for week ended noon 21st October, 1916.

Unit	O.	O.R.	Unit	O.	O.R.
46th Bde R.F.A.		4	5th Ox & Bucks L.I.		4
47th Bde R.F.A.		2	5th K.S.L.I.		5
48th Bde R.F.A.		2.	9th K.R.R.C.		6.
14th D.A.C.		4.	9th R.B.		5.
X.14 T.M. Bty.			42nd M.G. Coy.		2
X.14 T.M. Bty.		3.	42nd T.M. Bty.		Nil
Y.14 T.M. Bty.			6th Somerset L.I.		4.
Z.14 T.M. Bty.			6th D.C.L.I.		10.
8th M.M.G.Bty.		Nil.	6th K.O.Y.L.I,		8
61st Field Co. R.E.		Nil.	10th Durham L.I.		4.
62nd Field Co. R.E.		Nil.	43rd M.G. Coy.		1
89th Field Co. R.E.		1.	43rd T.M. Bty.		Nil.
14th Signal Co.R.E.		Nil.	11th L'pool R		3.
7th K.R.R.C.		5.	14t Supply Column,		2.
8th K.R.R.C.		3.	42nd F. Amb		Nil.
7th R.B.		6.	43rd F. Amb		1
8th R.B.		2.	44th F. Amb		Nil
41st M.G. Coy.		Nil.	14th Div. Train.		2.
41st T.M. Bty.		1.	25th Sanitary Section		Nil.
			26th Mob.Vet.Section,		Nil.

Total = Other Ranks 90.

LIEUT-COLONEL,
A.A.& Q.M.G.

14TH (LIGHT) DIVISION.

ROUTINE ORDERS.

24th October, 1916.

1857. STRAW.

The issue of straw at the weekly rate of 4 lbs per man is authorised for troops during the winter months.
Issue will be made through Supply Officer.

1858. RATIONS.

With reference to Corps Routine Order No.1273, dated 12/9/16, the full Cheese Ration of 3 ozs will be resumed from 24/10/16, the issue of potatoes in lieu being discontinued.
(Authority D.D.S.&.T., Third Army No. S/5078 dated 22/10/16.
VI Corps Q/341/12).

1859. BLANKETS.

Approval is given for the issue of a second blanket per man. Indents for same should be forwarded through the usual channel.

1860. FIRE ORDERS.

Copies of "Precautions against Fire" are circulated with DR.Os today. A copy will be prominently posted in every billet in the present area or in any area to which the Division may move in the future.

LIEUT-COLONEL,
A.A.&.Q.M.G.
14TH (LIGHT) DIVISION.

NOTICE.

LOST: Taken from No.7 Rue de Arras, WANQUETIN, on 27-9-16:
BICYCLE No. 24974, marked on Frame "No.103 Coy" Red Club on rear Mud-guard.
Information to A.P.M., 14th Division.

14TH (LIGHT) DIVISION.

ROUTINE ORDERS.

25th October, 1916.

1861. FIGHTING STRENGTH RETURN.

In the weekly Fighting Strength Return rendered to this office the heading of Column "B" will be altered to read "Detached to Trench Mortar Batteries".

No mention will in future, be made by Units in A.F. B.213 of men permanently detached to Tunnelling Coys who have been struck off the strength.

1862. ANIMALS.

The number of animals damaged from kicks has been unduly high during the past week. O.C. Units should see that bad kickers are kept separately.

C.C. Hamilton
LIEUT-COLONEL,
A.A.&.Q.M.G.
14TH (LIGHT) DIVISION.

NOTICE.

MISSING: From Hut, Rue de Dainville, WARLUS, on 20th inst, BICYCLE, Civilian pattern handlebars, Rim brake on rear wheel with Roller lever, Coaster hub: Rear Carrier only: Information to O.C., 14th Signal Co.R.E.

14TH (LIGHT) DIVISION.

ROUTINE ORDERS.

26th October, 1916.

1863. HONOURS AND REWARDS.

Under authority of H.M. THE KING, Military Medals have been awarded to the undermentioned N.C.Os and men :-

No. 16434.	Sergt. F.B. Blake,	5th Ox & Bucks L.I.
19080.	Pte J. Holloway,	-do-
23095.	Sergt. W. Brooke,	6th K.O.Y.L.I.
11498.	Sergt. A.J. Smith,	5th Bn. K.S.L.I.
16024.	Sergt. W. Bullock,	-do-
2938.	Sergt. V. Harrison,	7th Bn. K.R.R.C.
2384.	Sergt. J. Dawes	8th R.B.
7600.	Rfmn. P. Gorman,	9th R.B.
37787.	Sergt. J. Smith,	42nd F. Amb. R.A.M.C.

1864. LEAVE.

The address of every officer, N.C.O. and man who is permitted to go on leave will be recorded by the Officer who signs the "Combined Leave and Railway ticket".

1865. STOKES BOMBS.

An accident has occurred through handling a stack of 3-inch Stokes Bombs, fitted with detonators, and pistol heads, from which one of the two safety pins had been removed.
Both safety pins will always be in place until immediately before firing, and if for any reason a bomb is not fired after the safety pins have been withdrawn, both will be replaced and their ends splayed out.
(Authority Third Army O/50/52, dated 25-10-16, VI Corps Q/2/54).

1866. FUEL WOOD.

Units will not obtain fuel wood from any other source than through their respective Supply Officers, except in cases of emergency, when subsequent report will be made. Issues of wood out under Military arrangements will be made on a Supply Officer's indent.

1867. TRANSFERS OF UNITS.

Attention is drawn to VI Corps Routine Order No.1397 dated 24th October, 1916.

1868. POSTAL.

Brigade Post Offices will move on 27th to Headquarters of Brigades. Units will draw mails from Brigade Post Offices on and after that date.
R.A., R.E., Pioneers and Mobile Vet. Section will draw their mails from the Train Post Office at BAREY.

1869. BLANKETS USED FOR BURIALS.

In cases where blankets have been used for burial purposes, a report to that effect will be rendered to D.A.D.O.S., and the blankets so used will be struck off charge.

O.L. Hamilton
LIEUT-COLONEL,
A.A.&.Q.M.G.
14TH (LIGHT) DIVISION.

14TH (LIGHT) DIVISION.

ROUTINE ORDERS.

28th October, 1918.

1870. HONOURS AND REWARDS

Under authority of H.M. THE KING, the following decorations have been awarded :-

DISTINGUISHED SERVICE ORDER.

Bt.Major (Temporary Lieut-Col.) W.F.R. WEBB,
   22nd Punjabis,
      Comdg. 5th Bn. Ox & Bucks L.I.

MILITARY CROSS.

Captain S.E.L. TURNER,	14th D.A.C. attd. C/47th Bde R.F.A.
2/Lieut.K.G. Hadow,	A/47th Bde R.F.A.
Captain W. Morrison, R.A.M.C. attd. 7th Bn. K.R.R.C.	

1871. OFFICERS ADVANCE BOOKS.

All "Officers Advance Books" A.F. W.3241 F. in possession of Commanding Officers, who have not been issued to Officers, will be returned to Field Cashier, VI Corps, as early as possible.

1872. WATER CARTS.

The condition of water carts is not yet satisfactory.
Commanding Officers are responsible for the maintenance of their water carts in proper repair, for the completeness of the equipment and for the provision of an adequate Supply of chloride of lime in proper condition. They are also responsible that the water carts are treated in accordance with the orders issued on the subject.
Medical Officers of units will inspect the water carts of their units weekly and bring to the notice of Commanding officers any deficiencies or any need for repair. They will see that the supply of chloride of lime is sufficient and that the supply does not accumulate to such an extent that the tins become useless before use.
The A.D.M.S. will also arrange for frequent inspection of the water-carts of the Division by himself or the D.A.D.M.S.

1873. SIGNALLING EQUIPMENT.

All Aeroplane Signalling equipment in possession of Battalions is to be returned at once to 14th Div. Signal Coy for overhauling and repairs.

(Continued).

1874. **SALE OF ARTICLES PURCHASED IN CANTEENS.**

G.R.O.1414 is re-published for information :-
It has come to notice that soldiers are selling to French civilians goods purchased from canteens and regimental institutes. This practice will cease forthwith. It is pointed out that canteens have been established solely for the use and benefit of the British Army in the Field: all good sold therein being, through the courtesy of the French Government, imported into this country duty free and articles are therefore saleable at a cheaper rate than is possible in French Shops.

If further instances of soldiers retailing goods to civilians are brought to notice the question of closing all canteens and regimental institutes in the area affected will have to be considered.

The provisions of G.R.O.1414 apply to all French Citizens, including soldiers.

1875. **DAMAGE TO CROPS.**

Attention is again directed to A.R.O.127 which reads:-
"Troops are to be warned against riding over, or otherwise needlessly damaging land which has been newly sown. Notice boards should be supplied to farmers under arrangements made by Divisional Commanders for erection in fields as soon as they have been sown".

1876. **SALVAGE.**

The following is a list of articles salved by the 14th Div'l Salvage Company :-

WEEK ENDED 27-10-16.

No. Collected	Description of articles	Serviceable(S) or Unserviceable(US)	How disposed of
1	Rifle	S.	Div.School.
2 Boxes,	Smoke Helmets, P.H.	U.S.	D.A.D.O.S.
70	Waterproof Sheets,	S.	D.A.D.O.S.
81	Shovels,	S.	D.A.D.O.S.
12	Pick heads,	S.	D.A.D.O.S.
12	Steel helmets,	S.	D.A.D.O.S.
56 Pairs,	Boots,	S.	D.A.D.O.S.
13	Slings, leather,	S.	6th DCLI.
1 belt.	Web ,	S.	6th DCLI.
6	Valises (Web)	S.	6th DCLI.
9	Boilers (T.K.)	U.S.	D.A.D.O.S.
8 Boxes,	Horse-shoes,	U.S.	for
6 Bags	-do-	U.S.	Railhead.
14 Sacks,	Jackets, S.D.	U.S.	-do-
4 Sacks,	Greatcoats,	U.S.	-do-
3 Sacks,	Puttees,	U.S.	-do-
3 Sacks,	Pantaloons,	U.S.	-do-
9 Sacks,	Boots, F.S.	U.S.	-do-
14 sacks	Trousers, S.D.	U.S.	-do-

1877. **PETROL TINS.**

All empty 2-gallon petrol tins except those actually being used for carrying water to the trenches, will be collected at some convenient point for return to Base. Units will report by the 30th instant the numbers of petrol tins available for evacuation and where collected.

1878. FROST COGS.

Pending issue of horse-shoes with frost cogs, demands will be sent to Base for Frost Nails as required.
(Authority Third Army wire Z.2628, dated 27-10-18. VI Corps Q/444
(VI Corps R.O. 1409).

for LIEUT-COLONEL,
A.A.&.Q.M.G.
14TH (LIGHT) DIVISION.

NOTICE.
DIVINE SERVICE - OCTOBER 29TH.
C of E.

LE CAUROY :- Barn opposite H.Q. Cook-house, next Chateau:

    7.30 a.m. Holy Communion.
    9.30 a.m. H.Q. Service.
    10.0 a.m. Salvage Co. service, with Holy Communion.

The Deputy Chaplain General will hold Confirmation at VI Corps H.Q. at 3 p.m. Thursday November 2nd.

14TH (LIGHT) DIVISION.

ROUTINE ORDERS.

29th October, 1916.

1879. FIELD CASHIER.

Field Cashier will attend at Div'l Headquarters on Tuesdays and Saturdays from 10 a.m. to 12 noon.

1880. SICK WASTAGE.

The following is the Sick Wastage Return for week-ended 29-10-16 :-

	O.	O.R.		O.	O.R.
46th Bde R.F.A.	1		5th Ox & Bucks L.I.		5
47th Bde R.F.A.	1	2	5th K.S.L.I.	1	8.
48th Bde R.F.A.		3.	9th K.R.R.C.		5.
14th D.A.C.		8.	9th R.B.		5.
V.14 T.M. Battery,		1.	42nd M.G. Coy.		3.
X.14 T.M. Battery,		Nil.	42nd T.M. Bty.		Nil.
Y.14 T.M. Battery,		Nil.	6th Somerset L.I.		4.
Z.14 T.M. Battery,		Nil.	6th D.C.L.I.	2	2
8th M.M.G. Battery.		Nil.	6th K.O.Y.L.I.	2	2
61st Field Co. R.E.		Nil.	10th Durham L.I.		5.
62nd Field Co. R.E.		Nil.	43rd M.G. Coy.		1.
89th Field Co. R.E.		2.	43rd T.M. Bty.		3.
14th Signal Co. R.E.		Nil.	11th Bn. L'pool R.	1	4.
7th K.R.R.C.		9.	No.14 Div. Supply Column,		Nil.
8th K.R.R.C.		1.	42nd Field Ambulance,		1.
7th Bn. R.B.		8.	43rd Field Ambulance,		8.
8th Bn. R.B.		2.	-do- A.S.C. attd.		2.
41st M.G. Coy		Nil.	14th Div. Train,		4.
41st T.M. Bty.		2.	25th Sanitary Section		Nil.
			20th Mob. Vet. Section,		Nil.

Total Officers 8, Other Ranks 92.

1881. DISCIPLINE - SLEEPING ON POST.

On the 25th September 1915 the Commander-in-Chief had occasion to issue G.R.O.1168 to the effect that, in consequence of the frequency of cases in which soldiers posted as sentries had been found asleep on their posts, he would in future be obliged to confirm sentences of death passed by Courts-Martial for such conduct.

After a period during which the Army was immune from this most serious and dangerous offence, it has again become regrettably prevalent and the Commander-in-Chief orders that the troops are to be informed that if there is any recurrence of this crime after the present warning, he will have no alternative but to carry out the extreme penalty.
(G.R.O.1886).

1882. ARMY BOOK 64 - RETENTION BY THE SOLDIER.

The practice of withdrawing Army Book 64 from soldiers going into action, is to be discontinued.
(G.R.O.1895).

Continued/

LONG SERVICE AND GOOD CONDUCT MEDALS.

Officers Commanding Units in the field, will submit to the D.A.G., G.H.Q., 3rd Echelon, the names of Warrant Officers, Non-Commissioned Officers and men, who are eligible for, and are recommended for, the award of the medal. This medal can be awarded under Article 1234 of the Royal Warrant to a soldier who has qualified for such award before his death.

The medal so awarded would then become the property of the next of kin, as would any gratuity attaching to such medal.

G.R.Os 622 and 1050 are cancelled.
(G.R.O.1889).

1884. **LONG SERVICE AND GOOD CONDUCT MEDAL - GRATUITY WITH.**

A Warrant Officer Class II, who is in possession of, or entitled to the medal under Article 1232, is eligible for this gratuity on discharge, or on promotion to Class I. It is not however payable to a Non-Commissioned Officer on promotion to Warrant Officer Class II.

(Authority:- War Office letter No.68/General Number/2651 (F.2) dated 9th October, 1915).

G.R.O. 1213 is cancelled.
(G.R.O.1890)

1885. **TRENCH MORTAR BATTERIES.**

Officers employed with Trench Mortar Batteries will not in future be either seconded from their units or transferred to the General List.

They will be struck off the strength of their units, in order to admit of reinforcements being demanded, but will not create a vacancy for promotion.

Those Officers who have already been notified in the Weekly List of Appointments for seconding or transfer will not have such seconding or transfer cancelled.
(G.R.O.1893.)

1886. **GLYCERINE RESIDUE FOR MACHINE GUNS.**

Units will forward, to reach Div'l Headquarters by noon the 31st instant, their probable requirements of Glycerine Residue for Machine Guns, for the winter months, under the following headings :-
(a) Initial.
(b) Estimated probable requirements weekly.

1887. **COTTON RAGS FOR CLEANING PURPOSES.**

It is notified for information that cotton rags may be demanded for cleaning purposes in cook houses.

Steps will be taken to place a distinctive mark on the rags to prevent their being used for other purposes.
(Authority Q.O.S./851/A. dated 23-10-16. VI Corps Q/772).

for LIEUT-COLONEL,
A.A.&.Q.M.G.
14TH (LIGHT) DIVISION.

14TH (LIGHT) DIVISION.

ROUTINE ORDERS.

30th October, 1916.

1888. MOTOR CYCLES - Repair of.

In future, all Motor cycles sent to the Supply Column workshops either for repair or replacement will be sent in stripped of all equipment, tools, and accessories.

In the event of the Machine being evacuated the equipment, tools etc., will be handed over separately and a receipt obtained.

1889. FRENCH MONEY.

It has come to notice that certain shops and traders do not accept at their face value the notes of the various "Chambres de Commerce" in FRANCE.

Shops and stores which do not accept these notes at their face value are to be put out of bounds to all troops, by request of the French Authorities.

Brigadier-Generals in Command will take immediate action in accordance with this order, reporting their action to Div'l Headquarters.

All ranks are to assist in this matter by reporting the name of any trader who makes deductions from the face value of notes, to their immediate superiors.

1890. HORSE-SHOE BOXES.

With reference to G.R.O.No.1863, all horse-shoe boxes will now be returned to Base, where they are urgently required.

1891. SCRAP METAL.

With reference to Third Army Routine Order No.501, dated 4/9/16, it is observed that no old brass or copper has so far been sent to Heavy Mobile Workshop. As such material is valuable, every effort will be made to collect it.

1892. NOMINAL ROLL.

Officers Commanding Units will render through the usual channels so as to reach Div'l Headquarters by 6 p.m. on 2nd November, a nominal roll of Officers and Other Ranks of the Jewish Faith on the strength.

LIEUT COLONEL,
A.A.&.Q.M.G.
14TH (LIGHT) DIVISION.

14TH (LIGHT) DIVISION.

ROUTINE ORDERS.

31st October, 1916.

1893. UNDERCLOTHING.

Underclothing has been received by A.O.D. which has so shrunk in washing that it is too small for any soldier to wear.

The method of washing woollen articles is as follows:-
The Water should be luke warm only. On no account should woollen articles be put into boiling or even very hot water. The articles must be well rinsed in clean tepid water before drying - Yellow soap only is to be used. The use of washing powder is forbidden. A little ammonia may be added (one tablespoonful to 2 gallons of water) to remove perspiration. After the water has been completely wrung out of the articles they will be well pulled out before drying.

These instructions should be made known to every soldier who washes his own clothes or gets them washed away from the Divisional Laundry.

1894. SALVAGE OF UNSERVICEABLE CLOTHING.

Attention is drawn to the importance of salvage of unserviceable clothing.

The Stuff is readily consumed by the industry at home, the prices continuing to rise. That paid for old Service Dress is now about £26 per ton more than it was when salvage was started.

The following were recently the market rates for a few of the articles :-

	Price per Cwt.		Per Article
Jackets, SD,	76/-	equals	1/8¾
Trousers, SD.	87/-	"	1/6.
Greatcoats,	63/-	"	3/2½
Puttees,	80/-	"	5d.
Shirts, Silver grey,	66/-	"	9d.
Socks,	105/-	"	2d.

C. Rumsfeyt
for LIEUT-COLONEL,
A.A.&.Q.M.G.
14TH (LIGHT) DIVISION.

NOTICES.

FOUND: In a hedge in OXFORD STREET, SIMENCOURT, RIFLE and EQUIPMENT (with ammunition) marked "14 K.R.R." No. of Rifle 3995, No of equipment 1949 d- 12/15. Cut in small of butt, right side. "M.A.E".
Apply O.C., 48th Bde R.F.A.

FOUND: On 28-10-16 OFFICER'S CHARGER, with saddle, headcollar etc., on the road between MANIN and MONTENESCOURT. Brown Gelding, height 15.2, white socks hind feet, white streak on forehead. Marked "R.C.H." near haunch, 12 on near shoulder.
Apply A.D.V.S., 14th Division.

LOST: MULE, Brown Gelding, height about 14 hands, numbered 108 near fore, 1 over D.A.C. on off fore, broad arrow near hind-quarters. T near Hind-quarter, UD off hind-quarter.
Information to 14th Div'l Artillery.

DIVINE SERVICE - WEDNESDAY NOVEMBER 1ST. (ALL SAINTS DAY).
Celebration Holy Communion 7.30 a.m. in barn opposite H.Q. cook-house, next Chateau, LE CAUROY.

14TH (LIGHT) DIVISION.

ROUTINE ORDERS.

3rd November, 1916.

1896. COURT MARTIAL. Weeded

1897. BICYCLES - LOSS OF.

Several cases have recently occurred of bicycles, left unattended, having been stolen.
It is considered that more care should be exercised by the person in whose charge the bicycle is at the time, and, in future, Courts of Enquiry will take evidence to show that the bicycle was not left unattended longer than was absolutely necessary.
(C.R.O. 1428)

for LIEUT-COLONEL.
A.A.&Q.M.G.
14TH (LIGHT) DIVISION.

NOTICE.

Holy Communion, Div'l H.Qrs, 7.30 a.m.
Morning Service, 9.30 a.m. in H.Q.Unit Mess Room in Barn near Chateau.

ROUTINE ORDERS.

4th November, 1916.

1898. LEAVE.

B.O. 5/16

In future a printed note will be issued at ABBEVILLE to all men detained at that station on their return from leave, which should be produced on rejoining their Unit.

1899. RUM - ISSUE OF.

It is notified for information that Rum is only issued with the sanction of the Corps Commander.

1900. SALVAGE.

The following is a list of articles salved by the 14th Div'l Salvage Company :-

WEEK ENDED 3 - 11 - 16.

No Collected	Description of articles	Serviceable (S) or Unserviceable (US)	How disposed of.
9 Boxes	Horse Shoes,	U.S.	DADOS for
9 Bags,	" "	U.S.	Railhead.
9	Camp Kettles,	U.S.	"
125	Caps, S.D.	U.S.	"
223	Jackets, S.D.	U.S.	"
9	Greatcoats,	U.S.	"
108 Pairs	Puttees,	U.S.	"
60 "	Pantaloons,	U.S.	"
260 "	Boots, F.S.	U.S.	"
1	Telescopic Sights,	S.	"
2	Packs,	U.S.	"
70 Pairs	Trousers, S.D.	U.S.	"
5	Boilers, T.K.	U.S.	"
9	Fryers,	U.S.	"
20	Greatcoats,	S.	D.A.D.O.S.
2 Sets,	1914 Equipment,	S.	5th KSLI.
22 Pairs	Boots,	S.	D.A.D.O.S.
236	Greatcoats,	S.	Remaining
46	Jackets, SD.	U.S.	at dump.
4 Suits	Overalls,	U.S.	"
12 Pairs	Puttees,	U.S.	"
112	Smoke Helmets,	U.S.	"
34	Box Respirators,	U.S.	"
10 Pairs	Pantaloons,	U.S.	"
3	Rifles,	S.	"
45	M.G.Belt boxes,	S.	"
4	Leather tool cases,	S.	"
1	Gas Cylinder,	U.S.	"
8	Mess-tins,	U.S.	"
1	Saddle,	U.S.	"
6	Water bottles,	U.S.	"
1 Set	Traces,	U.S.	"
2	Steel Helmets,	U.S.	"
1	Lamp, hurricane,	U.S.	"
4	Tripods, L.G.	U.S.	"
1	L.G.Hand-cart wheel,	U.S.	"
5	L.G.Flame checks,	U.S.	"
2	Oil drums,	U.S.	"
1	Stretcher Carrier,	S.	"
4	Headcollars,	U.S.	"
4 Reels,	Cable wire,	S.	"

1901. **COTTON RAGS FOR CLEANING PURPOSES.**

Reference C.R.O.1436:
The report called for therein will be rendered to reach this office by Noon 7th instant.

J.W.Watson Maj for LIEUT-COLONEL,
A.A.&.Q.M.G.
14TH (LIGHT) DIVISION.

NOTICES.

FOUND. BLACK GELDING, Star, numbered on near Fore 34 over 34, Age 8 years, Height 15 hands.
Also BAY GELDING, Star and Snip, Numbered on near Fore 27 over 27, Age 6 years, Height 15.1.
Apply A.D.V.S., 14th Division.

DIVINE SERVICES. 5-11-16:
C OF E.
Holy Communion, Div.H.Q. 7.30 a.m. in Coach House, Chateau, Le Cauroy.

WESLEYANS, PRESBYTERIANS, ETC.

9.30 a.m. BERLENCOURT. for 9th K.R.R.C., 5th Ox & Bucks.
11.30 am. GIVENCHY, " 43rd F.Amb, 42nd F.Amb, 5th KSLI. 9th R.B.
3 p.m. IZEL LES HAMEAU. for 6th D.C.L.I. & 42.F.Amb, (voluntary).
6 p.m. LIGNEREUIL (School) Voluntary.

14TH (LIGHT) DIVISION.

ROUTINE ORDERS.

5th November, 1916.

1902. CLIPPING OF HORSES.

Reference C.R.O.1440.
Application to clip horses will be forwarded to Div'l Headquarters through the usual channels.

1903. PETROL - ISSUE TO FARMERS.

Reference C.R.O.1435, in places where threshing is being delayed for want of petrol, demands should be wired to Div'l H.Qrs without delay.

Hudvatson Major
for LIEUT-COLONEL,
A.A.&.Q.M.G.
14TH (LIGHT) DIVISION.

14TH (LIGHT) DIVISION.

ROUTINE ORDERS.

6th November, 1916.

1904. HONOURS AND REWARDS.

The KING has been graciously pleased to approve that the Insignia of an Order or Decoration conferred by HIS MAJESTY for distinguished or Meritorious services since August 4th 1914 upon an officer or soldier who has not survived to receive it may be publicly presented to the next-of-kin if they so desire and are resident in the United Kingdom.

The Victoria Cross and the insignia of G.C.B., G.C.M.G., K.C.B. and K.C.M.G. will be presented by His Majesty in person.

Other decorations will be presented on His Majesty's behalf by General Officers Commanding at parades of troops to be held from time to time throughout the country.

The wishes of the next-of-kin as to public presentation will be ascertained in the future in the case of W.Os, N.C.Os, and men by Officers i/c Records, and in all other cases by The Secretary, War Office.

In cases where Orders and Decorations have already been forwarded by post, presentation as above will be arranged on application of the next-of-kin, in writing, to the War Office.
(Extracts from Army Order XII dated 28th October, 1916).

1905. LEAVE.

All leave is temporarily suspended.

1906. SICK WASTAGE.

The following is the Sick Wastage Return for week ended 4-11-16 :-

Unit	O.	O.R.	Unit	O.	O.R.
46th Bde R.F.A.		1.	5th Ox & Bucks L.I.		2.
47th Bde R.F.A.		3.	5th K.S.L.I.		3.
48th Bde R.F.A.		3.	9th K.R.R.C.	1	2.
14th D.A.C.		2.	9th Rifle Bde.		9.
V.14 T.M. Battery.		Nil.	42nd M.G. Coy.		Nil.
X.14 T.M. Battery,		Nil.	42nd T.M. Battery,		Nil.
Y.14 T.M. Battery,		Nil.	6th Somerset L.I.		4.
Z.14 T.M. Battery,		Nil.	6th D.C.L.I.		5.
61st Field Co. R.E.		Nil.	6th K.O.Y.L.I.		8.
62nd Field Co. R.E.		Nil.	10th Durham L.I.		5.
89th Field Co. R.E.		Nil.	43rd M.G. Coy.		1.
14th Signal Co.R.E.		Nil.	43rd T.M. Battery,		Nil.
7th K.R.R.C.		5.	11th Bn, L'pool R.		4.
8th K.R.R.C.		5.	No.14 Supply Column,		1.
7th Rifle Bde,		4.	42nd F.Amb,		1.
8th Rifle Bde.		4.	43rd F.Amb,		2.
41st M.G. Coy.		Nil.	44th F.Amb.		1.
41st T.M. Battery,		Nil.	14th Div. Train.		Nil.
			25th San.Sec.ASC att.		1.

Total Officer 1, Other Ranks 76.

LIEUT COLONEL,
A.A.& Q.M.G.
14TH (LIGHT) DIVISION.

14TH (LIGHT) DIVISION.

ROUTINE ORDERS.

7th November, 1916.

1907. CLOTHING.

Demands for clothing continue to be abnormally high.
Attention is called to D.R.O.1850. 95% of the articles issued must be accounted for by returns of unserviceable clothing. D.A.D.O.S. will keep a ledger account and balance it twice monthly.

Clothing returned as unserviceable which is found to be fit for reissue will be issued to the same unit as returned it in lieu of new clothing.

1908. SANITARY.

On taking up new billets, Officers Commanding Battalions will place two Pioneers at the disposal of their Medical Officers for the construction of latrines, shelters, and ablution benches until the work is completed.

1909. REFILLING.

Refilling points on and after 8th instant :-

42nd Brigade on road LIENCOURT to LE CAUROY, near LIENCOURT.

On and after 9th :-

43rd Brigade on road SERICOURT to FREVENT, near SERICOURT.

LIEUT-COLONEL,
A.A.&.Q.M.G.
14TH (LIGHT) DIVISION.

14TH (LIGHT) DIVISION.

ROUTINE ORDERS.

8th November, 1916.

1910. HONOURS AND REWARDS.

Under Authority granted by H.M. THE KING, the following decorations have been awarded :-

MILITARY CROSS.

2/Lieut. M.M. O'Keeffe, "B" Bty. 48th Bde R.F.A.

MILITARY MEDALS.

No. 83786. Gnr. W. Crook, R.F.A.
89021. Dr. A. Childs, R.F.A.
83989. Gnr. W. Meacham, R.F.A.
98086. Gnr. C. Barber, R.F.A.
89305. Gnr. G. Miller, R.F.A.

1911. ADMINISTRATIVE.

The Senior Officer in each village is O.C. Troops. A Town Commandant will be appointed for each village under Brigade arrangements to assist the O.C. Troops, in the following matters, in addition to carrying out his ordinary duties :-
(1) Distribution of accommodation.
(2) Sanitary measures.
(3) Minor repair of roads within the village.
(4) Preparation of schemes for the improvement of the village and supervision of the work.

These Town Commandants will probably have to be left behind for a few days when the Division moves to hand over improvement schemes and ensure continuity of policy when another Division arrives. They would also be utilised for Salvage and collection of stores in case of a move. Suitable Officers must be chosen. Names will be communicated by Brigades to Divisional Headquarters by noon November 10th.

1912. MILLS GRENADES.

Attention is called to VI Corps Routine Order No. 1049 dated 12th July 1916 as regards the following paragraphs :-
"The 16 rifles per battalion ordered to be set aside for use in firing Rifle Grenades under Q.O.S./15/43/B dated 7th March, 1916 may be increased to 34 as soon as the cup attachments are issued.

Every effort must be made to prevent other rifles than those set aside for the purpose being used with the Mills or any other form of rifle grenade."

Rifles with bulged barrels will be obtained by D.A.D.O.S. and supplied to units requiring them.

Each Battalion will hand over two of its 34 rifles to Div'l School for instructional use there. On no account are serviceable rifles to be used for this purpose.

LIEUT COLONEL,
A.A.&.Q.M.G.
14TH (LIGHT) DIVISION.

NOTICE.

A PAPER CHASE will be held on Tuesday November 14th starting at 2.45 p.m. from the Chateau Gates at LE CAUROY.

The Camp Commandant has undertaken to provide a changing room at LE CAUROY, also tea if Units will notify him by the 12th inst the number of Officers and men wishing to attend.

Requested that this notice may be republished in Brigade and Regimental Orders.

14TH (LIGHT) DIVISION.

ROUTINE ORDERS.

10th November, 1916.

1915. HORSE SHOES.

The report called for in C.R.O.1460 will be rendered so as to reach Div'l Headquarters by 13th instant.

1916. FROSTBITE.

With reference to circular on the Subject of Cold and Frost Bite published with VI Corps Routine Order 1548 and amended by VI Corps Routine Order No. 1463:

The Orderly to Medical Officer in each Battal'on is to attend the course of massage at No.105 Field Ambulance, beginning 9 a.m. 13th and not a man of the R.A.M.C. as stated therein.

The men for the class will be collected from Battalion Headquarters of all battalions (including Pioneers) by the Field Ambulance situated in the same Brigade Area and taken to LIGNEREUIL by 8.30 a.m. 13th instant.

Each man is to take his full kit and his rations for the current day.

LIEUT-COLONEL,
A.A.& Q.M.G.
14TH (LIGHT) DIVISION.

NOTICE.

DIVINE SERVICES.
Sunday, 12th Novr.

R.C. Mass at IVERGNY Church at 9 a.m.
" " BEAUDRICOURT Church at 10.30 a.m.
" " SOMBRIN Church at 10.30 a.m.
" " GRAND RULLECOURT Church at 10.30 a.m.
Evening Service at IVERGNY Church at 5 p.m.

14TH (LIGHT) DIVISION.

ROUTINE ORDERS.

11th November, 1916.

HONOURS AND REWARDS.

Under Authority of H.M. THE KING, the following decoration has been awarded :-

MILITARY CROSS.

2/Lieut. G.A. Murray, "D" Battery, 47th Bde R.F.A.

1918. EMBLEMS TO DENOTE BARS TO DECORATIONS.

With reference to A.O.290, September, 1916, Indents for the emblems referred to should be put in on Ordnance Officers concerned.

The Army Order in which the award of the bar or bars was notified must be quoted, together with the name, regiment, etc, of the individuals concerned for whom the articles are required. The D.D.O.S. Woolwich Arsenal, will send the emblems by registered post to the O.C. Unit.

(Authority O.S.G./5283/1220, dated 5-11-16, VI Corps Q/803).

1919. SALVAGE

The following is a list of articles salved by the 14th Div'l Salvage Company :-

WEEK ENDED 10 - 11 - 16.

No. Collected.	Description of articles	Serviceable (S) or Unserviceable (US)	How disposed of.
70	Greatcoats,	S.	D.A.D.O.S.
2	Rifles,	S.	5th K.S.L.I.
27 Pairs	Boots,	S.	D.A.D.O.S.
14	Belts and Boxes, M.G.	S.	43rd M.G.Co.
1	L.G.Hand-cart wheel,	U.S.	DADOS for
2	Saddles,	U.S.	railhead.
144 Pairs	Boots,	U.S.	do.
40	Box Respirators,	U.S.	do.
11 boxes,	Smoke Helmets,	U.S.	do.
202	Jackets, S.D.	U.S.	do.
46 Pairs,	Pantaloons,	U.S.	do.
120 "	Trousers, S.D.	U.S.	do.
14	Steel helmets,	U.S.	Remaining
2	Kettles, T.K.	U.S.	at dump.
1 Bag	Leather equipment,	S.	do.
1 "	Web	S.	do.
4	Limber tail boards,	U.S.	do.
6	Oil drums,	U.S.	do.
34	M.G. Belt boxes,	U.S.	do.
1	Gas Cylinder,	U.S.	do.
3	Leather M.G.Tool cases	S.	do.
1	Stretcher Carrier,	S.	do.
1	Limber pole,	U.S.	do.
1 bag	Spare harness,	U.S.	do.
19	Nose-bags,	U.S.	do.
5	M.G.Flame checks,	U.S.	do.
120 Pairs	Boots, F.S.	U.S.	do.
220 Pairs	Trousers, S.D.	U.S.	do.
110	Jackets, S.D.	U.S.	do.
185 Pairs	Puttees,	U.S.	do.
2	Officers' Saddles,	U.S.	do.
4	Universal Saddles,	U.S.	do.
200	Greatcoats,	S.	do.
50	British Warm,	S.	do.
40 Pairs	Pantaloons,	U.S.	do.

Continued :-

16	Box Respirators	U.S.	Remaining at Dump.
4	Head collars,	U.S.	do.
1	Bandolier,	U.S.	do.
1	Spring balance,	U.S.	do.
4	Bayonets,	S.	

[signature]
Lieut-Colonel,
A.A.&.Q.M.G.
14th (Light) Division.

NOTICE.
DIVINE SERVICES, C. OF E.
SUNDAY 12th Nov.

Holy Communion 8.30 a.m. Div'l H.Qrs (Field Cashier's Room).
Morning Service 9.30 a.m.   "   "   (Recreation Room).
Evening Service 5.30 p.m.   "   "   (No.4 H.Q. Mess (by Canteen)

14TH (LIGHT) DIVISION.

ROUTINE ORDERS.

12th November, 1916.

1920. HONOURS AND REWARDS.

Reference D.R.O.1910 dated 8-11-16, for "No.98086, Gunner C. BARBER" read "No.98086, Gunner C. BARBET".

1921. SHIRTS.

A certain number of shirts have recently been received at the laundry in a mutilated condition, sleeves cut short, tails cut off, cut open down the front etc. Such mutilation is forbidden.

Apart from orders on the subject it will be realised that when those shirts are reissued, the men who receive them have just grounds for complaint.

1922. REFILLING.

Refilling Point for the 43rd Inf.Bde was established from the 11th November on the road between FREVENT and HOUVIGNEUL, West of HONVAL.

C.H.Hamilton
LIEUT-COLONEL,
A.A.&.Q.M.G.
14TH (LIGHT) DIVISION.

14TH (LIGHT) DIVISION.

ROUTINE ORDERS.

13th November, 1916.

1923. BLANKETS.

Reference O.R.O.1429:
Brigades and R.A. will report in what buildings they propose to store the second blanket in the event of a move of the Division. The exact buildings must be specified. Not more than one building per village will be selected and they must be capable of containing the blankets of all the men in that village. If possible one building per group of villages should be selected, but it must be borne in mind that the blankets will have to be taken there before the Division marches off.
Reports will reach this office by 17th instant.

1924. RESPIRATORS.

Indents for Box Respirators required and 10% spare will be submitted forthwith by units to D.A.D.O.S. showing clearly the numbers required of each of the three sizes in which respirators are provided.
After respirators have been received and fitted to each individual the spare will be returned to D.A.D.O.S.
Information as regards sizes may be obtained from Div. Gas Officer in any case in which the information has not already been obtained.

1925. LEAVE.

The names of any N.C.Os and men who become entitled to ONE MONTH'S leave under G.R.O.1679 up to the end of December, 1916, should be forwarded to this office as soon as possible.

LIEUT-COLONEL,
A.A.&.Q.M.G.
14TH (LIGHT) DIVISION.

14TH (LIGHT) DIVISION.

ROUTINE ORDERS.

Nov

14th September, 1916.

1926. OCCUPATION OF LAND.

Reports of occupation of land must be submitted to Div'l Headquarters by 18th instant on the pro-forma circulated herewith.

The following extracts from 14th Division AR/3/1 dated 3rd April, 1916 are republished for information and compliance:-

"Land may be hired for public purposes, e.g. Camps, Horse lines, and training, or for private purposes, e.g. Extra grazing or football fields. The proceeding is as follows in either case:

1. The O.C. of a unit on arrival in a commune should consult the Maire (in conjunction with the Town Major, Town Commandant or any similar official if existing) with a view to the selection of the most suitable ground for his purpose, in order to eliminate as far as possible the occupation of valuable pasture or of fields sown with expensive crops.

2. The Unit should then enter into occupation of the land. No price must be agreed upon until the Rent Officer is consulted.

3. The Rent Officer should then be informed through Div'l Headquarters :-
   (a) The site of the land must be clearly described.
   (b) Full particulars must be given as to the state of the land on the date of occupation.
   (c) The purpose for which the land is required must be stated.

4. The Rent Officer will then make an agreement with the farmer personally.

5. The Rent Officer should be immediately informed of the departure of the Unit. Units quitting hired ground will inform Div'l Headquarters of the fact even if the order to quit emanates from Divisional Headquarters.

There must be no delay in reporting the occupation of lands to Div'l Headquarters, so that if the occupation is not approved by the G.O.C., Division it may be evacuated at once. If there is any delay, the compensation to the owners will be chargeable to the unit concerned."

Should the O.C. Unit be unable to agree with the Maire as to the lands to be occupied, a report must be forwarded at once in order that the French Mission may intervene.

1927. RESTRICTION OF LIGHTING.

The Royal Flying Corps report that the illumination of villages on our side of the line is very marked in comparison that on the German side.

Steps will at once be taken to ensure that all windows are covered, so that lights at night do not shew through.

All lights in the open will be reduced to a minimum, and will be shaded. This applies specially to lights in horse lines and camps.

(over)

1928. STEEL HELMETS.

Army Routine Order No.339 is cancelled and the following substituted :-
1:- Steel helmets will be worn at all times by all ranks engaged in operations.
2:- When troops are not engaged in operations, steel helmets will be worn by all ranks on guard, on parade, when training or on the march.
(A.R.O.541)

1929. EXPLOSIVES.

Whenever an accident occurs with a grenade or any other form of explosive, every effort must be made at once to trace the maker of grenade, detonator, or other component. If possible, the box in which they were packed should be set aside for special inspection, with any grenades etc., that may be in it, or that have been taken from it.
Information thus obtained will be of great value in tracing defects and so lead to their removal.

Bombing Officer 15h

1930. SICK WASTAGE.

The following is the Sick Wastage Return for week ended 11-11-16 :-

Unit	O.	O.R.	Unit	O.	O.R.
46th Bde R.F.A.		7	9th K.R.R.C.		6
47th Bde R.F.A.		3	9th R.B.		5.
48th Bde R.F.A.		4.	42nd M.G. Coy.		14.
14th D.A.C.		5.	42nd T.M. Bty.		Nil.
V.14 T.M. Bty.		1.	6th Somerset L.I.		3.
X.14 T.M. Bty.		Nil.	6th D.C.L.I.		10.
Y.14 T.M. Bty.		Nil.	6th K.O.Y.L.I.		5.
Z.14 T.M. Bty.		Nil.	10th Durham L.I.		4.
61st Field Co.R.E.		Nil.	43rd M.G. Coy.		2.
62nd Field Co.R.E.		1.	43rd T.M. Bty.		Nil.
89th Field Co.R.E.		3.	11th Bn. L'pool R.		Nil.
14th Signal Co.R.E.		3.	No.14 Supply Column,		5.
7th K.R.R.C.	1	12.	42nd Field Amb.		4.
8th K.R.R.C.		7.	43rd Field Amb.		1.
7th R.B.		4.	44th Field Amb.		3.
8th R.B.	1	1.	14th Div. Train.		3.
41st M.G. Coy.		1.	-do- RAMC attd.		1.
41st T.M. Bty.		Nil.	25th Sanitary Section,		Nil.
5th Ox & Bucks L.I.		6.	26th Mob.Vet.Section,		Nil.
5th K.S.L.I.		7.			

Total Officers 2, Other Ranks 129.

C.L. Hamilton
LIEUT COLONEL,
A.A.&.Q.M.G.
14TH (LIGHT) DIVISION.

14TH (LIGHT) DIVISION.

ROUTINE ORDERS.

15th November, 1916.

1931. HONOURS AND REWARDS.

H.M. THE KING has been pleased to award the Military Medal to the undermentioned N.C.Os and men for services prior to June 30th 1916:-

ROYAL ARTILLERY.

96437.	Sergt.	F. Coggan,	14th D.A.C.
10772.	A/Bdr.	S. Bailey,	48th Bde R.F.A.
99881.	Corpl.	C. Robinson,	49th Bde R.F.A.
99892.	Bombr.	E.G. Strickland,	48th Bde R.F.A.
45538.	Bombr.	A. Copsey,	14th D.A.C.
96269.	Fitter	F.J. Pell,	48th Bde R.F.A.
27252.	Gr.	A.J. Brocklesby,	46th Bde R.F.A.
84022.	Gr.	G. Griffiths,	47th Bde R.F.A.
83939.	Gr.	J. Chamberlain,	48th Bde R.F.A.
60226.	Dvr.	W. Sims,	14th D.A.C.
85644.	Dvr.	S. Martin,	14th D.A.C.
41516.	Sergt.	G. Duff,	T.M. Batteries.
72577.	Bombr.	M. Fenwick,	49th Bde R.F.A.
84585.	Bombr.	A. Downie,	14th D.A.C.
81947.	Bombr.	W.G. Lord,	14th D.A.C.
98010.	Sergt.	D.A. Carse,	48th Bde R.F.A.
72683.	Gr.	J. Hargreaves,	49th Bde R.F.A.
116.	Corpl.	W. Gibson,	46th Bde R.F.A.
21657.	Sergt.	A. Knights,	14th D.A.C.
56592.	Bombr.	H. Price,	T.M. Batteries.
5508.	Gr.	J. Neary,	T.M. Batteries,
96251.	Sergt.	W. Kelly,	47th Bde R.F.A.
7398.	Sergt.	J.R. Watt,	48th Bde R.F.A.
72718.	Bombr.	J.J. Clarke,	49th Bde R.F.A.
98.	Gr.	G. Findlay,	46th Bde R.F.A.
84584.	Corpl.	F.W. Litchfield,	14th D.A.C.
89275.	Dvr.	C. Onions,	46th Bde R.F.A.
27217.	Corpl.	J.S. Balmer,	14th D.A.C.
83928.	Dvr.	D. Carter,	48th Bde R.F.A.
65943.	Dvr.	R. Morrell,	14th D.A.C.
93606.	Sergt.	W. Strachan,	49th Bde R.F.A.
82246.	Sergt.	C.H. Hindle,	46th Bde R.F.A.
7784.	Dvr.	J. McDonald,	14th D.A.C.
20066.	Bombr.	H. Turpin,	49th Bde R.F.A.
79905.	Bombr.	O. Clarke,	46th Bde R.F.A.

ROYAL ENGINEERS.

45148.	Sapper	H. Dunn,	89th Field Co. R.E.
42135.	Sapper	G. Bell,	62nd Field Co. R.E.
45181.	A/Corpl.	C.F. Searston,	89th Field Co. R.E.
42059.	Sapper	H. Hill,	61st Field Co. R.E.
40044.	Sapper	A. Thompson,	61st Field Co. R.E.
89394.	L/Corpl.	C.W. Shaw,	89th Field Co. R.E.
41851.	Corpl.	E.T. Sharpe,	61st Field Co. R.E.
41161.	Corpl.	A. MacMaster,	62nd Field Co. R.E.
26963.	Sapper	A. Johnson,	62nd Field Co. R.E.
42131.	Sapper	J. Smetten,	62nd Field Co. R.E.
40230.	Sergt.	R.H. Banks,	62nd Field Co. R.E.
48076.	Pioneer	A. Dale,	14th Signal Co. R.E.
58789.	D/Corpl.	H. Orchard,	14th Signal Co. R.E.
48048.	Pioneer	C. Ramsey,	14th Signal Co. R.E.
40004.	Sapper	L.J. Sutton,	14th Signal Co. R.E.

(Continued)

(2)

11TH BN. THE KING'S (LIVERPOOL) REGIMENT. (PIONEERS)

```
No.12581.   Private   J. Hoyle,
   20735.   L/Corpl.  A. Mather,
 3/12386.   Sergt.    W. Taylor,
   19908.   Private   E.L. Jones,
   23754.      "      J. Brown,
    9203.      "      A.L. Robinson,
   12332.      "      M. Bennett,
   21205.      "      J.H. Moss.
```

6TH SOMERSET L.I.

```
13761. Sergt.  P. Ford,
10209. L/Cpl.  E. George,
11542. Pte.    W. Elliott,
 8015. Sergt.  A. Baker,
 7171. Pte.    W. Hussey,
 9884.   "     T.J. Wren,
11167. Sergt.  G.G.A. Lambert,
 9946.   "     A.L. Grice.
```

6TH BN. D.C.L.I.

```
14027. Pte   H. Goodwin,
 5978. Sergt. R. Howe,
10423.   "    R. Treloar,
11027. Pte    E. Wakely,
10821. L/Sgt. F. Oxenham,
10613. Pte.   S. Price,
 5822. Corpl. J. Browning.
```

5TH OX & BUCKS L.I.

```
 9912. Sergt. A. Wheeler,
10694.   "    W.R. Hancock,
10514.   "    T. Maycock,
10698.   "    H. Graubner,
10889.   "    F. Godfrey,
 9268.   "    G. Hickman,
10130.   "    J.E.L. Hinton,
10277. Pte    W.W. Johnson,
10788. L/Cpl. R. Stevens,
10968. Pte.   E. Brickwell,
10638.   "    J. Wiley,
```

6TH BN. K.O.Y.L.I.

```
 3134. L/Cpl. J.C. Perkins,
18602.   "    S. Bottomley,
15271. Pte.   W. Bolton,
18653.   "    F. Johnson,
14673. Sergt. J.A. Boyd,
 2131. CQMS.  A. Dickenson,
11445. Sergt. W. Hull,
```

6TH K.S.L.I.

```
 9324. C.Q.M.S. J. Gimes,
 6446. Pte.    R. Lloyd,
11376. L/Sgt.  C.F. Cowper,
11128. Pte.    R. Lloyd,
10522. Corpl (Sgt) T. Williams,
14863. Pte.    G. Parsons,
15891.   "     S. Butterworth,
11420. Corpl (L/Sgt) J.F. Butler,
11260. Sergt.  F. Atkinson,
20157.   "     E.J. Davies,
10830. L/Cpl.  W.R. Chorley,
10981. Pte.    J. Lloyd.
```

7TH BN. K.R.R.C.

```
 2851. Sgt (CSM) J. Jones,
A.93.  CQMS.  E.J. Scroggs,
A.509. Sergt. S. Ellis,
 6364.   "    S. Wilson,
A.478. Corpl. H. Hoad,
A.173. L/Cpl. W. Fry,
A.3358. Sergt. W. Plant.
```

8TH BN. K.R.R.C.

```
  650.  Rfmn.  H. Booker,
 1706.    "    E. Lucas,
R.6018. L/Cpl. S. Liddiard,
 6019.  Rfmn.  G.E. Diggory,
 8244.  Sergt. W.E. Rooke,
 7199.  Rfmn.  J.H. Green,
 3682.    "    P. Pegg,
 1031.  Sergt. A. Leaver,
A.534.    "    F. Tass,
R.6008. Rfmn.  G.W. Hill,
A.1560. Corpl. W. Hooper,
A.3114. L/Cpl. H. Wakeford,
R.8092. Rfmn.  C. Baynes,
```

9TH BN. K.R.R.C.

```
10350.  Rfmn.  T. Underwood,
A.2333. L/Cpl. H. Mitchell,
A.1629. Rfmn.  R. Rickards,
R.7105. L/Cpl. G. Rayner,
R.10469. L/Cpl. S. Moorley,
```

(Continued)

10TH BN. DURHAM L.I.

No. 20840. Pte. P. Kileen,
12050. " J. Cunningham,
12275. " J. Lumsdale,
9071. " T. Brown,
9721. " W. Thompson,
24258. Sgt. C. Wakeham,
8780. " F. Mullett,
12773. " J. Pratt,
15995. CQMS. W. Moody,

7th BN. THE RIFLE BDE.

4409. Rfmn. F.R. Freer,
749. Corpl. W. Green,
2350. Sergt. F. Wedge,
13/709. Corpl. G. Tovy,
2682. Corpl. S. Burton,
2502. A/Cpl. H. Watts,
B.53. Sergt. A. Beckenham,
B.1509. Rfmn. H. Thomas,
B.1510. Rfmn. W. Hanson,
2665. A/Cpl. R. Perry,
S.961. Sergt. L.E. Pope,

8TH BN. THE RIFLE BDE.

No. B.683. Rfmn. H. Warden,
B.724. Sergt. F. Driver,
S.3057. " J. Buck,
S.1783. " C. Carson,
S.5472. A/Cpl. T. Murphy,
B.2857. " T. Austin,
S.7277. " M. Halliwell,
2341. CQMS. J. Holden,
580. Sergt. N. Hayward,
B.2870. Sergt. P. O'Hara.
S.898. Rfmn. J. McKeon.

9TH BN. THE RIFLE BDE.

906. Sergt(CSM) P. Wood,
3795. " " F. Brooker,
B.957. Sergt. T. Angel,
5935. Rfmn. J. Phillips,
S.4357. A/Cpl. G. Sulley,
B.3302. Corpl. H. Parrish,
S.6458. A/Cpl. A. Mellor,
B.2468. Corpl. A. Norris,
2429. Sergt(CSM) T. Moad,
B.3150. A/Cpl. F. Baker.

MACHINE GUN CORPS.

41ST M.G. COY.

No. 19742. Sergt. B. Adams,
19804. " A.M. McColl,
19805. " J. Knight,

42ND M.G. COY.

No. 19873. Sergt. W.G. Buttery
19879. Pte. E. Palmer,
19890. " J. Coupland.

43RD M.G. COY.

No. 20079. Sergt. J. Magnay,
20044. " R. Swallow,
20021. Pte. J.G. Isaac.

ARMY SERVICE CORPS

Attd. 43rd Inf. Bde H.Qrs.

S.26825. L/Cpl. (A/Sgt) W. Hull.

ROYAL ARMY MEDICAL CORPS.

31683. L/Cpl. J. Hunter,   42nd Field Ambulance.
31344. Sergt. W.T. Fairley,   -do-

BARS TO MILITARY MEDALS.

The awards of Military Medals to the undermentioned N.C.Os and men announced in D.D.Os as stated below against their names should now read "Bars to Military Medals".

No. 10772. A/Bombr. S. Bailey, R.A.   1777   24-9-16.
A.650. Rfmn. H. Booker, 8th KRRC.   1809.   9-10-16.
B.683. Rfmn. H. Warden, 8th RB.   1809.   9-10-16.
19804. Sergt. A.M. McColl, 43rd M.G.Co. 1909. 9-10-16.

(Continued)

(4).

1932. OFFICERS CLOTHING AND EQUIPMENT.

The following articles may be had on indent on repayment from A.O.D. :-

		£	s	d
Bags Sleeping Officers,	each	1	2	6
Braces Officers,	"		1	4
Brushes Hair Officers,	"		4	2
" Shaving "	"		1	5
" Tooth "	"			6
Braid Worsted Tracing Drab, per 144 yards,	"		6	5
Caps S.D. Officers,	"		11	2.
Coats Raincoat Officers,	"	1	16	7
Collars Officers Winter,	"			9½
" " Summer,	"			9
Crowns Gilt Officers,	"			7½
" Worsted "	per dozen		3	9
Drawers Woollen Officers Thin Short,	per pair		5	2
" " " Thick "	" "		5	2
Gloves Leather Lined Officers,	" "		4	4
" " Unlined "	" "		3	2
Jackets Pea Drab Officers,	each	1	16	0
" " Furlined "	"	3	4	0
Jackets S.D. Officers No.1 (Thick or Thin)	"	3	5	0
" " " 2 " " "	"	3	1	9
Handkerchiefs Khaki Officers Silk,	"		1	4.
" " " Linen,	"			10.
Lace Silk & Worsted Drab ½"	per gross yds		11	6
" " " " " 5/8"	"		8	10.
Leggings Leather Officers,	per pair		11	8
Razors Officers,	each		1	7½
Rugs K.C. Officers.	"	3	6	3
Scarves Silk Officers,	"		9	6
" Other than Silk,	"		2	4
Shirts Drab Flannel Officers Summer,	"		7	3
" " " " Winter,	"		8	10
Socks Woollen Officers,	per pair		1	4½
Stars Gilt Officers,	each			4
" Worsted "	"			3¾
Straps Valise Officers Kit,	per set.		14	10
Ties Knitted Officers,	each		1	1
Valise Officers Kit.	"		15	3
Vests Woollen Officers,	"		5	0
Waistcoats Cardigan Officers,	"		10	6.

(signed) C.L. Hamilton

LIEUT-COLONEL,
A.A.&.Q.M.G.
14TH (LIGHT) DIVISION.

NOTICE.

LOST:- A small Wristlet WATCH, between A.D.M.S. Office and
No.2 Mess, H.Qrs, 14th Division, about 11 a.m. on
13th inst.
Information to A.D.M.S., 14th Division.

14TH (LIGHT) DIVISION.

ROUTINE ORDERS.

16th November, 1916.

1933. PEAS AND BEANS.

Information has been received that beans or exotic peas, containing cyannidic acid (beans or peas of Birmanic or Java) are sold in the zone of the Armies at cheap prices.

Those dry vegetables, even if they contain only a slight proportion of acid, inferior to the quantity of 20 miligrams allowed per 100 grammes, are very dangerous when eaten regularly.

They cannot be mistaken for home grown beans, which have the regular shape of a kidney with a smooth surface. The forme has a triangular shape with unequal sides, which at first sight make them different from the latter. Moreover, the pod instead of being in a hole, as is the case with home grown beans, makes a sort of swelling, out of which many superficial ramifications issue. The difference can, therefore, be easily detected, but on account of the danger they offer, chiefly when eaten by troops in the Field, it is necessary that their introduction into the food supply of men should be avoided.

The circulation and sale of beans or peas called "of Birmanic or Java" is, therefore, forbidden in the zone of the British Army, and units, canteens and messes will only purchase their supplies of beans or peas through their respective Supply Officers.
(Authority D.D.S.&.T., Third Army S/449, dated 13-11-16. VI Corps Q/341/28).

1934. COTTON RAGS FOR CLEANING PURPOSES.

Reference C.R.O.1483:
Demands for cleaning rags will be kept within the following weights :-

	Per month.
Battalions,	35 lbs.
Batteries & Companies, other than Companies of Battalions,	14 lbs.
Field Ambulances,	21 lbs.
Other Units,	7 lbs.

C. Parsons Captain
for Captain
LIEUT COLONEL,
A.A.&.Q.M.G.
14TH (LIGHT) DIVISION.

NOTICE.

Officers Commanding Units are requested to afford facilities for N.C.Os and men of the Jewish Faith to meet the Senior Jewish Chaplain at BERLENCOURT at 10.45 a.m. on Sunday next. A Guide will be at H.Qrs, 9th K.R.R.C. to point out the place selected for the Meeting.

14TH (LIGHT) DIVISION.

ROUTINE ORDERS.

17th November, 1916.

1935. HONOURS AND REWARDS.

The following name should be added to those published in D.R.O.1931 of November 15th as having been awarded Military Medals :-

No. 11982, Corpl. H.H. Russell, 6th Bn. Somerset L.I.

1936. OFFICERS CLOTHING AND EQUIPMENT.

Reference D.R.O.1932, the first sentence should read "The following articles may be had on indent ON repayment from A.O.D".

1937. COURTS MARTIAL.

Officers having less than one complete year Commissioned Service are NOT ELIGIBLE as Members of a F.G.C.M. and must not be detailed.

LIEUT-COLONEL,
A.A.&.Q.M.G.
14TH (LIGHT) DIVISION.

NOTICE.
DIVINE SERVICES, SUNDAY 19TH NOVR.1916.

C OF E.

7.30 a.m. Holy Communion at Div'l Headquarters (Coach House)
9.30 a.m. Morning Service " " " (Recreation Room)
5.30 p.m. Evening Service " " " (No.4 Mess-room).

R. C.

9 a.m. Mass at IVERGNY Church for 9th R.B. & 5th K.S.L.I.
10 am. " " BERLENCOURT Church for 9th KRRC & 5th Ox & Bucks L.I.
10.30 a.m. " " SOMBRIN Church for troops in vicinity.
10.30 a.m. " " GRAND RULLECOURT for troops in vicinity.

-*-*-*-

SCA205

Thanks for your reply of
1938. the number now of
horses if any would be the
necessary information will
reach this office by 12
noon 22.11.16.

18.11.16
Street

Call for names — not those
now employed as post
find me name in 1/7/15

14TH (LIGHT) DIVISION.

ROUTINE ORDERS.

18th November, 1916.

1938. RETURN.

Each Infantry and R.F.A. Brigade will submit by 22nd instant the names of four qualified Post Office Servants to assist with Christmas Mails and Gifts of the Division. Only established (i.e. pensionable) P.O. Servants will be considered and the following particulars are required :- (a) Post Office rank (b) office at which employed, (c) length of Post Office Service.

Names of N.C.Os and men now employed as Post Orderlies should not be submitted as it is considered that they will be of more use with their units in their present capacity.

1939. CHRISTMAS MAILS.

The latest dates for posting in the United Kingdom for delivery in the Field by Christmas Day will be :-

    Letters,   17th December.
    Parcels,   13th December.

The latest dates for posting in the Field for delivery in the United Kingdom on Christmas Day are the same as those above.

1940. EFFECTS OF SICK, WOUNDED and DECEASED SOLDIERS.

It has been brought to notice that Units are not in all cases carrying out the instructions laid down in G.R.O.1358, dealing with Army Form W.3190, which is to be enclosed in the registered packets of men's effects sent to the D.A.D.R.T. Havre. When the instructions are not carried out, it is impossible to know whether the contents, as received, are correct or not.
(Third Army R.O. 547).

LIEUT COLONEL,
A.A.&.Q.M.G.
14TH (LIGHT) DIVISION.

14TH (LIGHT) DIVISION.

ROUTINE ORDERS.

19th November, 1916.

1941. BATHS.

Baths have been or are being erected at SOMBRIN, BERLENCOU OPPY, HOUVIN, BUNEVILLE and SERICOURT for the use of the Division.

Brigades will allot hours of bathing.

A.D.M.S. will arrange for the running of the baths and the provision of clean clothing.

Men must be put through the baths as quickly as possible to avoid waste of fuel. SOMBRIN Baths will work 56 hours a week, the remainder 36 hours a week only. Brigades will inform A.D.M.S. of the days and hours selected.

1942. CLEAN CLOTHING.

Clean clothes will be issued in exchange for dirty at all Baths under Divisional control for the men bathing there at the time of bathing.

If any balance of clean clothes accumulates at the laundry units will be informed where they may send for clean clothes in exchange for dirty. The dirty clothes should in that case be fastened in bundles or placed in sacks. Each sack or bundle must have a label showing the nature and number of its contents and the unit sending it. CLEAN boxes or CLEAN sacks must be sent in which to take away the clean clothes. If no CLEAN receptacles are provided, the clean clothes will not be handed over but a receipt only will be given for the dirty clothes.

1943. H.E. TRENCH MORTAR BOMBS.

Reference C.R.O.1503: Brigades will report by noon 20th the number of dummy T.M. Bombs which they estimate as being required.

1944. IMPROVEMENT OF ACCOMMODATION.

Brigades and Camp Commandant will render a report by 30th instant showing for each village the amount of work done since village was occupied by the Division up to and including the 25th inst, to increase and improve the accommodation, and the material expended on each item or group of items of similar nature.

C.R.E. will report the amount of material provided to each Brigade and to the Camp Commandant, Div'l H.Qrs.

An addendum to the report will show the use to which each Armstrong and Nissen Hut in the village is put.

1945. BRICKS.

Indents for bricks will be sent to C.R.E. through Brigad Headquarters.

Authority for issue signed by C.R.E. will be sent to uni who will present the authority at the Orderly Room, 11th King (Liverpool) Regiment, BUNEVILLE. Instructions as to drawing bricks will be given there.

A brick depot will shortly be formed at LE CAUROY for un whose distance from BUNEVILLE is more than 7 Miles. Notificat will be made when it is formed.

(Continued)

- 2 -

1946. PETROL - ISSUE TO FARMERS.

Corps Routine Order No. 1435, dated 3-11-16 is cancelled. Petrol is now only issuable for Threshing through Army Purchase Board. Units will forward to this office through the usual channel by noon the 22nd instant, all receipts, in duplicate, given by Maires for issues of Petrol that have been made, or a statement to the effect that no issue has been made.
(Authority D.D.S.& T. 3/Army S/448, dated 17-11-16. VI Corps Q/

1947. BOOTS F.S. SHOEPACK PATTERN.

Some of the F.S. Boots now coming up, although excellent in other respects have too thin a sole.
It is recommended that they be "clumped" under regimental arrangements before first issue.
(C.R.O. 1506)

1948. SALVAGE.

The following is a list of articles salved by the 14th Div'l Salvage Coy. for week ended 16th November, 1918.

No Collected	Description of Articles	Serviceable (S) or Unserviceable (US)	How disposed
120	Ammunition Brackets,	S.	D.A.D.O.S
29	" M.G. Boxes,	S.	DADOS for
14	" " Belts.	S.	Railhead.
648 Pairs	Boots,	U.S.	"
8 Boxes	Horse shoes,	U.S.	"
3 Bags	" "	U.S.	"
2 "	Spare Harness,	U.S.	"
1	Forge,	U.S.	"
5 Bags	Steel Helmets,	U.S.	"
1005	Jackets, S.D.	U.S.	"
549	Trousers, S.D.	U.S.	"
157 Pairs	Puttees,	U.S.	"
10	Ground sheets,	S.	"
135 Pairs	Pantaloons,	U.S.	"
110	Box Respirators,	U.S.	"
1	Spring balance,	U.S.	"
20	Cardigans,	U.S.	"
5	Saddles, Universal,	U.S.	"
2	" Officers,	U.S.	"
44	Greatcoats,	U.S.	"
25	Coats, British Warm,	U.S.	"
5 Boxes	Tube Helmets,	U.S.	"
8	Lamps, Hurricane,	U.S.	"
2	Saddles, complete, Unral	S.	D.A.D.O.S.
61 Pairs	Boots,	S.	"
188	Steel Helmets,	S.	"
168 Pairs	Puttees,	S.	"
½ Drum	Cresol,	S.	"
1	Vermorel Sprayer,	U.S.	"
2	Rifles,	S.	"
4	Bayonets,	S.	"
1	Sword, Cavalry,	S.	"
4	Periscopes,	S.	"
12	Haversacks,	S.	5th K.S.
2	Valises,	S.	"
4	Water Bottle Carriers,	S.	"
1 Set.	Supporting Straps,	S.	"
4	Entrenching tool Carriers	S.	"
1	Entrenching Tool,	S.	"
1 Pair	Stirrup leathers,	S.	D.A.D.O
1 "	Iron Stirrups,	S.	"
4	Tyres,	U.S.	25th Su
200	Greatcoats,	U.S.	Romainh
50	Coats, British Warm,	U.S.	Dump

1948. (Continued)

4 Boxes	: S.A.A.	S.	: Remaining at Dump.
3 "	: Empty S.A.A. cases,	S.	: "
1	: Water tank,	S.	: "
1	: L.G.Leather case,	U.S.	: "
3	: L.G.Leather spare parts case.	U.S.	: "
3 Bags	: Equipment,	S.	: "
36	: Boilers, T.K.	U.S.	: "
9	: Horse Shoe boxes,	S.	: "
10	: Box Respirators,	U.S.	: "
2	: Outer covers (Cycle)	U.S.	: "
2	: Inner Tubes, (Cycle)	U.S.	: "
5	: Groundsheets,	S.	: "
4	: Rifles, German,	S.	: "
10 Drums	: Oil	S.	: "
50	: Tube Helmets,	U.S.	: "
4	: Saddles, Cycle,	U.S.	: "
1 Bag	: Spare Harness,	U.S.	: "
1	: Bandolier,	U.S.	: "
1	: Rifle,	S.	: "
1	: Mincing Machine,	U.S.	: "
1	: Periscope case,	U.S.	: "
3 Suits	: Motor Cycle Overalls	U.S.	: "

J.W.Watson Major
for LIEUT-COLONEL,
A.A.&.Q.M.G.
14TH (LIGHT) DIVISION.

14TH (LIGHT) DIVISION.
ROUTINE ORDERS.

20th November, 1916.

1949. BILLETING ACCOMMODATION.

Reference C.R.O.1507:
The necessary orders will be issued by Brigade Area Commanders. A carbon copy of the Form will be sent by Town Commandants direct to this office.
This office No. A/86 is cancelled so far as it affects Form 'A' issued therewith.

1950. SELF-INFLICTED WOUNDS.

It is notified for information that in cases of Self-Inflicted wounds and Accidental Injuries, Third Army Form A/G/1017 properly filled up and accompanied by statements (vide instructions on back of form) is sufficient for all purposes. Courts of Inquiry are only necessary when accidents are thought to be due to faulty grenades, ammunition, or other defective material.

1951. DISPOSAL OF PRISONERS.

Units, other than the smaller Divisional Units which cannot furnish the necessary guards etc., are responsible for the custody of their own prisoners sentenced to Penal Servitude or Imprisonment. They are not to be sent to the A.P.M. for Commitment to Prison until the orders of the Army Commander directing the sentence to be 'carried out' or 'suspended' have been communicated to the unit concerned.

C.M. Hamilton
LIEUT-COLONEL,
A.A.&.Q.M.G.
14TH (LIGHT) DIVISION.

14TH (LIGHT) DIVISION.

ROUTINE ORDERS.

21st November, 1916.

1952. POSTINGS - OFFICERS.

Temp. Second-Lieutenant G.D. HARLE posted to 9th K.R.R.C. under M.S.510/10299 dated 3-11-16 is cross-posted to 7th Bn. Rifle Bde, with effect from 3-11-16, under the provisions of A.G., G.H.Q., No.A/17979.

1953. HEAVY BRANCH - MACHINE GUN CORPS.

Reference A.G. No.A/18532 dated 9th November, 1916 issued to all units.
Applications made by Officers and Other Ranks for employment in the Heavy Branch, Machine Gun Corps will be submitted through the usual channels and will be forwarded by Brigades to this office immediately they are received without waiting for the returns from each Unit to come in.
Attention is directed to Para.3(a).

1954. WAR DIARIES.

The instructions issued dealing with War Diaries are not in all cases observed.
The attention of all concerned is directed to General Routine Order No.1598, and particularly to the fact that War Diaries are Secret Documents.
(Third Army Routine Order 552).

1955. ADDITIONAL PAY AND WORKING PAY.

Time is constantly being wasted and unnecessary correspondence caused by the submission of applications for Additional and Working Pay to the Command Paymaster, Paymaster-in-Chief, or D.A.G., 3rd Echelon.
It is to be noted that the term "General Officer Commanding" for the purpose of Article XI Royal Warrant for Pay refers, for troops serving in an Army of the B.E.F. to the Army Commander only.
All applications for Additional and Working Pay will be rendered through the usual channels.

1956. MOTOR CYCLISTS - SPEED OF.

Attention is drawn to the excessive speed at which Despatch Riders and others on motor cycles, or motor cycles with side-cars, move. This speed is dangerous to other users of the road, to the cyclist himself, and it also damages the machine.
The maximum speed for motor cycles in the Third Army Area will be 10 Miles per hour through towns and villages, and 25 miles per hour elsewhere.
In the case of a despatch rider, if it is considered necessary to exceed these speeds, A.F. B.2501 - "Despatch Rider Docket" will be endorsed and signed by the Officer authorising the despatch rider to exceed the speeds laid down for the Third Army Area.
Officers Commanding Units having motor cycles on their charge will ensure that this order reaches their men.
(Third Army A.O.554)

1957. WATERING HORSES.

Horses and mules will be bitted when ridden or led to or from water, and strict march discipline is to be enforced.
The bits are to be removed when animals are drinking.

LIEUT-COLONEL,
A.A.&Q.M.G.
14TH (LIGHT) DIVISION

14TH (LIGHT) DIVISION

ROUTINE ORDERS.

22nd November, 1916.

1958. BATHS.

Hours for bathing at the Baths, BERLENCOURT, will be allotted in future by Camp Commandant, Div'l H.Qrs to whom applications should be made.

1959. LIGHT RAILWAY:- FREVENT - AVESNES.

Officers, N.C.Os and men travelling on duty by train to FREVENT may use the light railway AVESNES - FREVENT without further authority than the usual order from their Commanding Officer to proceed to ultimate destination.

Other Officers, N.C.Os and men using the railway either on duty or on pass must be provided with authority to travel.

This authority will be an endorsement signed by an officer on the written order to proceed on duty or on the written pass in the following form :-

"Movement order to travel by Light Railway
from .... to ....
(sd) ....

Officers, N.C.Os and men are not to use the Light Railway at their own or at the public expense unless provided with an authority as specified above.

1960. HORSE TRUCKS.

Complaints have been received from the French Railway Authorities that trucks used for the conveyance of horses are sent back without having been cleaned.

These trucks have to be used for transport of troops immediately on return.

In future, units to whom horses are despatched by rail will be responsible that trucks are cleaned before return to the Base.

A supply of shovels and brushes will be kept at Railheads for this purpose by the R.T.O.
(Authority Third Army QC/4869 dated 20-11-16. VI Corps Q/839).

1961. SICK WASTAGE.

The following is the Sick Wastage Return for week ended 18-11-16:-

Unit	O.	O.R.	Unit	O.	O.R.
46th Bde R.F.A.		3.	9th K.R.R.C.		2.
46th Bde R.F.A. AVC Attd.		1.	9th R.B.		3.
47th Bde R.F.A.		3.	42nd M.G. Coy.		1.
48th Bde R.F.A.		8.	42nd T.M. Bty.		Nil.
14th D.A.C.		4.	6th Somerset L.I.	1	3.
V.14 T.M. Bty.		Nil.	6th D.C.L.I.		1.
X.14 T.M. Bty.		Nil.	6th K.O.Y.L.I.		7.
Y.14 T.M. Bty.		Nil.	10th Durham L.I.		8.
Z.14 T.M. Bty.		1.	43rd M.G. Coy.		1.
61st Field Co. R.E.		1.	43rd T.M. Bty.		1.
62nd Field Co. R.E.		1.	11th Bn. L'pool R.		5.
89th Field Co. R.E.		2.	No. 14 Supply Column,		Nil.
14th Signal Co. R.E.		Nil.	42nd Field Ambulance,		Nil.
7th K.R.R.C.		6.	43rd Field Ambulance,	1	3.
8th K.R.R.C.		2.	44th Field Ambulance,		Nil.
7th R.B.		12.	14th Div. Train.		Nil.
8th R.B.		2.	25th Sanitary Section,		Nil.
5th Ox & Bucks L.I.		3.	26th Mobile Vety Sec.		1.
5th K.S.L.I.		7.			

Totals Officers 2 Other Ranks 88.

C. Parsons Capt.
LIEUT-COLONEL
A.A. & Q.M.G.
14TH (LIGHT) DIVISION

14TH (LIGHT) DIVISION.

ROUTINE ORDERS.

23rd November, 1916.

1962. THIRD ARMY COOKERY SCHOOL.

Officers Commanding Units desirous of sending the Quartermaster or Quartermaster-Sergeant to visit Third Army School of Cookery for one day in order that they may be shown the system adopted for improvising cooking ranges, using rations economically etc etc., should submit names through usual channels to reach this office by 9 a.m. on Monday 27th instant. Arrangements will then be made for the visit and Units will be informed.

1963. TENTAGE RETURNS.

A Certificate will be added to all returns of tentage rendered in future that tents held by units on their Mobilization Store Table are not included.

1964. STEEL HELMETS.

With reference to Corps Routine Order No.1113: It is apparent from pictures appearing in the Daily Press that Steel Helmets are still being used for illegitimate purposes.
Offenders, if detected, are to be severely dealt with.
(Authority Third Army O/67, dated 20-11-16. VI Corps Q/47).

LIEUT-COLONEL,
A.A.& Q.M.G.
14TH (LIGHT) DIVISION.

14TH (LIGHT) DIVISION.

ROUTINE ORDERS.

24th November, 1916.

1965. POSTING - Officers.

Temp. Second-Lieutenant H. STEWART, posted to 7th Bn. The Rifle Brigade under A.G., G.H.Q., No.A/1186/387 dated 12-11-16 is cross-posted to 9th Bn. K.R.R.C. with effect from 20-11-16 under the provisions of A.G., G.H.Q., No. A/17979.

1966. COTTON RAGS FOR CLEANING PURPOSES.

D.R.O.1934 is cancelled owing to the limited supply of cotton rags.

Demands will be kept within the following weights :-

	Per month.
Battalions,	4 lbs.
Batteries and Companies other than Companies of Battns.	1½ "
Field Ambulances,	3 "
Other Units,	1 "

1967. A.B. 64..

Officers Commanding Units will insert the customary abbreviations denoting religion below the line given for "Name in full" on page 2 of A.B.64 of all Soldiers in this country.

(G.R.O.1954)

1968. BINOCULARS.

Attention is called to the necessity for taking all possible steps to prevent the wastage of binoculars. It should be remembered that these are expensive and difficult to obtain, especially the prismatic pattern, and are easily misappropriated.

Information received from Bases indicates that there is want of supervision and check over the demands for these articles. Commanding Officers must ensure that the circumstances under which binoculars are lost are fully investigated before demands are submitted, and that those which have become deficient through neglect are paid for by the individuals concerned. Demands for replacement of unserviceable binoculars will not be passed until the unserviceable articles have been handed in to the Ordnance Officer of the Formation, or a satisfactory explanation of the deficiency has been given.

Officers in charge of Casualty Clearing Stations and other Medical Units will arrange that all binoculars in possession of casualties, not being the property of the individual as in the case of Officers, are returned to the Ordnance Officer of the nearest Formation or nearest Ordnance Depot.

(G.R.O.1956)

1969. UNSERVICEABLE TELEPHONES or PARTS OF TELEPHONES.

Telephones have been returned to Ordnance deficient of their platinum silver contacts. The removal of these contacts is forbidden.

(G.R.O. 1959).

(Continued)

1970. **MEN ENLISTED AT SPECIAL RATES OF PAY WHO ARE GRANTED TRANSFER TO HOME ESTABLISHMENT ON COMPASSIONATE GROUNDS.**

Attention is directed to G.R.O.1951 dated 19-11-16.

C. Parsons Captain
for
LIEUT-COLONEL,
A.A.&.Q.M.G.
14TH (LIGHT) DIVISION.

DIVINE SERVICES.
SUNDAY 26TH NOVEMBER, 1916.

C of E.

Holy Communion 8.30 a.m. Field Cashier's Room, Div.H.Qrs.
Morning Service 9.30 a.m. Signal Co.Recreation Room.

14TH (LIGHT) DIVISION.

ROUTINE ORDERS.

25th November, 1916.

1971. HONOURS AND REWARDS.

Military Medals.

The following names should be added to those published in D.R.O.1931 dated 15-11-16 :-

No.12088, Pte C.V. Gwynn,
 2nd Garr.Bn.Devon Regt, late 6th Somerset L.I.
No.S/4939. Sergt. J. Smith,
 9th Bn. The Rifle Bde.

1972. ROADS.

Officers Commanding Troops are responsible that sufficient parties are detailed to enable Town Majors to remove mud from the roads in Towns and Villages to some convenient place outside. Mud must not be allowed to remain in heaps at the side of the road.
 (C.R.O.1526).

1973. WOOD.

Units drawing wood from VI Corps Dump at AVESNES will forward A.B. 55, duly completed, with party sent to draw wood. In all cases a loading party will accompany the N.C.O. sent to draw wood.
 (C.R.O.1524).

1974. CHILLED FEET & FROSTBITE - Prevention of.

Every Officer and Senior N.C.O. is to be in possession of a copy of G.R.O.1275 dated 28-11-15.
Demands for the number of copies required to complete are to be sent to Div. H.Q. by 28th instant.

1975. BURIAL OF JEWISH SOLDIERS.

Officers Commanding Units will if circumstances permit communicate by wire with the Senior Jewish Chaplain, 9th C.C.S stating date, time and place at which the funeral is to take place. If he is unable to attend the funeral will be conducted under Regimental arrangements according to the Jewish Prayer Book, a copy of which may be obtained from the Church of England Chaplain attached to the Brigade or formation.

A.C.Hamilton

LIEUT COLONEL,
A.A.&.Q.M.C.
14TH (LIGHT) DIVISION.

14TH (LIGHT) DIVISION.

ROUTINE ORDERS.

26th November, 1916.

1976. HONOURS AND REWARDS.

Reference D.R.O.1931 dated 15-11-16, the Number of L/Corpl. C.W. Shaw, 89th Field Co. R.E. should read 49394 and not as stated.

1977. SALVAGE.

The following is a list of articles salved by 14th Div. Salvage Co. for week ended 25-11-16:-

No. Collected	Description of Articles	Serviceable (S) or Unserviceable (US)	How disposed of
354 Pairs	Trousers, S.D.	U.S.	D.A.D.O.S. for Railhead.
536	Jackets, S.D.	U.S.	"
504 Pairs	Boots,	U.S.	"
213 "	Puttees,	U.S.	"
22	Shovels,	U.S.	"
26	Ground sheets,	U.S.	"
147	Greatcoats,	U.S.	"
40 Pairs	Pantaloons,	U.S.	"
27	Leather valises,	U.S.	"
15	B.W. Coats,	U.S.	"
67	Haversacks,	S.	"
20 Pairs	Pouches, (Web)	S.	"
25	Belts,	S.	"
1 Bag	Equipment,	S.	"
1 "	" Leather,	S.	"
9 Pairs	Pouches, "	S.	"
72 "	Braces,	U.S.	"
6	Saddles, Bicycle,	U.S.	"
1	Chain,	S.	"
20	Rifle slings,	U.S.	"
4	Saddles Universal,	U.S.	"
1	" Officers,	U.S.	"
4	Sheep Skin Coats,	U.S.	"
6 Boxes	Horse shoes,	U.S.	"
2 bags	"	U.S.	"
1 Box	Tube Helmets,	U.S.	"
5 Pairs	Horse Clippers	U.S.	"
16	Box Respirators,	U.S.	"
3	L.G. Cart wheels,	S.	"
4	Rifles, German,	U.S.	"
1	" British,	U.S.	"
1 Bag	Harness,	U.S.	"
21 Pairs	Boots, F.S.	U.S.	"
3	Lamps, hurricane,	U.S.	"
1	Mincing Machine,	S.	D.A.D.O.S.
76 Pairs	Boots,	S.	14th Signals.
1 Pair	Stirrups, Iron,	U.S.	25th San.Sec.
4	Tyres, cyclo,	S.	9th R.B.
20	Braces, leather,	S.	5th K.S.L.I.
3	Drums, oil, empty,	S.	D.A.D.O.S.
30 Pairs	Puttees,	S.	Still at dump
3	Rifles,	S.	D.A.D.O.S.
2	M.G. Tripods,	U.S.	Still at dump
70 Pairs	Pantaloons,	U.S.	" " "
172 "	Trousers, S.D.	U.S.	" " "
8	Inner Tubes Cyclo,	U.S.	" " "
1	Outer Cover,	U.S.	" " "
150	Cardigans,	U.S.	" " "
100	Tunics,	U.S.	" " "
14	Greatcoats,	U.S.	" " "
2	Bandoliers,		

Continued/

14	Box Respirators,	U.S.	Still at dump
1 Bag	Equipment, (sundry)	S.	" " "
20 Boxes	Empty Cartridge cases	U.S.	" " "
2 "	Ammunition,	S.	" " "
2 "	Preserved Beef,	S.	" " "
1	Stretcher,	U.S.	" " "
25	Steel Helmets,	U.S.	" " "
1	100 Gall. Water tank,	S.	" " "
5	Bicycle wheels,	U.S.	" " "
4 Sets	Harness,	U.S.	" " "
1	Draught Pole,	U.S.	" " "

1978. **CARRIERS, MAGAZINE, Lewis Gun.**

Provision is being made for the repair of Carriers, Magazine, Lewis Gun, in Divisional Shops.
They may also be repaired in Regimental shops and the following articles may be indented for through D.A.D.O.S. per Carrier :-

Buckle, brass,	1.
Eyelets, oval, brass (complete with washer)	2.
Turnbuckle (complete with rivets and burrs where required)	2.
Material for repairing } Webbing	In Yards as required.

1979. **PUMPING MACHINERY.**

Reference C.R.O.1488:
Pumping Machinery includes Chain helice pumps & persian wheel pumps but not ordinary cottage wells with ropes and buckets. Town Majors requiring repair to these ordinary wells will wire to C.R.E. 14th Division.

C.L. Hamilton

LIEUT COLONEL,
A.A.& Q.M.G.
14TH (LIGHT) DIVISION.

NOTICES.

FOUND: RIDER, Black, 15.2 hands, aged, Clipped, 6 Nr.Quarter. Enquiries to H.Qrs 14th Division.

LOST: On evening of 24th inst between the hours of 4 and 7 p.m. on the WARLUS - DAINVILLE - ARRAS Road, Burberry WATERPROOF COAT. Initials H.A.G. on back of collar. Information to Capt. Gillespie, R.A.M.C. attd 5th Ox & Bucks L.I.

14th (LIGHT) DIVISION

ROUTINE ORDERS

27th November 1916.

1980. SICK WASTAGE

The following is the Sick Wastage Return for week ended 25/11/16:-

Unit	O.	O.R.	Unit	O.	O.R.
46th Bde R.F.A.		2			
47th Bde R.F.A.	1	8	42nd T.M.Bty		1
48th Bde R.F.A.		8	6th Somerset L.I.		4
14th .D.A.C.	1	5	6th D.C.L.I.		5
61st Field Co., R.E.		2	6th K.O.Y.L.I.	2	4
62nd Field Co., R.E.		1	10th Durham L.I		8
89th Field Co., R.E.		1	43rd M.G.Coy,		2
7 K.R.R.C.		13	43rd T.M.Bty.		Nil
8th K.R.R.C.		1	11th Bn.K.L'pool R.		5
7th Rifle Bde.		5	14th Div'l Train		3
8th Rifle Bde.		3	42nd Field Ambulance		2
5th Ox & Bucks L.I.		8	43rd Field Ambulance		1
5th K.S.L.I.		3	44th Field Ambulance		1
9th K.R.R.C.		1	25th Sanitary Section		1
9th Rifle Bde.	1	11			

Totals Officers 5 Other Ranks 107.

1981 FUEL

During the present scarcity wood will be issued at the rate of 5 lbs per man per week.

It is hoped now to maintain the Supply of Coal at the rate of 9 lbs per man per week after all deductions have been made for Divisional purposes.

Extra wood when available may be issued in lieu of coal to the extent of 2 lbs wood per man per week in place of 1 lb coal.

All Units will report weekly on Saturdays through the usual channels whether they have received fuel to the above scale or over if for the period Saturday to Friday Night.

1982. TRAFFIC

The main road from BEAUDRICOURT to LUCHEUX is closed to all traffic, except Staff Officers in cars, and vehicles with special passes.

1983 FUEL WOOD.

No purchase of wood, whether cut or uncut, will be made by Units in the VI Corps Area without reference to this office.
(C.R.O. 1533)

1984 CHAFF-CUTTERS.

Certificates will be rendered by every Unit, through the usual channels, of the number of Chaff-cutters in possession.

Returns showing the distribution in detail will be forwarded to reach Divisional Headquarters by 30th inst.

Privately owned chaff-cutters will be shown separately, and the certificate should state that they were not paid for out of Public Funds.

Continued/

1985. GUM BOOTS - REPAIR.

All concerned are reminded that Gum Boots beyond local repair are to be returned without delay to Ordnance for despatch to O.O., Pantin, Paris.
(C.R.O. 1537)

1986 OVERLOADING OF VEHICLES, ETC.

With reference to Corps Routine Orders Nos. 1434 and 1468, dated 3/11/16 and 9/11/16 respectively, it is notified that there is no objection to a light superstructure being placed
(a) on water carts to enable empty petrol tins to be carried when a Division is moving into the line during offensive operations.
(b) on the forward portion of the field kitchen, for the carriage of preserved rations.
In this case the cooking pots are to be empty.
Divisional Commanders are held responsible that the above concessions do not lead to overloading, and that the superstructures are not used for the carriage of any stores other than those mentioned.
(C.R.O. 1539)

1987 RANK TO BE GIVEN TO RE-ENLISTED EX-WARRANT OFFICERS, AND NON-COMMISSIONED OFFICERS.

Ex-Warrant Officers and N.C.O's who re-enlisted for the duration of the war previous to the passing of the Military Service Acts, and who were promoted forthwith to acting rank corresponding to the rank they held on discharge, will now be given substantive rank corresponding to the rank they held on discharge, provided they are still serving in that or in a higher rank.
N.C.O's who re-enlisted under A.O. 384 of 1914 and were only promoted acting Corporal will now be given that substantive rank, provided they are still serving in that or in a higher rank.
(G.R.O. 1962)

1988 DOGS

General Routine Order 1808 will remain in force until further orders.
General Routine Order 1843 is cancelled.

1989 CENSORSHIP - GREEN ENVELOPES (A.F.W.3078)

(1) Reference G.R.O. 1855 the scale of issue of Green Envelopes will shortly be increased to 50% on War Establishments or the ascertained average strength of units.
(2) To provide for Christmas and New Year correspondence an extra issue of Green Envelopes will be made for 2 weeks early in December at the rate given in Censorship Orders, para 2 (1)
(3) Attention is called to paragraph 3 of G.R.O. 1361, which is now republished for information:-
"Letters sent to the Base Censors for forwarding are not to be enclosed in any outer covering other than the officially issued green envelope".
The Censors at the Base have been instructed to forward to Officers Commanding Units any letters which contravene this order. If the unit cannot be traced, the letters are liable to destruction Regimental Censors are to be warned that they are not to pass such letters.

Continued/

1990.   **DISINFECTION.**

Attention is drawn to the indiscriminate use of bleaching powder (Chloride of Lime) for disinfecting purposes.
As it is unnecessary and wasteful to use bleaching powder as a disinfectant for latrine floors, gutters, refuse heaps, etc., this practice must cease, and where disinfection of this nature is required, cresol is to be used in its place.

Bleaching Powder (Chloride of Lime) will be used normally only for sterilization of water supplies. If it is required for any other purpose, it will only be issued on the authority of the medical officer, who will specify his reasons for the issue.

C.H. Hamilton

Lieut. Colonel,
A.A. & Q.M.G.,
14th (Light) Division.

14TH (LIGHT) DIVISION.

ROUTINE ORDERS.

30th November, 1916.

1991. SMALL BOX RESPIRATORS.

Units will report through the usual channels as soon as all ranks have been fitted with new small Box Respirators.

1992. DRYING ROOMS.

Drying accommodation is to be provided for its own use by each unit as soon as latrines and washing places are nearing completion.

One or more rooms will be set aside for this purpose and marked by a notice board "DRYING ROOM".

These rooms will be fitted up as well as possible with stoves and drying lines. Whatever fittings are made are to be considered as fixtures and they are to be left for the succeeding unit.

As soon as material is available R.E. will fit up drying rooms inside barns, making an inner structure capable of being raised to a considerable heat. The remainder of the barn will be used as mens' sleeping accommodation.

LIEUT COLONEL,
A.A.&Q.M.G.
14TH (LIGHT) DIVISION.

NOTICE.

PRIVATE TELEGRAMS.

Arrangements have been made with the French Civil Authorities for the despatch of private telegrams.

Messages written in block letters, bearing Censor's Stamp and the signature of an officer and accompanied by the exact cost of transmission, viz: 2d per word, must reach Signal Office at Div'l H.Qrs by 10.30 a.m.

Telegrams addressed to places in France must be written in French.

FOUND:

On 27th instant RIDER, Bay gelding, 14.3 hands, 7 years, Broad arrow Near Hip, Footmarks:- Q.F.20, O.H. A.S.C.

Also RIDER, Grey, gelding, 14.3 hand, 7 years, Footmarks:- O.F. 11, O.H. A.S.C. A.S.C.

Enquiries H.Qrs 14th Division.

14TH (LIGHT) DIVISION.
===========================

ROUTINE ORDERS.

1st December, 1916.

1893. RATIONS.

Troops proceeding from Bases and places on the Lines of Communication to the Front are now being issued with an extra day's rations.

They have therefore with them the rations for the day following that on which they are due to arrive.

This extra days rations is to be taken into account when indenting for daily rations.

LIEUT-COLONEL,
A.A.&.Q.M.G.
14TH (LIGHT) DIVISION.

NOTICES.

LOST: Taken from Football Field at HOUVIN, CYCLE, No.13954, B.S.A., with haversack on front carrier, leather bottom.
Information to 43rd Infantry Bde.

CHURCH SERVICES - Sunday 3rd December, 1916.

Holy Communion, in Field Cashier's Room, Div.H.Q. 8 a.m.
Morning Service in R.E. Recreation Room, Div.H.Q. 9.30 a.m.
Evening Service in H.Qrs Recreation Room, Div.H.Q. 6.30 p.m.

The authorised Monthly collection will be taken at Holy Communion and Morning Service, for Army Missionary Association.

14TH (LIGHT) DIVISION.

ROUTINE ORDERS.

2nd December, 1916.

1994. RESTRICTION OF LIGHTING.

Reference D.R.O.1927:
Town Majors will take steps within their respective jurisdictions to suppress any excessive lighting.
A.P.M. will instruct his police to assist, especially as regards civilian inhabitants. Any excessive lighting that is persisted in by either civilians or soldiers is to be reported to Div'l Headquarters.

1995. PIERRE DE FOSSE.

Pierre de Fosse is now being sent up to 14th Division. It will be allotted to villages in turn.
Town Majors are responsible that it is properly used. Road repairs must be done first. The top layer of horse standings may be made of this material after requirements of the roads have been met.
No other use is authorised.

[signature]

LIEUT-COLONEL,
A.A.&.Q.M.G.
14TH (LIGHT) DIVISION.

14TH (LIGHT) DIVISION.

ROUTINE ORDERS.

3rd December, 1916.

1996. HONOURS AND REWARDS.

Military Medals.

The following names should be added to those published in D.R.O.1931 dated 15th November :-

No.13789, Sergeant J. Donnelly,
10th Durham L.I.

No.11966. C.Q.M.S. T. Keating,
10th Durham L.I.

1997. RIFLES – Covers and Protectors for.

Every rifle should be provided with a cover either (a) a long cover referred to in G.R.O.581 or (b) a Breech cover referred to in G.R.O.1165.

In either case indents should be made on D.A.D.O.S. to replace covers lost or for first supply if none have been received.

D.A.D.O.S. will obtain supply from the Base or by local purchase in accordance with C.R.O.1101.

(2) Muzzle protectors, i.e. the metal plate which is fastened to the fore end of a rifle and can be closed over the muzzle may be demanded on indent but the supply is at present below demand and the issue is likely to be deferred.

Other methods for protecting the muzzle are (i) the long cover mentioned above or (ii) a canvas bag which will be obtained by D.A.D.O.S. by local purchase to meet any demands made upon him.

1998. COURTS MARTIAL.

Attention is drawn to the practice of attaching to Proceedings an extract from the accused's Conduct Sheet, (A.F. B.122). This practice is irregular. In future, a certified true copy, showing everything that appears on the Conduct Sheet, must be attached.
(C.R.O.1563).

1999. LOCKS FOR VICKERS GUNS.

Great difficulty is being experienced in the supply of Locks for Vickers Machine Guns.

This is due to the difficulty in manufacturing the casing.

All locks beyond repair, but which could be repaired at the Base, should be sent there with the least possible delay.

(Authority Third Army O/30/67, d/ 1-12-16. VI Corps Q/867).

2000. HORSE-SHOE BOXES.

Corps Routine Order No.1419, dated 29-10-16 is republished for information :-

"With reference to General Routine Order No.1863, all horse-shoe boxes will now be returned to Base, where they are urgently required.

(Authority Third Army O/36. dated 29-11-16. VI Corps Q/775).

(Continued)

2001. **TRAFFIC CONTROL.**

Third Army Routine Order No. 562 dated 30-11-16 is republished for information :-
"Columns of wheeled transport, guns, lorries, etc., are not to halt in the streets of towns or villages. When it is necessary to halt, the officer or non-commissioned officer in command will see that the rear of the column is clear of the town or village before giving the order to halt.

Whenever a block occurs on a road, it is the duty of any officer or non-commissioned officer who may happen to be present to take steps at once to clear it and provide a passage for passing vehicles.

Blocks are usually caused by a vehicle halting in the fairway when it could easily have been halted in another spot close by without interfering with traffic".

2002. **WORKING PARTIES.**

It is noticed that men employed on working parties waste their time. This is in a large measure due to the fact that the officer or non-commissioned officer in charge takes no interest in their work, and does not make it his business to see that the best use is made of their services, and that the men themselves are kept at work.

It is apparently the general impression on the part of officers and non-commissioned officers that their duty ends with handing their men over to those at whose disposal they are placed for work.

It is to be impressed on all who may be in charge of working parties that it is their duty to supervise the work of their men and to check all waste of time, labour and energy.
(Authority Third Army AC/5922, dated 29-11-16. VI Corps A/2829).

2003. **USE OF ROADS DURING A THAW.**

In order to provide against a Thaw after hard frost and the closing of roads to M.T. Vehicles:
O.C. 25th Sanitary Section will arrange to draw his rations in future with Div'l Headquarters.
O.C. other M.T. Units will arrange to draw 3 days preserved rations for their personnel and 3 days forage for their horses and maintain the same as a reserve. O.C. these Units will report on the last day of each month to Div'l Headquarters the number of rations and the amount of forage on hand with a certificate that the same are in good condition and have been turned over within the past month.

2004. **WASTAGE OF FOODSTUFFS.**

Third Army Routine Order No.560 dated 29-11-16, is republished for information :-
Attention of Officers Commanding Units is again directed to the necessity for avoiding waste. Certain commodities, particularly preserved meat, M & V Rations, and biscuits continue to be drawn up to the scale when not actually required, and when unconsumed rations are in hand. In view of the vital public interests involved, Commanding Officers should ensure that the commodities not required to be drawn are shewn daily on A.B.55 (France) in the space for the purpose.

Accumulated rations may be used up by underdrawal, or may be returned to Railheads in unbroken cases, or may be collected by Salvage Companies and brought to account. In fact, all machinery for avoiding waste exists, and Commanders must ensure that full use is made of it.
(C.R.O.1551).

Continued)

2005. CORRESPONDENCE WITH STRANGERS.

General Routine Order No.1503 is re-published for information :-
All ranks are forbidden :-
(i) To insert advertisements or to have letters inserted in any publication, inviting strangers to communicate with them.
(ii) To answer the advertisements of strangers who offer to write letters to the troops.
(iii) To advertise or to have letters inserted, in any publication asking for gifts or loans of articles of personal equipment for themselves, and for gifts of clothing and necessaries and medical comforts for the use of the troops.

When acknowledging gifts received, the greatest care must be taken to avoid giving information of military value.

It has come to knowledge that hostile agents (especially females) are making use of the means indicated above to collect information of value to the enemy, and that in corresponding with them, officers and men are playing into the hands of the enemy's spy system.

This order is to be republished in orders issued by all formations and units, and is to be promulgated to all troops now serving in this country, and to all troops who may arrive in this country in the future."

From the constant reports which are received, it is clear that this order is not generally known to the troops. It is to be republished forthwith in the orders of all formation and units.

Disciplinary action will be taken in cases which bring to light any infraction of G.R.O.1503.

2006. CENSORSHIP ORDERS AND REGULATIONS.

The attention of all ranks will be directed to S.S.393 - "Censorship Orders and Regulations for Troops in the Field".

2007. SPEED OF VEHICLES.

Officers concerned will forward a report to reach this office by noon 5th instant that C.R.O.1557 dated 30-11-16 has been read out on 3 successive parades.

2008. LAMPS, STOVES ETC.

Reference C.R.O.1553,
Stoves, lamps, buckets and other barrack stores will be accounted for in future by Town Majors.

Officers Commanding will notify Town Majors in this Div'l area of the quantities on hand by 5th instant. Town Majors will report them on their reports rendered to Div'l H.Qrs on 7th 14th 21st and 28th of each month. Units will no longer report them.

LIEUT-COLONEL,
A.A. & Q.M.G.
14TH (LIGHT) DIVISION.

14TH (LIGHT) DIVISION.

ROUTINE ORDERS.

4th December, 1916.

2009. RECREATION.

Mounted paper chases are forbidden.
When arranging for cross-country runs care is to be taken that Crops are not damaged.

2010. SICK WASTAGE.

The following is the Sick Wastage Return for week ended 2-12-16 :-

	O.	O.R.		O.	O.R.
46th Bde R.F.A.		6.	42nd T.M. Bty.		Nil.
47th Bde R.F.A.		2.	6th Somerset L.I.		4.
48th Bde R.F.A.		2.	6th D.C.L.I.	1	4.
14th D.A.C.		3.	6th K.O.Y.L.I.	1	6.
Z.14 T.M. Bty.		1.	10th Durham L.I.		1.
61st Field Co. R.E.		3.	43rd M.G. Coy.		Nil.
62nd Field Co. R.E.		Nil.	43rd T.M. Bty.		Nil.
89th Field Co. R.E.		1.	11th Bn. L'pool R.		6.
14th Signal Co. R.E.		Nil.	14th Div'l Train.		Nil.
7th K.R.R.C.		3.	ASC(MT) att. Div.Train,		1.
8th K.R.R.C.		1.	R.A.M.C., 42nd Field		
7th R.B.		7.	Ambulance,		Nil.
8th R.B.		4.	R.A.M.C., 43rd Field		
41st M.G. Coy.		Nil.	Ambulance,		1
41st T.M. Bty.		1.	R.A.M.C. 44th Field		
5th K.S.L.I.		Nil.	Ambulance,		1
5th Ox & Bucks L.I.	1	1	25th Sanitary Section,		Nil.
9th K.R.R.C.		4.	26th Mob.Vet.Section,		Nil.
9th R.B.	1	3.	M.M.P.		Nil.

Total Officers 5 Other Ranks 65.

2011. SALVAGE.

The following is a list of articles salved by 14th Div. Salvage Co. week ended 30-11-16 :-

No. Collected	Description of Articles	Serviceable (S) or Unserviceable (U.S)	How disposed of
1	Tripod, M.	S.	D.A.D.O.S
1	Rifle, German,	S.	D.A.D.O.S
2	Wheels, bicycle,	S.	D.A.D.O.S.
8	Drums, lime, empty,	S.	C.R.E.
4	Drums, oil, empty,	S.	C.R.E.
25 pairs	Boots, ankle,	S.	D.A.D.O.S.
30 "	Puttees,	S.	D.A.D.O.S
18 boxes	Horse-shoes,	U.S.	D.A.D.O.S
6 "	Helmets, Anti-Gas,	U.S.	for rail-head.
4	Saddles, Universal,	U.S.	"
2	Saddles, Panel (incomp)	U.S.	"
120	Cardigans,	U.S.	"
40 pairs	Puttees,	U.S.	"
54	Helmets, Steel,	U.S.	"
3 bags	Harness, spare,	U.S.	"
156	Box Respirators,	S.	"
70 pairs	Pantaloons,	U.S.	"
290	Trousers, S.D.	U.S.	"
45	Coats, Great, D.M.	U.S.	"
310	Jackets, S.D.	U.S.	"
1 Pair,	Boots, Gum, Knee,	U.S.	"

Continued/-

14	Baskets, Ammunition,	S.	D.A.D.O.S. for
3	Lamps, hurricane,	U.S.	railhoad.
10	Sheets, Waterproof,	U.S.	"
14	Coats, British Warm,	U.S.	"
120	Coats, Great, D.M.	U.S.	Remaining at
130	Jackets, S.D.	U.S.	dump.
100 Pairs	Trousers, S.D.	U.S.	"
270	Box Respirators,	U.S.	"
100 Pairs	Puttees,	U.S.	"
50	Cardigans,	U.S.	"
40 Pairs	Pantaloons,	U.S.	"
15	Sheets Waterproof,	U.S.	"
6 Bags	Equipment, spare,	U.S.	"
120 Pairs	Boots, Ankle,	U.S.	"
2	Stretchers,	U.S.	"
1	Marquee, complete,	U.S.	"
4	Wheels, Bicycle,	U.S.	"
1	Pipe, hose,	U.S.	"
1	Rifle German,	U.S.	"
1	Rifle bucket, leather,	U.S.	"
2 Boxes	Preserved Beef,	S.	"
12 Boxes	Helmets, Anti-gas,	U.S.	"
2 Bags	Helmets, Anti-gas,	U.S.	"
40 boxes	S.A.A. (empty) cases,	U.S.	"
8 Boxes	S.A.A.	S.	"
6 bags	S.A.A.	S.	"
20	Helmets, steel,	U.S.	"
2	Covers, cycle, outer,	U.S.	"
5	Tubes, cycle, inner,	U.S.	"
1	Saddle, Officers,	U.S.	"

for
LIEUT-COLONEL,
A.A.&Q.M.G.
14TH (LIGHT) DIVISION.

14TH (LIGHT) DIVISION.

ROUTINE ORDERS.

5th December, 1916.

2012. HONOURS AND REWARDS.

The conditions governing the grant of the Annuity and Medal for Meritorious Service under Article 1227 Royal Warrant and Para. 1747 King's Regulations are in no way affected by Army Order of 6th October, 1916.

Recipients of the Medal who may be eligible for the Annuity are not registered until they qualify for registration under the conditions laid down in Para. 1747 King's Regulations.
(W.O. 68/Gen.No./2845 (M.S.3).

2013. AMENDMENT TO WAR ESTABLISHMENT.

The following amendment should be made to W.E. 351/70 and 351/71 - Transport of Infantry and Pioneer Battalions :-

Headquarters,	Vehicles.	Drivers.	Draught Horses.
for Wagons Limbered) G.S. for S.A.A.)	5	5	10
road Wagons Limbered) G.S. for S.A.A. and) grenades,)	7	7	14

(Authority Q.M.G.No.Q/5449 dated 1-12-16. VI Corps Q/870).

C.M. Hamilton

LIEUT-COLONEL,
A.A.&Q.M.G.
14TH (LIGHT) DIVISION.

14TH (LIGHT) DIVISION.

ROUTINE ORDERS.

6th December, 1916.

2014. STRENGTH.

Sufficient information is to be given on the back of the perforated sheet of A.F. B.213 to explain the difference between the present and the previous week's strength.

Drafts posted to battalions will not be taken on the strength as shown on B.213 until they have actually arrived and reported at the Battalion Headquarters or at the Battalion Transport lines when the battalion is in the trenches.

[signature]
LIEUT-COLONEL,
A.A.&.Q.M.G.
14TH (LIGHT) DIVISION.

NOTICE.

LOST: On night of 2nd/3rd inst Brown MULE, Gelding, 15.1. Old scar about 6 inches long on near shoulder, suspected lesion on base of near side of neck in front of shoulder.
Information to Headquarters, 14th Division.

14th (LIGHT) DIVISION

ROUTINE ORDERS

9th December 1916.

2015. MARCH DISCIPLINE

It is constantly observed that officers or N.C.Os. in charge of convoys of horse transport are a considerable distance away from their column, and not attending to march discipline, which is consequently bad.

The officer or N.C.O. will always have the convoy under his personal control, and be responsible for its march discipline.
(CRO 1586)

2016. AMMUNITION BOXES

Empty 3-inch Stokes Trench Mortar bomb boxes are required at Ammunition Railheads and should therefore be returned.
(C.R.O. 1587)

2017. TRAFFIC

Loaded vehicles are to be given the "right of way", and empty convoys will halt when necessary to allow them to pass. Motor Cars, motor ambulances, and horsed transport will always give way to motor lorries and leave them the centre of the road (C.R.O. 1576)

2018. EMPTY AMMUNITION BOXES.

When the Division is in a Rest Area, empty boxes required to be returned to Ammunition Railheads are to be collected into dumps at Infantry Brigade Headquarters and a request for transport forwarded to Divisional Headquarters, when a sufficient quantity is collected. On no account are any empty boxes which are required to be returned to be left lying about.

2019. DEFICIENCIES IN SPECIALISTS

With reference to G.R.O. 1702 para C. "Deficiencies in "Specialists" personnel should not be demanded on the perforated sheet of A.F. B. 213 if this deficiency can be filled up by personnel already serving in the unit.

In the event of this being impracticable the demand should be made weekly until the deficiency is filled."

J.W. Watson Major
for LIEUT-COLONEL.
A.A. & Q.M.G.
14th (LIGHT) DIVISION.

NOTICES

CHURCH SERVICES - Sunday 10/12/16.
Holy Communion, in Field Cashier's Room, Divisional H.Q. 8-30 A.M.
Morning Service, in R.E., Recreation Room. do.   do. 9-30 A.M.
Evening Service, in H.Q., Recreation Room, do.   do. 6-30 P.M.

14th (LIGHT) DIVISION

ROUTINE ORDERS

10th December 1916.

2020. SALVAGE

The following is a list of articles salved by 14th Div. Salvage Co. week ended 8th December 1916:-

No. Collected	Description of Articles	Serviceable (S) or Unserviceable (U.S)	How disposed of
37 Prs.	Boots Ankle	S.	D.A.D.O.S
6	Bicycle Covers Outer	U.S.	25th Corps.
5	Helmets Steel	S.	A.P.M.
13	" "	S.	D.A.D.O.S.
3	Rifles British	S.	D.A.D.O.S
3	Rifles German	S.	D.A.D.O.S.
2	Sights Lewis Gun	S.	D.A.D.O.S.
594 Prs	Boots Ankle	U.S.	D.A.D.O.S.
517	Jackets S.D.	U.S.	for rail-
452 Prs	Trousers S.D.	U.S.	head
78 "	Pantaloons	U.S.	"
135 "	Puttees	U.S.	"
70	Cardigans	U.S.	"
72	Greatcoats	U.S.	"
135 boxes	Helmets Anti-Gas P.H.G.	U.S.	"
45 "	" " " P.H.	U.S.	"
1 "	" " " P.H. Drill	U.S.	"
19 bags	" " " Satchels	U.S.	"
84	Helmets Steel	U.S.	"
3	Covers Tent	U.S.	"
1	Covers Marquee	U.S.	"
11	Poles Marquee	U.S.	"
12	Saddles Universal	U.S.	"
51 boxes	Shoes Horse	U.S.	"
5 bags	Equipment Leather	U.S.	"
2 "	" Web	U.S.	"
1	Pump Trench	U.S.	"
2	Plates Signalling	U.S.	"
7 bags	Harness spare	U.S.	"
2	Swingletrees	U.S.	"
1 bag	Traces rope	U.S.	"
1	Sprayer Vermin	U.S.	"
1	Lamp Motor	U.S.	"
1 bag	Signalling Equip.	U.S.	"
2 Prs	Boots F.S.	U.S.	"
1	Coil Rope	U.S.	"
1	Pole Draught	U.S.	"
12 boxes	Meat Preserved	S.	Remaining at dump
60	Helmets Steel	S.	"
35 prs	Boots Ankle	U.S.	"
1	Pipe Hose	U.S.	"
1	Handcart L.G.	U.S.	"
6 boxes	Lewis Gun	S.	"
120	Greatcoats	S.	"
600	Box Respirators (Large)	S.	"
50	" " (Small)	U.S.	"
1	Rifle Bucket	U.S.	"

Continued.

(2)

2	Stretchers	U.S.	Remaining at dump
60 boxes	S.A.A. Empty cases	S.	"
20 bags	S.A.A. Empty cases	S.	"
5 boxes	S.A.A.	S.	"
1	Saddle Universal	U.S.	"
2	Saddles Officers	U.S.	"
1 bag	Shoes-horse	U.S.	"
4	Magazines L.G.	U.S.	"
5	Shovels G.S.	U.S.	"
1	Belt L.G.	U.S.	"
1	Tubes, Inner, Cyclo	U.S.	"
2	Covers, Cyclo, outer.	U.S.	"
100	Jackets S.D.	U.S.	"
40 Prs.	Pantaloons	U.S.	"
3	Covers Wagon	U.S.	"
1 Cask	Soda Carbonate	U.S.	"
300	Helmets Anti-Gas-P.H.G.	U.S.	"
150	" " " P.H.	U.S.	"
1	Periscope	U.S.	"
4 Reels	Wire Tracing	U.S.	"
4	Rifles British	S.	"
1	Saw Hand	U.S.	"
2 Sets	Iron Stirrups	U.S.	"

2021. **SICK WASTAGE**

The follwoing is the Sick Wastage Return for week ended 9/12/16:-

	O.O.R.		O.O.R.
48th Bde R.F.A.	2	5th Ox & Bucks L.I.	4
14th D.A.C.	2	9th K.R.R.C.	1
V/14th T.M.B.	1	9th Rifle Bde	3
61st Field Coy. R.E.	1	6th Som.L.I.	4
62nd Field Coy R.E.	1	6th D.C.L.I.	3
89th Field Coy R.E.	1	6th K.O.Y.L.I.	6
14th Signal Coy R.E.	1	10th Durham L.I.	1 6
7th K.R.R.C.	5	11th Bn.K.L'pool R.	1 5
8th K.R.R.C.	1 1	A.S.C. Div'l Train	1
7th Rifle Bde	5	RAMC 42nd Fld Ambce.	2
8th Rifle Bde	1 1	RAMC 43rd Fld Ambce	2
41st Machine Gun Coy	2		

Total Officers 4   Other Ranks 60

2022. **NO.5 GRENADES**

When it is found that the igniter of a No.5 Grenade cannot be removed through corrosion due to damp or any other cause no attempt is to be made to throw the grenade as it may explode prematurely.

A report is to be made by wire to Divisional Headquarters showing where and in whose custody the grenade or grenades may be. The C.R.E. will then be directed to make arrangements for their destruction.

Continued

(3)

2023 DISCIPLINE

Complaints are constantly received from inhabitants of wood being taken by soldiers for fuel.
This practice is to be stopped and the offenders severely dealt with.

[signature]

for LIEUT-COLONEL.
A.A. & Q.M.G.
14th (LIGHT) DIVISION.

14th (LIGHT) DIVISION

ROUTINE ORDERS

11th December 1916.

2023. CLEARING OF BARNS

The question of clearing barns will in future be undertaken by the Third Army authorities in conjunction with the French Mission, and not by Divisional Representatives.
Brigades will forward a list to Divisional Headquarters, by noon the 14th inst, showing, in order of importance, the barns in the villages in their area that are required to be cleared.

2024. CHAFF-CUTTERS.

All Chaff-Cutters, excepting those privately owned, (i.e. not paid for out of public funds), are area stores, and will be handed over to the nearest Town Major.
Reports of numbers will be sent to Divisional Headquarters by last D.R. on the 14th instant, accompanied by a copy of the Town Major's receipt.
In ARRAS where the Town Major does not hold area stores, units in possession will hand over to their successors and obtain receipts.

2025. FUEL Reference D.R.O.1981 dated 25/11/16 . The Fuel Return will in future be rendered on the Form Circulated herewith

A.L. Hamilton
LIEUT-COLONEL,
A.A.& Q. .G.
14th (LIGHT) DIVISION.

NOTICES

LOST : on FREVENT - AVESNES ROAD, Nr LIENCOURT on the 9th inst. Kit Bag marked M2/043541 Pte Martin A.R. finder please communicate with O.C., 14th Divisional Supply Column.

LOST : Taken by mistake from 14th Divisional School, on 10th inst a "British Warm"; marked A.L.C.Cavendish (Captain's Stars) Black Gloves in pocket. Information to Major Cavendish 14th Divisional School.

RETURN SHEWING AMOUNT OF FUEL DRAWN FOR WEEK ENDED

Unit	Quantity entitled to		Amount Received		Excess		Deficient	
	Coal	Wood	Coal	Wood	Coal	Wood	Coal	Wood

14th (LIGHT) DIVISION

ROUTINE ORDERS

12th December 1916.

2026. TRANSPORT

Cases have occurred in which lorries engaged on transport work have been detained all night, or sent on extended duty by units without any reference to Corps Headquarters. It is to be clearly understood that under no circumstances will such action be taken without reference to Corps Headquarters.

2027 SMALL BOX RESPIRATORS

No officers or other ranks will be taken into the trenches until they have been fitted with Small Box Respirators and trained in their use.

JHWatson Major
/o
LIEUT-COLONEL,
A.A.&.Q.M.G,
14th (LIGHT) DIVISION.

14th (Light) DIVISION

ROUTINE ORDERS

13th December 1916.

2028. LEAVE WARRANTS

The Base Commandant, Boulogne reports that officers and other ranks are arriving at his Port with leave Warrants endorsed "Via Havre".

All ordinary leave from this Division being now Via Boulogne care is to be taken that no Warrants for ordinary leave are endorsed "Via Havre".

N.C.Os, and men who are given one month's special leave on re-engagement are to travel Via Havre with Warrants endorsed "Via Havre". These men are not on any account to go to the Port of Boulogne and must be told so at the time of departure from their unit.

2029. DAMAGE TO GUN EMPLACEMENTS

All ranks are to be warned against removing timber from or in any way damaging gun emplacements whether in use or not.

If any such damage is at any time found to have been done the nearest troops may be required to furnish guards over gun emplacements.

J. Robertson Major

for LIEUT.-COLONEL,
A.A. & Q.M.G.
14th (LIGHT) DIVISION.

14th (LIGHT) DIVISION.

ROUTINE ORDERS

15th December 1916.

2030. LIGHTS

Corps Routine Order No. 854 of 21st May, 1916, is cancelled and the following substituted:-

(a) Between the hours of dusk and dawn, all motor vehicles will, except as specified below, have both side lamps lighted in areas where lights are allowed. If in possession of headlights these will be used in addition.

(b) Headlights may not be used east of the following line:- Road Junction L.1.d. - AGNES-LES-DUISANS - GOUVES -MONTENESCOURT - WANQUETIN - GOUY-EN-ARTOIS - DAVINCOURT - SAULTY. (All places exclusive with the exception of DAVINCOURT).

NOTE. Headlights may not be used on the DOULLENS - ARRAS Road east of BEAUREPAIRE.

(c) No lights may be used east of the MARŒUIL - DAINVILLE Railway, or south of Dainville - Berneville - Simoncourt - Monchiet Road exclusive.

No lights may be used east of the BAC DU SUD on the DOULLENS - ARRAS Road (inclusive)

(d) Bicycles and motor bicycles are exempted from the above regulations, and may use their lights up to ARRAS, except on the ARRAS - DOULLENS Road east of the BAC DU SUD.

(e) Tail lights should be used on all occasions, but must be so arranged that only a RED light is shown in the Forward area.
(C.R.O. 1610.)

2031. CARTRIDGES FOR TRENCH MORTARS

When reports as to defective 3-inch Stokes Cartridges are forwarded, five cartridges if available from the same box should be forwarded with the report, as, owing to the absence of any marking on these cartridges, there is no means of investigating defects which are reported.
(C.R.O. 1615).

2032. CARTRIDGES ILLUMINATING

With reference to C.R.O. No. 1613. Brigades will notify this office by noon 20th, numbers of these Cartridges to be collected.

2033. ORDERS FOR TOWNS AND VILLAGES

The following Circulars were issued to Divisional Artillery and Infantry Brigades with O.R.Os. of yesterday's date for distribution to Town Majors of Villages in their areas.
(a) Standing Orders for Town Majors.
(b) Precautions against fire.
(c) Orders for Policing Towns and Villages.
These Orders supersede all those previously issued.

2034. CARTRIDGES FOR TRENCH MORTARS.

Attention of all concerned is drawn to C.R.O. No. 1612. Reports called for in para 4 will be forwarded to this office in all cases of failure of cartridge-containers.

for LIEUT.-COLONEL.
A.A.&.Q.M.G.

14th (Light) DIVISION

ROUTINE ORDERS

16th December 1916

2035 POSTAL-REGISTERED LETTERS AND PACKETS

General Routine Order No. 1985, dated 7/12/16, is re-published for information:-

"(i) To enable Post Orderlies to keep a proper record of the receipt and disposal of registered letters, etc., Army Book 426,
"Post Orderly's Receipt Book", will shortly be issued to all units by the Army Printing and Stationery Services.

(ii) Commanding Officers are responsible that the instructions contained in Army Book 426 are fully understood and carried out by Post Orderlies."
(C.R.O. 1603)

2036 SALVAGE

The following is a list of articles salved by 14th Div. Salvage Co. week ended 15th December 1916:-

No. Collected	Description of Articles	Serviceable (S) or Unserviceable (U&S)	How disposed of
4	Belts Leather	(S)	10th D.L.I
1	Waterbottle Carr. (L)	(S)	"
3	Entrench.Tool "	S	"
4	Helve Carriers "	S	"
3 Pairs	Supporting Straps "	S	"
1	Frog (Bayonet)	S	"
3 Pairs	Pouches	S	"
6	Chests Lewis Gun	S	D.A.D.O.S.
1	Lamp Motor	U.S.	"
3	Cycles	U.S.	"
10	Rifles	U.S.	"
1	Rifle (German)	U.S.	"
1	Boxes Magazine L.G.	S.	"
1	Saddle - Officer's	U.S.	"
10	Ground Sheets	U.S.	"
24	Small Box Respirators (No.3)	S.	"
22	" " " (No.2)	S	"
21	" " " (No.4)	S	"
30 Pairs	Boots Ankle	S	"
12 Boxes	Preserved Meat	S	D.S.S.
11 Bags	" "	S	"
1 Tin	Biscuits	S	"
6 Boxes	S.A.A.	S	D.A.C.
60 "	S.A.A. Empty cases	S	"
20 Bags	" "	S	"
2 Boxes	" Clips	S	"
20 "	" empty cases	S	"
299	Jackets S.D.	U.S.	D.A.D.O.S.
279	Trousers S.D.	U.S.	for
175	Great Coats S.D.	U.S.	railhead
115	Pantaloons	U.S.	"
10	Cardigan Jackets	U.S.	"
782	Helmets Anti-Gas (P.H.)	U.S.	"
2176	" " " (P.H.G)	U.S.	"

CONTINUED/

(2)

1650		Sadhols Helmet	U.S.	D.A.D.O.S.
1130		Large Box Respirators (used)	U.S.	for
26		Bags-Washing	U.S.	railhead.
28		Helmets-Steel	U.S.	"
10		Inner Tubes (Cycle)	U.S.	"
16		Outer Covers "	U.S.	"
240	Pairs	Boots - Ankle	U.S.	"
12		Bolts M.G. (Vickers)	U.S.	"
3	Boxes	Belts " "	S.	"
1		Saddle Officer's	U.S.	"
3		Saddles Universal	U.S.	"
2		Machine Gun Periscopes	U.S.	"
2		Poles - Measuring	U.S.	"
1		Level	U.S.	"
2		Rifle Buckets	U.S.	"
12		Capes Waterproof	U.S.	"
50	Pairs	Puttees	U.S.	"
10	Bags	Equipment	U.S.	"
1	"	Telephone Apparatus	U.S.	"
1	"	Spare Harness	U.S.	"
61		Boiler T.K.	U.S.	D.A.D.O.S.
?		Frying Pans T.K.	U.S.	for Heavy
24		Camp Kettles	U.S.	Mobile
4		Machine Gun Flame Shades	U.S.	"
2		Springs (G.S)	U.S.	"
2		Couplings - Limber	U.S.	"
1	Bag	Brake Blocks	U.S.	"
1	"	Lamps	U.S.	"
8		Rasps	U.S.	"
123		Jackets S.D.	U.S.	Still on
97	Pairs	Trousers S.D.	U.S.	dump.
32		Great Coats	U.S.	"
52		Pantaloons	U.S.	"
130	Pairs	Boots Ankle	U.S.	"
20	"	Boots F.	U.S.	"
?	Capes	Waterproof	U.S.	"
200		Helmets Anti-Gas (P.H)	U.S.	"
375		" " " (P.H.G)	S.	"
3		Boxes (L.G.Magazine)	S.	"
1		Handsaw	U.S.	"
50		Steel Helmets	U.S.	"
22		Box Respirators Small	U.S.	"
78		" " Large (used)	U.S.	"
10	Boxes	Horseshoes	U.S.	"
6		Shovels G.S.	U.S.	"
2		Cleavers	U.S.	"
1		Stretcher	U.S.	"

2037 DISCIPLINE

Attention of all concerned is drawn to G.R.O.1619. dated 15th December 1916.

[signature]
for LIEUT-COLONEL,
A.A. & Q.M.G.
14th (LIGHT) DIVISION.

DIVINE SERVICES
SUNDAY DECEMBER 17th 1916.

Holy Communion 7-45 a.m. H.Q. Canteen Room.
Morning Service 9-30 a.m. R.E., Recreation Room.
Evening Service 6-30 p.m. H.Q., Recreation Room.

14th (LIGHT) DIVISION

ROUTINE ORDERS

18th December 1916.

2038 SICK WASTAGE

The following is the Sick Wastage Return for week ended 16/12/16:-

	O.	O.R.		O.	O.R.
14th Div.H.Q.	2		41st Machine Gun Coy.		1
14th Div.R&A.,H.Q.		1	5th Ox.& Bucks L.I.		9
46th Bde R.F.A.		1	5th K.S.L.I.		4
47th Bde R.F.A.		2	9th K.R.R.C.		4
48th Bde R.F.A.		8	9th Rif.Bde.	1	5
14th D.A.C.		8	6th Somerset L.I.	2	5
X 14th T.M.B.		1	6th D.C.L.I.		5
Y 14 "		1	6th K.O.Y.L.I.	1	6
Z 14 "		1	10th Durham L.I.		2
61st Field Coy R.E.		2	43rd Machine Gun Coy.		2
62nd " " "		1	11th King's L'pool R.	2	6
14th Signal Coy		1	A.S.C. Divisional Train		1
7th K.R.R.C.		3	R.A.M.C. 42nd Fld. Amblce		3
7th Rif. Bde		7	" 43rd " "		1
8th K.R.R.C.		4	" 44th " "		2
8th Rif.Bde.		1			

Total Officers 8 Total Other Ranks 96

2039 WATER BOTTLES

Water Bottles are to be cleaned twice monthly with strong solution of Chloride of Lime, under regimental arrangements. Any surplus solution must be thoroughly washed out of the bottles with water made fit for drinking.

2040 PIT PROPS SUPPLY OF

As the supply of pit props is inadequate, they must be not be used for making corduroy roads till further orders.

for A.A.&.Q.M.G.
14th (LIGHT) DIVISION.

14th (LIGHT) DIVISION

ROUTINE ORDERS

20th December 1916.

2041. **Xmas Puddings**

The following arrangements have been made for the distribution of the Xmas Puddings.

They will be packed with the M.F.Parcels in M.F.E. trucks and sent via the Regulating Stations by the formation Supply Trains to Railheads.

The first consignment will be calculated at ½ lb per man and when this amount has been despatched to each formation by its supply train a second despatch of ½ lb per man will be similarly arranged for.

The first consignment will be available at refilling point tomorrow.

2042. **Baths**

Brigades will submit their programme of bath parades completed for following week by 7 p.m. on Thursdays.

Troops can be provided with clean clothing once a fortnight on the average.

Bath parades will commence on Sunday next the 24th instant.

LIEUT.-COLONEL,
for A.A.&.Q.M.G.
14th (LIGHT) DIVISION

14th (LIGHT) DIVISION

ROUTINE ORDERS

21/12/16.

2043 FIELD CASHIER

The Field Cashier will attend at Divisional Headquarters on Tuesdays and Thursdays between the hours of 2-30 p.m. and 4-30 p.m.

2044 RUM, ISSUE OF

Rum will not be issued to men in trenches.
Two issues of rum a week may be made to all other troops. Units should indent for requirements which will be complied with whenever possible.

[signature]

LIEUT-COLONEL,
A.A. & Q.M.G.
14th (LIGHT) DIVISION.

NOTICE

LOST.   Brown Gelding clipped out except legs, bald face, carrying set of officer's appointments, snaffle bridle and white head rope.
Was last seen at junction of ACHICOURT and ARRAS - DOULLENS Roads going in direction of DAINVILLE Station.
Information to Lieut. O'Kelly A Battery 43rd Bde. R.F.A., 12th Division.

14th (LIGHT) DIVISION

ROUTINE ORDERS

22/12/16.

2045. AERIAL GUNNERS

Reference Third Army Routine Order No. 542 of the 12th November, 1916, no more applications from N.C.Os and men as Aerial Gunners are required.

2046. LEAVE

Owing to an outbreak of Measles, leave will not be granted to the following places until further orders:- FISHERGATE, SOUTHWICK, LANCING, and KINGSTON-ON-SEA.

2047 LEAVE

The return called for in Third Army Routine Order No. 586 dated 19/12/16, will be rendered to Divisional Headquarters by noon 28th of each month.

2048 DRESS- SHAVING OF UPPER LIP.

General Routine Order No. 1854, dated 10/10/16, is re-published for information:-
"The following amendment is made to King's Regulations, paragraph 1698, by Army Order 340 (3), of 1916:-
"Line 2 delete 'but not the upper lip'."
It being now optional whether the upper lip be shaved or not by officers and men, if a moustache is worn no portion of the upper lip shall be shaved.
(Authority:- W.O. letter No.105/Gen.No./2301 (A.G.3) dated 4/10/16). This order will published in all Brigade and Battalion orders.

(C.R.O. No. 1638)

LIEUT.-COLONEL,
A.A. & Q.M.G.,
14th (LIGHT) DIVISION.

NOTICES

CHURCH SERVICES

R.C. Services for Sunday December 24th

Mass at 8 a.m. in Parish Church BEAUMETZ
" " 8-30 a.m. " " DAINVILLE
for 9th K.R.R.C.
Mass at 9-30 in Parish Church WANQUETIN
" " 10 a.m. at AGNY for the King's Liverpool Regt and 5th Oxford & Bucks L.I. at Company Headquarters of King's Liverpool Regt.
Mass at 10-20 a.m. at Cures House, Riviere.

ROUTINE ORDERS

23rd December 1916.

2049. 3" STOKES MORTARS, REPAIR OF

When sending in 3" Stokes Mortars to the shops for repair, care should be taken to see that small stores are not sent in at the same time. When Divisions have several guns in the shop small stores are liable to be inadvertently exchanged.

2050. TRENCH AND AREA STORES.

Attention is directed to Corps Routine Order No. 1175, dated 15/8/16. Disciplinary action will be taken in all future breaches of this order.
(C.R.O. 1640)

2051. GUM BOOTS

All concerned are reminded that Gum Boots, with the exception of those allowed to specified units by G.R.O. or A.F. G 1098, are Area Stores, and do not form part of a unit's equipment. (C.R.O. 1643)

2052. PAILLASSES

With reference to Corps Routine Order No. 1817, dated 14/12/16, all are reminded that
(a) The paillasses are kept in the areas for which they are issued, and are removed by troops when moving, nor taken into the trenches.
(b) The paillasses are not used in tents.
(Authority:- Third Army O/103/65, dated 26/9/16. VI Corps Q/730).
(C.R.O. 1644)

2053. TRAINING IN ARRAS

The training of specialists may be carried out by small parties under the trees in ARRAS except on clear days when enemy aircraft are active.
Care is to be taken that ARRAS TOWN ORDER No.13 is strictly obeyed at all times.

H.A. Boyce.

for LIEUT.-COLONEL,
A.A. & Q.M.G.,
14th (LIGHT) DIVISION

NOTICES

LOST. Officer's Charger, Bay Gelding, 14·2 hands, clipped out, Race, Two Hind Socks, Carrying set of Officer's saddlery marked D.M.11.
Taken from Cavalry Barracks ARRAS on the night of 21/12/16.
Information to Adjutant, 10th Durham L.I.

Church Services

Sunday December 24th   C. of E.

Church Army Hut BERNEVILLE, Holy Communion 8 a.m.
        Morning Service   10-30 a.m.
Church Army Hut WARLUS Morning Service 9-30 a.m.
Service for preparation for Christmas Communion 6-30 p.m.

CHRISTMAS SERVICES

ARRAS   <u>Cavalry Barrack Chapel</u> Holy Communion 7-30 and 8-30 a.m.
                                    Morning Service 9-30 and 10-15 a.m.
<u>RONVILLE</u> Canteen   Holy Communion 11 a.m.

<u>ACHICOURT</u> Reformed Church Holy Communion 9-30 a.m. and
               12 noon.
           Morning Service and Holy Communion. 10 a.m.
<u>DAINVILLE</u>   Church of England Chapel Holy Communion 7-30 and
           8-30 a.m. Station 10-15 a.m.
           Recreation Room Evensong and Preparation Xmas Eve 6 p.m.
           Xmas Day Holy Communion 10-30 and Carol Service 6 p.m.
<u>AGNY</u>   No. 3 Happy Villa Holy Communion 7-30 and 11-30 a.m.
           Carol Service 6 p.m.
<u>WARLUS</u> Cross Roads Church Army Hut Xmas Eve 6-30 p.m. Preparation
           Service Xmas day Holy Communion 7-15 a.m. and 9-30 a.m.
           (Choral)
<u>BERNEVILLE</u>   Evensong and preparation service Xmas eve 6 p.m.
           Xmas day Holy Communion 8 a.m. and 10-30 a.m. Choral.

<u>WANQUETIN</u>   Church Army Hut, Holy Communion 7 and 8 a.m.
           Morning Service 10 a.m. 44th Field Ambulance
           Xmas Eve Service 3 p.m. Xmas day Holy Communion 6-45 and
           7-30 a.m.

<u>SIMENCOURT</u>   Xmas Eve only. 10-30 and 11-30 a.m. Places to be found
           by Town Major.

<u>MONCHIET</u>   Xmas Eve only. 'Theatre Royal' Hut 2-15 p.m.

<u>HAUTEVILLE</u>   10-45 a.m. Morning Service and Holy Communion Field Amb.

<u>BARLY</u>   Morning Service and Holy Communion 11-15 a.m.
           Divisional Rest Camp.
<u>GOUY</u>.   10 a.m. Morning Service and Holy Communion 43rd Fld.Amb.

<u>RIVIERE</u>   Church of England Chapel as in local notices or
           apply Rev. T.W.A.Jones 41st Infantry Bde.
<u>BEAUMETZ</u>   apply Rev. T.W.A.Jones 41st Infantry Bde.

Sunday Services
<u>Divisional Headquarters,</u>   8-30 a.m. Holy Communion 9-30 a.m. Morning
                                                            Service.

Roman Catholic
Christmas Day

Holy Mass at 7-30, 8, and 9-30 a.m. in Parish Church. WANQUETIN
"   "   "   7 a.m.   "   "   "   SIMENCOURT
"   "   "   8-30 a.m.   "   "   "   DAINVILLE
"   "   "   9-0 a.m.   "   "   "   BEAUMETZ
"   "   "   10 a.m.   at AGNY (Ling's Liverpools).
"   "   "   10-30 a.m.   at Cures House, RIVIERE.

14th (LIGHT) DIVISION

ROUTINE ORDERS.

24th December 1916.

2054 KILLING OF GAME

General Routine Order No. 1297 and Third Army Routine Order No. 230 are re-published for information :-
" G.R.O.1297. As cases still occur of Officers and other ranks pursuing and killing game, it is notified for information that the hunting, shooting or killing of game (which includes hares and rabbits) by nets, snares or other methods is strictly prohibited."
" A.R.O. 230. Leave to shoot game has been given by the French Government to certain French civilians. British Officers are not allowed to shoot with them even if invited. "
The above orders will be published in all Brigade and Battalion Orders.
(C.R.O. 1649.)

2055. TIMBER.

The situation in regard to the supply of timber for the use of the British Armies is causing serious anxiety and the necessity for rigid economy must therefore be exercised in the use of timber of all kinds, the demands of which are growing at an alarming pace.

2056. SICK WASTAGE.

The following is the Sick Wastage Return for week ended 23/12/16 :-

	O.	O.R.		O.	O.R.
14th Div. H.Q.	1		9th K.R.R.C.		1
46th Bde R.F.A.		1	9th Rif. Bde.		2
47th Bde. R.F.A.		4	6th Somerset L.I.	1	5
48th Bde. R.F.A.		1	6th D.C.L.I.		2
14th D.A.C.		1	6th K.O.Y.L.I.		4
62nd Field Coy. R.E.		1	10th Durham L.I.		2
89th " " R.E.		1	43rd Machine Gun Coy.		3
8th K.R.R.C.		3	11th King's L'pool R.		1
7th Rif. Bde.		6	6th D.C.L.I. att'd Div.Sal.Coy.		1
8th Rif. Bde.		4	R.A.M.C. 43rd Fld. Amblce.		2
5th Ox. & Bucks L.I.		4	A.S.C. (M.T.) No.14 Supply Coln.		3
5th K.S.L.I.		2			

Total Officers 2.   Total Other Ranks 54.

2057. TUBE HELMETS.

As it is found that P.H. helmets can be worn for considerable periods without losing their efficiency, and as the "Drill Helmets" carried by units give rise to difficulties in transport, it has been decided to withdraw all "Drill Helmets" from units.
The P.H. helmet carried as the second anti-gas appliance on the man should, in future, be used for purposes of helmet drill.
These P.H. helmets should be exchanged when they have been worn for a total time of 24 hours in drill or in shell gas attacks. They should, however, invariably be exchanged if used in cloud gas attacks.

(2)

2058. RUM.

        Reference D.R.O. 2044 : under normal circumstances Rum will not be issued to men in the Trenches. In event of exceptionally cold and wet weather, the Corps Commander is prepared to consider applications for an issue of Rum to men in the Trenches, provided such Rum is issued under strict supervision and drunk in the presence of an Officer.

        To enable such issues to be quickly made, a small amount of Rum (not exceeding one day's ration) may be maintained by Divisional Commanders, but issues will only be made on the Corps Commander's authority.

H.W.Watson Major for   LIEUT.-COLONEL.,
                            A.A. & Q.M.G.,
                          14th (LIGHT) DIVISION.

N O T I C E S.

LOST.   Plain Silver Cigarette Case, on 19th Decr. at BERNEVILLE. Engraved "J.H.TEMPLE Presented from LOFTUS HOCKEY "TENNIS" CLUB, 1911."
Information to TOWN MAJOR, BERNEVILLE.   Reward offered.

Church Services.

Christmas Day.   C of E.

    RIVIERE, C. of E. Chapel.- Holy Communion 8.0, 9.30
                                          and 10.45 a.m.
                            Carol Service   5.0 p.m.
    BEAUMETZ. (Place arranged by Battn. in rest.)
                            Morning Service 11.30 a.m.
                            Holy Communion 12.0 noon.
    WAILLY.   Holy Communion 8.0 a.m.

14th (LIGHT) DIVISION.

ROUTINE ORDERS.
------:0:------

25th December, 1916.

2059. DIVISIONAL CINEMA.

The Divisional Cinema will open on Wednesday, 27th instant. The Entertainment will continue nightly, including Sundays, commencing at 5.30 : doors will open at 5.0 p.m.

Admittance for Officers will be 1 franc and for men 25 centimes. A few reserved seats for N.C.O.'s will be available at 50 centimes.

2060. LEAVE.

Owing to an outbreak of measles at BIRKENHEAD and WALLASEY (Cheshire) England, leave will not be granted to soldiers to proceed to these places until further orders.

2061. ARMY BOOK 64.

In consequence of frequent transfers of soldiers it is essential that an accurate record should be kept in A.B.64.

Commanding Officers will ensure that the correct regimental number, name and unit are clearly shown in the pay book of all soldiers serving under their Command.
(G. R. O. 2009.)

2062. IDENTITY DISCS.

Reference G. R. O. 1922, Green Identity Discs have now been distributed and Commanding Officers will ensure that the correct regimental number, name, unit and religion, are clearly shown on the identity discs of all Soldiers under their Command.
(G. R. O. 2010.)

2063. SHELL BASKETS - 18-POUNDER.

Under no circumstances will shell baskets of 18-pounder Limbers and Wagons be removed and utilised for the carriage of ammunition.
(C. R. O. 1655.)

2064. HORSE TRANSPORT - CARE OF.

The attention of all concerned is directed to the absolute necessity of keeping the wheels of horse-drawn vehicles in good order. They should be thoroughly cleaned every third day - inspected and greased. In this connection it is pointed out that it is necessary periodically to remove the wheels to ensure that they are thoroughly greased.
(C. R. O. 1657.)

LIEUT.-COLONEL,
A.A. & Q.M.G.,
14th (LIGHT) DIVISION.

14th (LIGHT) DIVISION.

ROUTINE ORDERS.

27th December, 1916.

2065. **FIELD CASHIER.**

D.R.O. 2043 of 21st December is cancelled. In future the Field Cashier will attend at WARLUS from 2.30 p.m. to 4.0 p.m. every Monday and Thursday.

2066. **LEAVE.**

(1) Owing to an outbreak of Measles at LOFTUS AND LIVERTON MINES (LOFTUS URBAN DISTRICT), Yorkshire, England, leave will not be granted to soldiers to proceed to these places until further orders.

(2) Owing to an outbreak of small pox at PRESTON, Lancashire, England, leave will not be granted to soldiers to proceed to this place until further notice.

LIEUT.-COLONEL,
A.A. & Q.M.G.,
14th (LIGHT) DIVISION.

14th (LIGHT) DIVISION.

ROUTINE ORDERS.

29th December, 1916.

2065. GAS APPLIANCES.

The Return called for in D.R.O.s 1056 and 1111 will in future include Box Respirators.

2066. DIVISIONAL CINEMA.

There will be change of programme on Monday Wednesday and Friday each week.

2067. TRAFFIC.

The road from BEAUMETZ Station to Roadside Copse is to be used, by daylight, only by Orderlies with urgent messages. They must be in possession of passes or of envelopes marked "Urgent", signed by an officer.

2068. RAT POISON - PRECAUTIONS AGAINST.

In order to guard against accidental poisoning, warning is to be given when phosphorus paste, extract of Squills or any other Rat Poison is laid.
Receptacles containing the poison are to be labelled and the bait unconsumed by rats destroyed.
(A.R.O. 588, 24-12-16.)

2069. ISSUE OF CARD PASSES.

1. A new British Card Pass will come into force on January 1st, 1917. The conditions of issue will be as stated in A.R.O.534.
2. Applications for Passes for the new period will be made to A.P.M.s of Formations by 26th December; the reasons for the demand are to be stated, and also the number of the Car in the case of drivers of Motor Cars.
3. All out of date passes are to be returned to the P.M. or A.P.M., who issued them, by January 6th, to be cancelled.

2070. DRILL HELMETS.

Attention is directed to C.R.O. 1665 of 27th Decr.
All Drill Helmets in possession of units should be returned to D.A.D.O.S. forthwith.

2071. WOOD.

Attention is directed to Corps Routine Order No. 1524, dated 24-11-16. No wood will, in future, be issued from VI Corps Dump unless A.B.55 duly completed, is sent with the loading party.
(VI Corps Q/24/16. C.R.O. 1662.)

Continued.

8072. ORDNANCE STORES.

Commencing January 1st, 1917, Ordnance Stores will be indented for as follows :-

STORES.	Indents should be handed or sent in on -	Stores should be available for issue on -
Boots, Clothing S.D., Greatcoats, Woollen Drawers, Vests and Puttees, Nose Bags and Saddle Blankets.	Thursday.	Thursday week.
Accoutrements, Oil and Grease	Sunday.	Monday week.
Picketing Gear, Camp Kettles, Blankets, Ground Sheets, Entrenching Implements, Buckets Water Canvas, Sponge Cloths, Cotton Waste, Flannelette and Horse Rugs.	Monday.	Monday week.
Horse Shoes, Clothing, Shirts, Socks and Balance.	Saturday.	Saturday week
Winter Clothing	Wednesday.	Wednesday week.

NOTICES.

A performance will be given by Miss LENA ASHWELL'S "Firing Line" Party in the Divisional Theatre at BERNEVILLE on 31st December. Performance will commence 5.30 p.m.- Doors open 5.0 p.m. No charge will be made for admittance.

LOST - It is desired to trace following horse, formerly the charger of Brigadier-General H. R. Davies, 3rd Inf. Bde., evacuated to No. 7 Veterinary Hospital on 14th July last with shell wound :-
Dark Brown Gelding Rider, 15 years, 15.1 hands, faint star, saddle marks. Scar of wound near fore forearm. Branded on both fore feet with the letter "D".
It is presumed to have been discharged cured to Remount Service and re-issued.
Search should be instituted and report made to Deputy Director of Veterinary Services.

LOST - Decr. 23rd, 1916, at BERNEVILLE :
Black mule, 15 hands, lame near hind, white patch off shoulder
Dark brown mule, 13 hands, white saddle patches near and off
Information to Hd.Qrs. 14th Division.

J H Watson Major
for LIEUT.-COLONEL,
A. A. & Q.M.G.,
14th (LIGHT) DIVISION.

14th (LIGHT) DIVISION.

ROUTINE ORDERS.

30th December, 1916.

2073. **HONOURS & REWARDS.**

H.M. THE KING has been pleased to award the Military Medal to the following N.C.O. for services prior to June 30th, 1916 :-

No. R/5985 Sergt. F. Downes, 8th Bn. K.R.R.C.

2074. **POSTING - OFFICERS.**

Temp. 2/Lieut. E. H. HARVEY posted to 8th Battn. The Rifle Bde. under A.G. G.H.Q. No.A/1186/371 dated 17-12-16 is cross posted to the 9th Battn. The Rifle Bde. with effect from 29-12-16 under the provisions of A.G. G.H.Q. No.A/17979.

2075. **PASSES.**

With reference to G.R.O. 2006 of 21st December, 1916, the Green Card Pass now in force will continue to be used until further notice.

[signature] Major

for LIEUT.-COLONEL,
A.A. & Q.M.G.,
14th (Light) DIVISION.

NOTICE.

FOUND — On GOUY - MONCHIET Road at 3.20 P.M., 29th instant, Bay Mare, Rider, Aged, about 15 hands, Star, White Coronet near fore, White fetlocks both hind feet, Saddle gall near side, Head Collar and chain.

Apply Headquarters, 14th Division.

14th (LIGHT) DIVISION.

ROUTINE ORDERS.

31st December, 1916.

2076. CUTTING OF WOOD.

Damage has been caused to woods and forests in the Third Army area by the indiscriminate cutting of wood by units and individuals without reference either to the owners or to higher authority.

Wood can only be cut after the necessary arrangements have been made with the owners by Corps Hd.Qtrs., the Chief Engineer, or the D.D.S. and T. of the Army.

All applications for cut wood will be referred to Corps and Divisional Hd.Qtrs. for Corps and Divisional Troops, and to the Chief Engineer and D.D.S. and T. of the Army for Army Troops.

It is forbidden to cut wood in the Third Army area until application has been made and sanction received as above.

This order will be republished in the orders of all formations and units in the Third Army every month.
(A.R.O. 591, 29-12-16.)

2077. SICK WASTAGE.

The following is the Sick Wastage Return for week ended 30-12-16 :-

	O.	O.R.		O.	O.R.
46th Bde. R.F.A.		1	9th Rif. Bde.	1	9
47th Bde. R.F.A.		1	6th Somerset L.I.		7
14th D.A.C.		1	6th D.C.L.I.		7
14th Signal Coy. R.E.		1	6th K.O.Y.L.I.	1	5
7th K.R.R.C.		11	10th Durham L.I.		6
8th K.R.R.C.		4	43rd Machine-Gun Coy.		1
7th Rif. Bde.		10	11th Bn.K. L'pool R.		5
8th Rif. Bde.		4	R.A.M.C.43rd Fld.Amb.		1
5th Ox. & Bucks L.I.		6	R.A.M.C.44th Fld.Amb.		1
5th K. Shrops. L.I.		3	A.V.C. 26th Mobile Sec.		1
9th K.R.R.C.		2			

Total Officers 2.   Total Other Ranks 87.

2078. BOXES FOR LATRINES.

Units must hand over daily as many 50-lb. biscuit boxes as possible to O.C. Sanitary Section, 14th Division. The boxes will be sent in whenever available.

Town Majors will notify their requirements of latrine seats to the O.C. Sanitary Section.

It is very important to satisfy the demand, but if units carry out these instructions, the demand can be satisfied and the boxes will then be available for other purposes.

LIEUT.-COLONEL,
A.A. & Q.M.G.,
14th (LIGHT) DIVISION.

www.ingramcontent.com/pod-product-compliance
Lightning Source LLC
Chambersburg PA
CBHW080836010526
44114CB00017B/2316